WEAKNESS OF WILL FROM PLATO TO THE PRESENT

STUDIES IN PHILOSOPHY
AND THE HISTORY OF PHILOSOPHY

General Editor: Jude P. Dougherty

Studies in Philosophy
and the History of Philosophy Volume 49

Weakness of Will from Plato to the Present

Edited by Tobias Hoffmann

THE CATHOLIC UNIVERSITY OF AMERICA PRESS
Washington, D.C.

The paper used in this publication meets the minimum requirements of American National Standards for Information Science—Permanence of Paper for Printed Library Materials, ANSI Z39.48-1984.
∞

LIBRARY OF CONGRESS CATALOGING-IN-PUBLICATION DATA
Weakness of will from Plato to the present / edited by Tobias Hoffmann.
p. cm. — (Studies in philosophy and the history of philosophy ; v. 49)
Includes bibliographical references (p.) and index.
ISBN 978-0-8132-1520-4 (cloth : alk. paper) 1. Free will and determinism. I. Hoffmann, Tobias, 1967– II. Title. III. Series.
BJ1461.W39 2008
128'.3—dc22 2007033940

Contents

Preface vii

Tobias Hoffmann, Introduction ix

1. KENNETH DORTER, Weakness and Will in Plato's *Republic* 1

2. TERENCE H. IRWIN, Aristotle Reads the *Protagoras* 22

3. LLOYD P. GERSON, Plotinus on Weakness of the Will: The Neoplatonic Synthesis 42

4. JAMES WETZEL, Body Double: Saint Augustine and the Sexualized Will 58

5. DENIS J. M. BRADLEY, Thomas Aquinas on Weakness of the Will 82

6. TOBIAS HOFFMANN, Henry of Ghent's Voluntarist Account of Weakness of Will 115

7. GIUSEPPE MAZZOTTA, Dante: Healing the Wounded Will 138

8. ANN HARTLE, Montaigne's Marvelous Weakness 159

9. JOHN C. MCCARTHY, Descartes's Feeble Spirits 175

10. THOMAS E. HILL JR., Kant on Weakness of Will 210

11. TRACY B. STRONG, Nietzsche, the Will to Power, and the Weak Will 231

12. ALFRED R. MELE, A Libertarian View of Akratic Action 252

13. ALASDAIR MACINTYRE, Conflicts of Desire 276

Bibliography 293

Contributors 309

Index of Names 313

Preface

This volume collects thirteen original papers on the topic of weakness of will. Most of them were originally delivered in the fall 2004 lecture series entitled "Weakness of Will," sponsored by the School of Philosophy at the Catholic University of America. Terry Irwin presented his paper on a different occasion, while James Wetzel and Denis Bradley wrote their papers purposely for this volume. I am very grateful to the authors for their contributions and for their cooperation during the preparation of the manuscript.

The book would not have come about without the generous support of Rev. Dr. Kurt Pritzl, O.P., dean of the School of Philosophy, who deserves my special appreciation. I am obliged to Risto Saarinen (University of Helsinki) and Hugh McCann (Texas A&M University), who refereed the manuscript and provided useful comments. I also wish to thank Dean Emeritus Dr. Jude Dougherty, series editor, and Dr. David McGonagle, director of the Catholic University of America Press, for publishing this volume in the Studies in Philosophy and the History of Philosophy, as well as my colleagues at the School of Philosophy, who assisted me in organizing the lecture series. In addition I want to express my gratitude to Janelle Livesay, who helped with the practical details of preparing the lecture series, and to Thérèse Scarpelli and Emily Yang for proofreading the manuscript. I am grateful as well to the Matchette Foundation for financial support for the lecture series.

Introduction

TOBIAS HOFFMANN

That I may do something contrary to what I consider best to do is not necessarily perplexing: I want to score a goal at a soccer game but fail to do so because of lack of skill; I want to drive south but unknowingly drive north instead; I fall from my bike because the road is slippery. However, that I act against my better judgment intentionally, that is, knowingly and freely, is puzzling indeed: no one wants to kick wide of the net, get lost on the road, or take a painful tumble, while judging that it would be desirable to score a goal, to arrive at one's destination on time, or to avoid a fall.

Weakness of will (i.e., incontinence) names the phenomenon of acting, voluntarily, contrary to one's better judgment. In such action, something has evidently gone quite wrong, but it is not immediately apparent what.

Since the reawakening of interest in incontinence about forty years ago, most literature has focused on the question of whether and how it is possible. The renaissance of philosophical inquiry about incontinence was initiated by R. M. Hare's denial of its possibility and above all by Donald Davidson's argument to the contrary.[1] Since then, discussions have centered either on whether incontinence is possible in light of a specific theory of practical rationality, or, conversely, on how practical rationality must be conceived so as to account for the possibility of incontinence.

In incontinent action, the connection between rational judgment and rational desire, or between rational desire and action, is interrupted. The practical judgment is not translated into action. Incontinence

1. R. M. Hare, *Freedom and Reason* (Oxford: Clarendon Press, 1963), 68–69; D. Davidson, "How Is Weakness of the Will Possible?" in *Moral Concepts,* ed. Joel Feinberg (Oxford: Oxford University Press, 1970), reprinted in D. Davidson, *Essays on Actions and Events* (New York: Oxford University Press, 1980), 21–42. For a brief historical sketch of the discussions from Hare until the recent past, see Sarah Stroud and Christine Tappolet, eds., *Weakness of Will and Practical Irrationality* (Oxford: Clarendon Press, 2003), 1–9.

differs from compulsive action and from thwarted action, for in incontinent action the chain that normally connects judgment, rational desire, and action together is not violently or unwillingly severed. One does not, however, intentionally break a link of that chain; one typically does not form an intention to desire differently from what reason judges best, or to act differently from one's rational desire. A more subtle explanation must be given.

Practical reasoning is not a disembodied calculation. It does not have a sharply definable beginning and a clear-cut end, but rather extends over time. It tends to have a reflective nature: one can look back on the deliberation and judge whether one's reasoning was good. Practical reasoning is conditioned by our emotional and physical states, by our acquired dispositions, by our explicit and implicit interests, and by the norms that govern our society, our work environment, our family, and so on. When affected by strong passions, when experiencing pain, when craving for something, when being exposed to peer pressure, I reason differently than when I am calm and alone. Under such conditions, I may even fail to deliberate altogether and act compulsively. The practical principles and moral convictions that normally inform my actions may in such circumstances be without effect, and thus I can act against my better judgment.

But does incontinence simply mean that I change my mind about what is best to do, or rather that at the very moment when I sincerely judge something to be the better action, I do the opposite? Consider these two examples: (1) I judge that I should not drive if I have drunk more than one beer. Being offered a second one, I think I shouldn't accept it. Yet I also begin to look at it in a new light: I enjoy the company, the beer is good. . . . I now shape a new judgment: it is good to have another beer, because it is pleasurable. I have not abandoned the view that I should not drink too much, but at present I do not pay attention to it. (2) In the same situation, I continue to be fully convinced that I should not drink more, but I do so anyway. The first is an example of diachronic weakness of will, whereas the second is an instance of synchronic weakness of will, also called "clear-eyed" or "open-eyed" akrasia. Diachronic weakness of will may be seen as a weakness of practical reason (the failure to draw the correct conclusions from my own convictions), whereas synchronic weakness of will appears to be weakness of the power of willing (the failure to will in accordance with what I judge best here and now).

Most of us experience incontinence or weakness of will as a frustrating experience. Hence the question arises what we can do to counter it, that is, how we can strengthen our reason and will, how we can achieve a firmer and more consistent character. Whereas many recent discussions have approached the problem of incontinence mainly from the point of view of action theory, asking how it is possible and what notion of practical rationality it implies, traditionally this phenomenon was also viewed within the larger viewpoint of character development. Some philosophers who showed little interest in weakness of will in the narrow sense as acting against one's better judgment paid attention to weakness of will taken broadly as weakness of character. Yet to describe character types as either strong or weak, as balanced or wavering, as abiding by reason or by the passions, is not yet to offer a theory of moral education. In the present volume, the three perspectives find attention: weakness of will as a phenomenon that calls for a philosophical explanation, weakness of will as weakness of character, and the challenge of weakness of will to moral progress. The papers of the present volume address these issues either by critically discussing the views of the major thinkers of the history of philosophy or by examining them in their own right.

Currently one can observe a growing interest in the historical approach to weakness of will.[2] The historical and contemporary perspectives offered in this volume will enrich current debates, not only by suggesting answers, but also by broadening the usual range of questions, such as these: Is there conceptual space for incontinence? Can incontinence be overcome, that is, can reason gain full control of a person? Should reason even rule over the passions? Should one give up the struggle with the passions and find a modus vivendi with one's own weakness? How can we learn from our own experience of weakness? What are the remedies for weakness of will? Do situations of weakness of will leave room for free choice or are they a matter of good or bad luck? How does weakness of will differ from other deplorable character states?

The philosophical examination of weakness of will brings to the fore central problems of action theory, such as the connections among desire, conviction and action, between intellect and will, and between rationality and emotions. In addition, it addresses important ethical issues, such as the diversity of character dispositions, moral progress and moral

2. For recent historical studies, see Christopher Bobonich and Pierre Destrée, eds., Akrasia *in Greek Philosophy: From Socrates to Plotinus* (Leiden: E. J. Brill, 2007); Risto Saarinen, *Weakness of the Will in Medieval Thought* (Leiden: E. J. Brill, 1994); and Tobias Hoffmann, Jörn Müller, and Matthias Perkams, eds., *The Problem of Weakness of Will in Medieval Thought* (Leuven, Paris, and Dudley, Mass.: Peeters, 2006). See also Fabienne Pironet and Christine Tappolet, "Faiblesse de la raison ou faiblesse de volonté: Peut-on choisir?" *Dialogue: Canadian Philosophical Review* 42 (2003): 627–44, which is an introductory essay to a special issue of this journal that collects papers more or less closely related to incontinence. It contains individual essays on Xenophon, Aristotle, Descartes, Spinoza, and Locke, as well as an essay on Aquinas, Gerald Odonis, and Buridan.

education, the limits of virtue, and moral responsibility. The problem of weakness of will is so intimately connected with other key themes in moral philosophy that the historical and thematic studies contained in this book also provide an overview of moral philosophy as a whole.

Synopsis

Kenneth Dorter. In the *Protagoras,* Socrates famously rejects the view that knowledge can be overcome by our passions. By contrast, in Book 4 of Plato's *Republic,* where Socrates argues for a tripartite soul, he holds that the appetitive, spirited, and rational parts may well conflict with one another: hence the need for self-mastery, by which the better part of the soul rules over the worse parts. Socrates argues repeatedly that the better part of the soul is reason and that it is therefore best for reason to rule. Self-mastery consists thus in the rule of reason, and the failure of reason is weakness of will. How can reason be weak? According to Book 7 of the *Republic,* knowledge is indeed virtue and invulnerable to weakness of will, if it is more than mere opinion or belief, namely, if it is wisdom. When wisdom is attained, that is, when one leaves the cave of the visible world and contemplates the Form of the Good, the soul as a whole is turned to the Good. Thus the soul is no longer divided, and self-mastery is no longer required. Because true knowledge entails an undivided soul, it cannot be defeated by the passions. Accordingly, the *Republic* is not at odds with the *Protagoras* when one takes into account that Socrates himself insists on the inadequacy of the treatment in Book 4 and that the conception of knowledge, as presented in Book 7, is sufficient for virtue and invulnerable to temptation.

Terence H. Irwin. When Aristotle attributes to Socrates the denial of the possibility of incontinence, his account of Socrates' position is based on the *Protagoras.* But Aristotle's attitude toward the *Protagoras* is different in the *Magna Moralia*—which Terence Irwin considers substantially authentic—and the later treatment of *Nicomachean Ethics* 7 (which is common to the *Eudemian Ethics*). Only in *EN* 7 does Aristotle refer to Socrates' view in the *Protagoras* that knowledge is not dragged around like a slave by passion. Irwin stipulates that Aristotle adds this specific reference in his later treatment because he now recognizes that Socrates says something true here. Only perceptual knowledge, not knowledge in the full sense, is dragged around by passion. Perceptual knowledge furnishes the minor premise to a practical syllogism. This knowledge is dragged from a "good" syllogism to a "bad" one. Instead of connecting the minor premise that "this is sweet" to the major premise forbidding sweet things, incontinent individuals connect it instead to the major premise that permits sweets. They thereby lack the knowledge that this particular thing ought not to be tasted; they do not sincerely judge while acting incontinently that they ought not to do what they do. Aristotle thus admits with the *Protagoras* that a certain kind of knowledge is not dragged around, and yet he grants against the *Protagoras* the possibility of incontinence.

Lloyd P. Gerson. Plotinus incorporates Peripatetic and Stoic teachings into his Platonic moral psychology. Lloyd Gerson briefly rehearses the Platonic, Aristotelian, and Stoic accounts of incontinence that are presupposed by what he calls "Plotinus's Neoplatonic synthesis." Common to the three accounts is the distinction between what individuals desire and what they desire to desire (in Harry Frankfurt's terms, between first- and second-order desires). Conflicting desires and weakness of will result from the ignorance of what is truly one's own good. It is characteristic of the Stoa to minimize the difference between incontinence and vice, on the one hand, and between continence and virtue, on the other. For Plotinus, what makes conflicts of desire possible is that human beings are double, that is, they are the composite (body and soul) and the self. Passions (πάθοι), bodily states, elicit desires, which can be either involuntary (i.e., not endorsed by a second-order desire) or voluntary (i.e., endorsed). One should not identify with involuntary desires resulting from the fact that human beings are embodied, but rather with second-order desires, so that one may identify one's own good with the Good. Moral virtue disposes one to desire that which intellect determines as good. The vicious and incontinent, conversely, are ignorant of self, unable to transcend the domain of first-order desire, and forgetful of their true identities and of their own good. Weakness is to turn away from the real good due to the failure to separate the real good that one truly desires from the apparent goods proposed to the embodied persons.

James Wetzel. Involuntary desires are a major preoccupation of Augustine, in particular those that are of the sexual sort, resulting from what he calls "*consuetudo carnalis,*" which James Wetzel translates as "sexual habit." The struggle with sexual habit reaches farther than that with *akrasia;* incontinent actions may result from sexual habit, but even when one resists the carnal desires one cannot avoid being affected by them. As in Stoicism, the distinctions between temperance and continence, and between incontinence and vice, fade. Even continent and virtuous persons—for example, St. Paul as he sees himself in *Romans* 7—are victims of sexual habit. Though they may avoid doing what they hate, they still desire what they hate. Wetzel concentrates on *Confessions* 7–8, where Augustine describes the struggles of his conversion and where he investigates the origin of evil. The desires that pull him away from what he considers most worthy of being desired—God and things of the spirit—are summed up in sexual habit, which results from *concupiscentia,* an innate disordered attachment to things of the flesh. Concupiscence and sexual habit are inherent to the person and make it impossible to avoid sinning, except by grace. This wound is an inheritance from Adam, understood by Augustine as a historical individual (rather than taken figuratively). Adam's free decision to sin mysteriously entails the inability of all his descendants to avoid sinning. Wetzel argues that Augustine is self-deceived in that he fails to see that human weakness is not due to an original free choice of a historical first man, but rather to the condition of being a mortal creature, of being flesh. Failing to accept one's mortality makes one desire a body double that never dies.

Denis J. M. Bradley. In the works of Thomas Aquinas, the problem of weakness of will receives ample treatment. As Denis Bradley shows, for Aquinas incontinence is only one of several notions that specify the general concept of weakness of will. The contexts in which Aquinas treats weakness of will are the discussion of the conflict between flesh and mind described by St. Paul in Romans 7, the treatment of "sin from weakness," that is, from passion; the close analysis of Book 7 in the commentary on the *Nicomachean Ethics;* and his account of original sin and the need for grace. In his *Ethics Commentary,* Thomas gives a careful analysis of the Aristotelian account, as Bradley shows, concentrating on its explanation of the practical syllogisms that constitute the incontinent person's practical reasoning. In his theological works, however, Aquinas introduces, in addition to the Aristotelian explanation, the notion of the will as a distinct power of the intellectual soul that mediates between reason and the sense appetite. Whereas Aristotle denies that incontinent individuals choose to act incontinently, Aquinas holds that they do—they do not choose the action as such, but they choose to satisfy their passions. Although he introduces the will into the fundamentally Aristotelian account of incontinence, Thomas does not think that there can be "open-eyed *akrasia,*" that is, an action against reason in full knowledge that it is unreasonable. While passions cloud the rational judgment, the incontinent ignore that this thing at hand should not be chosen here and now, mistakenly thinking that it is best to satisfy concupiscence. Like Augustine, Aquinas considers the weakness of human nature to be innate due to original sin. Even a temperate person like St. Paul continues to experience disordered movements of concupiscence in the sense appetite, unless a person is miraculously saved from original sin, as Christian theology says of the Blessed Virgin Mary.

Tobias Hoffmann. Aristotle and Aquinas explain incontinence within the Socratic presupposition that one cannot do evil in full knowledge that the action is evil. For them, incontinent action presupposes ignorance of what is best to do here and now. By contrast, according to Henry of Ghent, ignorance follows upon incontinent action. A cognitive defect does not explain moral evil. The root of moral evil is in the will alone. Once an evil choice is made, the judgment of reason is clouded. Over time, repeated evil choices destroy practical knowledge entirely: someone who initially thought that theft is bad comes to think that it is good. The overall concern of Henry is to save the freedom of the will's choice, including the incontinent person's choice. If a choice were caused by anything else than the will, it would not be free, for nothing else than the will can contingently cause its own effect. Not even reason and practical deliberation can cause free decision, for, in Henry's view, reason's operation is deterministic. The will cannot choose without prior knowledge, but when knowledge is available, the will's choice is entirely self-caused. It can even choose contrary to the judgment of what is best here and now. Though for Henry the possibility to act against reason is a necessary condition for free decision, freedom of the will *(libertas voluntatis)* consists in adhering to the good, not in free decision *(liberum arbitrium).* The more firmly one adheres to the good, the freer one is and the stronger is one's will. What strengthens the will are the moral virtues, which are essentially virtues of the will.

Giuseppe Mazzotta. Philosophy cannot adequately express all of reality. For example, it cannot fully describe the experience of love. When Dante falls in love with Beatrice, he experiences the powerlessness of the will, not mainly because his love for her comes about as a sudden and nondeliberate experience, but above all because Beatrice dies without his being able to do anything about it. Dante desires to write a poem about Beatrice. This poem is the *Divine Comedy.* As Giuseppe Mazzotta shows, the focus of the *Divine Comedy* is moral and spiritual education. In *Hell,* Dante dramatizes the wounds of the will and the soul's proneness to sin; in *Purgatory,* he depicts education to moral virtue; and in *Paradise* he portrays the education of the intellect to truth and knowledge of God. Only in the unity of intellect and will can knowledge and affection accomplish the healing of the wounded will. Mazzotta provides examples of personalities of the *Divine Comedy* who illustrate the wounds and the healing of the will in the domain of ethics and politics. What accomplishes the healing is art, understood as work (the shaping of nature), which is depicted as the foundation of the moral life and the corrective of the disorders of the will and the intellect.

Ann Hartle. Despite the great diversity of ethical conceptions and theories of ancient and medieval thinkers, they share some fundamental convictions: that ethics regards the accomplishment or perfection of the human being; that practical reason is a guide to such perfection, and that the moral virtues dispose us to act according to the ethical ideal. Failure to act in accordance with the dictates of reason is seen as a weakness that one should endeavor to overcome. Montaigne, by contrast, is content with his being weak. Ann Hartle spells out how he develops this theme in his *Essays.* Instead of striving for victory in moral struggles, he tries to avoid them. He considers himself unable to moderate his passions, and so he rather avoids them. He calls the character trait that he embodies "goodness," a natural distaste for vice, but he ranks it lower than "imperfect virtue" (overcoming vicious inclinations by force) and "perfect virtue" (when the seeds of vice are rooted out). Whereas virtue depends on the rule of reason in the soul, goodness does not. Montaigne opposes himself to the idea that there is a form common to all human beings, that this form is reason, and hence that the standard for all human affairs is reason. He instead posits individual forms that are peculiar to particular human beings. One cannot propose the same ethical ideal to all; philosophy has in fact failed in proposing an ethical path that is common to all. Each person should rather live according to his or her individual form, without trying to imitate anyone who is presumably better. Montaigne's own form is weakness. This weakness is marvelous, for it opens one up to the transformation of the traditional moral life of the virtues through the theological virtues of faith, hope, and charity.

John C. McCarthy. Descartes's published writings contain scarcely anything on ethics. The French philosopher never discusses weakness of will as such, for in his view it is sufficient to judge well to do well and to acquire all the virtues. Yet he does depict a character type that has a certain likeness to the incontinent, even if, on closer inspection, it can be seen also to be comparable to the continent: those he calls "feeble spirits." John McCarthy explores Descartes's portrayal of feeble spirits in the *Discourse on Method* and in particular in *The Passions of the Soul.* These weak spirits are inconstant and prone to remorse. Their counterpart, the strong spirits, are self-confidently self-reliant; they are also, as McCarthy observes, an emblem for the (Cartesian) philosopher. Although Descartes does not exhibit any concern about weakness of will in the traditional sense, he shows considerable interest in the possibility of the conflict—or rather "battle"—that takes place between a person's will and his or her passions. This battle is not a conflict within the soul, but rather between body and soul, for the passions of the soul are actions of the body. The "weapon" the soul should employ against the agitation of the passions is the judicious use of passions against passions, that is, to use one passion to control the other. Rather than in terms of rational emendation, Descartes likens the soul's mastery over the passions to animal training. And since this "domestication" does not bring the corporeal and the psychic into a mutually beneficial harmony, the conflict cannot be eradicated, but only regulated. Morality's main objective is the rule of desire. The principal means to this goal is the virtue of generosity, understood as the capacity to distinguish between those things that entirely depend upon us and those that do not, and then to limit our desires to that which is in our own power. Generosity is the virtue of self-reliance, and in this office, it is the key to all the other virtues and the remedy against all the disorders of the passions. The opposite of the generous are the base, that is, the weak in spirit or soul, who believe that they cannot subsist by themselves and who make the fulfillment of their desires dependent on others.

Thomas E. Hill Jr. Weakness of will, as traditionally conceived, is no topic of interest for Descartes, because in his view correct knowledge entails right action. For the English empiricists Hobbes and Hume, there is not even conceptual room for weakness of will, for the will is nothing but an inevitable event in a chain of natural causes: the desire that happens to be strongest (according to Hobbes) or the "impression" that happens to be felt (according to Hume). Kant, contrarily, thinks of the will as an active power of the mind, not as something we passively experience. We have control of our actions, and likewise we are to be praised or blamed for our character. Kant distinguishes among several character types. Moral perfection, that is, virtue, is fundamentally a developed strength of will to do what is right. Weakness or frailty is when there is a commitment to follow the moral law, yet on occasion one is too weak to do so. Kant distinguishes this from impurity (a qualified commitment to the law) and depravity (to subordinate the moral law to one's own interests). Morally weak *and* vicious people are aware of what is right and willfully disregard the standard of the law (momentarily the former, systematically the latter). Hill interprets Kant's account of weakness of will as having two dimensions: (1) our will to do right is vague and inexplicit with regard to its implications: once we see the costs of doing the right thing, we abandon our resolution to do what is right; (2) we will weakly; we resolve half-heartedly and in a wavering fashion. In neither case does weakness of will mean to be literally overpowered, for throughout temptation the will remains in control of our choices. The culpability for doing wrong under the influence of strong passions is mitigated, but not fully excused.

Tracy B. Strong. While Kant emphasizes the possibility of free choice even under strong temptation, Nietzsche stresses the fact that the will's choices in the present are entirely conditioned by the past. But this is not what makes Nietzsche's view unconventional. Its originality is that he holds that rationality is not that which helps to overcome weakness of will, but rather that which makes it possible in the first place. What characterizes the will originally is not weakness or strength, but its inherent will to power. There is no will that is not will to power, but it comes in two opposed character types: either as masterly and nobly moral will to power, or as slavely moral will to power—as strong or as weak. The first is the mark of the dominators, the second of the dominated, the oppressed. Being oppressed, the slavely moral types want the masterly types to be what they are not, that is, to be weak rather than strong. Nietzsche illustrates this with a parable: The lamb, the eagle's prey, wants the eagle not to behave as an eagle. The lamb demands that strength not express itself as strength, that it may not become a master. It wants the eagle's will to be weak, and to this end, it asks the eagle for a reason for what it does; it demands that it have a choice, and that there be a common framework in terms of which the lamb and eagle can make judgments. Thus instinct, the creative-affirmative power, is replaced by reflective rationality. The eagle now learns to be weak-willed: rather than doing what it desires, its weakness consists in doing what is rationally good. This is the triumph of the slave over the master: he places the master under the demands of a choice that the master did not make in the past. It is thus that rationality makes weakness of will possible.

Alfred Mele. What may cause individuals to act contrarily to their better judgment is that although they have a good reason (or reasons) not to perform an action, they have an insignificant reason to do it. Supposing that the decision to act one way or the other is made by a free agent, understood in the libertarian sense that the person had alternative possibilities of action, how does one account for the the actual choice of one alternative? In other words, what accounts for the difference between the fact that one of two alternative possibilities is chosen and the fact that, in another possible world, the other one is chosen? "Event-causal libertarians" who are committed to the view that the situation up until the very moment of choice is identical in both cases, so that the only difference consists in the choice itself, would have to hold that there is nothing that accounts for this difference and that the difference is a matter of luck. A choice contrary to the person's conscious belief of what is best to do would then be a matter of bad luck, not of weakness of will. Alfred Mele investigates how an event-causal libertarian view that admits these premises can account for the fact that an akratic agent acts freely and responsibly. In addition, he discusses how such a view explains the difference between akratic actions and radical breakdowns of agency. He also gives an account of how the capacity to form free actions for which one is responsible is developed in childhood.

Alasdair MacIntyre. It is generally assumed that it is normal for a human being to act in a principled and consistent way, and that actions at variance with one's better judgment require special explanation. Against this presumption, Alasdair MacIntyre argues that lapses from what we know to be best are rather a normal human condition, for we are not in full control of our desires. For moral development, it is important to develop the habit of pursuing objects that we have reason to desire, rather than simply those that we in fact desire. MacIntyre develops this point against the foil of rational decision theory. Exponents of this theory as a theory of practical rationality provide criteria for the rational pursuit of what one desires, but fail to provide a critique of the desires themselves, and thereby they do not protect us from becoming victims of our own desires. Such a critique of desires presupposes a rank ordering not only of desires, but also of goods. A good is that which contributes to my flourishing; this is precisely what makes it reasonable to desire a good. To desire what we have reason to desire requires learning to be patient, to defer satisfaction, and to respond to the desires or needs of others. It also involves learning how to rank-order goods and how to solve conflicts of desire, so as to acquire a conception of what is best for us as human beings. Since conflicts of desire and the lapses and inconsistencies that they entail are a normal condition of life, virtuous persons are not immune to such lapses. What characterizes the virtuous is rather their ability to respond to them. Inconsistent behavior is not a sign of weakness of will, but of an imperfect ordering of our desires, even in the best individuals. Weakness of will, or lack of strength to pursue our good, consists in the incapacity to respond adequately to the inconsistencies, either by ignoring them or by consenting to them. Lapses into temptation should be the occasion for further reflection, for a continued dialogue with ourselves and others that is devoted to resolving conflicts of desire and to attaining the judgments about what we have reason to desire.

1 Weakness and Will in Plato's *Republic*

KENNETH DORTER

The central problem in determining Plato's attitude toward moral weakness lies in the apparent discrepancy between what Socrates says in dialogues like the *Protagoras, Laches, Charmides,* and *Meno,* on the one hand, and Book 4 of the *Republic,* on the other. The former are characterized by moral intellectualism, the view that since we always want good things for ourselves, once we know that something is good we will act in accordance with that knowledge; they argue that knowledge has an intrinsic power too great for it to be enslaved by inferior principles like appetite and spiritedness.[1] While the *Protagoras* scornfully ascribes to "the multitude" the view that knowledge alone is not strong enough to rule over its rivals—that without the help of something like moral strength it can be enslaved by our emotions (352b–c)—the *Republic* seems to defend precisely the view that the *Protagoras* dismissed as that of the multitude. According to Book 4, it is possible for us to know what is good and yet fail to act on that knowledge because we are too weak to master our temptations or fears, so that if our knowledge is not accompanied by moral strength or self-mastery, our rational faculty can indeed be overmastered by its inferiors:

> Self-control [σωφροσύνη] is surely some kind of order, the self-mastery [ἐγκράτεια] of certain pleasures and appetites, as they say, using the phrase "master of oneself" [κρείττω αὑτοῦ]—I don't know how—and other such phrases that are like traces that it has left behind. . . . Yet isn't the expression "master of oneself" ridiculous? He who is master of himself would also be subject to himself, and he who is subject master. The same person is referred to in all these statements. . . . But the saying seems to me to want to say that in the same person there is something in

I would like to thank Tobias Hoffmann for his helpful comments on an earlier version of this paper.

1. Some passages say this not only about knowledge but also belief (e.g., *Protagoras* 358b–d, οἰόμενος, οἴεται), which complicates the issue because it is more difficult to maintain that mere belief is too noble to be enslaved. We will consider the claim about belief after discussing the claim about knowledge.

the soul that is better and something that is worse, and when the part that is better by nature is master of the worse, this is what is meant by speaking of being master of oneself. . . . But when, on the other hand, because of bad upbringing or bad company the better part which is smaller is mastered by the multitude of the larger, we blame this as something shameful, and call it being subject to oneself and licentious. (430e–31b)[2]

In the soul of the tyrant, explicitly, "the most reasonable part of it is dishonorably and wretchedly enslaved" (577c).

It is tempting to resolve the inconsistency by supposing that Plato has simply changed his mind and come to recognize, like Aristotle,[3] that we quite regularly act against our better judgment under the pressure of our appetites and fears. There are two reasons to be cautious about that solution, reasons that seem to point in opposite directions. On the one hand, the dialogues that assert moral intellectualism all end at an impasse; they fail to resolve the issue to which they are devoted, and leave us uncertain about precisely what we are meant to learn. Conceivably, we may be meant to learn that the inquiry foundered because the doctrine of moral intellectualism leads to a dead end. In that case the *Republic* would present positively what the other dialogues imply negatively: the need to accommodate the possibility of weakness of will.

On the other hand, the *Republic* presents its self-mastery thesis in a way that undermines our confidence in it as much as if it too had led to an impasse. Just prior to his introduction of the concepts of self-control and self-mastery, Socrates says, "Two things still remain to be discerned in our city, self-control and . . . justice. How then might we find justice without having to bother any more about self-control?" (430d). He seems to be suggesting that the most adequate conception of justice would not require reference to self-control (or self-mastery), but Glaucon replies that he does not want to skip over self-control in any case, so whatever lay behind Socrates' question remains unexplained. Socrates renews his misgivings more forcefully midway through the ensuing discussion: "in my opinion we will never get an accurate answer using our present methods of argument." But when he adds that "perhaps we can get an answer that's up to our previous standard," Glaucon is satisfied, so the source of Socrates' dissatisfaction once again fails to be explained (435c–d; cf. 504b). After

2. Translations are my own.

3. "It is problematic how someone with correct understanding can lack self-mastery. Some say this is not possible for someone who has knowledge; for it would be strange, as Socrates thought, if when someone possessed knowledge something else should master it and 'drag it around like a slave.' Socrates in fact used to attack the account altogether, on the grounds that there is no such thing as lack of self-mastery; for no one understands himself to act against what is best, but they do so only through ignorance. Now this account clearly goes against the evidence" (*Nicomachean Ethics* 7.2.1145b21–29).

these warnings it is not surprising that Socrates sums up their eventual conclusion with something less than enthusiasm: "if we said that we discovered the just person, and the courageous one . . . I think we would in some way not completely seem to be lying" (444a).

It seems, then, that if the intellectualistic claims of dialogues like the *Protagoras* are thrown into question by their aporetic conclusions, the self-mastery thesis of the *Republic* is made to look equally uncertain in other ways, and it is conceivable that the *Republic* may ultimately not be opposed to moral intellectualism after all.[4] As I intend to show in this paper, no interpretation can do full justice to the *Republic*'s position that does not accommodate Socrates' insistence that the treatment in Book 4 is inadequate, and the way that the conception of knowledge changes in the next three books, especially after the Divided Line. The conception of knowledge presented in Book 7 will be sufficient for virtue—no longer vulnerable to temptation and fear or in need of supplemental reinforcement—which means that the *Republic* is not ultimately at odds with the *Protagoras;* the discrepancy appears only if we take Book 4 to be the *Republic*'s final word on the subject, instead of seeing it as a preliminary treatment that is superseded in what follows.[5]

The first quotation shows that the concept of self-mastery requires (1) a conception of the soul or self as divided, and (2) the identification of one part as better and another as worse. In what follows we shall consider, first, how Socrates establishes in Book 4 that the soul has three parts, and then the arguments in Book 9 for regarding rationality as in some sense the best of them (both claims are contentious, and their contentious nature will be pointed out by Socrates himself). Only then will we return to the argument for the tripartition of the soul to discover

4. Cf. Samuel Scolnicov, "Reason and Passion in the Platonic Soul," *Dionysius* 2 (1978): 35–49, at 45, and *Plato's Metaphysics of Education* (London: Routledge, 1988), 102 and 112; W. K. C. Guthrie, *A History of Greek Philosophy,* vol. 4 (Cambridge: Cambridge University Press, 1975), 435–36; Emile de Stryker, "The Unity of Knowledge and Love in Socrates' Conception of Virtue," *International Philosophical Quarterly* 6 (1966): 428–44, at 440–41; and Horace Fries, "Virtue Is Knowledge," *Philosophy of Science* 8 (1940): 89–99, at 91 and n. 5.

5. Explorations of this issue usually focus on Book 4. See, e.g., Christopher Bobonich, *Plato's Utopia Recast: His Later Ethics and Politics* (Oxford: Clarendon Press, 2002), 235–58; Gabriela Roxana Carone, "*Akrasia* in the *Republic:* Does Plato Change His Mind?" *Oxford Studies in Ancient Philosophy* 20 (2001): 107–48, Terence H. Irwin, *Plato's Ethics* (New York: Oxford University Press, 1995), 223–24; Amélie Oksenberg Rorty, "The Limits of Socratic Intellectualism: Did Socrates Teach Arete?" in *Proceedings of the Boston Area Colloquium in Ancient Philosophy,* vol. 2, ed. John Cleary (Lantham, Md.: University Press of America, 1987), 317–30, at 328–29; Lloyd P. Gerson, "Platonic Dualism," *Monist* 69 (1986): 352–69, at 359; Glenn Lesses, "Weakness, Reason, and the Divided Soul in Plato's *Republic,*" *History of Philosophy Quarterly* 4 (1987): 147–61, at 148; and Charles Kahn, *Plato and the Socratic Dialogue: The Philosophical Use of a Literary Form* (Cambridge: Cambridge University Press, 1996), 240.

why Socrates disparaged it, and how it is superseded by the conception of knowledge introduced in Books 5–7. Because of the *Republic*'s "arch" structure, it is in those central books that the discussion reaches the highest level, after which it explicitly returns to the discussion of Book 4 (543c). Why Plato proceeds in this way will be considered subsequently.

Since the concept of will does not appear directly in Plato (the term usually translated as "weakness of will," ἀκράτεια as at 461a, simply means "weakness"), we will formulate the problem in terms of Socrates' statement that moral weakness ("being subject to oneself") means that the better part in us is overpowered by the worse. In that case, for our purposes Plato's question in Book 9, "Which is our best part?," can be taken to mean, "Which is our true will?"[6]

1. The Tripartite Soul

Books 2 and 3 develop Socrates' model of the soul writ large, the depiction of the formation of a city as a visible analogue of the soul, to facilitate our understanding of the nature of justice (368c–69a). When the city evolved into three classes—productive workers, military auxiliary, rulers—the definitions of the virtues were based on the relationship of the classes to one another. Consequently the definitions will be transferable to the soul only if it has an analogous triadic structure. It is obvious that the distinctive characteristics of the three classes—appetite in the productive class, spiritedness in the auxiliaries, rationality in the rulers—are in each of us since we all enjoy pleasures, have a degree of ambition, and care whether things are true or false. It is also obvious that they sometimes lead to conflicting goals and desires; but that does not mean they must be discrete parts within us. It is doubtful, for example, that we ever experience rationality when it is not accompanied by some emotion, or emotion that is completely devoid of rationality, so our experience does not seem to support a model of the self in which these functions are anything like separate parts. Socrates raises the problem himself: it may be, he says, that our soul acts as a unity when it learns, gets angry, and desires, rather than doing each of these with a different part of itself (436a). My hand can reach for objects of pleasure, swing a tennis racket in competition, and turn pages in pursuit of truth, but that does not mean it has different parts for each of the three functions. Why should it mean that in the case of the soul? To eliminate that possibility

6. In the moral context of weakness of will, will is not necessarily distinguished from reason, as it is in the debate between voluntarism and intellectualism (i.e., whether reason or will predominates in us).

Socrates constructs an argument around the principle of opposition, an ontological equivalent of the principle of contradiction:

(1)The same thing cannot be opposed to itself in the same respect, in relation to the same thing, at the same time. So, if this happens in the soul we are not dealing with one thing but many (436b).

(2) Standing still while moving our arms and head is not an exception because we are not standing still and moving in the same respect: our feet are at rest and our arms are moving (c–d).

(3) The same is true of a spinning top that stays in one place: "it's standing still with respect to its axis . . . and moving in a circle with respect to its periphery" (d–e).

(4) Sometimes we are thirsty but decide not to drink, so there is something in us that tells us to drink, namely, appetite, and something else that tells us not to, namely, rationality, the two of which must then be different species in our soul (439c–e).

(5) Sometimes we get angry at ourselves because of our appetites, in which case our spiritedness fights against our appetite as one thing against another (439e–40d).

(6) When we rationally restrain our anger, then spiritedness and rationality are in opposition (441a–b).

We will consider the cogency of this argument in section 6, but for now we can say that it provides at least prima facie grounds for believing that appetite, spiritedness, and rationality are distinct parts of us. Our next step is to see how Socrates establishes that rationality is the best of the three, and must be obeyed for self-mastery to occur—in which case rationality is what would correspond to our true will and be the referent of weakness of will. That conclusion is by no means self-evident. Most people are governed by their appetite, the next largest group by spiritedness, and the smallest by rationality, so the concept of weakness of will is seen in different ways by different people. Appetitive or spirited people sometimes feel that if they listened to the warnings of reason and refrained from doing what their appetites or spiritedness prompted, it would show not strength of will but timidity. Thrasymachus has nothing but contempt for the "weak," "fearful" people who do not try to maximize their pleasures and power (344c), a view that Glaucon echoes as a devil's advocate (359a–60d), and that resurfaces again in Book 8 (549c–50a). Rational people may appear weak to the spirited, and unadventurous to the appetitive. Throughout the history of philosophy hedonists have championed appetite over rationality, and, especially since Schopenhauer and Nietzsche, voluntarists have championed something like spiritedness over rationality. Outside the philosophical community there is even stronger disagreement with the claim that the pursuit of truth is preferable to the pursuit of pleasure or power. Here again Socrates himself calls attention to the problem: although to rational people rationality seems like what is best in us, to appetitive people appetite appears to be best and rationality is good only as an instrument of our appetites, while to spirited people spiritedness seems best and rationality is good only if it brings us honor (580c–81c).

To establish his claim that reason alone deserves to be our ruling faculty—our will—(and that therefore the just life, the rule of reason, is the best life), Socrates offers three arguments to the effect that only a life that follows reason will bring true and lasting happiness, while the others lead only to ambiguous and temporary satisfaction. In terms of the question of weakness of will, it makes sense to call reason our true will if it is the only drive that can bring us fulfillment.

2. First Argument: Fitness to Rule

Socrates' first argument compares the inner life of the most just and the most unjust person. The most just person is ruled by rationality, while the most unjust is ruled by the most extreme of the three forms of appetite. The three forms are distinguished by first dividing appetite into necessary and unnecessary appetites, and then unnecessary appetites into lawful and lawless species. Necessary appetites are those that are indispensable or beneficial, like the desire for healthy food. Unnecessary appetites are neither indispensable nor beneficial, and are "harmful both to the body and to the soul with respect to wisdom and self-control," like the desire for unhealthy food (558d–89c). Socrates' description of lawless appetites could have come straight out of Freud:

> They are probably in all of us, but when restrained by the laws, and by the better desires together with rationality, in some people they are gotten rid of completely or only a few weak ones remain, while in others they are stronger and more numerous. . . . They are aroused during sleep when the rest of the soul slumbers—the rational, gentle, and ruling part of it—but the bestial and wild part, full of food or drink, springs up and, pushing away sleep, seeks to go and satisfy its dispositions. You know that in this condition it dares to do everything, as though released from and rid of all shame and wisdom. It shrinks from nothing, and tries to have sex with its mother, as it believes, or with any other person, god, or beast; nor does it shrink from any murder or refuse any food. In a word, it stops short of no folly or shamelessness. . . . There is then a terrible, wild, and lawless form of appetite in each of us, even in some of us who seem to be most moderate, and this becomes clear in our sleep. (571b–d, 572b)

Once we relax control over our appetites, things that were once unthinkable become at first conceivable and then irresistible, as we become driven by an appetite for the excitement and adventure of novelty. The belief that every appetite no matter how extreme deserves to be gratified cannot help but be felt eventually as an insatiable craving. But those who are in the grips of an insatiable craving cannot be happy; they are rather the most unhappy and least free kind of person, slaves to their most violent appetites. Socrates had already argued in Book 7 that the life of rationality leads to a vision of goodness that brings complete happiness (516b–19d). Now, by contrast, we find that the most appetitive life has the opposite effect and leads to the greatest unhappiness. The argument gives us one reason to believe that if weakness of will means that the worse part of us rules over the better, it is those ruled by appetite who most fit this description.

3. Second Argument: Criteria of Truth

The next argument could hardly begin more hesitantly: "Look at this second one if indeed you think there's anything in it" (580d). This is where Socrates points out the relativity we noted earlier, that appetitive, spirited, and rational people all love their defining pleasure—material things, honor, or wisdom, respectively—so if we ask them which of the three kinds of life is most pleasant they would each choose their own: lovers of material things will not care much about learning or honor except where they are materially profitable; lovers of honor have contempt for money, which they consider vulgar, and for learning, which they regard as smoke and nonsense (some things never change), except where these can bring them honor; and lovers of wisdom regard the other two not as true pleasures but only as necessities, which they would ignore if possible. How then can we decide which of the three is correct (580c–81c)?

It seems odd that Socrates would ask which way of life is most pleasant, since he was only challenged to show that just people are *happier* than unjust ones, and Socrates is the last person we would expect to equate happiness with pleasure, especially after he pointed out that some pleasures are bad (505c).[7] It would be more in keeping with his preceding analyses to maintain that even if the life of a voluptuary is more pleasant than that of the philosopher, the philosopher's life is more noble, and

7. Cf. N. R. Murphy, *The Interpretation of Plato's* Republic (Oxford: Clarendon Press, 1951), 209–11, 223; Julia Annas, *An Introduction to Plato's* Republic (Oxford: Clarendon Press, 1981), 306–14.

nobility is closer to the good (and happiness) than is pleasure. Socrates insists, however, that this argument is not about nobility or goodness but only about pleasure and pain (581e–82a). He wants to show that even if he accepts the terms of the lovers of appetite his conclusion still follows. When people object against hedonism that they are not motivated by pleasure but by nobility or morality, hedonists reply that the moralists have not chosen morality instead of pleasure, but that being moral gives them the *most* pleasure—that people who say they prefer something else to pleasure are really only saying that they prefer a less common form of pleasure to a more common one. Accordingly, Socrates now classifies all three parts of the soul as species of appetite that pursue corresponding species of pleasure (580d), and seeks to show that even by this criterion the life of rationality will still turn out to be the best (as Epicurus later concluded as well).

Socrates suggests three criteria for determining the truth of the matter: experience, intelligence, and rationality (582a). In the main argument, which deals with experience (the other two are dealt with quickly afterward at 582d), Socrates asks which of the three types of people has the most experience of all three kinds of pleasure: appetitive, spirited, and rational. They conclude that while lovers of wisdom have ample experience of all three, lovers of material things and lovers of honor have never experienced the pleasure of contemplating reality (582a–d). Philosophers are the only ones in a position to compare the three on the basis of experience, and so their verdict has the greatest claim to truth.[8]

A hedonist might object to this that Socrates' three criteria—experience, intelligence, and rationality—all belong to the rational part of the soul, so even though the argument takes pleasure as its standard, its criteria are those of rationalism. But this would be problematic only if those criteria were arbitrary, whereas they are in fact the most reasonable ones that could be appealed to. Could the hedonist object to this reply on the same grounds—that it appeals to the criterion of reason-

8. Cf. John Stuart Mill's similar argument in *Utilitarianism,* chap. 2, par. 6–7. R. L. Nettleship believes the argument is unsatisfactory because "a man who had no experience of a kind of pleasure which he was asked to believe was better than his own could not be convinced by the experience of another"; see *Lectures on the Republic of Plato,* 2nd ed. (London: Macmillan, 1901), 321. However, the goal of the argument is not to convince appetitive and spirited people that their belief about what is most pleasant is wrong, but to provide evidence to show which of the three beliefs has a stronger claim to truth. Theodor Gomperz claims that the argument "overlooks the fact that greater susceptibility to one kind of pleasure is usually coupled with a smaller capacity for enjoying other kinds" (*Greek Thinkers: A History of Ancient Philosophy,* vol. 3 [London: John Murray, 1905], 100), but he offers no evidence that—assuming his generalization to be correct—the capacity itself is smaller rather than the pleasure seeming less important by comparison.

ableness? In the *Philebus,* when the life of reason and the life of pleasure compete against each other, and Socrates proposes to decide between the two claims rationally, Philebus replies that as far as he is concerned, pleasure will be the winner regardless of what happens in the argument (12a–b), and refuses to take any further part. It is an understandable course for him, for why should the competing claims of hedonism and rationalism be judged by the criteria of reason? If Philebus finds the pursuit of pleasure more pleasant than the pursuit of truth, then for him that is the only criterion that counts. There is no common ground on which Socrates can meet someone like that, and in the *Philebus* Plato shows that he understands this. Hence the caution with which Socrates introduced this argument: "See if you think there's anything in this." The most that can be said against Socrates' procedure here is that he has not demonstrated all of his premises, but it is never possible to demonstrate all premises, and we must be satisfied if we begin with what is self-evident in the sense that to deny it is to deny the possibility of rational inquiry. Socrates' assumption meets that standard.

If this argument presupposes rationality as the criterion, that cannot be said of the next one, which will proceed not from the character of knowledge but from the character of pleasure itself. The three arguments by which the rational life defeats the appetitive life correspond, in fact, to all three of the values manifested by the three parts of the soul and the city. The first argument was based on a civil war model wherein not only do the three parts of the city and the soul compete for supremacy, but a further power struggle takes place within the appetitive part, either between rich and poor classes or between necessary and unnecessary appetites. In the end the just life is preferred because in the unjust soul the better parts are enslaved by the worse. That argument relied on the categories of spiritedness—warfare, enslavement, and domination—while the present argument relies on the rational categories of experience, intelligence, and rationality. The third and final argument will rely on the categories of appetite: which life has the most pleasure and the least pain.

4. Third Argument: True and False Pleasure

Socrates distinguishes three conditions: pain, pleasure, and an intermediate calm. When people in pain call it pleasant to be free of pain, they are mistaking calm for pleasure: as they move from the bottom to the middle they mistake the middle for the top (583d). Since it is also true that when someone ceases to feel pleasure the state of calm feels painful (the psychological basis of addiction), the intermediate state can be both painful and pleasant. But it is not "possible for what is neither to become both" (583e), so this state is not true pleasure (or true pain).

It is often objected that if people find this condition pleasant, it makes no sense to say they are not feeling pleasure: pleasure is a subjective state and only the individual can pronounce on its presence or absence.[9] But the argument rests on more than telling people that they do not feel what they think they feel. Socrates' point is that because these perceived pleasures depend on a prior condition of pain, a life devoted to them is equally a life devoted to pain, and thus only an apparently pleasant life. Still, if one person is content because of pseudopleasures like relief from pain, and another is content because of real pleasures, both are nevertheless content. If ignorant people are happy because they do not know any better, are they any less happy than wise people?

The answer is implied in the next stage of the argument. Ignorance and being unwise are empty states of the soul, as hunger and thirst are empty states of the body—the latter filled by food and drink, and the former by knowledge and reason. We are more truly filled, Socrates says, when we are filled with what more truly is, namely, the form (εἶδος) of true opinion, knowledge, reason, and all of virtue, rather than the class of food, drink, and nourishment in general. The latter never *is*, but is in a constant state of becoming, while the former "is always the same, and immortal, and true" (585b–d). Consequently it fills us with something that is stable and pure, and thus with more reality than other pleasures do (586a). It is not enough to say that as long as we feel pleasure, the basis of that feeling is unimportant—for pleasure turns out to be not just a feeling but a state of being and a change in our condition; and we can scarcely say that changes in our condition make no difference as long as what we feel is pleasant. Guided by rationality, we will even be able to pursue the pleasures that the realms of appetite and spiritedness have to offer, and enjoy them in their truest forms (586d–e). Under the guidance of rationality, spiritedness and appetite will devote themselves to pursuits that are most likely to achieve the desired results, rather than if our spirited pursuits were reckless and self-defeating, or our appetitive pursuits sought pleasure in ways that also bring the most pain. Here again what Socrates is proposing is the conception of pleasure maximization through rationality that was later championed by Epicurus.

9. Cf. R. C. Cross and A. D. Woozley, *Plato's* Republic: *A Philosophical Commentary* (London: Macmillan, 1964), 266, and Guthrie, 541. But as Annas points out, "it is up to us to argue, and not just assert, that pleasantness can *never* be an objective matter"; see *An Introduction to Plato's* Republic, 314, and her discussion at 308–14 generally.

5. Problems with the Tripartite Soul

At this point the *Republic*'s position seems clear. Weakness of will is possible because our soul is divided into three parts, one of which deserves to be identified as our will because it is what is best in us. When we ignore the best part in order to follow one of the inferior parts, we are weak-willed, or, in Plato's terms, subject to ourselves rather than masters of ourselves. Contrary to what most people believe, the best part is rationality, so that is our true will or best self.

But we have not yet dealt with Socrates' reservations about the first argument, the division of our soul into three parts. We must now try to understand the reasons for his warnings and see where that leaves us. Are there any obvious limitations with the tripartite model of the soul that might explain Socrates' repeated warnings? Most obvious was the assumption that if these are parts of the soul there are just three of them. The demonstration argued why there are not fewer than three, but gave no reason why there might not be more than three. In fact, a few pages later Socrates casually refers to the three parts of the soul together with "any others that may be in between them" (443e).[10] It is not hard to imagine borderline cases between the frustration of unfulfilled appetite and the anger of spiritedness, or between the striving of spiritedness and the striving for truth. Is there any limit to the number of parts in the soul, or could we keep finding additional intermediate cases until the soul looks more like a continuum than a troika? Does it even matter whether or not there is a finite number of parts?

As the dialogue proceeds, not only does Socrates allude to intermediate parts between the original three, but each of the original parts is further subdivided. At the end of Book 6, in the Divided Line section, rationality is divided into four parts. Spiritedness too is subdivided, sometimes taking the form of anger, sometimes love of honor, and sometimes love of victory (436a, 581b, 586c–d). As for appetite, in Book 9 Socrates goes so far as to say that there is *no common quality* to all the things called appetite: "because of its multiple forms, we could not designate it with one appropriate name, but we named it by what was biggest and strongest in it" (580d–e). In the course of the dialogue the soul looks less and less like a triad, and more and more like a continuum that at one end pursues the most brutish pleasures, and at the other end the most transcendent truth.

Let us look more closely at steps 2 and 3 of the argument for tripar-

10. Similarly, the appetitive, spirited, and rational classes of the city that serves as a visible analogue of the soul are only "the primary three classes" (581c) because there can be any number of intermediate cases and subdivisions among them.

tition, the example of the man waving his arms and the example of a spinning top. Both were examples of apparent contradictions that were resolved by distinguishing different parts, in anticipation of the way different parts would be attributed to the soul. In the first case, although the man was both standing still and moving, it was his feet that were standing still and his arms and head that were moving. If we think of the soul on that model, then it is composed of parts that are absolutely distinct: if an arm, leg, or even the head were lost, the others would still remain. On that model appetite, spiritedness, and rationality are three entirely distinct parts of the soul, which is how the soul appeared when the model was first formulated. But the example of the top is different. If we removed the periphery of a top, whatever is left would still be the periphery—we cannot remove it but only narrow it. Similarly if we tried to remove the axis by drilling a hole through the center of the pin, the axis would remain but it would be hollow. Periphery and axis are not separable parts like arms and legs, but abstractions that stand to each other as relations. If we apply this model, the tripartite soul looks quite different. If appetite, spiritedness, and rationality are related to one another like the axis and periphery of a top, then they too are abstractions and relative to one another, more like locations on a continuum than discrete parts.

But if the parts of the soul are like locations on a continuum, how can we account for the oppositions that Socrates pointed to? In the discussion of step 4, Socrates illustrates the relationship between thirst and drinking with two kinds of examples of how one thing can stand in relation to another. In the first, greater is in relation to less, double to half, heavier to lighter, and so on (438b–c). In the second, knowledge of building stands in relation to building, while knowledge of medicine stands in relation to healing (438c–d). The second model obviously fits the context: thirst is the species of appetite that is related to drinking, as medicine is the species of knowledge that is related to healing. But the first model seems irrelevant. How can we say that thirst is related to drinking the way the double is related to the half? Either Socrates lost track of what he was talking about or the example serves a less obvious purpose. But he must have thought it was important because he gave us nine versions of it.[11] In fact it gives us a model of how things can be called opposites simply because they are different degrees on a continuum. The examples show that if the soul is more like a continuum than a triumvirate, we can still account for the oppositions that arise in

11. Greater to less, much greater to much less, formerly greater to formerly less, about-to-be greater to about-to-be less, more to fewer, double to half, heavier to lighter, faster to slower, hot to cold, "and all similar cases."

it. When rationality and appetite are in conflict, for example, we can say that the opposition is between, on the one hand, greater rationality and less appetite, and, on the other hand, greater appetite and less rationality, or between short-term gratification ("about-to-be less") and long-term gratification ("about-to-be greater").

At this point all these implications are merely implicit, but they become explicit later, although Socrates does not call attention to the way the model has changed. In another passage that could have been taken from Freud's discussion of the libido, Socrates says,

> We surely know that when the appetites strongly incline toward some one thing they are thereby weakened toward others, like a stream from which there is a diversion into another channel. . . . So when they flow toward learning and all such things, they will be concerned, I suppose, with the pleasures of the soul itself by itself, while those that come through the body it will abandon, if someone is . . . a true philosopher. (485d–e)

Rationality was called the love of learning and was opposed to appetite, the love of pleasure, but now we are told that the love of learning is itself a kind of appetite. Here all three "parts" of the soul are regarded as channels through which eros (to use the word that Socrates employs in leading up to this quotation) flows toward different kinds of gratification (485b1, b8, c7). Later Socrates makes it even more explicit that rationality and spiritedness can be conceived as species of appetite, when he says that each part of the soul has its distinctive kind of appetite (580d), and he even calls philosophy (the love of wisdom) a kind of appetite (561c–d). If we conceive of the soul as a continuum extending between appetite at one end and rationality at the other, we can conceive of everything on it as a degree of appetite. But we can also conceive of them as degrees of rationality, as Socrates does when he says that all three parts of the soul are governed by their beliefs (ὁμοδοξῶσι, 442d1). Again, we can also conceive of the three parts of the soul as species of spiritedness, such as when Socrates portrays them as waging war against one another (440b, 440e, 442d, 444b) or "biting and fighting against each other" (589a). Even if we conceive of the soul as a continuum, then, appetite, spiritedness, and rationality may be regarded as its primary features.

Why, however, does Socrates take the trouble to establish a tripartite soul if he does not believe it to be an adequate model—why does he allow Glaucon to veto his misgivings and reluctance? For one thing, Plato often formulates a clear, simple model to provide an easily grasped answer to a question, but then introduces complicating factors that enable us to see beyond the limitations of the first model and to notice a subtler but more adequate model that begins to emerge.[12] Nowhere is that more true than in the *Republic*, which begins with an apparent victory by Socrates over Thrasymachus that is subsequently disparaged by Socrates himself as meaningless at the end of Book 1; then follows it with the elaborate development of a political constitution to illuminate the nature of the soul, at the climax of which Socrates again denigrates the accuracy of his methods. At that very point, however, ignored by Glaucon, he added, "although there is another longer and fuller road that does lead to such an answer" (435c). Although Glaucon showed no curiosity about this longer, more satisfactory way, a different kind of dissatisfaction by Polemarchus and Adeimantus (450a) forces Socrates to take that longer road and develop the material that will become Books 5–7. From that standpoint we will be able to see why Socrates progressively transformed the tripartite model of the soul into a continuous model.

At the end of the longer road, Socrates speaks of our ability to leave the cave of the visible world and perceive the ultimate reality of the principle of goodness that is the source of all being. In Book 7 he says that for those who have attained that vision, through what Socrates calls a conversion (518c, 521c), weakness of will is no longer a danger because it is a vision that cannot be attained by a divided soul:

> [T]he instrument by which everyone understands is like an eye that cannot be turned to light from darkness except together with the whole body. Thus that instrument must be turned from the realm of becoming together with *the whole soul* until it becomes able to contemplate that which is, and what is brightest of that which is; and we say that this is the good. (518c–d, emphasis added)

If the whole soul must turn to it together, then there can be no discord within the soul, no weakness of will, and no need for self-mastery. If we can achieve this knowledge, the relative poverty of other kinds of goods is so clear to us that we can no longer be tempted by them. Those who have had this experience and recall the goals that most other people pursue would "go through any sufferings rather than share their opinions and live as they do" (516d). The gradual erosion of the distinctions between the parts of the soul, and the emergence of a conception of soul as a continuum, is the bridge between the simplified "inaccurate" model of Book 4 and the more elusive but more adequate conception of Book 7.

12. As Grace Hadley Billings puts it, "one of Plato's favorite methods of developing a theme [is that a] partial or superficial view of the subject is first presented, only to be superseded or supplemented by further discussion. The *Republic* [is among the] notable examples of this method"; see *The Art of Transition in Plato* (Menasha, Wis.: George Banta, 1920), 21 and n. 64.

6. Indefeasible Knowledge

If we want to understand the position of the *Republic* as a whole, and not only that of Book 4, on the question of whether knowledge is sufficient for virtue, we must first see what the *Republic* means by knowledge, and for that we must turn to the Divided Line. The Line draws an absolute distinction between knowledge and opinion, not only in the expected way that knowledge is certain and opinion uncertain (477e), but in the stronger and more surprising sense that knowledge corresponds to the intelligible realm of being (the forms) while opinion corresponds to the visible realm of becoming (509d–10a). We have no knowledge of the visible world, only opinion. If we apply that to the context of Book 4, we can see that what may have been called knowledge there can never be more than opinion. The entire project of the dialogue between Books 2 and 4 is to construct a visible analogue of the soul, a city, to serve as a model for our understanding of the soul. Throughout that stage of the argument, and again in Books 8 and 9, after Socrates returns from the longer road to pick up from where he had left off at the end of Book 4, the soul is treated as if it is nothing more than a smaller version of the city (368e–69a), in other words, as if it could be assimilated to visible models. Similarly, since in Plato divisibility is always the mark of visible objects,[13] a tripartite conception of the soul in which the parts are fully distinct from one another would assimilate the soul to visible things. Thus at the end of Book 10, with the intelligible world brought into the picture in a way that had not yet happened in Book 4, Socrates says,

> We must see the soul as it is in truth, not maimed by communion with the body and other evils, as we now see it, but discern it adequately with reason when it has become pure. . . . Now, however, we told the truth about the soul as it appears at present. . . . But we must, Glaucon, look elsewhere, . . . [namely,] to its love of wisdom, and we must understand what it touches upon, and what kind of things it yearns to associate with, as being akin to the divine, and to the immortal, and to what always is . . . And then one might see whether in its true nature it has many forms or one form, or in what way it is and how. (611c–12a)

Books 2–4 never introduce the theory of forms, but remain entirely within the visible world of becoming. Although the rational guardians are educated to philosophy, the love of wisdom (410e, 411e–12a), and are called wise (428e), their wisdom consists only of good judgment (εὔβουλος, 428b) and has nothing to do with a love of the intelligible realm of forms, which becomes the hallmark of the true philosopher in

13. E.g., *Phaedo* 78c.

Book 5 (475e–80a). Their education comprises only physical training and fine arts (376e). From the point of view of the Divided Line, then, what is called knowledge in Book 4 turns out to be, once the forms are introduced, only a kind of opinion. In Book 4 weakness of will is possible and self-mastery is necessary, because the rational element of our souls has not yet attained knowledge in the fullest sense of the word. True knowledge, once we attain it, can no longer be defeated, as we saw in the passages quoted above from 518c–d and 516d.

The need of the account in Book 4 to be reevaluated as the dialogue progresses is a function not only of Plato's practice of using simple models as starting points for more nuanced ones, but also a function of his practice of illustrating doctrines before they are explicitly formulated.[14] The *Republic* does this in the case of the Divided Line: by the time the doctrine is actually stated, the dialogue itself has passed through each of its stages. The war of words with Thrasymachus in Book 1 was an example of "image thinking" (εἰκασία), the lower kind of opinion; the construction of a city as a visible model of the soul represented "conviction" (πίστις), the higher kind of opinion; and Books 5–7 illustrate the two kinds of knowledge, inferential (διάνοια) and intellective (νόησις).[15] If it seems misleading of Socrates to present a doctrine in Book 4 that is only meant to be superseded later on, at least we cannot say he did not warn us. To say that the account of Book 4 has been superseded by that of Book 7 is not to say that the former has been rejected. For the vast majority of us who have not achieved the true knowledge described in Book 7, the model presented in Book 4 is where we must begin.

When we look at Book 4 in isolation from what follows, it seems indeed as if Plato has abandoned the intellectualism of dialogues like the *Protagoras*. But when we take seriously Socrates' expressed dissatisfaction with the approach of Book 4, and follow his longer road to the present account, we find that true knowledge really is sufficient for virtue. It eliminates the need for self-mastery and the danger of weakness of will—but only if it is knowledge in the fullest sense.

The paradoxical nature of Socrates' intellectualism in the other dialogues, where virtue is defined in terms of knowledge, can be seen to turn on a similar kind of systematic ambiguity in the way the term "knowledge" is used there (although the ambiguity is not as compartmentalized as in the *Republic*), vacillating between wisdom and conventional kinds of

14. In the *Phaedo*, e.g., Simmias is made to anticipate the Method of Hypothesis at 85c–d.

15. I have provided evidence for this in "The Divided Line and the Structure of Plato's *Republic*," *History of Philosophy Quarterly* 21 (2004): 1–20, and throughout *The Transformation of Plato's* Republic (Lanham, Md.: Lexington Books, 2006).

knowledge. In the *Laches,* Nicias proposes that virtue follows from being wise (σοφός) and Socrates agrees, but when Laches asks what kind of wisdom (σοφία), Socrates restates the question as, "What is this knowledge [ἐπιστήμη]?" (194d–e), and the discussion ends in an impasse. The *Meno* hypothesizes that virtue can be taught if (and only if) it is a kind of knowledge (ἐπιστήμη) (87c), but the actual proof is a demonstration that virtue is a kind of wisdom (φρόνησις).[16] The shift occurs at 88b and remains in effect until 89c, when "knowledge" returns, to be replaced again by "wisdom" in Socrates' later recapitulation: "Didn't virtue seem to us to be teachable if it was wisdom . . . and if it was teachable it would be wisdom?" (98d). However, in a passage reminiscent of the paradoxes at the end of the *Protagoras,* Socrates argues that since knowledge and teachability are equivalent, the fact that there are no teachers of virtue implies that virtue is not a kind of knowledge after all (89d and following). This passage, like that of the *Protagoras,* suggests that the difference between knowledge and wisdom in these dialogues is that wisdom is a species of knowledge that cannot be taught, at least not in the straightforward way that other kinds of knowledge can be taught. It is not information or technique. Knowledge is virtue, and invulnerable to weakness of will, only insofar as the kind of knowledge meant is wisdom. A comparable ambiguity is at work in the *Protagoras.* After reminding Protagoras of their agreement that knowledge is indefeasible (357c), Socrates smoothly extends the claim to belief: "no one who knows [εἰδώς] or believes [εἰόμενος] that other things are better than the ones he is doing, and are possible, then does these if the better ones are available" (358b–c). This extension bears on the aporetic ending of the dialogue which, like the *Laches* and the *Meno,* concerns the teachability of virtue. For if virtue is a kind of knowledge, and "knowledge" is broad enough to include "belief," then since beliefs are teachable, virtue (including wisdom) would have to be teachable.

In Book 4 of the *Republic,* too, knowledge is not clearly distinguished from belief. When Socrates defines self-control as when appetite and spiritedness "share the belief" (ὁμοδόξωσι) of reason about who should rule (442d), "belief" refers to what he had just called "knowledge" (ἐπιστήμη, 442c).[17] The change of terminology implies that in cases of this kind, appetite and spiritedness cannot have true knowledge but only opinion, but when we turn to the kind of knowledge that is firmly

16. Σοφία is used at 91a and at 99b, where it is used interchangeably with ἐπιστήμη.

17. Carone shows that the rest of the tripartite soul discussion is consistent with 442d; see "*Akrasia* in the *Republic,*" esp. 117–24. Space does not permit consideration of the interpretive difficulties of these texts, but I have discussed them in "Wisdom, Virtue, and Knowledge," *Review of Metaphysics* 51 (1997): 313–43.

distinguished from opinion, in Books 5–7, appetite and spiritedness no longer merely share the belief of rationality about who should rule, but also its knowledge of the good (518c). What the *Republic* and these other dialogues have in common is a systematically ambiguous employment of the term "knowledge," so that in some places it seems to mean what we ordinarily call knowledge, but in others it refers to the perfection of knowledge as wisdom. The aporetic conclusions of the shorter dialogues invite us to discover what went wrong, and thereby to reflect on the difference between the knowledge that requires self-mastery and the wisdom that does not. The *Republic* does the same thing in a nonaporetic way, in terms of Socrates' warnings in Book 4, and the higher point of view developed in Books 5–7.

7. Strengthening the Will

To combat weakness of will we must attain at least self-mastery of the kind described in Book 4, or, ideally, the conversion described in Book 7. Since both conditions are achievements of the rational part of our nature, the strategy for preventing weakness of will is the same in either case: we must make every effort to strengthen our rationality. One way of achieving this, good upbringing (409a), is beyond our control, but there are two things we can do: we can weaken whatever undermines our rationality, and we can strengthen rationality itself. Since rationality is by nature impartial, operating according to what is right rather than according to self-interest, we need to avoid anything that promotes biased behavior or emotions like self-indulgence, rage, and self-pity. In addition to not behaving that way ourselves, since behavior shapes character, we must also avoid associating too closely with people who do behave that way, because of the power of peer pressure (492b–c). We should even employ the same kind of restraint with respect to our entertainment. When we watch a play (or now a television program or movie) or read a book, we experience vicariously ("imitate within ourselves") the behavior of the protagonists. If they behave unjustly or exhibit self-indulgence or self-pity, their behavior echoes within us and we imagine ourselves behaving that way. The more we imagine ourselves doing something that we disapprove of, the less unthinkable it is for us to behave that way ourselves. Even arts as abstract as music without words can convey emotions like self-pity and can make them dangerously beautiful and seductive. Plato gives examples in the music of his day (397c–99c), and there is no lack of examples in our own music. Examples are even more abundant in the case of music *with* words, from opera to all forms of popular music. These are the sort of influences we must be careful of, to avoid weakening our will by strengthening the opponents of rationality. But how do we strengthen rationality itself?

The most obvious way is by making it more effectively rational—to be rational rather than to rationalize. Although rational behavior shows strength of will, while rationalization shows weakness of will, it is not easy to distinguish rationality from rationalization since rationalization means disguising as rationality what actually conflicts with rationality. It is the attempt to convince ourselves that we are behaving rationally (correctly) when we have ignored the promptings of reason in favor of those of appetite or spiritedness. It can be hard to tell whether we are rationalizing or being rational because we can easily mistake a lesser good for a greater one if the lesser good offers more immediate gratification—the way a small thing seems bigger than a large one if it is closer to us (*Protagoras* 356c–57b). We may choose the smaller rewards of appetite over the larger ones of rationality, or the smaller rewards of injustice over the larger ones of justice, because their rewards are more immediate. Moreover, the very impurity of the bodily pleasures is a source of their appeal: because they are mingled with pains, they are intensified by the contrast between the pleasure and the pain, which can make them madly exciting (586b–c). We must learn to recognize that pleasures that depend on relief from pain are less truly pleasant and will make us less happy than pleasures that are independent of pain, even though they are more intense.

In the case of pleasures that seem bigger only because they are closer, and provide immediate gratification instead of delayed gratification, we must develop the ability to measure goodness independently of its nearness or farness. The educational system of the *Republic* is designed to give us the ability to make this kind of measurement, but it is not a precise calculation like that of utilitarianism. At the end of the Myth of Er, Socrates says that someone's ability to "distinguish the good from the bad life" involves

> knowing how beauty, combined with poverty or wealth and with what kind of character of the soul produces good or evil, good birth and bad birth, private life and governing, strength and weakness, ease of learning and difficulty of learning, and all such things regarding the soul, both natural and acquired, so that from all these things—and looking at the nature of the soul—he will be able to choose rationally between the better and worse life, calling a life worse which leads him to become more unjust, better if it leads him to become more just, and disregarding all other considerations. . . . He would know how to always choose the mean among such lives, and avoid each of the extremes. (618b–19b)

If the good is a mean between extremes, we cannot calculate it because the extremes do not have a precise value. Unlike a mathematical mean, where we know the extremes first and then calculate a midpoint, here we must know the mean in order to know the extremes. We only know that something is an extreme because we recognize that it goes too far or not far enough, and we can recognize those cases only if we can identify the point that is just right.

As long as rationality needs to continually assert itself against appetite and spiritedness by means of self-mastery, and our emotions push us through rationalization toward the extremes, it will be difficult for us to recognize the mean. Only if we can attain the complete understanding of goodness that removes all temptation (516d, 518c–d) can we reliably discern the mean in all situations. Plato recommends two paths that can bring us to that understanding—one that operates at the level of appetite and another at the level of rationality. The first is eros and the second dialectic. There is also a path that operates at the level of spiritedness, namely, the self-discipline of purification that is present throughout the *Republic* in the mission of spiritedness to make appetite obedient to rationality, but the privative nature of discipline must be combined with a positive goal furnished by eros or dialectic. The path of eros is explored especially in the *Symposium* and the *Phaedrus* and is only briefly indicated in the *Republic,*[18] which, like the *Meno,* the *Phaedo,* the *Timaeus,* and the *Philebus,* is more concerned with dialectic as an extension of mathematics.

The higher education of the rulers (523a–33a) begins with arithmetic because arithmetic begins in the realm of appetite but leads to that of rationality: its employment is in the visible world but its principles are intelligible. We cannot perceive numbers themselves—as distinct from their written symbols—with our eyes but only with our mind. If the study of mathematics makes us realize that the visible world is governed by principles that are perceived only by the mind, we are on the first step of the road to a dialectic that concerns itself only with intelligible being rather than visible becoming, and which leads to the source of the intelligible principles in the Idea of the Good. This "turning" of our attention from the physical world of becoming to the intelligible world of being leads to Socrates' designation of it as a conversion (518c–d). The more we attend to intelligible reality, the more effectively will our own

18. E.g., 499b–c. For a discussion of the relation between the *Republic*'s references to eros and Plato's doctrine of eros generally, see Irwin, *Plato's Ethics,* chap. 18. This positive sense of eros in the *Republic* should be kept in mind together with the negative sense that has been noted by Leo Strauss, *The City and Man* (Chicago: Rand McNally, 1964), 111; Stanley Rosen, "The Role of Eros in Plato's *Republic,*" *Review of Metaphysics* 18 (1965): 452–75; and Jacob Howland, "The *Republic*'s Third Wave and the Paradox of Political Philosophy," *Review of Metaphysics* 51 (1998): 633–57, at 646–55.

rationality function within us; and the more we appreciate the relative unimportance of physical things, the less power will our appetites have over us.

However convincing we may find Socrates' account, his words and our intellectual acceptance of them can do no more than give us the morally fragile kind of knowledge described in Book 4 that is not immune to weakness of will and must be enforced by self-mastery. The complete knowledge that turns the whole soul toward the good can only come from inner experience:

> You will no longer be able, my dear Glaucon, to follow me, although for my part I would not willingly omit anything. But you would no longer see an image of what we are saying, but the truth itself. . . . And the power of dialectic alone can reveal it to someone who is experienced in the things we just went through, and it is not possible in any other way. (533a)

Few of us will ever get that far; for the rest of us weakness of will continues to be a danger, and so at the beginning of Book 8 Socrates turns away from the whole preceding discussion of Books 5–7 as a digression (543c), and returns to the divided self of the tripartite soul, proceeding to illustrate in detail how, if we do not take the necessary steps to achieve self-mastery, what starts out as weakness of will may become in the end the unexamined life of those in whom what is best in them is enslaved by what is worst.

Conclusion

We praise strength of will but not willfulness, because only "will" in the first sense implies that our goal is worthy. Thus the strength of will that Plato calls self-mastery implies that it is our better self that leads; but to demonstrate that one of our motivations is better than another is no easy matter. The discussion of self-mastery in Book 4 simply assumes that our better self is (to update the terminology) not the pleasure principle, nor the will to power, but the love of truth. Not until Book 9 does Socrates attempt to redeem that assumption with arguments. But even that is not the whole story. The *Republic* is a book of levels, and beyond the level at which strength of will is necessary to resist the temptations and fears that threaten to undermine our morality is a kind of knowing that is inviolable so that supplemental considerations of strength or mastery become irrelevant. It is important to remember that just as the discussion of Book 1 was declared inadequate (354b–c) and superseded by that of Book 4, that of Book 4 was disparaged as well (435c–d) and is superseded by that of Book 7.

2 Aristotle Reads the *Protagoras*

TERENCE H. IRWIN

1. Aristotle, Socrates, and Incontinence

The discussion of incontinence in the *Nicomachean Ethics* mentions only one philosopher who held views on this topic. Aristotle begins by criticizing Socrates, but ends by agreeing with him, with qualifications, on one important point. We might hope to understand Aristotle's discussion better if we can see what view he ascribes to Socrates and why he rejects and accepts different parts of Socrates' position. But if we try to answer these questions, we face some prior questions: (1) What does Aristotle mean by attributing a view to "Socrates"? Does he intend a historical claim about the historical Socrates, or is he simply alluding (for instance) to something in the Socratic literature without any commitment to its historical accuracy? (2) What is his source for the view on incontinence that he ascribes to Socrates? (3) How accurate is his report of Socrates? Accuracy might refer to different things, depending on our answer to the first question. (4) The treatment of incontinence in the book we know as *EN* 7 is not the only treatment of the question in the Aristotelian corpus. The *Magna Moralia* presents another treatment.[1] How are the two treatments related?

An earlier version of this paper was presented at a seminar in the series "Aristotle Reads Plato" at the Institute for Classical Studies in the University of London. I received helpful questions from members of the seminar, especially Mary Margaret McCabe and Verity Harte. I am also grateful to David Charles for much discussion and for showing me a draft of his paper for the 2005 Symposium Aristotelicum (since I have only seen a draft, I have not commented on this work).

1. The authenticity of the *MM* is disputed. I believe it is substantially authentic, following Franz Dirlmeier; see Aristoteles, *Magna Moralia,* Werke in deutscher Übersetzung, vol. 8 (Berlin: Akademie Verlag, 1964); and John M. Cooper, "The Magna Moralia and Aristotle's Moral philosophy," *American Journal of Philology* 94 (1973): 327–49, reprinted in his *Reason and Emotion: Essays on Ancient Moral Psychology and Ethical Theory* (Princeton: Princeton University Press, 1999), 195–211. Its authenticity is denied by Christopher J. Rowe, "A Reply to John Cooper on the *Magna Moralia,*" *American Journal of Philology* 96 (1975): 160–72, and by Anthony J. P. Kenny, *The Aristotelian Ethics* (Oxford: Clarendon

Some of these questions are both familiar and difficult. On the large issues about Aristotle's treatment of Socrates and about the three Aristotelian ethical treatises, I will give rather short answers without detailed argument. My remarks will introduce some of the issues that I will discuss in more detail in connection with incontinence. But I believe these issues are worth mentioning because they throw some light on the discussion of incontinence. In particular, I hope to show that if we attend to Aristotle's reflections on Socrates on incontinence, we can also understand some aspects of the development of Aristotle's treatment of incontinence. The revisions in his portrayal of Socrates correspond to revisions in his conception of incontinence.[2]

2. Aristotle on the Historical Socrates

I believe that in many passages Aristotle intends his remarks on "Socrates" to apply to the historical Socrates, and that the passages that mention Socrates' views on incontinence are among those that make this historical claim.

This view is worth comparing with the alternative view that Aristotle uses "Socrates" to refer to the character with that name in Plato's dialogues or in some other part of the Socratic literature. Sometimes, admittedly, he uses "Socrates" simply to refer to the dialogues. He even treats the *Laws* as a Socratic discourse, though Socrates does not appear in it (*Pol.* 2.6.1265a10–13).[3]

Sometimes, however, Aristotle's use of "Socrates" suggests that he does

Press, 1978). In this paper I offer only one consideration favoring the view that the *MM* is early and genuine. A decision on this question requires a decision on a much more complex body of evidence on each side.

2. I have not tried to cite or to discuss most of the large secondary literature on Aristotle on incontinence. Apart from older books and papers, some of the contributions I have found especially helpful are A. J. P. Kenny, "The Practical Syllogism and Incontinence," *Phronesis* 11 (1966): 163–84; David Charles, *Aristotle's Philosophy of Action* (London: Duckworth, 1984); Sarah W. Broadie, *Ethics with Aristotle* (New York: Oxford University Press, 1991); Norman O. Dahl, *Practical Reason, Aristotle, and Weakness of the Will* (Minneapolis: University of Minnesota Press, 1984); John H. McDowell, "Incontinence and Practical Wisdom in Aristotle," in *Essays for David Wiggins: Identity, Truth and Value,* ed. Sabina Lovibond and S. G. Williams (Oxford: Blackwell, 1996), 95–112; and Terence Penner, "Socrates on the Strength of Knowledge: *Protagoras* 351b–357e," *Archiv für Geschichte der Philosophie* 79 (1997): 117–49. I have also drawn on two papers of mine: "Some Rational Aspects of Incontinence," *Southern Journal of Philosophy* 27 Suppl. (1988): 49–88, and "Will, Responsibility, and Ignorance: Aristotelian Accounts of Incontinence," in *The Problem of Weakness of Will in Medieval Thought,* ed. Tobias Hoffmann, Jörn Müller, and Matthias Perkams (Leuven, Paris, and Dudley, Mass.: Peeters, 2006), 37–56.

3. If we suppose that Aristotle refers to an earlier draft of the *Laws* in which Socrates was the main speaker, we confirm the point that sometimes he uses "Socrates" simply to refer to the character in the dialogues.

not simply refer to the character in the dialogues. He attributes incompatible views to Socrates and to Plato; but if "Socrates" simply named the speaker in the dialogues, he would have no reason to distinguish Socrates' views from Plato's. He asserts that Plato disagrees with Socrates on some important points. In the *Metaphysics* (1.6, 13.4) he claims that Socrates did not separate the forms, whereas Plato separated them.

He also contrasts Socrates' ethical theory with Plato's, most explicitly at the beginning of the *MM*. In this passage, as in the passages in the *Metaphysics* on separation, Aristotle ascribes the views of the dialogues we normally count as "early" to Socrates, and ascribes those of the "middle" dialogues to Plato.[4] Aristotle ascribes a purely cognitive view of virtue to Socrates, but never to Plato. He believes that Plato agrees with him in distinguishing rational from nonrational parts of the soul, and in drawing conclusions for the account of virtue (*EN* 2.3.1104b11–13, 5.11.1138b5–14).

Aristotle claims that Socrates denied the existence of incontinence. Since this denial fits a cognitive view of virtue, he probably attributes it to the historical Socrates. We can support this conclusion from two further features of the passage: (1) Aristotle uses the proper name "Socrates" without the definite article. According to "Fitzgerald's canon," he uses the name without the article to refer to the historical Socrates, but the name with the article simply to refer to a dialogue. If Fitzgerald's canon is correct, Aristotle's omission of the article in our passage indicates that he treats the *Protagoras* as a reliable source for the views of the historical Socrates.[5] (2) Aristotle speaks of Socrates' views in the imperfect tense. He normally uses the present tense, as we do in English, when he is referring to what someone says in a written source (e.g.), and uses the imperfect to refer to the views someone actually held. Hence, for instance, when he is recalling something Plato used to say, but not referring directly to a passage in the dialogues, he uses the imperfect (*EN* 1.4.1095a32–b1).

These points give us a reasonable prima facie case for believing that in some passages, including the discussion of incontinence, Aristotle intends to discuss the views of the historical Socrates. They do not show whether Socrates held these views. We might wonder whether Aristotle's historical claims rest entirely on the observation that in different Platon-

4. The evidence for Aristotle's contrasting Socrates with Plato on ethics does not depend on the genuineness of the *MM*. The same contrast is clear in the *EE* and in *EN* 6–7. See Section 3.

5. For sensible discussions of Aristotle on Socrates, see W. David Ross, ed., *Aristotle's Metaphysics: A Revised Text with Introduction and Commentary,* 2 vols. (Oxford: Clarendon Press, 1924), Introduction, pp. xxxiii–xlv; and Gregory Vlastos, *Socrates, Ironist and Moral Philosopher* (Ithaca: Cornell University Press, 1991), chaps. 2–3.

ic dialogues Socrates appears to defend different views. Did he conjecture, without supporting evidence, that these different views belonged to Socrates and to Plato?[6]

In reply to this question we may ask why Aristotle should have accepted this particular conjecture. Why should he not simply have conjectured that Plato changed his mind, or (as some later readers supposed) concealed some of his views in some dialogues? Plato's contemporaries were interested in what Socrates had actually said, and in whether Plato had got him right (cf. *Rhet.* 2.23.1398b30–32). If Aristotle had rashly assumed without further evidence that some dialogues presented Socrates' actual views, he could have expected to be criticized for his rashness. It is more likely that he relied on evidence outside the Platonic dialogues. But we need not pursue this question further at the moment.

Probably, then, Aristotle believes he is discussing the views of the historical Socrates. Does his discussion rest on an accurate report of these views? We cannot answer this question with complete confidence since we have nothing besides Plato's Socratic dialogues to test Aristotle's claims about Socrates, and we have to rely on Aristotle's testimony if we are to believe that these dialogues tell us about the historical Socrates. Our sources on Socrates outside Aristotle and Plato are not detailed enough either to confirm or to refute Aristotle's claims. Still, we can reasonably be confident in Aristotle's accuracy to a more limited extent. If we believe that Aristotle is right to suppose that some of the Platonic dialogues tell us about Socrates, we are right to believe what he tells us about Socrates; for what he tells us fits the relevant Platonic dialogues.

This is rather a large claim about Aristotle on Socrates' ethical theory. I would not want to defend it on every single point that he ascribes to Socrates. But I believe it is correct about one important aspect of Socrates' ethics: his treatment of belief, motivation, and action. To support this claim, I will discuss Aristotle's remarks on Socrates' treatment of incontinence.

3. The Three Ethics on Socrates

Aristotle's discussion of Socrates on incontinence is part of the recurrent discussion of Socratic ethics in his ethical treatises. But the three treatises take instructively different attitudes to Socrates. A survey of these attitudes will help us to understand the passages on incontinence.

6. The view that Aristotle's account is a conjecture based entirely on the dialogues (perhaps supplemented by Xenophon's dialogues) is held by Charles H. Kahn, *Plato and the Socratic Dialogue: The Philosophical Use of a Literary Form* (Cambridge: Cambridge University Press, 1996), 83–87. See especially his criticism of Ross at 81–82.

In the *Magna Moralia* Aristotle (as I will call the author, simply for convenience) introduces Socrates at the very beginning, in his historical survey of ethical thought.

After him (sc. Pythagoras) came Socrates, who spoke better and further about this subject, but even he was not successful. For he used to make the virtues into sciences, and this is impossible. For the sciences all involve reason, and reason is to be found in the intellectual part of the soul. So that all the virtues, according to him, arise in the rational part of the soul. The result is that in making the virtues into sciences he is doing away with the nonrational part of the soul, and is thereby doing away also both with passion and character; so that he has not been successful in this respect in his treatment of the virtues. After this Plato divided the soul into the rational and the nonrational part—and in this he was right—assigning appropriate virtues to each. (*MM* 1.1.1182a15–26)

Aristotle offers some unspecific praise of Socrates, and adds the specific criticism that Socrates was wrong to identify virtue with knowledge. This criticism introduces Aristotle's opposition to Socrates' purely cognitive account of the virtues.

Neither was Socrates right in making the virtues sciences. For he used to think that nothing ought to be pointless; but from the virtues being sciences it turned out for him that they were pointless. Why? Because in the case of the sciences, as soon as one knows what the science is, it results that one is scientific. . . . But this result does not follow in the case of the virtues. . . . It follows then that the virtues are pointless and that they are not sciences. (1.1.1183b8–18)[7]

In the light of all these criticisms, it is not surprising that Aristotle also attacks Socrates for his denial of incontinence, which follows from at least one plausible interpretation of his cognitive account of virtue. The *MM* is uniformly critical of Socrates, and especially of his cognitive account of moral virtue. His errors on this point are strongly emphasized. No specific positive contribution is acknowledged.

The *Eudemian Ethics*, including the Common Books,[8] has several passages on similar themes. Some of them agree with the criticisms in the

7. All translations are my own. See also *MM* 1.9.1187a5–13; 1.20.1190b28–32; 1.34.1198a10–21.

8. Aristotle's fullest discussion of incontinence appears in *EN* 7, which is one of the books common to *EN* and *EE*. I am convinced by arguments that have been given to show that these three common books originally belong to the *EE*. Some of these arguments are presented by Kenny, *The Aristotelian Ethics*, chaps. 2–3. But I believe they are appropriately called "common" books since I believe Aristotle probably intended them to be part of the *EN* as well, and I would not exclude the possibility that he revised them to fit them into the *EN*. But even if that speculation is right, we need to compare them initially with the rest of the *EE*.

MM, and attribute an excessively cognitive view of virtue to Socrates.[9] But without retracting these criticisms, the *EE* also emphasizes the point on which Socrates' claims about virtue and reason are correct.[10] In sharp contrast to the other two Ethics, the *Nicomachean Ethics* has very little explicit comment on Socrates.[11] It scarcely mentions Socrates at all, outside the Common Books, and it scarcely criticizes him by name, even when it refers to Socratic doctrines (e.g., *EN* 1.5.1096a1).

It would be rash to draw sweeping conclusions about the order of the treatises from this evidence alone. Still, the order *MM, EE, EN* readily explains the differences we have found. The *MM* is most concerned to separate Aristotle from Socrates, but later Aristotle takes a more conciliatory attitude (*EE* and the Common Books). Later still he even loses interest in mentioning Socrates *(EN).* These facts are not quite as easy to explain if we suppose the *MM* to be spurious and later than the other two Ethics. Why should a post-Aristotelian writer be so concerned to underline the differences between Aristotle and Socrates? This concern seems easier to understand if we attribute it to the young Aristotle.

It is useful to compare the references to Plato in the three Ethics. The *MM* mentions him once critically (1.1.1182a24) and once neutrally (1.33.1194a6). The *EE* does not mention him by name at all. The *EN* mentions him a few times (1.4.1095a32, 2.3.1104b12, 10.2.1172b28), always favorably. When it discusses the Form of the Good, it does not name Plato, just as the *EE* does not name him; it prefaces the discussion with the famous passage about honoring truth above our friends (1.6.1096a11–17), which is absent from the other two Ethics.

Though it may be misleading to confine ourselves to places where Aristotle mentions Socrates and Plato by name, these passages suggest that the *MM* is the most explicitly critical of Socrates and Plato, the *EN* is the least critical, and the *EE* is in the middle. We have a choice between two reasonably plausible arrangements. If the right order is *EN, EE, MM,* the young Aristotle is conciliatory to Socrates and Plato, the older Aristotle is more critical, and the post-Aristotelian writer is the most critical. If the right order is *MM, EE, EN,* the young Aristotle is the most critical, and the older Aristotle becomes gradually less inclined to open dispute with Socrates and Plato.

Given these systematic differences in the treatment of Socrates and

9. See especially *EE* 1.5.1216b3–25. Cf. 3.1.1229a14–16, 3.1.1230a7–10, 7.1.1235a35–39, 8.1.1246b32–36. The *EE* drops one objection that the *MM* raises against Socrates, about whether it is up to us to be virtuous.

10. See especially *EN* 6.13.1144b17–21, 28–30.

11. See *EN* 3.8.1116b4–6, 4.7.1127b25–26.

of Plato in the three Ethics, the treatment in the *MM* probably does not reflect careless notes by a student. Carelessness or lack of understanding may explain some passages in the *MM*, but they do not explain the systematic differences from the other Ethics on Socrates. If the *MM* is post-Aristotelian, the critical treatment of Socrates and Plato probably reflects a deliberate decision by the author. But if its substance expresses Aristotle's early views, it shows that the young Aristotle is more openly critical of Socrates and Plato than he becomes later on.

4. The *Magna Moralia* and the *Protagoras*

These questions are relevant to the discussion of Socrates on incontinence in the *MM* and the *EN* 7.[12] In both works Aristotle attends closely to Plato's *Protagoras*, but the two works attend to different passages in the dialogue. Aristotle's treatment suggests that he reread the dialogue and found different points to discuss.

The discussion in the *MM* 2.6 begins with a statement of Socrates' position.

> Now Socrates the elder used to do away with incontinence altogether and to deny that there was any such thing, saying that no one knowing bad things that they are bad would choose them, but the incontinent seems, knowing that they are base, to choose them nonetheless, being led by passion. Because of this sort of argument, then, he thought there was no incontinence. But there he was wrong. For it is absurd for us, having been persuaded by this argument, to do away with something that persuasively comes about; for human beings are incontinent, and they themselves, knowing that things are base, nonetheless do them. (2.6.1200b25–32)

This statement follows to the *Protagoras*. Aristotle takes over Socrates' formulation of what incontinence would have to be like if there were any such thing:

> For I say that . . . your argument turns out to be ludicrous, whenever you say that often a human being knowing [γιγνώσκων] bad things that they are bad, nonetheless does them, it being open to him not to do them, being led and disturbed by pleasures. (*Protagoras* 355a7–b1)

Aristotle changes the cognitive verb from "γιγνώσκειν" to "εἰδέναι." Perhaps he simply makes Plato's usage more uniform; for Plato uses εἰδέναι in

12. As I have said, this book is a common book, and may be more appropriately compared with the rest of the *EE* than with the rest of the *EN*. But I will follow convention hereinafter, and refer to it by its Nicomachean name and number.

saying that no one chooses the worse either εἰδώς or οἰόμενος (358b7).[13]

According to Socrates, passion or pleasure leads (ἄγειν) us, but does not prevent us from acting freely. Socrates insists that it must be open to us (ἔξον) not to do the bad thing we do. Perhaps Aristotle alludes to this condition; he says that when incontinents act, "they themselves" (αὐτοί) do the bad things in knowledge of their badness. Though neither Plato nor Aristotle explains this condition further in the immediate context, it is important that incontinence appears to be voluntary and blameworthy action, and therefore up to the agent.

After stating Socrates' position, Aristotle rejects it, and offers to show how incontinence is possible, so that people can know that actions are bad (φαῦλα), but nonetheless do them. His solution removes any puzzle by pointing out that it is possible to have (ἔχειν) knowledge without actualizing (ἐνέργειν) it. In Aristotle's view, this is the condition of incontinents:

> But there is no paradox in the incontinent man's doing something base [τι φαῦλον], whether he has knowledge [ἐπιστήμη] or opinion such as we speak of. For there are two ways of knowing, one of which is having knowledge . . . and the other of which is actualizing the knowledge. And so the one who has knowledge of fine things, but does not exercise it, is incontinent. And so, whenever he does not exercise this knowledge, it is not at all absurd that he does base things having the knowledge. (2.6.1201b9–17)

The incontinent's action is first mentioned in the singular as "something base," but then his knowledge is "knowledge of fine things," and he "does base things having the knowledge." The same plural appears in Socrates' description of the incontinent as the one who "knowing bad things that they are bad, nonetheless does them" (*Protagoras* 355a5–b1).

These plurals may be significant. They are ambiguous between (a) several instances of particular knowledge and (b) one instance of universal knowledge. I might be said to do bad things knowing they are bad in either of two cases: (a) I eat one piece of cake too many today, knowing that this particular action is bad, and I do the same thing tomorrow knowing that that particular action is bad; (b) I eat one piece of cake too many today and I know that eating too much cake is bad. In case (b) Aristotle does not ascribe to me any particular knowledge that this action here and now is bad.

Having said that the incontinent has knowledge of what is better without exercising it, Aristotle offers two apparently distinct explanations of

13. To describe the badness of incontinent actions, both Plato and Aristotle use "κακόν." Plato also sometimes uses "πονηρόν" (353c7) and Aristotle uses "φαῦλον."

how this happens. The first explanation compares the incontinent to a dreamer:

Having but not actualizing knowledge happens when we are asleep; this is analogous to the case of the incontinent. For the case is the same as that of sleepers. For they, though they have knowledge, nevertheless in their sleep both do and undergo [πάσχουσιν] many disgusting things; for their knowledge is not actualized in them. So it is in the case of the incontinent. For he seems like one asleep and does not actualize his knowledge. In this way, then, the puzzle is solved; for the puzzle was about whether the incontinent expels his knowledge or falls away from it at this time [sc. when he acts incontinently], since both of these would seem to be absurd. (1201b17–24)

This explanation does not say what sort of knowledge the sleeper has and does not exercise. Nor does it say much to persuade us that the incontinent is relevantly like a sleeper. Contrary to this explanation, it seems quite possible for him to be occurrently aware that what he is doing is bad and still to do it.

In the second explanation Aristotle tries to say more precisely what happens to the incontinent to prevent the exercise of his knowledge.

But, again, the point may be made evident from the following. As we said in the *Analytics*, deduction depends on two premises, and of these the first is universal, while the second falls under it and is particular. For instance, I know how to cure any one with a fever, and this man has a fever: therefore I know how to cure this man. And so there is something I know with universal knowledge, but not with particular knowledge. And so in this case also a mistake comes about for the one who has knowledge; for instance I know how to cure anyone with a fever, but I do not know [οἶδα] if this man has a fever. In the same way, then, in the case of the incontinent who has knowledge the same mistake will come about. For it is possible for the incontinent to have universal knowledge that things of this sort are base and harmful, but still not to have particular knowledge [εἰδέναι] that these things are base, so that while he has knowledge in this way he will make a mistake; for he has the universal knowledge, but not the particular. In this way also, then, nothing absurd will come about in the case of the incontinent, that the one who has the knowledge does something base. (2.6.1201b24–1202a1)

This second explanation relies not on the previous distinction between having and using, but on the distinction between universal and particular knowledge expressed in universal and particular premises. If I lack a particular premise, I am ignorant of the fact that this action here and now has some property; if I had known, I would have known that this action is one of those that I recognize I ought not to do.[14]

14. Aristotle uses "ἐπίστασθαι" for the knowledge of the universal premise and the

In this second explanation Aristotle states, more clearly than in the first explanation, what the incontinent knows or does not know when he is said to know or not to know that "these things are bad." We do not need to explain how his knowledge that this action here and now is bad is not actualized; for he lacks this knowledge. He acts contrary to his universal knowledge, because he does not know how this universal knowledge applies to his particular situation.

In Aristotle's view, the second explanation makes the incontinent similar to a drunk who does not apply his universal knowledge to a particular case.

> For it happens as it does in the case of drunk people. For drunk people, whenever the drunkenness has worn off, are the same people again. Reason was not expelled from them, nor was knowledge, but it was overcome by the drunkenness; and when they have got rid of the drunkenness, they are the same people again. The same applies, then, to the incontinent. For his passion, having overcome, made reasoning inactive; but whenever the passion, like the drunkenness, has gone away, he is the same person again. (2.6.1202a1–7)

This example tries to make the second explanation more plausible by telling us how it happens that the incontinent has only universal knowledge when he acts incontinently. He has clearly not lost his universal knowledge, since he is the same person before and after his incontinent action; he does not need to relearn the universal principle he previously knew that he ought not to eat too many pieces of cake. But his passion has temporarily interrupted his normal course of reasoning, so that he does not believe he ought not to eat this cake when he eats it.

Aristotle now claims to have shown that the situation rejected by Socrates is possible and nonparadoxical. Socrates rejected incontinence because he did not see how someone could "know bad things that they are bad" and nonetheless do them "led and disturbed by pleasures" (*Protagoras* 355a5–b1). These features that seemed paradoxical to Socrates are in fact the key to seeing how incontinence is not paradoxical. In Aristotle's view, "knowing bad things that they are bad" is consistent with choosing bad things, provided that we take the relevant knowledge to be universal. Socrates' phrase "led and disturbed by pleasures" shows us the point of resemblance between the incontinent and the drunk; for the incontinent's appetites and passions interrupt his reasoning so that he does not apply his universal knowledge to this particular situation.

In Aristotle's view, this solution is preferable to the Socratic dissolu-

---

conclusion, but "εἰδέναι" for the knowledge of the particular premise, which is not a matter of ἐπιστήμη.

tion of incontinence. For he believes that Socrates needs to say that the incontinent "is not the same person" before and after his incontinent action. If Socrates were right, the incontinent would have lost his universal knowledge, and would have to relearn it, or else he would have abandoned it, and so would have to relearn the habit of acting on it.[15] We can avoid these paradoxical claims about the incontinent if we acknowledge that his passions temporarily interrupt his reasoning so that he lacks the relevant particular knowledge.

Still, some questions may be raised about Aristotle's solution: (1) The discussion of having and actualizing knowledge does not seem to be properly connected to the rest of the discussion, and does not seem to offer a very plausible solution in its own right. To the extent that an alleged case of incontinence is like the case of a sleeper, to that extent it seems less like real incontinence. (2) Similarly, the second explanation seems to overlook one major question about incontinence. The formulation in the *Protagoras* says only that the incontinent person "knowing bad things that they are bad, nonetheless does them." This does not make it clear whether Socrates refers to universal or to particular knowledge. Aristotle takes him to refer to universal knowledge; but we might suppose that incontinence is possible in the face of particular knowledge. Aristotle seems to assume that this sort of incontinence is impossible.

And so, despite Aristotle's criticism of Socrates, his solution seems rather Socratic. Unlike Socrates, he believes that nonrational desires help to explain why the incontinent lacks the relevant sort of knowledge. But he assumes that Socrates is right to appeal to ignorance.

5. *Nicomachean Ethics* 7 and the *Protagoras*

The discussion of incontinence in the *EN* 7 also refers to the *Protagoras*, but not to quite the same passages.

> We might be puzzled about in what way someone supposing correctly acts incontinently. First of all, some say he cannot [act] knowingly. For it would be terrible—Socrates used to think—for knowledge to be in someone, but mastered by something else, and dragged around like a slave. For Socrates used to oppose the account [of incontinence] altogether, on the ground that there is no incontinence; for [he held] no one supposes that he is acting contrary to the best, but because of ignorance. (*EN* 7.2.1145b21–27)

Aristotle's remarks about knowledge as being mastered as a slave, and as being dragged around, all echo Socrates' introduction of the common

15. These seem to be the two possibilities referred to in "expel" and "fall away" in *MM* 2.6.1201b22–23.

view of incontinence (*Protagoras* 352c1: ἀνδραπόδου, περιελκομένης; c5: κρατηθῆναι).[16] He introduces Socrates as someone who argues that the "correct apprehension" of an incontinent cannot be knowledge because it would be terrible for knowledge to be dragged about like a slave. But he explains (γάρ, 1145b25) that Socrates held this view on the strength of three further claims: (1) There is no incontinence. (2) No one does what he supposes to be worse. (3) If anyone does what is actually worse, it is because of ignorance.[17]

These three claims go beyond the initial claim that Aristotle ascribed to Socrates. We might claim that one cannot act against knowledge of what is best, but allow the possibility of acting against correct belief. Only the claim about knowledge appears in the passage in the *Protagoras* that Aristotle follows most closely. But two further passages support Aristotle: (1) At 357c6 the many ask Socrates and Protagoras: "If this condition [πάθημα] is not being overcome by pleasure, what is it at all, and what do you two say it is?" Socrates answers that he has vindicated the answer that they would at first have ridiculed, that the condition is ignorance (ἀμαθία) (357d1–3). Hence they must agree that "[t]his is what being overcome by pleasure is: the most serious ignorance" (357e2). (2) At 358c6–d5 the many accept Socrates' view that "no one is willing to go toward what one thinks [οἴεται, 358c7, d1; cf. 358e5: ἡγεῖται] to be bad."

These two passages support Aristotle's claims about Socrates' denial of incontinence. In the first passage Socrates' position might seem contradictory. The many take him to have shown that the condition he has described is not a case of being overcome by pleasure; he does not correct them, but he says that being overcome by pleasure is ignorance. One might argue that if he offers to say what being overcome by pleasure is, he must believe there is such a thing. This apparent conflict, however, is easily resolved; Socrates' claim that being overcome by pleasure is ignorance is parallel to the claim that witches are hysterical women. Someone who accepts the latter claim does not believe in witches; the claim means "the people who used to be thought to be witches are really not witches, but hysterical women." Socrates offers an eliminative reduction of incontinence to something that is not incontinence—to ignorance of the good. His conclusion vindicates Aristotle's view that he denies the existence of incontinence.

In the second passage Socrates correctly supposes that his explicit

16. Kahn, *Plato and the Socratic Dialogue,* 86, describes Aristotle's use of the *Protagoras* with some exaggeration, by saying that "Aristotle is literally quoting the text of the *Protagoras.*"

17. These claims (2) and (3) are my expansion of "οὐθένα γὰρ . . . ἀλλὰ δι' ἄγνοιαν," *EN* 7.2.1145b26–27.

argument against incontinence applies no less to belief than to knowledge. If he had allowed that we can act against our current correct belief about the good, his eliminative reduction would be undermined; for if choosing the worse is consistent with correct belief that it is worse, it cannot simply be the result of ignorance. Aristotle sees this, and so he is justified in ascribing to Socrates a more extreme thesis than the initial claim that knowledge cannot be dragged about by nonrational desires.

These points suggest that Aristotle has not only read the passage on knowledge being dragged around, but has also studied the argument that follows and the conclusions that Socrates draws from that argument. The argument and the conclusions justify him in ascribing to Socrates the extreme view that denies the possibility of incontinence. Though Aristotle begins this discussion by looking for the kind of correct apprehension that the incontinent person acts against, he does not count Socrates as one of the people who thinks there is such a correct apprehension. Since Aristotle believes that we recognize incontinence only if we recognize that one can act against such a correct apprehension, he takes Socrates to deny incontinence. In the *Protagoras* Socrates takes the same view.

If we compare *EN* 7 with the *MM* on incontinence, we notice that Aristotle has not only read but reread the *Protagoras*.[18] He now inserts the remark on knowledge being dragged about like a slave, which he does not mention in the *MM*. Though he still affirms that Socrates denies incontinence, and he still rejects this denial, he does not say Socrates was wrong to think it would be terrible if ἐπιστήμη were dragged around.

> This argument, then, contradicts things that appear manifestly. If ignorance causes the incontinent to be affected as he is, we must look for the type of ignorance that it turns out to be; for it is evident, at any rate, that before he is affected by passion [πρὶν ἐν τῷ πάθει γενέσθαι] the one who acts incontinently does not suppose. (*EN* 7.2.1145b27–31)

Aristotle disagrees with Socrates' reason for believing that knowledge is not dragged around. Socrates believes incontinence is impossible. Aristotle suggests that we ought to look for a different reason, and where we might find a solution to the problems that led Socrates to eliminate incontinence.

In Aristotle's view, we should consider the type of ignorance that might be relevant, and recognize that the incontinent does not think

18. The list of puzzles about incontinence is fairly similar in the two works, except that the *EN* lists some puzzles that the *MM* omits at first, but takes up in the course of discussion. Cf. *EN* 7.2.1146a4 with *MM* 2.6.1204a5, and 1146a31 with 1203a7.

he ought to do the incontinent action before he is influenced by his passion. If Aristotle is so careful to say that this is true of the incontinent only before he is influenced by passion, we may gather that he thinks it is false once the incontinent is influenced by the relevant passion. These glosses on the Socratic position, anticipating Aristotle's solution, are absent from the *MM.*

This is difficult to explain on the assumption that the author of the *MM* was simply excerpting the *EE,* including *EN* 7. I am not sure why he would bother to delete the reference to one passage of the *Protagoras* (on knowledge being dragged around) and then to insert a reference to another passage. It is more likely that Aristotle added the reference to knowledge being dragged around because he had come to see that Socrates was right about something. Whether this is a reasonable explanation or not depends on what we think about the rest of Aristotle's discussion.

6. Second Thoughts on Incontinence

Despite Aristotle's expressions of sympathy with Socrates, *EN* 7 expands the discussion of incontinence in ways that seem to depart from a Socratic solution. Several times in Book 7 Aristotle affirms that the incontinent has the right decision (προαίρεσις) and acts against it.[19] The *MM* describes what is sound in the incontinent person by saying that he has correct reason that opposes his going after the things that his appetite leads him toward.[20] It does not mention the right decision.

Does this difference of expression mark a difference of doctrine? That depends on what the *MM* means by saying that the incontinent's reason "opposes" (ἐναντιοῦται, 1203a5) or "fights against" (μάχεται, 1203b27) his passions. Does this mean that he actually forms a rational desire or prescription forbidding him to do this particular thing that he has the bad appetite for? If Aristotle means this in the *MM,* one might argue that he implicitly ascribes the right decision to the incontinent. But he probably does not mean this; he suggests that the incontinent is inhibited from forming any desire with a particular content that would present him with this particular prescription (not to eat this piece of cake now). Probably, then, Aristotle means in the *MM* that the incontinent has the right general principles, but not the right particular pre-

19. *EN* 7.4.1148a13–17, 7.8.1151a5–7 (cf. 7.8.1150b29–31), 7.9.1151a29–33 (cf. 7.9.1152a4–6, οἰόμενος δεῖν), 7.10.1152a17.

20. *MM* 2.6.1203a5; cf. a14: "λόγον ὀρθόν," b18–19: "λόγον ὀρθόν," b26–27: "ὁ λόγος τοῖς πάθεσι μάχεται."

scriptions and desires. That is why he takes the claim that the incontinent has correct reason to be equivalent to the claim that he has the correct principle (ἀρχή, 1203a15).

The claim in the *EN* that the incontinent has not only the right principle, but also the right decision, commits Aristotle to a more definitely particular prescription. When he speaks of a decision, he normally refers to the outcome of deliberation, starting from the wish (βούλησις) for an end and ending with a desire that is determinate enough to be the immediate preliminary to action. As the *EE* puts it, questions for deliberation are such questions as "whether they will go to war" (2.10.1227a13), and one continues the deliberation until one "brings it back to oneself" (1227a17). If this is what Aristotle means in claiming that the incontinent has the right decision, he ascribes more to the incontinent than he ascribes in the *MM*. Nothing in the *MM* implies that the incontinent has a rational desire not to eat this piece of cake, whereas the *EN* implies just this.

We might try to avoid this argument by suggesting that Aristotle does not use "decision" in its normal sense when he ascribes the correct decision to the incontinent. Perhaps he just means the same as he means in saying (in both treatises) that the incontinent has the right principle.

We can test this suggestion about the sense of "decision" by examining another element in the *EN* that has no *MM* parallel. Before the incontinent acts, he has formed a "good syllogism," a practical syllogism based on wish and deliberation, reaching a conclusion that expresses his decision (7.3.1147a25–28). He will act on this conclusion at once if he is able to act and is not hindered (7.3.1147a29–31).

> Further, we may also look at the cause in the following way, from the point of view of nature. For the one is a universal belief; the other is about particulars, of which perception is now in control. And whenever one [belief] comes to be from them, it is necessary, in one case, for the soul to affirm what has been concluded, but, in the case of beliefs about production, to act at once on what has been concluded. If, for instance, everything sweet must be tasted, and this, some one particular thing, is sweet, it is necessary for someone who is able and unhindered also to act on this at the same time. (*EN* 7.3.1147a24–30; cf. b9–13)

The conclusion that he reaches prohibits the very action that he later does because of incontinence.

> Suppose, then, that someone has the universal [belief] hindering him from tasting; he has the second, that everything sweet is pleasant and this is sweet, and this is active; but it turns out that appetite is present in him. The one, then tells him to avoid this, but appetite leads him on, since it is capable of moving each of the [bodily] parts. (*EN* 7.3.1147a31–35)

Moreover, he may still be able to say the words of the good conclusion when he is acting incontinently.

The summary I have just given could be disputed at every stage. Still, it is difficult to deny that the incontinent person forms a rational desire not to do the very thing that he eventually does. We already have good reason to expect this from the fact that Aristotle says the incontinent makes the right decision; but if that is not enough for us, the description of the incontinent person's inferences implies that he forms a correct rational desire directed to a particular action.

In claiming that the incontinent makes the right decision and that he draws the conclusion of the good syllogism, Aristotle rejects the account in the *MM* of the incontinent's error. The *MM* relies on the distinction between universal knowledge, which the incontinent keeps, and particular knowledge, which he lacks (*MM* 2.6.1201b29–1202a1). The *EN* retains the distinction between universal and particular knowledge, but it inserts a new section that examines the question "from the natural point of view" (φυσικῶς, 1147a24). This section describes the practical inferences of incontinent people, showing that they reach a conclusion about particulars. The *MM* does not suggest this. When it says that incontinent people's passion takes control of them (ἐπικρατῆσαν) and makes their reasoning inactive (ἠρεμεῖν ἐποίησε τὸν λογισμόν, 1202a6), it suggests that their passions prevent them from completing the practical inference that would show them that this particular action is bad. The *EN* implies, on the contrary, that incontinents complete their practical inference.[21]

We can now see the point of Aristotle's remark that to solve the puzzles about incontinence we need to find the relevant type of ignorance. The text, literally translated, says: "for that the one acting incontinently does not suppose, before he comes to be in the passion, is evident" (*EN* 7.2.1145b30–31). We need to supplement this literal rendering of the Greek: What is it that the incontinent does not suppose before he comes to be in the passion? It would be irrelevant to apply this remark to universal knowledge of general moral principles, for the incontinent always accepts the right principles, before, during, and after his incontinent action. Aristotle's remark fits a judgment about a particular action, since

21. A fuller defense of this claim would need to take account of Aristotle's remarks on the "rash" and the "weak" incontinents in 7.7.1150b19–28. Aristotle says the rash incontinent does not stop to deliberate, but is led on by his passion. We should not infer, however, that he has not completed the relevant practical inference. We can perform a complete inference and make a decision without stopping to deliberate on that occasion. The case that Aristotle mentions in 3.8.1117a17–22 helps to explain his view about the rash incontinent. I have said a little more on this in "Some Rational Aspects of Incontinence," 58–59.

this changes under the influence of passions. Probably he is not simply saying that the incontinent lacks the positive belief that he ought to eat this piece of cake now before he is influenced by passion. That would not show that he is acting incontinently in eating it. Aristotle probably also means that before the incontinent is influenced by his passion, he believes he ought not to eat this piece of cake now. That is the judgment he ascribes to the incontinent person on the basis of the conclusion that forbids him to eat this.

In these ways the *EN* tries harder than the *MM* to accommodate the phenomena of incontinence. Aristotle gives up the suggestion that the incontinent has only potential knowledge of the minor premise that would lead to the particular prescription forbidding the action he eventually does.

7. Is Knowledge Dragged Around?

I mentioned earlier that the *EN* differs from the *MM* in picking out Socrates' rejection of the view that knowledge is dragged about like a slave. We can see Aristotle's reason for picking out this idea once we look more closely at the next step of his account of how incontinence happens. He claims that the incontinent acts on appetite, not on decision (*EN* 7.3.1147a33–34, 3.2.1111b13–14). He is moved by the conclusion of a "bad syllogism," based on appetite and perhaps on some deliberation, focused on the action prohibited by the conclusion of the good syllogism.[22]

We may wonder how this is possible, given that the incontinent has already formed the conclusion of the good syllogism. Aristotle answers our question by claiming that when incontinents act, they lack the minor premise of the good syllogism, and so are ignorant (7.3.1147b6–12).

This claim that the incontinent "lacks the minor premise" has puzzled many readers. A plausible account of the inference leading to the incontinent action suggests that the good and the bad syllogisms share a minor premise, "This is sweet." If the incontinent lacked this premise, he could not focus his appetite on this particular sweet thing. In the face of this difficulty, some readers have suggested that the Greek phrase translated "minor premise" (τελευταία πρότασις) should be translated "last proposition," referring to the conclusion of the good syllogism.

This suggestion is unnecessary (whether it is right or wrong), since

22. I have followed the exegesis of this passage that attributes two practical syllogisms to the incontinent. But the main point I make about losing the minor premise would still stand even if appetite does not operate through a second practical syllogism.

we can give a reasonable sense to the claim that the incontinent lacks the minor premise of the good syllogism when he acts incontinently. In Aristotle's view, incontinents believe the proposition that is the content of the minor premise, but they lack a belief that is serving as a premise of the good syllogism. If a belief serves as a premise, one must not only hold the belief, but also combine it and "view it together" (συνθεωρεῖν, *Prior Analytics* 2.21.67a37) with the other beliefs in the inference.[23] Incontinents do not combine their perceptual belief with the good general principle in the appropriate way to make two premises of a good syllogism. They have disconnected the minor premise from the major premise with which they combined it (when they made the right decision).[24]

These references to combination and disconnection explain why Aristotle mentions Socrates' objections to knowledge being dragged around. For the belief that is initially the minor premise of the good syllogism is indeed "dragged around." Under the influence of passion it is dragged from the good syllogism to the bad, so that the good syllogism is destroyed.

Aristotle points out this connection with Socrates when he says how one of Socrates' claims turns out to be right.

> And since the last term does not seem to be universal, or expressive of knowledge in the same way as the universal term, even the result Socrates was looking for would seem to come about. For the knowledge that is present when someone is affected by incontinence is not the sort that seems to be fully knowledge, nor is it dragged about because of his affection, but only perceptual knowledge. (*EN* 7.3.1147b13–17)

Only perceptual knowledge is present when one acts incontinently; it is not clear whether Aristotle means to say that it is also dragged around.[25] But if we have given the right account of the stages leading to incontinent action, he believes that it is dragged around, from one syllogism to another.

But what does Aristotle mean in saying that what seems to be "knowledge strictly speaking" (or "full knowledge") is not present to be dragged around when one acts incontinently? The previous contrast between the "last term" and the "universal" and "scientific" ("expressive of knowl-

23. On συνθεωρεῖν, see *APr* 2.18.66b18–67b11, *APo* 1.1.71a7–b8, and H. H. Joachim and D. A. Rees, *The Nicomachean Ethics: A Commentary* (Oxford: Clarendon Press, 1951), 226–28.

24. On reasons for taking the τελευταία πρότασις, *EN* 7.3.1147b9, to be the conclusion ("last proposition"), see Charles, *Aristotle's Philosophy of Action,* 120–28.

25. Grammatically ἀλλὰ τῆς αἰσθητικῆς, *EN* 7.3.1147b17, is connected to παρούσης in b16. The remark about dragging around, "οὐδ᾽ αὕτη περιέλκεται διὰ τὸ πάθος" in b16–17, applies grammatically only to "τῆς κυρίως ἐπιστήμης εἶναι δοκούσης" in b15–16.

edge," ἐπιστημονικόν) term might suggest that strict knowledge is universal knowledge.[26]

But Aristotle cannot deny that this is present, for the incontinent still knows that (e.g.) one ought not to taste too many sweet things. The incontinent lacks the knowledge that this particular thing ought not to be tasted, for since he simply says the words of the minor premise, he also simply says the words of the conclusion, and so he does not know that this ought not to be tasted. To know it, he would have to infer it from the correct general principle that he ought not to taste sweet things, but since the good syllogism has been dissolved, he no longer infers it from that principle. He knew it previously, when he made the right decision.

I am inclined to speculate, therefore, that Aristotle's rereading of the *Protagoras* leads him to notice the remark about dragging around, and so suggests a way to improve the explanation of incontinence. Socrates' claim that knowledge is not dragged around suggests to Aristotle a distinction between beliefs that are dragged around and those that are not; and this distinction suggests a way of endorsing Socrates' claim that knowledge is not dragged around. We can agree that a certain kind of knowledge is not dragged around, while admitting, contrary to Socrates, the possibility of incontinence.

8. For and Against Socrates

I have argued that Aristotle becomes more sympathetic to Socrates in the *EN* than he was in the *MM*. Instead of simply saying that Socrates was wrong about incontinence, he also tries to explain the important respect in which he was right. But this does not mean his position is more Socratic in the *EN*. As far as I can see, the reverse is true.

The *MM* and the *Protagoras* agree on one claim about incontinence that many people would find counterintuitive: incontinents do not act against a sincere rational judgment that it is better not to do what they eventually do. Socrates believes that if they ever formed this judgment, they must have abandoned it and replaced it with the judgment that it is better to do the allegedly incontinent action. The *MM* holds that Socrates was wrong not to recognize that appetite interferes with practical reasoning so as to prevent the formation of the good syllogism (the

26. Most commentators take the relevant knowledge to be universal knowledge, and then have to resort to rather implausible accounts of why it is not present. See the helpful note in John Alexander Stewart, *Notes on the Nicomachean Ethics*, 2 vols. (Oxford: Clarendon Press, 1892), ad loc. The view that he rejects (Ramsauer's, p. 163)—that κυρίως ἐπιστήμη requires the presence of both the major and the minor premise—seems the most plausible to me.

one that would forbid their doing what they eventually do). Incontinence, on this view, consists in acting against one's principles because of the influence of appetite.

The *EN* comes closer to common sense, and hence moves further from Socrates. Instead of saying that incontinents act against their general principles, Aristotle agrees with common sense, against Socrates and the *MM,* that they form the correct decision, including the correct particular prescription against the incontinent action. He concludes, therefore, that they do the particular thing they believe they ought not to do. He retains the Socratic claim, which many regard as counterintuitive, that incontinents do not sincerely judge at the time they act incontinently that they ought not to do what they do. They lose the conclusion of the good syllogism under the influence of appetite, even though they still say the words. In neither work does Aristotle agree with Socrates' view that alleged incontinents really judge it best to do what they do at the time when they act incontinently.

I will not discuss Aristotle's reasons for saying that the incontinent just says the right words, but does not make a sincere judgment. I have simply tried to point out the anti-Socratic elements in the *EN.* They show that Aristotle's expressions of sympathy with Socrates do not lead him closer to acceptance of the Socratic position. If I were to conclude with a speculation, I would suggest that when Aristotle is no longer so concerned to separate himself from Socrates, he is readier to appreciate him. Whereas the outlook of the *MM* is polemical, the later works aim at the outlook of the impartial judge.

3 Plotinus on Weakness of the Will: The Neoplatonic Synthesis

LLOYD P. GERSON

Porphyry tells us that "mixed in" with Plotinus's *Enneads* are "concealed Stoic and Peripatetic teachings."[1] Nowhere is this more apparent than in his understanding of moral psychology, broadly speaking. At the same time, Plotinus thought of himself as an unwavering adherent of Platonism, certainly more a "paleo-Platonist" than a "neo-Platonist." It is misleading to suggest that this Platonism is a type of syncretism, which I understand to be the view that an amalgam of philosophical positions is thought to result in something new. Rather, it is an application of the principle that Aristotle's philosophy and, at least in psychological and ethical matters, Stoic philosophy, were in harmony with Platonism. This is the position that Hierocles of Alexandria attributes to Plotinus's teacher, Ammonius Saccas.[2] The claim that with regard to an account of weakness of the will Plato, Aristotle, and the Stoics are in harmony is bound to appear dubious. For Aristotle seems to consciously develop his account in opposition to Plato; and at least for the Old Stoa, weakness of will seems to be ruled out by the account of the actions of rational creatures. Accordingly, I begin with a brief survey of what I believe Plotinus took to be the received wisdom of the three great schools that preceded his own. I then turn to Plotinus's synthesis of this material.

1. Plotinus's Predecessors

Plato

In *Protagoras,* Plato has Socrates argue *against* the possibility of weakness of the will.[3] As Socrates argues against the many, that which is

1. *Life of Plotinus* 1.4.
2. Photius, *Bibliotheca* 214.2, 172a2–9; Porphyry, *De regressu animae* fr. 302F, 6 Smith.
3. *Protagoras* 352a1–c7.

commonly called "being overcome by pleasure though one knows the right thing to" is in fact "ignorance" (ἀμαθία).[4] The basic argument is as follows: (1) Assume, with those who believe that being overcome by pleasure is a fact of life, that someone chooses X over Y knowing that Y is better but being overcome by the pleasurableness of X (353a5–b2); (2) "Pleasurable" and "good" are two names for the same thing (353b3–c1); (3) So, then, someone chooses X over Y, knowing that Y is better because he is overcome by the goodness of X (355c3–8). This conclusion is taken to be absurd and therefore to reveal the falsity of (1) (355d1–3). That is, assuming that "pleasure" and "good" mean the same thing, it makes no sense to say that someone does what he knows to be not good because he is overcome by pleasure.

Plato and Aristotle both came to believe that on the model of action assumed in this argument, weakness of the will is impossible. This model holds that persons are rational agents, that is, that reasons are the immediate causes of action, where action includes refraining from acting. In addition, it holds that the reasoning that causes action is a unified or coherent process, that is, if the reason for doing something is a belief that *p*, then one cannot simultaneously believe that not-*p*. Alternatively, we might put this by saying that the only reasons for acting are effective beliefs, beliefs that, all things considered, doing something is the way to achieve one's good insofar as one understands that. If I believe that in this instance refraining from doing something is good for me, I cannot be overcome in the relevant sense, for being overcome implies that the action springs from a belief that contradicts what I believe is good for me. If I do act, it is because I have an effective belief that, all things considered, this is the way to achieve my good.[5] Such action may be ill-informed or vicious, or even self-destructive, but it is not akratic.

The recognition of the possibility of ἀκρασία by Plato demanded a new model of action. The possibility is acknowledged in the *Republic* with the pathetic Leontius who yearns to gaze upon the naked corpses despite his belief that he ought not do so.[6] The new model of action is based upon the hypothesis of a partitioned soul. This new model seeks to provide the grounds for maintaining that the explanation for an action, the ἀρχή of the action, can be other than reason. In the case of

4. *Protagoras* 357d1 provides the correct name for what at 352e8–53a2 is described as "being overcome by pleasure."

5. An "effective belief" is close to what is indicated by Plato in his claim that "no one does wrong willingly." See *Apology* 37a5; *Gorgias* 488a3; *Protagoras* 345d8, 358c7; *Republic* 589c6; *Timaeus* 86d7–e1; and *Laws* 731c–d. An action done "willingly" (ἑκών) is one done on the basis of a belief that such an action will achieve one's own good. Cf. Aristotle, *Nicomachean Ethics* 3.3.1113a2–7.

6. *Republic* 439e6–40a3.

Leontius, the ἀρχή is his desire to satisfy his lurid appetite. This desire is resisted by his belief that it is wrong to seek such satisfaction.

How does partitioning of the soul permit us to say that someone acted against his own belief regarding what is best for him in the situation? As I have argued elsewhere, partitioning of the soul is partitioning of an embodied self or person.[7] This amounts to the recognition of an essential recursiveness or reflexivity in embodied rational desire. Beings capable of reason or λόγος have, normally, desires and desires in regard to these desires. One can, following Harry Frankfurt, call these first- and second-order desires if one likes, though Frankfurt himself eschews any interest in the metaphysics of personhood.[8] For Plato, this capacity is an example of the equivocal ontological status of all that is embodied.[9] Leaving the metaphysics aside for the moment, what this means is that embodied persons can be simultaneously the subject of one desire and the subject of the desire to have the first desire not be an effective cause of action. This hypothesis about personhood alone—whatever the explanation of the fact that the first desire prevailed—accounts for the possibility of ἀκρασία. The nature of embodied personhood is such that I can want to do something and simultaneously want not to do that identical thing. For Plato, no contradiction follows upon such a hypothesis because the subject of each desire is not unequivocally the same. In the case of Leontius, the subject of the desire to gaze upon the corpses is not unequivocally the same as the subject of the desire to refrain, though these are not unequivocally *different* subjects either. Leontius has a (second-order) desire that arises from a criticism of his own (first-order) desire, so there is no question that he is unequivocally two subjects; on the other hand, insofar as the identity or individuation of a subject is constituted by, among other things, its desires, he also cannot be unequivocally one subject.

It is important to realize that both the first- and the second-order desires are rational, in the sense that both are conceptualized by the subject. The so-called quarrel between reason and appetite that is supposed to entail the attribution of reason *to* appetite or to an appetitive faculty

7. See Lloyd P. Gerson, *Knowing Persons: A Study in Plato* (Oxford: Oxford University Press, 2003), chap. 3.

8. See especially Harry Frankfurt, "Freedom of the Will and the Concept of the Person," *Journal of Philosophy* 68 (1971): 5–20, reprinted in his *The Importance of What We Care About* (Cambridge: Cambridge University Press, 1988), 11–25. For a sympathetic yet critical analysis of Frankfurt's distinction, see Eleonore Stump, "Persons: Identification and Freedom," *Philosophical Topics* 24 (1996): 183–214.

9. In Timaeus 35a–b, the soul is "constructed" out of both divisible and indivisible οὐσία, reflecting the fact that we stand between mere images and that which is really real.

is in fact no such thing.[10] Reason does not argue with a "rationalized" appetite, whatever that is supposed to mean. There is also no need to posit a *homunculus* representing the appetite in the quarrel. The akratic event occurs *after* practical reasoning has occurred. If this were not the case, then the action taken as a result of the putative quarrel would not be akratic; it would be action resulting from the "all-things-considered" judgment of how one's good is to be achieved.

Leontius is faced with his belief that his good is achieved by satisfying his first-order desire to gaze and his belief that his good is achieved by satisfying his second-order desire to refrain from gazing. Leontius's dilemma is that he is insecure in his identity. He does not know whether acting or refraining from acting is his real good because he does not know whether he is really a subject of the first- or the second-order desire. His confusion is understandable since *both* his first- and his second-order desires are rational in the relevant sense, that is, they are conceptualized.[11] Why after all *should* Leontius prefer to act on his second-order desire rather than on his first-order desire? For Plato, the only possible reason for choosing to act on one desire rather than another is that at the moment of action, or in general, Leontius is sufficiently alienated from one self-conception and sufficiently identified with another that *his* good appears to him only as the object of the desire of the latter. The idea of "alienation" from one's own desire can be given a fairly perspicuous sense if we consider that the ultimate form of such alienation is when the desire is recognized by the subject as being like the desire of another person.[12] Conversely, the "identification" with the subject of a desire is the other extreme, whose ultimate achievement would occur

10. For the view that appetite is somehow capable of engaging in reasoning see Jon Moline, *Plato's Theory of Understanding* (Madison: University of Wisconsin Press, 1981), 61. See also Julia Annas, *Platonic Ethics, Old and New* (Ithaca: Cornell University Press, 1999), 133–36. See also William W. Fortenbaugh, *Aristotle on Emotion* (London: Duckworth, 1975), 38–44; Glenn Lesses, "Weakness, Reason, and the Divided Soul in Plato's *Republic*," *History of Philosophy Quarterly* 4 (1987): 147–61; Charles H. Kahn, "Plato's Theory of Desire," *Review of Metaphysics* 41 (1987): 77–103, at 85; Christopher Bobonich, "Akrasia and Agency in Plato's Laws and Republic," *Archiv für Geschichte der Philosophie* 76 (1994): 3–36, at 4, n. 3, with references, and p. 12; Terence H. Irwin, *Plato's Ethics* (New York: Oxford University Press, 1995), 217–22; Christopher Gill, *Personality in Greek Epic, Tragedy, and Philosophy* (Oxford: Clarendon Press, 1996), 243–60; and Dominic Scott, "Plato's Critique of the Democratic Character," *Phronesis* 45 (2000): 19–37, at 30–32.

11. *Republic* 437e7–8: "αὐτή γε ἡ ἐπιθυμία ἑκάστη αὐτοῦ μόνον ἑκάστου οὗ πέφυκεν, τοῦ δὲ τοίου ἢ τοίου τὰ προσγιγνόμενα." These "additions" include, minimally, conceptualization of a particular type of object of desire, e.g., lemonade, as opposed simply to drink. Since all desire is for the good, the conceptualization of the object is conceptualization of it as a good, e.g., lemonade is good for me now.

12. One may compare the extreme case of the psychotic who does not recognize himself as being identical with the individual who committed the crime.

if one *only* located one's good in the object of such a desire.[13] In such a person, there would be a coincidence of first- and second-order desires.

The subject of second-order desires is specifically the "man within the man" Plato refers to in *Republic* 589a7–8. His desires are also rational in a way that the first-order desires are not: they do not belong to a subject with which he is not really or ideally identical. That is, they do not belong to a subject of bodily appetites. This ideal subject is unquestionably a disembodied one for Plato; embodiment always entails at least a residual attachment to the subject of bodily appetites.

According to Plato, "giving in" to one's own appetites amounts to a false belief that one's identity is located as the subject of these appetites. Because there is a belief here, albeit a false one, there is rationality; because one has "given in" to the nonrational appetite, we can say that the ἀρχή of the action is other than reason. Alternately, we can say that the ἀρχή of the action is against "right reason."[14] Those who think that Plato has mistakenly forsworn the account of *Protagoras* by allowing the nonrational a part in the account of action do not, I believe, sufficiently acknowledge the ambiguity of the subject as rational and as image of the rational.[15] Identifying oneself as the latter is manifestly both a rational act and an abnegation of rational identity.

Aristotle

Turning to Aristotle, I begin with the perhaps surprising fact that Aristotle's account of ἀκρασία rests upon the same doctrine as Plato's, namely, a distinction between the idea "man within the man" and the embodied person or, in Aristotle's terminology, the "composite" organic ἄνθρωπος. In *Nicomachean Ethics,* Book 10, chapters 6–8, Aristotle distinguishes "that which we are especially" from the composite.[16] The former is intellect; the latter is the subject of embodied psychical states. Intellect, as in Plato, is immortal whereas the soul/body composite is not.[17] The relationship between intellect and soul is in Aristotle a vexed topic, especially in regard to cognitive matters. Nevertheless, it is with the dis-

13. *Republic* 443e1; 554d9–10.

14. See for ὀρθὸς λόγος in this sense *Statesman* 310c4; *Laws* 696c9.

15. See especially Terence Penner, "Plato and Davidson: Parts of the Soul and Weakness of the Will," *Canadian Journal of Philosophy,* Suppl. 16 (1990): 35–74; "Knowledge vs. True Belief in the Socratic Psychology of Action," *Apeiron* 29 (1996): 199–230; and "Socrates on the Strength of Knowledge: 'Protagoras' 351b–357e," *Archiv für Geschichte der Philosophie* 79 (1997): 117–49.

16. *EN* 10.7.1178a7: "τοῦτο [ὁ νοῦς] μάλιστα ἄνθρωπος." Cf. *EN* 10.7.1177a12–19; 1.7.1097a25–b21; 10.5.1175b36–1176a29; 10.8.1178a9–22; b3–7.

17. For the immortality of intellect, see *De anima* 3.5.430a23. Cf. 1.4.408b18–19.

tinction between the soul/body composite and the *real* person that we must approach Aristotle's account of incontinence.

Second, Aristotle, like Plato, distinguishes between the part of the soul that "has reason" and the part that, though it is nonrational, can "obey" reason.[18] This is "the appetitive part" (τὸ ἐπιθυμητικόν) of the soul.[19] Aristotle allows, however, that obeying reason requires "reason-involvement" of some sort, that is, the conceptualization of desire.[20] As in Plato, the subject of the incontinent person's desire is the same as the subject of the desire to refrain from acting. There is no need for *homunculi* here either. But Aristotle will not allow for embodied psychic dividedness, despite his acknowledgment of the distinction between the man and the "man within the man." Instead, he accounts for incontinence by distinguishing senses of "knowing" and "believing."

Basically, the Aristotelian akratic acts on a syllogism the major premise of which is a general statement indicating the general desirability of the satisfaction of an appetite. And though there must also be in the akratic a belief in a universal premise stating the *undesirability* of that appetite's satisfaction, the akratic acts according to the former, not the latter. He acts according to the universal premise, though his belief in the particular premise is, as Aristotle says, authoritative over the action.[21] But in order to avoid the paradox of saying that the akratic has contradictory beliefs, he says that it is the desire that contradicts reason, not belief.[22]

Aristotle seems to differ from Plato in maintaining that if there is occurrent knowledge in an agent indicating that he ought to refrain from acting, then he will not—or cannot—act.[23] Would Aristotle say then that Leontius could not know or truly believe that gazing on the corpses was bad for him? Not exactly. What Leontius could not have is "knowledge in the principal sense" (κυρίως ἐπιστήμη). He *could* have knowledge, but only in the way a drunkard or a madman has it. The distinction between knowledge (or belief) and "knowledge in the principal sense" in-

18. *EN* 1.7.1098a4; 1.13.1102a27–1103a3.

19. *EN* 1.13.1102b30.

20. *EN* 1.13.1103a1–3. It is clear from the characterization of the incontinent man at 7.3.1147a32–b3 that desire is conceptualized in order that he can be represented as syllogizing.

21. *EN* 7.3.1147b9–10.

22. *EN* 7.3.1147b2–3. Donald Davidson gives an analysis of weakness of the will that is essentially Aristotelian in form. Davidson thinks that the akratic acts against his "all-things-considered" judgment and in accord with his "unconditional" judgment of what he desires. I take it that this unconditional judgment arises from a desire that is unincorporated into the all-things-considered judgment; see "How Is Weakness of the Will Possible?" in *Moral Concepts,* ed. Joel Feinberg (Oxford: Oxford University Press, 1970), reprinted in D. Davidson, *Essays on Actions and Events* (New York: Oxford University Press, 1980), 21–42.

23. *EN* 7.3.1147b15–19.

dicates the a priori nature of the claim. The only way to tell what sort of knowledge Leontius has is by his report after the fact that he indeed had knowledge. If, however, he acted against this knowledge, then it is stipulated that he did not *really* have knowledge. What is the supposed difference between knowledge and knowledge in the principal sense? As Aristotle describes it, the difference is that in the former case there is a disconnect between belief in the universal proposition and belief that it applies to oneself or to oneself now.

This disconnect may occur for two different reasons: "impetuosity" (προπέτεια) and "weakness" (ἀσθένεια). In the first case, one of the particular premises in the practical syllogism is not applied; in the second case, the conclusion of the syllogism is rendered ineffective.[24] In either case, there is a failure to actualize fully the knowledge of the universal proposition, which evidently means a failure either to embrace the obvious fact that the particular falling under the universal is before one or to embrace the conclusion of the syllogism.[25]

All the explanatory content here is supposed by Aristotle to fall upon the "failure to embrace." But the analogy with the drunkard or the madman is opaque, for the problem is precisely that the akratic is neither drunk nor mad. To say that he fails to embrace or assent to the truth of what is before his eyes or to the truth of the conclusion of his own reasoning owing to "physiological" reasons is either to claim implicitly that incontinence *is* drunkenness or madness or it is to offer no explanation at all. In the former alternative, we undercut the culpability of the acractic; in the latter, we merely point to a psychological cause supposedly analogous to the putative physiological one.

Leontius could acknowledge that corpse gazing was bad, but that it was not bad for him here and now. What Leontius believes is that in his present circumstance he is an exception to the rule, or, stated otherwise, his good now, all things considered, is achieved by gazing. Even if he were to agree that it is wrong *for him* to gaze now, he still believes that, all things considered, his good is achieved now by gazing. Knowledge in the principal sense for Aristotle does not differ from any other knowledge by content, but by its being authoritative in action. And since all agents act to achieve a good, such knowledge is not authoritative when the agent conceives of his good otherwise, that is, in this case, by the satisfaction of an appetite to gaze.

24. *EN* 7.3.1147a4–10; 1147a24–b1; cf. 7.7.1150b19–23.

25. Anthony Kenny, *Aristotle's Theory of the Will* (New Haven: Yale University Press, 1979), 160–66, argues that just because the verbal criterion for the acceptance of the universal premise is different from the behavioral criterion for the acceptance of the particular, Aristotle does in fact explain incontinence.

In the light of Aristotle's explicit distinction between the human being and "what we really are," that is, intellects, his account of how weakness of the will is possible does not seem really to differ significantly from Plato's. It is perhaps Aristotle's denial in *De anima* that "the soul thinks with one part and desires with another" that leads one to suppose that he is taking a different line.[26] Plato, though, like Aristotle, needs to have the subject of desire be the same as the subject of thought. Weakness of the will for both Plato and Aristotle indicates confusion about self-identity. Such confusion is contrary to the fixity of character present both in the virtuous and in the vicious man.

Stoicism

There is a consensus among contemporary scholars that the Old Stoa rejected both the Platonic and the Aristotelian explanations of weakness of the will and reverted to the "Socratic" position of *Protagoras*.[27] Part of the scanty evidence for this view is that the Middle Stoa, particularly Posidonius, seems to counter this position by positing some sort of division within the soul.[28] I am not convinced, however, that, viewed from the perspective of issues of identity, the position of the Old Stoa really does constitute a rejection of the phenomenon of weakness of the will as opposed to a variation on its explanation.[29] This variation embraces the rationality of desire or impulse on behalf of a unitary concept of the soul. The actions of the putative akratic, for Chrysippus, originate in "excessive impulse" (ὁρμὴ πλεονάζουσα) which is itself or originates in "assent" (συγκατάθεσις), that is, assent to presentations contrary to the deliverances of right reason.[30] It is supposed by Galen and Posidonius, among others, that the mental conflicts from which akratic action ensues is inconsistent with a monistic psychology. This would be true if this psychology precluded the sort of conflict between first- and second-

26. *De anima* 1.5.411b5–6. But cf. *EN* 9.8.1168b34–35.

27. See, e.g., Brad Inwood, *Ethics and Human Action in Early Stoicism* (Oxford: Clarendon Press, 1985), 132–39.

28. Galen says that Posidonius agrees with Plato and Aristotle; see *De placitis Hippocrates et Platonis* fr. 143, in *Posidonius,* Vol. 1: *The Fragments,* ed. Ludwig Edelstein and I. G. Kidd (Cambridge: Cambridge University Press, 1972), 135.

29. Cf. Chrysippus's view, as recounted by Galen, see *De Placitis Hippocrates et Platonis* (Stoicorum Veterum Fragmenta [SVF] 3 § 476): "Διὸ καὶ οὐκ ἀπὸ τρόπου λέγεται ὑπό τινων τὸ τῆς ψυχῆς πάθος εἶναι κίνησις παρὰ φύσιν, ὡς ἐπὶ φόβου ἔχει καὶ ἐπιθυμίας καὶ τῶν ὁμοίων. πᾶσαι γὰρ αἱ τοιαῦται κινήσεις τε καὶ καταστάσεις ἀπειθεῖς τε τῷ λόγῳ εἰσὶ καὶ ἀπεστραμμέναι . . . Οἷαι καὶ ἀκρατεῖς αἱ τοιαῦται καταστάσεις εἰσίν, ὡς ἂν οὐ κρατούντων ἑαυτῶν, ἀλλ᾽ ἐκφερομένων, καθάπερ οἱ τῷ τόνῳ τρέχοντες προσεκφέρονται, οὐ κρατοῦντες τῆς τοιαύτης κινήσεως."

30. See Galen, *De Placitis Hippocrates et Platonis* (SVF 3 § 473, § 478); and Diogenes Laertius, *Lives and Opinion of Eminent Philosophers* 7.110.

order reasons, that is, the sort of conflict I interpret Plato and Aristotle to endorse. But it does not.[31] The question is rather as to the status of one's identification with the deliverances of second-order reasons. For the Old Stoa, this identification is as much an ideal one as it is for their two great predecessors. All nonsages are fools because they do not identify their own good with the will of Zeus or they do identify it as such but only in a way that does not constitute genuine assent.

The distinction between a dualistic and a monistic psychology a propos an account of weakness of the will is, I believe, something of a red herring. This is because the actions of creatures capable of weakness of the will are *essentially* dualistic *and* monistic in the relevant senses. That is, the agent who formulates the desire to act on appetite in despite of his own reason must be capable of the dualism of first- and second-order desires and also must be the selfsame subject of both. What, if anything, separates the three accounts of weakness of the will I have hitherto mentioned is a difference more in emphasis than anything else in regard to the way to understand the endowment and the ideal achievement of personhood.

The specific Stoic contribution to the understanding of weakness of the will is to minimize the difference between it and vice as well as the difference between strength of will or continence and virtue.[32] This minimizing is implied by the analysis of weakness of the will as rooted in a failure to identify one's own good as exclusively rational or, in Stoic language, as given by "right reason." Absent this identification, one could not unequivocally assent to its deliverances as applying to oneself. Hence, the difference between weakness of the will and vice becomes exiguous.[33] The akratic's notional commitment to right reason could not constitute assent.

31. See Inwood, 163. See also the interesting discussion in A. A. Long, *Stoic Studies* (Cambridge: Cambridge University Press, 1996), 275–85, on Epictetus's efforts to deny the phenomenon of weakness of the will at the same time as he acknowledges mental conflict.

32. Stobaeus, *Eclogues* 2.60.9 Wachsmuth (SVF 3 § 264), where ἐγκράτεια is listed as a virtue, specifically, one type of σωφροσύνη. The elision of weakness of the will and vice comes out simply as "weakness in the soul" in Chrysippus. See, e.g., Galen, *De Placitis Hippocrates et Platonis* (SVF 3 § 473). This weakness or ἀσθένεια is neither ignorance nor incompetence. See Stobaeus, *Eclogues* 2.58.5 Wachsmuth (SVF 3 § 95). Vice is called a weakness in the soul by Plato; see *Gorgias* 477b3–4 and *Republic* 444e1. Note that the type of weakness of the will said by Aristotle to be owing to "impetuosity" is dropped.

33. Similarly for the distinction between weakness of the will and compulsion. The latter, like weakness of the will, consists in acting against one's judgment of what is best for oneself. But the desire upon which one does act is thought to be irresistible. The idea of an irresistible desire is not easily distinguished from a desire that was not, at the time, resisted. There is, it seems, no way to establish the falsity of the counterfactual claim that if one had only tried harder, one could have resisted the desire. If one could do this, then

Another facet of the Stoic contribution is the formulation of an account of assent that makes of it a nascent concept of the will.[34] This is another story, to be sure, one that cannot be told adequately here. Chrysippus can maintain that "impulse in man is reason prescriptive of action for him."[35] Such reason is equivalent to the universal premise in a practical syllogism so long as we acknowledge that everyone desires their own good. The assent to the proposition that initiates action is assent to a statement of the specification of the good for oneself now.

As we turn to Plotinus, and what I have termed "the Neoplatonic synthesis," we shall see, I think, how all these strands come together.

2. Plotinus's Neoplatonic Synthesis

The reasons for thinking that Plotinus wished to be considered a "paleo-Platonist" rather than a "neo-Platonist" do not need to be rehearsed here. It should be added, however, that Plotinus was more than willing to appropriate Aristotelian and Stoic insights into what Proclus praised as Plotinus's "exegesis of the Platonic revelation."[36] I assume that he was deeply impressed by the convergence of Aristotelians and Stoics with Platonism on the bipolarity of identity as endowment and achievement. Plotinus asserts: "Each of us is double: one being the composite and one being the self."[37]

But the self, we are told, is the soul, whereas the composite is the soul plus the body.[38] This seems puzzling at first, since the soul appears to be "counted" twice. In fact, each person is the composite insofar as he acts on desires originating in the composite; he is his self when he acts on or identifies with his reason.[39] The claim that the composite is "me," but not the *real* or *true* "me," captures this duality exactly.[40] Frankfurt's

---

one could distinguish those cases in which the desire was not resisted, though it could have been. These latter cases are cases of weakness of the will.

34. See, e.g., Charles Taylor, *Sources of the Self* (Cambridge, Mass.: Harvard University Press, 1989), 137, on the Stoic contribution. Also see Richard Sorabji, *Emotion and Peace of Mind: From Stoic Agitation to Christian Temptation* (Oxford: Oxford University Press, 2000), 42–44, 319–40, who disputes the idea that the Stoics had a "full blooded" concept of the will.

35. See Plutarch, *De Stoicorum repugnatiis* 1037F (SVF 3 § 175): "Καὶ μὴν ἡ ὁρμή [according to Chrysippus] . . . τοῦ ἀνθρώπου λόγος ἐστὶ προστακτικὸς αὐτῷ τοῦ ποιεῖν . . ."

36. Proclus, *Platonic Theology* 1.6, 16.

37. *Enneads* 2.3.9, 31–32; cf. 4.4.18, 14–19.

38. *Enneads* 4.7.1, 24–25. Cf. Plato, *Alcibiades* 1.130c.

39. *Enneads* 1.1.9, 15–18.

40. Cf. *Enneads* 4.4.18, 11–16. Cf. Plato, *Laws* 959a4–b7, who identifies the true self with what remains after the death of the composite. That this is a rational entity alone seems to follow from *Timaeus* 90b1–d7.

distinction between first- and second-order desires expresses the psychological continuity between the two. In the Plotinian context, a person's first-order desire aims at a good of the composite. It is always a rational desire in the sense that it must be conceptualized as a good. If it could not be conceptualized as such, it could not be resisted or suppressed. But a first-order desire is *not* rational in the way that a second-order desire is rational. The latter includes nothing of the idiosyncratic or the particular. The manifest psychological continuity between the two consists in our ability to bring our theoretical reasoning to bear on our practical reasoning about actions related to our first-order desires. The very possibility that I could desire not to possess a desire or not to have that desire be the effective source of action constitutes, for Plotinus at any rate, the irreducible duality of the embodied person.[41]

A person must be able variously to identify himself as the subject of each type of desire. The plight of every such person concerns the choice of desires or the choice of self-identification. But it is the specific cause of the first-order desire that is the focal point of weakness. The cause is always a bodily state or πάθος such as sensations or feelings of pleasure and pain or emotions.[42] The desires elicited by these states are either voluntary or "involuntary" (ἀπροαίρετον). An involuntary desire is one that has not been endorsed by a second-order desire; a voluntary desire is one that has.[43] For example, someone who conceptualizes a desire for the elimination of a pain by an illicit pleasure is acting on an involuntary desire. The ideal state of the embodied person—the state arising from purificatory virtue—is one in which there is no involuntary desire at all.[44] This is the way Plotinus describes this state:

> But will we say that he has this perfect life in himself as a part of himself? In fact, one who has it in potency has it as a part, whereas the one who is at once happy is the one who is this actually and has transformed himself in the direction of being identical with this. Everything else is something he is carrying around at the same time, which no one would suppose to be a part of him, since he does

41. *Enneads* 6.8.2, 35–37 on the "mixed" nature of the actions of embodied persons.

42. By "bodily states" I mean states of the embodied soul for which the possession of a body is necessary.

43. See especially 1.2.5. A voluntary desire is also called by Plotinus "natural"; see ibid., line 19.

44. Cf. Plato, *Phaedo* 64d3–6, and Aristotle, *EN* 7.3.1147b23–31, on "necessary pleasures." The concept of τὰ ἀπροαίρετα is especially prominent in the Roman Stoa. It refers primarily to things outside of the control of our will or moral purpose. See, e.g., Epictetus, *Discourses* 1.18.21; 1.29.24; and 3.16.15. But Epictetus, 4.1.84, also distinguishes the desires for things within our control and the desires for things that are not. The latter would be involuntary desires. Plotinus certainly had a knowledge of Epictetus's *Discourses*.

not want to carry these things around. They would be parts of him if they were connected to him according to his will [κατὰ βούλησιν].[45]

The last sentence needs to be understood as indicating the person who endorses or wills the first-order desires arising from embodiment. By contrast, one who identifies exclusively with his second-order intellectual desires has, as Plotinus says, transformed himself, that is, he has embraced his identity as an intellect. In Plato's language, he has "become one out of many."[46]

The terrain on which any distinction between vice and incontinence can be made is to be found among those who more or less connect their first-order desires with themselves "according to their will." That is, they identify themselves more or less as subjects of involuntary desires. Like the Stoics, Plotinus believes that the distinction between those who make no such identification and those who do is far more significant than any distinction among the latter.[47]

For this reason, we are concerned with its [i.e., the body's] pleasures and pains, the more concerned the weaker we are, and to the extent that we do not separate ourselves, but posit it as the most honorable part of us and the human being and sink ourselves into it.[48]

Our weakness consists in transforming states of embodied life into involuntary desires. It is odd that they should be called "involuntary." The central idea is that the state causes the desire involuntarily, provided one has identified oneself with the subject of the state. The desire will be as spontaneous or automatic as is the state. The idea that we can control such involuntary desires and even eliminate them depends upon our primary identification with that which is essentially alien to this subject. An involuntary desire is only involuntary if we accept our embodied state. Plotinus is abundantly clear that the cause of the soul's weakness is matter.

This is the fall of the soul, to come in this way to matter and to become weak, because all of its powers are not activated; matter prevents their presence by oc-

45. *Enneads* 1.4.4, 11–17.

46. *Republic* 443e1; 554d9–10; *Phaedo* 83a7.

47. See above, note 33. Though all wrongdoing arises from involuntary desires, we may wonder if there is a distinction between resistible and irresistible involuntary desires. Even if such a distinction could be made, the main motive for making it seems to be evaluative, that is, for purposes of assigning blame or responsibility. But this sort of approach to moral matters is not central for Plotinus.

48. *Enneads* 4.4.18, 15–19. The soul-body composite is the human being, but not the true human being or self.

cupying the place that soul holds and in a way by making its condition constricted and by making evil what it got hold of by a sort of theft, until soul is able to escape. Matter is thus the cause of weakness in the soul and the cause of evil.[49]

Plotinus's complex and subtle account of matter deserves far more attention that can be here given.[50] What is paramount for our purposes is that matter is distinct from body, that it is identified with privation and evil.[51] It is thus via embodiment that we acquire the weakness in the soul that makes us susceptible to evil.

First-order desires arise out of our concern for the composite, hence concern for that which is inseparable from evil.[52] But because the composite or body is not itself evil but a mixture of matter and form (evil and good), bad first-order desires, that is, involuntary ones, are only secondarily evil.[53] Since desire is, unqualifiedly, for the Good, even bad desires reflect good ones. The appetites or ἐπιθυμίαι that are, for both Plato and Aristotle, the locus of acts of incontinence, have enough goodness in them, so that even those who identify them as their own and act on them are implicitly acknowledging their basic orientation to the Good. The desire toward "intellect" (νοῦς), or second-order desire, is, by contrast, different; it is uncontaminated with evil.[54]

3. Weakness of the Will and Freedom

In order to fill out the picture of Plotinus's account of weakness of the will, we need to consider his analysis of freedom or, as he puts it, what is "up to us." This analysis is best viewed as a commentary on Plato's claim that "no one does wrong willingly."[55] Literally, this claim comes close to being an analytic truth. The verb ἁμαρτάνειν ('to err') indicates a failed effort to achieve an explicit goal. *Of course,* no one willingly fails to achieve that which they *aim* to achieve. Combined with the premise

49. *Enneads* 1.8.14, 44–50.

50. See Denis O'Brien, *Plotinus on the Origin of Matter* (Naples: Bibliopolis, 1991), and his "Plotinus on Matter and Evil," in *The Cambridge Companion to Plotinus,* ed. Lloyd P. Gerson (Cambridge: Cambridge University Press, 1996), 171–95.

51. On matter as bodiless, see *Enneads* 2.4.8, 2; 2.4.9, 5; 2.4.12, 35. On matter as privation, see 2.4.16, 3–8; 1.8.5, 6–13; 1.8.11, 1–7. On matter as evil, see 1.8.7, 1–4; 1.8.7, 17–23.

52. *Enneads* 1.8.15.

53. *Enneads* 1.8.8, 41–44.

54. *Enneads* 1.8.15, 21–23.

55. That no one does wrong willingly is held consistently by Plato; see *Apology* 37a5; *Protagoras* 345d8, 358c7, 345d8; *Gorgias* 488a3; *Republic* 589c6; *Timaeus* 85d2, e1; and *Laws* 731c–d. It should be emphasized that Plato held that no one does wrong willingly both when he held that incontinence is impossible and when he held that incontinence is possible if the soul is tripartite.

that everyone aims at their own good, the nonparadoxical conclusion is reached that no one willingly fails to achieve their own good as they conceive of it. The *paradoxical* conclusion that no one willingly does what is *simpliciter* wrong is reached via the additional premise that there is an identity between what is wrong or bad *simpliciter* and what is wrong or bad for oneself. Thus, wrongdoing is caused by ignorance, specifically ignorance of this identity.[56]

How is this ignorance to be remedied? The simple answer might seem to be: by acquiring knowledge of that which is good or of goods, such as virtue. But it is precisely the existence of the incontinent individual that indicates the inadequacy of this response. For such a person can know what is good and also know that what is good is good for him and *still* do wrong. He does wrong unwillingly. According to Plotinus's analysis, the difference between one who acts willingly and one who does not is this:

> For this reason, we will not designate the actions of evil persons, who do many things according to [their] imaginings, as "up to them" or voluntary, whereas we will designate those as self-determining who, owing to the activities of intellect, are free from the affections of the body. Referring "up to us" to the most noble principle, the activity of intellect, we will designate as really free the premises that come from there and claim that the desires that arise from thinking are not involuntary, and we will say that [self-determination] is found among the gods who live in this manner.[57]

The "really free premises" are universal premises in practical syllogisms.[58] The desires that arise from thinking are voluntary, in contrast to those arising from states of the body. The premises are free from impediments thrown up by the latter, involuntary, desires. Self-determination is the coincidence of desire and true identity.[59] Plotinus then proceeds to raise a profound objection to this line of thinking.

> Still, one might seek to determine how that which comes about according to desire will be self-determining, since desire is directed to something outside us and indicates a lack, for that to which desire is led, even if it is led to the Good.[60]

56. Cf. Plato, *Alcibiades* 1.118a–b; *Protagoras* 360b7; *Theaetetus* 176c5; *Philebus* 22b6–8; and *Laws* 863c1; Plotinus, *Enneads* 1.8.8, 41.

57. *Enneads* 6.8.3, 17–26.

58. Aristotle, *EN* 7.3.1147a1. See Kenny, 164–65, who shows that for Aristotle the universal premise never fails to be effective; the failure is always with respect to cognition of the minor premise or of the conclusion. Analogously, Stoics equate assent with impulse to act.

59. At *Enneads* 4.4.44, 5–6, Plotinus contrasts one self-determined by reason with one whose "premises" for action arise from bodily states. The former identifies himself with the object of his contemplation, whereas in the latter, there is no such identification.

60. *Enneads* 6.8.4, 1–4. Cf. 3.8.11, 22–24.

The point is that any desire is already determined by its object. In that case, how can anything done according to desire be self-determining? Plotinus's concise answer is this.

> How could something borne toward the Good be forced, since its desire is voluntary, if knowing that it is good, it goes toward it as good? For that which is involuntary is a diversion from the Good and toward that which is forced, if something is borne toward that which is not good for it.[61]

The last words of this passage make explicit the crucial qualification. Every person desires his or her own good. He who is borne toward that which is not good for himself acts unwillingly because he does not know that it is not good for himself. He does not know that nothing is good for himself except the Good. Even one who desires that which is in fact good for himself does not do so in the manner of one who identifies his own good with the Good. The only way to do this is to identify oneself exclusively as the subject of the desire for the Good.

Plotinus proceeds to acknowledge that the complete identification with intellect is impossible for the embodied person. Hence, self-determination for one embodied has to be found in virtue, by which Plotinus means "moral virtue." But here yet another problem arises, namely, that virtuous actions are themselves determined by externals, and so are not free. As Plotinus puts it, a virtuous person would not choose to have wars, disease, and poverty just in order to be able to practice his virtue.[62] So, the presence of these in a way compels him. How, then, can it be, as Plato says, that "virtue has no master?"[63]

Virtue is self-determining since it "intellectualizes the soul."[64] One of the basic principles of Plotinus's metaphysical system is that Soul is, in general, an expression of Intellect.[65] What does the "intellectualization of soul" that arises from virtue add to this? Recognizing the identity of soul and self, we may interpret this as indicating the self-identification with second-order desire. This desire is the provenance of embodied intellect. Virtue intellectualizes the soul because it disposes one to desire that which intellect determines is good.

Moral virtue is, accordingly, a "kind of intellect" (νοῦς τις). When it is present, and only when it is present, one who acts is free, and what he does is "up to him."[66] He acts "without impediment" (ἀνεμποδίστως),

61. *Enneads* 6.8.4, 12–17. Cf. Aristotle, *EN* 3.1.1110a1–b16.

62. *Enneads* 6.8.5, 13ff.

63. *Republic* 617e3.

64. *Enneads* 6.8.5, 35. Cf. 6.7.35, 4–6.

65. Cf. *Enneads* 1.8.11, 17; 3.3.3, 34; 3.5, 9, 19–20; 5.1.3, 9; 5.1.6, 45–56; 5.1.7, 44; and 5.3.8, 36.

66. *Enneads* 6.8.6, 30–31.

both externally and internally; the former, because external circumstances did not produce an involuntary desire in him and the latter, because no first-order desire was determinative of his action. In this regard, moral virtue is an image of contemplative virtue, wherein is to be found the perfect coincidence of thinking and desiring, that is, second-order desiring.[67] This type of desiring, βούλησις, is an "imitation" (μίμησις) of the activity of intellect. For it desires the Good that intellect possesses.

Vice, and its next of kin, incontinence, are thus ignorance of self, as Plotinus puts it in the famous beginning to *Ennead* 5.1. Souls or persons, wanting to be "by themselves," end up honoring "everything more than themselves."[68] They end up honoring everything that can be an object of first-order desire, and thus forget their own identities.

Plotinus, like his predecessors whom I have briefly discussed, conflates "will" with one type of "desire" (ὄρεξις), namely, βούλησις, or "rational desire."[69] I have interpreted this as a second-order desire. Weakness of the will is, on this account, owing to a confusion in regard to one's own good based on a deeper confusion in regard to one's own identity. Whether the confusion is chronic or sporadic or even remediable is a secondary question.

Conclusion

What I have tried to show in this paper is that Plotinus appropriates Peripatetic and Stoic insights into his expression of Platonic moral psychology. His use of Stoicism is especially impressive because he was not deterred by what he certainly took to be the inadequacies of Stoic metaphysics. As Aristotle remarked, rational desire is for the unqualified, not the apparent, good. Plotinus wants to insist that the weakness that is a turning away from the real good is based on a failure to separate the real good that one truly desires from the apparent goods proposed to the embodied person. This failure is nothing more nor less than an inability to give the correct answer to the question "Who am I?"

67. *Enneads* 6.8.6, 32ff.: ἡ δὲ βούλησις ἡ νόησις (line 36).

68. *Enneads* 5.1.1ff.; cf. 4.4.3, 1–3; 4.8.5, 28; and 6.9.8, 31–32.

69. When βούλησις is analyzed into intellect plus will, as it is in the later medieval tradition, intellect becomes the final cause of will, and will the efficient cause of intellect. One may usefully compare here Aristotle's analysis of substantial form as both efficient cause and final cause. What is one in being is two in λόγος.

4 Body Double: Saint Augustine and the Sexualized Will

JAMES WETZEL

"What I do, I do not understand. For I do not do what I want, but I do what I hate." So says Paul in Romans 7, where he is describing the torment of not being able to keep God's law, despite a desire to do so. Many readers of Paul, including Augustine for a time, assume that Paul is adopting a persona in Romans 7 for dramatic purposes and so is not speaking directly about an inner torment that is his own. Augustine changes his mind about this as he begins to engage in a long and bitter argument with the Pelagian Bishop Julian of Eclanum, who, to Augustine's mind, had only bad, Pelagian motives for wanting to protect the image of an unconflicted Paul.[1] It is in the first of two polemical letters directed against Julian and his supporters that Augustine definitively concludes, contrary to what he once believed, that Paul must be talking about himself in Romans 7: the voice that speaks of doing what it hates to do is now the voice of Christ's last apostle, the champion of God's grace.[2]

I am not going to be concerned with whether Augustine gets Paul right. My interest lies with what Augustine's embrace of a self-conflicted

This essay has benefited from the careful reading of numerous friends and colleagues, above all from Tobias Hoffmann.

1. For a succinct history of Augustine's reading of Romans 7, see A. C. De Veer, note complémentaire 27, *Premières polémiques contre Julien,* Œuvres de Saint Augustin 23 (Paris: Desclée de Brouwer, 1974), 770–78. I would add to his bibliography three works: William Babcock, "Augustine's Interpretation of Romans (AD 394–396)," *Augustinian Studies* 10 (1979): 55–74; J. Patout Burns, *The Development of Augustine's Theory of Operative Grace* (Paris: Études augustiniennes, 1980); and Paula Fredriksen, "Paul and Augustine: Conversion Narratives, Orthodox Traditions, and the Retrospective Self," *Journal of Theological Studies,* n.s., 37 (1986): 3–34.

2. *Contra duas epistulas Pelagianorum* (A Refutation of Two Pelagian Letters) 1.10.22, ed. Carol Urba and Joseph Zycha, CSEL 60 (Vienna: F. Tempsky/Leipzig: G. Freytag, 1913); cf. Augustine's *Retractationes* (Reconsiderations) 1.22.1 and 2.1.1., ed. Almut Mutzenbecher, CCSL 57 (Turnholt: Brepols, 1984).

Paul tells us about Augustine's take on what the Greeks called *akrasia,* the Romans *impotentia,* and the rest of us now call "weakness of will." If I were to claim, like Augustine's Paul, to be doing what I hate to do, I would not necessarily be suffering from weakness of will. I may just be opting for the lesser of two evils. I may, for instance, hate to yell at my toddler, but if I find her about to run into the street, I will end up doing what I hate to do. Presumably I would understand my own motives for taking such an undesired course of action. Paul, on the other hand, speaks of *not* understanding why he does what he hates to do. Whether he is affecting this lack of understanding or, as Augustine has come to think, he is confessing to it, his admission makes it likely he is speaking about weakness of will.[3]

I intend to argue nevertheless that the Paul who enters into Augustine's confessional voice and becomes his chief ally against Pelagian ethics is not suffering from weakness of will, as it has been classically conceived, but from a form of self-deception. Again this is an argument about Augustine's appropriation of Paul and therefore an argument about Augustine, not about Paul. The argument comes in three stages. I begin by looking at Augustine's departure from a classically conceived conception of virtue—a conception that continues to inform Pelagian ethics. The terms of his departure make it unlikely that he could be attributing weakness of will to Paul, when Paul speaks of doing what he hates to do, or describing weakness of will in his own case, when he speaks of not willing his own will in Book 8 of the *Confessions.* In the next section, I look carefully at the confessional psychology that makes it seem as if Augustine were suffering from weakness of will on the eve of his conversion and begin to suggest an alternative interpretation. I finish that interpretation in my final section, where I frame Augustine's confessional psychology in terms of his myth of original sin. The self-deception that knots Augustine's will and renders him a mystery to himself is as common as it is chameleon: it is to think that one has accepted one's mortality when one has not. Often this kind of self-deception distorts a person's will to live. It distorted Augustine's will, and he called the result of that distortion his sexual habit. I will be especially concerned in this paper to understand what manner of habit that could be.

3. Stanley Stowers, who is much concerned to liberate Paul's letter from Augustinian misrepresentations, does believe that Paul is speaking about akrasia, though not in his own person: "Romans 7 stands forth as a Jewish Christian adaptation of Greco-Roman discourse about the problem of akrasia, in service of an argument against gentiles attempting to gain self-mastery by following the law." See Stowers, *A Rereading of Romans: Justice, Jews, and Gentiles* (New Haven: Yale University Press, 1994), 279.

1. The Eclipse of Temperance

In the classical analysis of weakness of will—and Aristotle is the touchstone here—the akratic, or weak-willed, person judges rightly but acts badly and so acts without sufficient reason. *Akrasia* is not quite a vice, says Aristotle, in that the akratic person has virtuous principles, but nor is *akrasia* a virtue. Knowledge of the good, placed in a person of weak character, is no virtue.[4] If Augustine is prepared to claim that as great a saint as Paul is weak-willed, the grace of God not availing, then it is a short step for him to claim that weak character is the general human condition and that the life of virtue, at least as it was classically understood, is unattainable.

The classically conceived life of virtue has to be able to sustain two distinctions. The first defines the difference between being able to resist temptation and being beyond the need to resist it. For Aristotle this is roughly the distinction between a self-restrained person, who resists an immediate pleasure to pursue a principled course of action, and a temperate person, who desires rightly and does so without ambivalence. I say "roughly" because the second distinction that is germane to a classically conceived life of virtue bears on the meaning of the first. A person of vicious or perverse disposition, who thinks of vice as a personal virtue, is not tempted to act other than basely. Vice, like virtue, is an unconflicted disposition to act in character, but virtue and vice are as different as day and night. The distinction between vice and virtue frames the struggle of the akratic person to cultivate self-restraint and ultimately a well-tempered disposition. As the poles of character development, pure virtue and pure vice are experienced without internal conflict. It is only the person of virtue, however, who is beyond the need to face such conflict. The vicious person, to make moral progress, needs to turn the pleasures of vice into temptations to be resisted.

Augustine insists on the importance of the distinction between virtue and vice while abandoning the distinction between self-restraint and temperance. In Book 19 of *City of God,* composed around 426 (Augustine dies in 430), he speaks of virtue's "endless war" *(perpetua bella)* with temptation, and he identifies the struggle to win this war specifically with the virtue "that goes by the name of *sōphrosunē* in Greek, *temperantia* in Latin."[5] Aristotle would have been perplexed by Augustine's apparent

4. Aristotle's extended discussion of pathological conditions of character, akrasia among them, is Book 7 of *Nicomachean Ethics.* His distinction between akrasia and a vice can be found in *EN* 7.8.1150b29–51a28.

5. *De civitate Dei* (City of God) 19.4, ed. Bernard Dombart and Alphonse Kalb, CCSL 48 (Turnholt: Brepols, 1955): "quae Graece σωφροσύνη, Latine temperantia nominatur."

inability to distinguish between a labored effort at self-control and the cultivated ease of a temperate disposition. It is both possible and natural, thinks Aristotle, to take pleasure in virtue; only an unrefined personality gets unhinged by less articulate pleasures, like sex. When Augustine insists to the contrary that the spirit perpetually struggles against the flesh, even in a virtuous person, he may be taken to be ignoring or grossly misreading what the classical virtue of temperance meant to the likes of an Aristotle. I think it more likely, however, that he is revising the classical view and not simply describing it. The Greeks may have claimed that the wisely tempered person is temptation-free, but if Paul is going to be for Augustine a conflicted saint, then Augustine is certainly not going to credit a pagan sage with having had a better virtue than self-restraint.

Whatever his intent, Augustine certainly understood the difference between a conflicted and an unconflicted personality. Before he gets into the thick of his polemic against Pelagianism and its faith in virtue, he is happy to assume that Paul fully desired the life to which he was called. On his way to thinking of Paul as conflicted, Augustine leaves Aristotelian temperance for another life and begins to focus more intently on the pathologies of human desire.

The pathologies divide into three basic forms: a confusion of virtue with vice (ignorance), an ineffectual knowledge of virtue *(akrasia),* and a lingering attachment to vice (temptation). Aristotle thought of vice as worse than *akrasia,* and he treated the two conditions as distinct kinds of pathology, given that *akrasia,* but not vice, presupposed a knowledge of virtue. Augustine does not make a sharp distinction between vice and weakness of will,[6] and, as his thinking about Paul changes, he appears to

6. In his instructive study of medieval perspectives on weakness of will, Risto Saarinen suggests more radically that there is no important distinction in Augustine between vice and weakness of will: "Aristotle distinguishes between evil and akratic actions, but Augustine thinks that all blameworthy actions result from consenting to the wrong alternative"; see *Weakness of the Will in Medieval Thought* (Leiden: E. J. Brill, 1994), 37. Saarinen's view is in keeping with the conventional way of distinguishing Aristotelian and Augustinian approaches to akrasia or weakness of will (assuming that these terms refer to roughly the same phenomenon). In the conventional reading, the Aristotelian thinks of akratic action as voluntary but not chosen; the Augustinian thinks of weak-willed action as involuntary but chosen. The *locus classicus* of the Augustinian view is *De spiritu et littera* (The Spirit and the Letter) 31.53, the passage where Augustine explains that an action taken involuntarily *(invitus)* is yet done with a will *(voluntate)* and therefore expresses the agent's power of will *(potestas).* See CSEL 60.

I have a number of reasons for dissenting from the conventional reading. Since I am not convinced that Aristotle's notion of choice *(prohairesis)* is much like Augustine's notion of will *(voluntas),* it isn't clear to me that a chosen action (in Aristotle's sense) is a willed action (in Augustine's); hence I have no basis for concluding that an unchosen but voluntary action differs from an involuntarily willed action. But let's leave the comparison with Aristotle to the side and just focus on Augustine's appeal to willingness. His appeal makes

weaken the distinction between weakness of will and simple temptation. Usually weakness of will implies a loss of self-control. But the Paul who, in Augustine's revised reading, owns to doing what he hates to do is still literally doing the right thing. The hated thing is not an act of vice but the residual appeal of a rejected vice, a holdover desire. In the first book of *Marriage and Sexual Desire,* Augustine tells us that the man in Romans 7 who says, "It is not I who act, but the sin within me," speaks the truth if he only desires *(concupiscit)* to sin, but not if he consents to that desire or acts it out bodily.[7]

It makes for a very odd reading of Romans 7, almost too odd, to equate doing what one hates with merely having a hated desire. Given that Augustine thinks of the offending desire as sexual in nature, it is hard to resist the conclusion that he is distorting the Pauline text in order to authorize a sexual ethic that avoids both Manichaean hatred of the flesh and Pelagian sex education. While I do not discount the polemical motives for Augustine's double-take on Paul, I also think it important not to retreat too quickly from the oddness of the second take. It is as if Augustine were attributing to Paul the power to will his own sexual desires; having this power, Paul wills to have sexual desires that his wiser self would prefer to disown.

In philosophical genealogies, Augustine is often honored or lamented as one of the founding fathers of voluntarism.[8] A "voluntarist" is someone who thinks of will as the third force of human personality, along with reason and appetite, and as the driving force of the three. Whatever one

---

no distinction between the case where he does something undesirable in itself to avoid a greater evil (e.g., he takes foul-tasting medicine to heal a stomach ailment) and the case where he does something pleasant in itself in disregard of a greater good (e.g., he takes on another mistress rather than come to terms with his lack of fidelity to women). The second kind of case is much more likely than the first to raise a question of self-knowledge for Augustine, but that possibility is occluded by his vacuous appeal to will. The only action that is not done "with a will" is no action at all but a forced movement, like being blown off the deck of a ship by a strong wind. The distinction between vice and weak-willed action cannot then be a matter of willingness. It is instead a matter of knowledge, or more accurately, a matter of the desire for self-knowledge. A weak-willed person is likely to wonder about his or her motives; a vicious person is not. Augustine showcases the psychological turn from vice to self-questioning in his *Confessions.*

7. *De nuptiis et concupiscentia* (Marriage and Sexual Desire) 1.29.31, ed. Carol Urba and Joseph Zycha, CSEL 42 (Vienna: F. Tempsky, 1902).

8. One of the standard and most commonly referenced accounts of Augustine's voluntarism in the context of classical thought is Albrecht Dihle, *The Theory of Will in Classical Antiquity* (Berkeley and Los Angeles: University of California Press, 1982). I offer a detailed response to Dihle and to voluntarist readings of Augustine in general in "Will and Interiority in Augustine: Travels in an Unlikely Place," *Augustinian Studies* 33 (2002): 139–60. See also the fine study of T. D. J. Chappell, *Aristotle and Augustine on Freedom* (New York: St. Martin's Press, 1995), who argues that the usual contrast between Aristotle and Augustine is overblown and that Augustine is more rationalist than voluntarist.

thinks of voluntarism, it is hard not to notice, upon a close reading of his texts, that Augustine is not a very consistent voluntarist. It is mainly when he is offering a psychological analysis of original sin, and in particular of Adam's motive for preferring his partner to God's command, that Augustine sounds the most voluntarist. He insists that Adam's resolve to stay bound to his partner was insufficiently motivated by either his reason (his sense of the good) or his sexual desire (his craving for pleasure). Adam's will determines his choice with God-defying autonomy. When Augustine turns his attention to human psychology outside the garden, in the thickets of mortal history, he no longer sounds voluntarist. His analysis defies easy categorization. Take the case of Paul. Does he willfully desire to do what he hates? Augustine suggests that the answer to this is both yes and no—yes inasmuch as the original Adam is in Paul, no inasmuch as Christ, the second Adam, has taken Adam's place. As a conflicted saint, Augustine's Paul is neither Adam nor Christ but a man whose will is neither original nor ultimate. In that regard, Paul's condition, his sainthood aside, is utterly common.

To a classical and especially Aristotelian way of thinking, Augustine can seem to have a bad conscience about human finitude. He seems to think of the punctuation of life by birth and death as a constraint on life, one that ideally should be removed. No wonder, if this is really his view, that he never feels at home in his world. He cannot afford to feel at home; the lack of conflict would leave him unresolved between Adam and Christ and destined to be defeated by death. In his masterly study of Augustine's relationship to classical thought, John Rist throws out the provocative suggestion that while Aristotle thinks of *akrasia* as an occasional problem for most people and only a chronic condition for a few, Augustine universalizes the phenomenon and writes as if everyone were akratic all of the time.[9] Rist does not mean to attribute to Augustine the wildly implausible view that no one ever acts according to his or her best judgment. The view is more that the habitual convergence of will and good judgment in a person is never sufficient to fix character. No matter how virtuous a person may seem, no one is ever completely free from temptation; vice is always lurking outside the tent of virtue. In keeping with this view, it makes a certain amount of sense that Augustine's Paul would bemoan temptation as if temptation were itself the equivalent of vice.

While I grant the force of Rist's analogy between *akrasia* and temptation, the analogy should not be overplayed. Augustine is not just a pes-

9. John M. Rist, *Augustine: Ancient Thought Baptized* (Cambridge: Cambridge University Press, 1994), 184–85, cf. 135–40 ("Difficultas and Concupiscentia").

simistic version of a classical virtue theorist, or someone who believes in virtue but not in human abilities. He is transforming as well as rejecting some of the basic features of the classically conceived life of virtue. As I have been discussing, he redefines the virtue of temperance to mean self-restraint and then blurs the distinction between self-restraint and weakness of will—moves that are likely to make him seem morbidly preoccupied with involuntary desires, especially of the sexual sort.[10] It is too dismissive, however, simply to note Augustine's darkening views of sexual desire and then assume that he is getting old and cranky and giving in to misanthropy. At the heart of his evolving view of the life of virtue and its limits is his complex notion of *consuetudo carnalis,* a notion I will translate—with some hesitation—as "sexual habit."[11]

Augustine's better commentators will caution us not to overly sexualize his idea of carnal desire; it is rarely just about sex.[12] This is true, but it is not *just* about sex because Augustine has such a complicated view of sex and not because the desire is about something else. The translation of '*consuetudo*' as 'habit' is also tricky. Habits are usually the things that shape character and stabilize personality, and they can be virtuous, vicious, or merely innocuous. When Augustine speaks about sexual habit, he is referring to a habit of desire that an enlightened soul would never want to have. It is the negative connotation of sexual habit that suggests the analogy to *akrasia,* but, unlike *akrasia,* sexual habit is *always* about sexual desire, and the problem of sexual habit, if Augustine is to be be-

10. Richard Sorabji concludes his Gifford Lectures with a critique of what he takes to be Augustine's contempt for human sexuality: "To many, myself included, the Pelagian view that lust is a good thing, which may be put to a bad use, is far more attractive than Augustine's view that lust is a bad thing which may, in marriage, be put to a good use." See his *Emotion and Peace of Mind: From Stoic Agitation to Christian Temptation* (Oxford: Oxford University Press, 2000), 417. Sorabji reads Augustine to be locating the badness of sexual desire in its involuntary nature, and, not surprisingly, he is surprised that Augustine does not see that this same kind of badness could be attributed (absurdly) to desires like hunger and thirst. But Augustine does not contend that hunger and thirst were *originally* subject to rational control; he does claim this about sexual desire. See, for instance, *De civitate Dei* (City of God) 14.23–24. Admittedly it is hard to know what to make of Augustine's claim about original sexuality, but unless one tries to make something of it, his claim that sexual desire has become involuntary won't have any ethical content—as Sorabji has discovered. For a brilliant attempt to give Augustine's notion of an original sexuality a sympathetic reading, see John C. Cavadini, "Feeling Right: Augustine on the Passions and Sexual Desire," *Augustinian Studies* 36 (2005): 195–217.

11. There is precedent for my choice. Henry Chadwick renders *consuetudo carnalis* as 'sexual habit' in his widely used translation of the *Confessions* (New York: Oxford University Press, 1991).

12. As Mathijs Lamberigts points out, "A Critical Evaluation of Critiques of Augustine's View of Sexuality," in *Augustine and His Critics,* ed. Robert Dodaro and George Lawless (London: Routledge, 2000), 179–81.

lieved, is everyone's problem all of the time; even Saint Paul struggled with it. If *akrasia* were a similarly pervasive kind of problem, the classical view of virtue would be unsustainable. It makes no sense to claim that virtue is natural and then observe that no one naturally desires to be virtuous.

Augustine's critics and many of his defenders have been quick to point out that he rejects classical virtue outright—in favor of something unnatural, say his critics; in favor of something better than natural, say his defenders. Personally I find Augustine's attitude toward classical virtue more ambivalent than dismissive. I would consider his attitude dismissive if he were truly thinking of sexual habit as an endemic form of akrasia. I don't think that he is, even conceding that there is a resemblance between akratic dysfunction and what Augustine describes as the disruptive power of sexual habit.

Obviously the time has come to look more closely at sexual habit. Augustine develops the notion with great richness, though not with great consistency, in the *Confessions,* espccially Books 7–8, where he describes the strangely obstructive power that a discredited habit can have. I will concentrate most of my attention there, but afterwards I will need to devote some time to his sense of the bigger story. When Augustine tries, in his fateful way, to turn Genesis into a book about the origin of evil, he roots sexual habit in an original act of will—Adam's opting for knowledge of the flesh. The most striking feature of this rooting is that Adam's choice becomes everyone else's habit, excepting Christ, that other Adam. As I put together Augustine's confessional psychology with his mythic sense of sin, I will be heading to the conclusion that sexual habit is best read not as the baleful product of a sexualized will but as the sign of a difficult and imperfect self-knowledge. It will prove hard to decide with any definitiveness what is natural about this burden of self-knowledge and what is not.

2. A Mysterious Inability

Books 7–8 of the *Confessions* are the most important books for understanding Augustine's conversion. He opens Book 7 by announcing the death of his adolescence—a good riddance, he thinks, but then he quickly adds that his new frame of mind was painfully limited. He could think of spirit only in terms of matter, and so his God, though not much like a human being in appearance, still occupied space and interacted with other material beings, albeit in a very refined way. Augustine offers the image of sunlight in airy places. Later in that book, we get his very famous and much debated description of an interior apocalypse.[13] Augustine describes being led by God into the mystery of immaterial spirit. He gets his best sense of that mystery while he is most within himself, in an interior depth known perhaps only to a couple of Platonists, whose books Augustine was reading at the time.[14] His revelation ends when his sexual habit disrupts his enjoyment of spiritual beauty, and he is returned to his senses and to a familiar, if now somewhat hollow, world of material beauties.

In Book 8, Augustine starts off by suggesting that he was done with having to conceive of God. His prior revelation had given him his conception of living spirit, the incorruptible source of his own soul, and now he desired only to be more stable in that source. Most of the rest of Book 8 is his description of his own strange resistance to that very stability. The resistance is strange because it derives its motive power from a discredited good. Augustine no longer believes that sexual pleasure is preferable to a life of chastity, but he cannot bring himself to will his preference: "[B]y now," he confesses to God, "I was no longer savoring secular delights more than your sweetness and the beauty of that house of yours that I loved, but still I found myself inextricably tied to women."[15] Augustine describes his sexual habit as will-like; it is as if

13. The key stretch of text extends from *Conf.* 7.10.16 through *Conf.* 7.17.23, though someone like Pierre Courcelle, who counts three distinct descriptions in Book 7 of an ultimately "vain attempt at Plotinian ecstasy," would extend the stretch through *Conf.* 7.20.26. The debate surrounding this somewhat variable stretch of text concerns Augustine's debt to Platonism. Is the sense of spirit that comes out of the *Confessions* fundamentally Platonist in inspiration, or does Augustine's conversion to Christ profoundly alter or even end his Platonism? Pierre Courcelle has more or less convinced everyone not to think of Christianity and Platonism as exclusive alternatives for Augustine (they weren't for the Milanese Christians who were listening, like Augustine, to Ambrose). See Courcelle, *Recherches sur les Confessions de Saint-Augustin* (Paris: E. de Boccard, 1950), esp. 157–67.

Despite Courcelle's "Copernican Revolution" (O'Donnell's term), many scholars of Augustine continue to find Augustine more Platonist (though perhaps not more Platonist than Christian) in his earlier writings, the ones that predate the *Confessions.* On this way of construing Augustine, his critique of Platonism in Book 7 of the *Confessions*—right God, wrong path—would have to be considered a retrospective judgment. He doesn't become disillusioned with Platonism until close to the *writing* of the Confessions; his conversion to Catholic Christianity takes place ten years or so prior to that. My own view is that his experiential description of spirit in Book 7 is best read as an answer to his question about evil's origin and not as a good or bad example of a Platonically inspired mystical experience. I develop my alternative reading of that book in what follows.

14. The authors of the *platonicorum libri,* the books first mentioned in *Conf.* 7.9.13, are undoubtedly Plotinus and probably Porphyry, but no one knows the precise extent of Augustine's reading in these authors. For a succinct and insightful discussion of the question of the *platonicorum libri* in Augustine scholarship, see James J. O'Donnell's comments on 7.9.13 in the second of his three-volume edition (text and commentary) of the *Confessions* (Oxford: Clarendon Press, 1992), 413–26.

15. *Conf.* 8.1.2: "iam enim me illa non delectabant prae dulcedine tua et decore domus tuae, quam dilexi, sed adhuc tenaciter conligabar ex femina." The "illa" refers to secular

there were two imperfect wills within him, each struggling against the other for ascendancy. Imperfectly he wills to be tied to a woman, and imperfectly he wills to be God's man. As an adolescent he used to make this his prayer to God, "Give me chastity and self-restraint, but not yet."[16] With his adolescence supposedly dead and buried, he is now more puzzled than ever by his lack of self-restraint.

But what he means by "self-restraint" *(continentia)* is not so clear. He does not seem to be lamenting some akratic episode of having given in to sexual desire despite a chaste resolve; he seems more to be lamenting his lack of resolve in the face of dogged sexual temptation, a bad habit of desire. He will deliberately obscure the difference between *akrasia* and temptation in his future readings of Romans 7. In Book 8 of *Confessions,* he confesses to a deliverance of unintended ambiguity. While anguishing in a garden, he overhears a child's voice chanting, "pick up and read" *(tolle, lege),* and he hears in these words a personal directive. He opens up a nearby book of Paul's letters, and his eyes fix upon a verse from Romans 13: "No more wild parties and drunken fits, bedroom antics and indecencies, rivalries and wrangling; just clothe yourself in Jesus Christ, your master, and don't look to care for your flesh with lusts."[17] Augustine is transformed by what he reads. "Right after the end of the sentence," he writes, "it was as if a light of security radiated into my heart and dispelled all the shadows of my doubt."[18]

The ambiguity of Augustine's deliverance stems from the obscurity of his doubt. What was he doubting? Not the existence of God, not the wisdom of Christ and his church, not the urgency of those truths to his own life. If Augustine can be said to have converted to Christianity in a garden in Milan in the summer of 386, it was not to the idea of Christianity that he was converted. He came to the scene having already embraced that idea. Readers of Augustine who see the religious experiences of Books 7–8 of the *Confessions* as a two-step movement tend to read his discovery of God's spirit as the conversion of his intellect and his discovery of God's flesh as the conversion of his will. At a surface level, this kind of reading works. There is an obvious struggle of will going on in Book 8. Augustine

---

goods and more particularly to the secular goods of fame and money. Augustine is declaring that he takes no further delight from being a professor of rhetoric. My source for the Latin of the *Confessions,* here and elsewhere, is James J. O'Donnell, *Augustine: Confessions,* Text and Commentary, 3 vols. (Oxford: Clarendon Press, 1992).

16. *Conf.* 8.7.17: "da mihi castitatem et continentiam, sed noli modo."

17. I am translating Paul (Romans 13: 13–14) as he appears in Augustine's text (*Conf.* 8.12.29): "non in comessationibus et ebrietatibus, non in cubilibus et impudicitiis, non in contentione et aemulatione, sed induite dominum Iesum Christum et carnis providentiam ne feceritis in concupiscentiis."

18. *Conf.* 8.12.29: "statim quippe cum fine huiusce sententiae quasi luce securitatis infusa cordi meo omnes dubitationis tenebrae diffugerunt."

is struggling to give up his sex life. Sympathetic readers of Augustine may be reluctant to put the matter so baldly, but, as James J. O'Donnell is happy to remind us in his recent biography of Augustine, when it comes to Book 8, "the issue is sex."[19]

What this reminder does not tell us, of course, is why the issue *should* be sex. If flesh is not anathema to God—who, as Jesus of Nazareth, gestated in Mary—why should Augustine try so hard not to be tied to a woman? Assuming that he has had his doubts about his own willingness to disown this tie, it is unclear whether he is hoping in Book 8 for a wholly new disposition or more modestly for a will to resist temptation.

The ambiguity is important. Ignore it, and Book 8 is about weakness of will. Augustine knows that he lacks the will to resist carnal knowledge, and so he must get from God an extra dose of willpower. This sort of reading makes him out to be an akratic personality, with a weakness for sexual pleasure, and it rests upon the supposition that he has nothing further to know about God once he has Platonized God's spirit. The Aristotelian notion of akrasia strikes a compromise between the Socratic thesis that virtue is wholly a matter of having the right knowledge and the worry, later dubbed voluntarist, that the motivating power of knowledge is never sufficient. Applied to Augustine's angst in Book 8, the Aristotelian reading would go something like this: the lure of sexual pleasure continues to distract Augustine from his knowledge of God, and in this state of suspended knowledge, he is liable to act against his better judgment. Admittedly Aristotle would have found in Augustine an odd case of akrasia; to Aristotle's way of thinking, it is not sexual desire that is distracting, but its distorted forms, as in a desire for too much sex or too little.

If we nevertheless stick with the quasi-Aristotelian reading of Book 8, where Augustine hopes to stabilize his knowledge of God by resisting sex, we get an uncomfortably clear idea of why sex is a problem for him. It is a problem for him because desire for God is being made out to be the opposite of sex. On the supposition that the soul is the life of the body, and God, an immaterial spirit, is the life of the soul, the soul looks in the wrong direction when it looks to be tied to a woman: that turn invites a confusion of spirit with flesh. Seeking sex for the oblivion of pleasure, with no hope of discovering a greater, less death-hounded kind of life, is still the same kind of confusion, expressed more myopically: it is to confuse spirit with one's own flesh. In neither case would there be knowledge in carnal knowledge.

19. *Augustine: A New Biography* (New York: HarperCollins, 2005), 74. O'Donnell's sympathies with Augustine are, to say the least, veiled and complex. See my review of his biography in *Journal of Early Christian Studies* 13 (2005): 528–30.

But this reading of Augustine is only as good as the idea that his God is pure spirit, no body. I do not find him defending this idea in Book 7 of the *Confessions;* I find him looking for an absolute difference between spirit and flesh and struggling with the idea that the Word was made flesh. It is in the context of that struggle that he will begin to efface the distinction between akrasia and temptation and treat temptation as if it were already a failure of will. For those apt to find in Augustine a cranky old ascetic, his moralization of involuntary sexual desire is going to seem like a demonization of sex. I understand this reaction and sympathize with it to an extent (the old man was certainly cranky in his responses to Julian), but I cannot rest with it. To think that sexual desire is sinful is to hope for either the end of the desire or its redemption. Augustine looks for the redemption of sex, and this commits him to the idea that sexual desire is originally good. To get at the nature of this goodness, particularly as it informs Augustine's own conversion, we have to stop reading Book 8 as a book about weakness of will and start entertaining a more radical possibility: that Augustine is getting a new conception of God there, at a time when he least feels the need for one.

I am suggesting, then, that Augustine's conception of spirit is more impoverished in Book 7 than he was willing to concede. He does not get to the meaning of spirit, only to fail to take that meaning to heart. He misses the meaning. I say this, not by way of an external critique (I do not myself profess to know what spirit *really* means), but by way of an immanent one. The fault lines show up in Augustine's own description of his spiritual awakening. He says that he needed to be awakened on account of his dullard imagination for God—as big stuff. Being stuck with a material God is not Augustine's root problem, however; it is an exacerbation. His root problem is the problem of the origin of evil, the conundrum that has tied him into knots for most of his adult life. The evil of most concern to him in his *Confessions* is his sin, his disposition to waste his spirit on petty self-indulgence, vainglory, and resentment. He is not so interested in explaining why he has such a disposition—he thinks in fact that such a disposition *cannot* be explained[20]—but he is keenly hopeful that the disposition is a perversion of his spirit and not its native expression. He needs, in order to sustain this hope, some reason to believe that he remains connected to an incorruptible source of goodness, a source that has made him essentially what he is. And here is where his material God has been less than helpful to him. If God is

20. The cause of an evil will, says Augustine, is always deficient *(deficiens)*. By "cause" *(causa)* he means motive; his claim is that an evil will is always deficiently motivated—there is never a good enough reason to express an evil will. For his most extensive discussion of the logic of deficient causality, see *De civitate Dei* 12.6–8.

material and Augustine is of God's same material, then Augustine's assumption is that God too would have to be corruptible. Matter, it would seem, always begets more of the same.

But why should spirit be any different? Augustine takes it as axiomatic that incorruptible being is superior to corruptible things. If matter spells corruption, then God, as the superior being, must be immaterial. Augustine is convinced of that conclusion at the beginning of Book 7; he just has no *conception* of what incorruptible being is. He has been hearing from Ambrose and some of the other Christian Platonists in Milan that he ought to be thinking of the will and its capacity for free choice *(liberum arbitrium)* as the source of sin in human life. He tries to think about sin this way, but the idea of free choice does nothing to help him resolve his interior confusion. He may well be freely choosing to waste his gifts, like the prodigal son in Luke's parable, but if God is the origin of his will, why is not God also, Augustine wonders, the author of his freedom? "These suffocating thoughts were bringing me down again," he writes, "but not all the way down to that hell of error where no one confesses to you, God, because everyone supposes that bad things are what you suffer and not what a human being does."[21]

In attempting to assess what Augustine is able to take from his new, divinely inseminated, conception of immaterial spirit—the one most scholars think of as fathered by Plotinus—it is crucially important to remember two things. One is that Augustine's conception of spirit is intimately connected in his mind with the problem of sin's origin. The other is that the problem of sin's origin is not fundamentally for Augustine a problem of theodicy; it is more deeply the challenge of having God for a father. A mortal son who loves his mortal father is often glad to be like his father. He does not desire, unless his love is pathological, to be his father. Likeness is a remarkable, if not paradoxical, combination of sameness and difference that in most ordinary contexts we simply take for granted. In an originary context, where creation has no precedent, likeness seems virtually impossible. Begin with God the father, who is without another, add nothing, and then try to imagine that the conjunction of being and nonbeing is a perfect something, having an existence of its own, and something like God. The problem of sin's origin, as Augustine struggles with it, is intimately related to this conceptual conundrum.

The conundrum does not go away if Augustine begins to think of God as willpower ad infinitum; it just gets worse. Imagine that matter is not

21. *Conf.* 7.3.5: "his cogitationibus deprimebar iterum et suffocabar, sed non usque ad illum infernum subducebar erroris ubi nemo tibi confitetur, dum tu potius mala pati quam homo facere putatur."

what God is but that matter's substance, its very materiality, is divinely willed into being. Matter will have ceased to supply Augustine with a medium for likeness to God, and he will be forced to look elsewhere—in this case to his own finite power of will—to supply him with his differentiating principle. Somehow he will have to be able to will other than as God wills, but without alienating himself from God.

Augustine understood better than many of his interpreters that the will cannot do the job here—certainly not in an originary context, where there is nothing to mediate between divine will and human inception. In this kind of idealization, which has no use for time, God is eternally willing Augustine out of nothingness and supplying him his materiality. Inasmuch as it defines his difference from God, materiality is doing so in an alienating way. Matter differs from God in its absoluteness, and we have been postulating that, absolutely considered, matter is nonbeing, or what God is not. If Augustine is to be what God is not, and yet still be something, he will have to crave a materiality that is not God's to will. That is, in effect, to crave a world where God is absent. In the first book of the *Confessions,* he ends his reflections on his earliest transgressions—those of infancy and early childhood—with these words: "My sin was this, that I was seeking pleasures, sublimities, truths not in God but in his creatures—me and the rest—and in this way I was dashing into miseries, confusions, errors."[22] Given the notions of matter and will developed thus far, his characterization of sin comes perilously close to a formula for individuation. Augustine seems most himself while sinning, for that is the use of will most likely to be his own.[23]

He is confused even about that, however, in Book 7. Faced with the thought of God's omnipotence, he has trouble imagining in himself an independent will to sin. It is only his repulsion at the idea of God's injustice that leads him to embrace his human initiative in sin. Still his

22. *Conf.* 1.20.31: "hoc enim peccabam, quod non in ipso sed in creaturis eius me atque ceteris voluptates, sublimitates, veritates quaerebam, atque ita inruebam in dolores, confusiones, errores."

23. In an essay that deserves a wide reading among students of Augustine, John Freccero argues that the literary genre of the conversion narrative, making as it does a distinction between a self who narrates change and a self who endures it, has to assign individuality to the changing sinful self: "All that happens in a confession has happened to the sinner; as every reader of Dante knows, the truly interesting people are in hell." Augustine would have hated that kind of irony; the question is, could he have avoided it? I will be arguing that he does avoid it. *Sin* is not what individuates Augustine in the *Confessions;* it is his *confession* of sin that does that work. Freccero's provocative reading of confessional writing calls for greater attention to that distinction. See his "Autobiography and Narrative," in *Reconstructing Individualism: Autonomy, Individuality, and the Self in Western Thought,* ed. Thomas Heller, Morton Sosna, and David E. Wellbery (Stanford: Stanford University Press, 1986), 16–29. The quote is taken from p. 21.

concern with theodicy is secondary to his interests in original sin. That claim may seem hard to sustain, given that his most extensive discussion of sin and freedom, the treatise *On Free Choice (De libero arbitrio),* is also his most developed theodicy. He opens that work on the question of God's responsibility for sin, and he goes on to argue that human beings invent sin all on their own. I am not suggesting that there is a better way to read *On Free Choice,* a work that Augustine started years before the *Confessions,* but not long after his baptism and the unexpected death of his mother. I am suggesting that Book 7 of *Confessions* is a much better study of the question of sin's origin and that its focus is not on theodicy. When Augustine is taken up into the mystery of spirit, his will is in abeyance and the only beauty that is ever directly visible to him is material.

Consider the details of his description. From the books of certain undisclosed Platonists, Augustine takes a directive to enter the inmost precincts of himself and look around with his soul's eye. He claims to have been able to do this with divine guidance *(duce te),* but he quickly dispels the notion that he was being given a guided tour of immaterialities by a gentle spirit. "When I first became aware of you," he says to God, "you gathered me up so that I might see that what I was seeing existed, and that I who was seeing it did not exist yet."[24] Did Augustine take himself to be seeing God, whose immaterial brilliance shocked his system and caused him to shake "with love and terror" *(amore et horrore)*? That is a good question. An even better one is how someone who does not exist yet can see anything.

Augustine says that he found himself far from God, in "a place of unlikeness" *(regio dissimilitudinis).* Not existing is certainly a way of being unlike God, who exists absolutely, but not existing is also a way of being unlike anything. I note that Augustine is associating his point of view and not himself with absolute unlikeness. A point of view that puts a viewer in the position of being unlike anything else, God included, is not a sustainable or even possible point of view. I believe that it is just this revelation about point of view that Augustine describes being offered in Book 7 and not some quasi-Platonic taste of immaterial spirit. He does not describe getting the point of that offering until Book 8, when his problem with sexual habit gets clarified in a spirited vision of the flesh.

The reading of Book 7 that has Augustine traveling in metaphysical space, moving from flesh to the fleshless spirit within, is admittedly inviting. For he does seem to gain from his travels a new conception of existence, one of nonextended substance. "It cannot be, can it," he asks,

24. *Conf.* 7.10.16: "et cum te primum cognovi, tu assumpsisti me ut viderem esse quod viderem, et nondum me esse qui viderem."

"that the truth that is not spread out over limited or unlimited space is nothing?"[25] The question has become merely rhetorical for him. Of course this truth cannot be nothing. In fact it must be the God who calls his people home from exile, the one who gives as his name "I am."

Augustine's place of exile is his place of unlikeness, the place far in affection, but not in distance, from his original source. It is the confessional context of his self-description that generates the meaning of his peculiar exile. Augustine has in his ordinary life, the one he imagines to be body fixated, been denying himself a viable conception of his own uniqueness, of his difference from his source. By refusing to think of matter as a differentiating principle, he leaves his self-definition to the devices of will. Fancying himself the inventor of his own sin, he assumes responsibility for the only form of will that has a chance of being originally his own, even given the complication, which I will discuss shortly, of being upstaged by an original Adam and his sin. The ironic result of all this, as I have already suggested, is that Augustine ends up tying his individuation to his capacity to reject God. In the experience he describes in Book 7, he is able to *see* the result of what he has been doing. It looks like unlikeness; Augustine has been living a life that is nowhere, or, more promisingly, a life that is not yet.

The principal failing of the generically Platonic reading of Augustine's new insight—the one that makes such a big deal out of his discovery of immaterial spirit—is that it encourages us to think of unlikeness as immateriality. The unlikeness that has interposed itself between Augustine and his self-perception, leaving him with an unmade life, is more radical than that. Once assumed into his unlikely place, he is unlike God, who is presumptively spirit, and unlike the created order, which is presumptively material. If spirit is no more in conception than the negation of matter, or material substance minus the extension in space and the placement in time, then Augustine, being unlike either, is not left with much to be. If he identifies himself with matter, he identifies with what is not God, and that is a trip to nowhere. If he identifies with immaterial spirit, he commits himself to a body-fleeing anorexia whose logical end is death. The God Augustine hears, but does not see, from his place of unlikeness seems to confirm for him the dilemma I have just described. He reports hearing these words from on high: "I am the food of grown-ups: grow and you will be feeding on me. But you will not change me into you, like the food your flesh eats; you will be changed into me."[26]

25. *Conf.* 7.10.16: "numquid nihil est veritas, quoniam neque per finita neque per infinita locorum spatia diffusa est?"

26. *Conf.* 7.10.16: "'cibus sum grandium: cresce et manducabis me. nec tu me in te mutabis sicut cibum carnis tuae, sed tu mutaberis in me.'"

Augustine is remarkably silent about the awful implication of these words, that communion with God is a withering away of human flesh. Perhaps he had an inkling of another implication, one more about living than dying. The kind of feeding that changes the feeder into the source of food is either a form of starvation, where the body is forced to feed upon itself, or it is a gestation, a feeding from within the womb. The son is of his mother, flesh of her flesh, bone of her bone, until the moment of birth, when material separation makes two out of one, but without effacing all the signs of an original unity. When Augustine is most concerned to define the nature of his difference from his father in heaven and take the responsibility for that difference upon himself, he is given a vision of himself as not yet, a soul still in gestation, awaiting a life-defining deliverance from its source. It is a vision of being forgiven, of being released from an impossible burden of responsibility, but it is also a vision that requires the acceptance of death—both the death that is conjoined to birth and separable from it only by an indeterminate "not yet," and the death that is the loss of a fundamental illusion of life. In Augustine's case, the loss of the illusion is a matter of coming to accept death, not as a punishment for being a son of Adam, but as a natural consequence of it.[27] It is usually the illusion of a grown-up to confuse the life of the body with an image of changeless perfection, a body double that never dies; children, by and large, wish to grow up and experience change. Augustine is being given a reminder from on high of what a grown-up can learn from a child.

He obviously has trouble taking in the reminder. In the other revelatory moment of his experience of unlikeness, he discovers to his great astonishment that he really loves God, not the God of his imagination, but the real one. I am inclined to think here of a son who discovers that he loves his mother, not as he thinks she ought to be, but as she is. It is the kind of discovery that can, if only for a moment, reveal perfection in imperfection. Augustine never claims to be able to see divine perfection other than in the visible things of creation, whose corruptibility is his

27. In Book 3 of *On Free Choice,* written early in his priesthood, Augustine does not associate inherited human incapacities of will and intellect with a culpable birth. "A natural inheritance of ignorance and inability," he writes, "does not make a soul guilty, but not seeking knowledge studiously and not bothering to acquire facility in acting rightly does." Translated from *De libero arbitrio* 3.22.64, ed. W. M. Green, CCSL 29 (Turnholt: Brepols, 1970): "Non enim quod naturaliter nescit et naturaliter non potest, hoc animae deputatur in reatum, sed quod scire non studuit et quod dignam facilitati conparandae ad recte faciendum operam non dedit." Augustine begins to speak of a "guilty birth" (*reatus originalis,* literally an "original guilt") in *Ad Simplicianum* (To Simplician), the first work of his episcopate. From then on he sticks to his difficult conviction that unbaptized infants are damned, albeit to the mildest part of hell. See *De diversis quaestionibus ad Simplicianum* 1.2.20, ed. Almut Mutzenbecher, CCSL 44 (Turnholt: Brepols, 1970).

usual notice. When he loves God in these things, he sees something immortally beautiful in a mortal offering. But he does not stay long in that perception. He speaks of being quickly pulled away by the force of his own weight. "This weight," he explains, "was sexual habit."[28]

In his comprehensive history of the early Christian practice of permanent sexual renunciation, or the once-and-for-all giving up of sex, Peter Brown says of Augustine—who plays a starring role in the narrative—that he always considered death and not the fugitive quality of bodily pleasure to be "the most bitter sign of human frailty." "For death," says Brown, "frustrated the soul's deepest wish, which was to live at peace with its beloved, the body."[29] I think that Brown is right; Augustine hated death mainly for its frustration of erotic longing. And apart from some such recognition about him, it is easy to misconstrue his sense of the weightiness of sexual habit. Unlike a classically minded philosopher, Augustine is not especially concerned about habit-forming bodily pleasures and the liability of carnal habits to divert a person from a serious-minded pursuit of truth. He is not unconcerned with this problem—which is why Augustine can sometimes sound in confession like an akratic sex-addict—but his deeper worry lies elsewhere. The weight that pulls him away from immortality is, in his mind, his own perverse and inexplicable love of the corruption of things, as if he were harboring a death wish for what he loves.

In Book 8 of the *Confessions,* Augustine agonizes over his inability to will abstinence. I have been urging a reading of this inability that does not take him to be describing weakness of will. The case against the akratic reading rests principally on two observations. One is that Augustine never claims that sexual habit was impairing his knowledge of God. He speaks of having turned his back on his old trifling loves, and for all the violent desperation of his dying persona, he says that sexual habit spoke to him with less than half his heart *(tepidissime)* when it hit him with this refrain, "Do you think you will be able to live without these loves?"[30] The point to underscore here is that Augustine was sober-minded enough to conclude, before his conversion, that sexual pleasures were doing him no good. And this leaves one further thing to observe. Since Augustine's struggle of will seems not to have been resolved by his resolve of abstinence, his climatic conversion is no deus ex machina of resolve. It is not more willpower that Augustine gets from God, mediated (rather redundantly) by the Pauline injunction to "just

28. *Conf.* 7.17.23: "et pondus hoc consuetudo carnalis."

29. *The Body and Society: Men, Women, and Sexual Renunciation in Early Christianity* (New York: Columbia University Press, 1988), 405.

30. *Conf.* 8.11.26: "'putasne sine istis poteris?'"

say no." It is illumination that is given. I concede that it is not clear from Book 8 alone that Augustine is more concerned there about the wisdom of his sexual desires than about his ability to withstand them, but when he insists, well into his episcopate, that the saint who does what he hates is still managing somehow to will what he knows is right, he invites that retrospective reading of the *Confessions*.

So what, then, is going on in Book 8, if not the strengthening of a will whose weakness is for sex? In one particularly telling part of Book 8, Augustine describes the condition of his soul after he had convinced himself that he had no further reason not to prefer a life of spirit over flesh: "Wordless trepidation remained; my soul dreaded like death being held back from the flow of habit that was sickening it to death."[31] If it is mortal knowledge that Augustine's soul is seeking to avoid, then it is not sex of the procreative sort that has been its habit. The intertwining of sex with new and renewed life is a memento mori—a reminder of the fragility, as well as the aching beauty, of human attachment. The only way to avoid the reminder is to divest sexual desire of its carnal knowledge and pursue the desire as a practice of detachment. Inasmuch as hedonism and abstinence can be, and probably were in Augustine's case, two sides of the same asceticism, his resolve of abstinence would have done nothing to dispel the illusion of his hedonism. It is only when he is enjoined to put aside his usual provisions for his flesh and live in the flesh of God—sinless and yet mortal—that he recovers, if only for a moment, an original knowledge.

3. A Myth of Original Choice

So if I am right, it is not lust but self-deception that is Augustine's impediment to conversion. The self-deception is woven into his desire for an immortal body, a double of his mortal one, but cramped into some unspecified and deathless perfection. It is not the bare desire for immortality that is troublesome here, but the way in which this desire has been clothed. It is impossible to get to spirit simply by relieving flesh of its disposition to surrender to different flesh. In a thinking animal, the surrender can be done poorly or perversely, but it cannot be willed away, even at the behest of some infinitely powerful spirit. Augustine's alternative to the immaterial God who creates and devours flesh is the mother of Jesus, who offers her flesh to her son. He in turn offers his to the humanity he loves, but absent her, he has no flesh to offer. The

31. *Conf.* 8.7.18: "remanserat muta trepidatio et quasi mortem reformidabat restringi a fluxu consuetudinis, quo tabescebat in mortem."

incarnate redeemer remains tied, in birth and in death, to a woman. Augustine, after all his travels in a place of unlikeness, remains likewise tied. Would he have the faithful believe that it is bodily resurrection that finally undoes the soul's tie to women, corrects for birth, and returns flesh to motherless spirit? My answer is a qualified no.

There is no getting around the fact that Augustine values abstinence over sex within the bounds of marriage. In this preference he approaches the classical ideal of the sage, who gives up the bother of childrearing and a sex life so as to have more time for philosophy, or to use language closer to Paul's, to have more time for things of the spirit. No doubt Augustine would have insisted on the great difference between a pagan and a Pauline option for abstinence, but I confess I have trouble seeing that difference myself. In the chapter of *Marriage and Sexual Desire* that he devotes to Paul's comparative assessment of abstinence and sexual continence, Augustine makes two basic points.[32] One is that Paul's view of the matter is time-sensitive. Paul thought that he was living in the brief span of time between the death of Jesus and the triumphal return of Christ. The need for men and women to have sex and thereby increase the body count of potential saints is not characteristic of this time. There are already bodies available in sufficient number to make up the ranks of the redeemed. Assuming, then, that the spiritual use of sex is over and done with, it follows—and this is Augustine's second point about Paul—that it would be better not to make a carnal use of sex. In a spiritually pregnant time, a carnal use of sex is sex, but at least sex of procreative intent, set within the sacramental context of marriage, recalls a spiritual act, albeit one no longer needed. Augustine concludes that Paul takes an indulgent view of sex within marriage, and Paul's view, Augustine has been telling us, is also his own.

Pagan assessments of the good of sex are not qualified by eschatology, but so what? Is it clear to anyone why one particular count of saints, say 144,000, should be spiritually more propitious, than another, say 143,000? Augustine speculates that had the first man and woman not sinned, they would have remained in Eden and engaged in spiritually appropriate sex, but only until the number of their children and their children's children matched the predestined number of the saints. With that number met and spirit and flesh ideally proportioned, God would transform all living human beings, who had to then been enjoying a probationary freedom from death, into genuine immortals. After this, there would no longer be a spiritual point or a fleshly desire for sex.

32. *De nuptiis et concupiscentia* 1.13.15. Augustine's gloss is principally on 1 Corinthians 7: 29–31.

As it turns out, the man and the woman do sin, and their act of disobedience introduces into the history of human sexuality an ineliminable dose of carnal chaos. When Augustine revises his reading of Romans 7 and seems virtually to identify sin with this chaos, he undermines the basis for his Pauline preference for abstinence over sexual fidelity. For if it is the mere unruliness of desire and not a lack of self-restraint that allows flesh to intrude upon spirit, why is abstinence a greater boon to spirit than a limited sexual partnership? The abstinent saint is as liable to experience concupiscent desire as the happily married man, arguably even more so. Augustine's departure from the classical ideal of the sage, and maybe from Paul himself, really has nothing to do with Augustine's interest in a final, predetermined tally of the saints; it has to do, once again, with his view of sexual habit.

I have already discussed sexual habit in the context of Augustine's confessional psychology. He casts this habit as the greatest obstacle to his conversion, but it is too simple a reading to suppose that he has been pitting pleasure against goodness. He does not suggest, except in a superficial and misleading way, that his desire to know the touch of flesh is opposed to his love of God; he does suggest, and this insight is revelatory for him, that he has desired to have touch without knowledge. It is this desire of his to undo knowledge that stands opposed to his love of the incarnate, and therefore mortal, God. To love a mortal being wholeheartedly is not, as Augustine once feared, to love death; it is to love a life apart from the need to possess it. Augustine's God dispossesses Augustine and consigns him to a place of unlikeness by allowing Augustine his sin; this same God turns dispossession into love by enduring birth, growing up, and suffering death. It is a single life that the human God lives and not all lives at once. The singularity of that one life is what allows Augustine his own humanity and his possibilities for love.

Think of it this way: the parent can love only the child that is different. The child that is the same as the parent is yet to be born, not in the literal sense of having yet to exit the womb, but in the sense of having the difference of its flesh go unrecognized. If the God that Augustine is trying to love is, like any one of us, uniquely human, then Augustine can do no better in his love than to love the difference in and between one nearby human being and the next. Love of God is, in this life, always the knowledge of a different flesh. It is the sort of knowledge that enables parents to claim, with some credibility, that they love all their children the same—*and* differently.

Augustine obscures the byways of divine love whenever he leaves his students the impression that abstinent love is categorically better than procreative sex. It is not categorically better because abstinent saints, like Augustine himself, have no immunity to dispirited forms of desire; it is not categorically worse because having children is not a guaranteed immunity-booster either. The dispiriting quality of sexual habit, as Augustine has come to experience it, is indifferent to whatever policing he or anyone else may wish to exercise upon it. Restraining the habit does not make the originating desire go away. Julian of Eclanum does a lamentably good job of getting Augustine to focus ever more obsessively on the culpability of involuntary desire—as if the most important question about a life-threatening pathology were whether it could be justly punished. Julian does this by exploiting an ambiguity in Augustine's sense of an originally human choice for mortal flesh and nudging Augustine toward the Pelagian side of the ambiguity.

The Pelagian Adam is the first man in history, unique in not having a human mother or father, but still human like the rest of us. When this Adam consents to his woman's desire and tastes death and life in conjunction, he gives in to a temptation—one he could have resisted. Up to here, Augustine and the Pelagians have no disagreement. Augustine says of Adam that he was able not to sin *(posse non peccare)*. He was not being torn apart by an inner conflict between flesh and spirit, and he knew well enough that defying God was wrong.[33] His descendants, on the other hand—and now we have Augustine's great divergence from Pelagianism—are from birth locked into sin and can do nothing else; they are not able not to sin *(non posse non peccare)*. From a Pelagian point of view, there is no such thing as a congenital moral disorder. If someone cannot help but sin, then at some time in the past that person must have freely willed a sin that only later, through much repetition, became an irresistible habit. In direct answer to his Pelagian critic, who is making a sharp distinction between will and desire and insisting on a historical frame of reference, Augustine has only one response, and it is a bad one. He will have to claim that Adam's original act of sin, which meets the Pelagian standard of accountable freedom, is the act of will that results in the irresistibly bad habits of his descendants.

The problem with this response is that it ignores the inconvenient

33. More than that, Augustine's Adam lived in a material and spiritual paradise and had no previous history of deviant psychology. See *De civitate Dei* 14.10. In fact, Augustine makes Adam's situation so good that his original sin seems wholly unmotivated and therefore more a surd happening than an intentional act. For a criticism of Augustine's reading along these lines, see William Babcock, "Augustine on Sin and Moral Agency," *Journal of Religious Ethics* 16 (1988): 28–55. For a response to Babcock and a defense of Augustine, see Scott MacDonald, "Primal Sin," in *The Augustinian Tradition*, ed. Gareth B. Matthews (Berkeley and Los Angeles: University of California Press, 1999), 110–39. Since I do not think that Augustine's Adam is best read as an historical figure, I feel no need to take a side in this debate.

fact that Adam, once cast as a historical individual, is just one individual. A father who abuses his freedom may compromise the happiness of his children in all kinds of ways, but the one thing he cannot do is preempt their use of their own freedom. Augustine wants to say that Adam's heirs are free only to sin; this is as much to say that people who cannot see past their prejudices are nevertheless free to live by them. If there is a sensible notion of freedom somewhere in that sentiment, it is not the notion that is naturally of interest to Augustine, who has had his prejudices returned to him on at least one occasion as unlikeness. In his confessional psychology Augustine emphasizes the preemptory nature of grace; in his polemics against the Pelagians, he more often gives the nod to sin for originality.

I want to conclude my look at sexual habit by sketching the mythology of sin that fits best with his confessional sensibilities. Although Augustine committed himself early in his theological career to offering a literal interpretation of Genesis, he found the task arduous, and he failed at it twice before he began his magnum opus on just the first three chapters of Genesis, a work that took him about a dozen years to complete.[34] I am generally at a loss to say what he meant by 'literal' *(ad litteram),* but in the case of the character of Adam, the literalness at issue is fairly clear. Literally, Adam would be a man, the first one in history; figuratively, he would represent the humanity that all human beings, male and female, find troublesome. Augustine tries to embrace both readings, but I doubt whether the result is coherent. The Pelagians incite him to be more literal. I think he ought to have been less so. A figurative Adam would have caused him less unnecessary trouble.

In the various readings that Augustine gives of the first sin, he assigns separate roles to the man and the woman. Her sin is first in time, but his is paradigmatic of what sin is. She eats of the tree of knowledge, thinking that the serpent is telling her the truth: that divine knowledge is bound to the life in mortality. The man is somehow not fooled, but he refuses to be parted from his partner, who has already taken her irrevocable bite. In his literal commentary on Genesis, Augustine comes close to making the man sound compassionate in his motives: "He did not want her to grieve," he writes, "believing that she would waste away if deprived of his counsel and left without his care and that the separation would altogether do her in."[35] In *City of God,* Augustine corrects for

34. He began *De Genesi ad litteram* (On Genesis: A Literal Commentary) in 401. His previous two tries were *De Genesi contra Manichaeos* (On Genesis: Against the Manichees) and *De Genesi ad litteram opus imperfectum* (On Genesis: An Unfinished Literal Commentary).

35. *De Genesi ad litteram* 11.42.59, ed. Joseph Zycha, CSEL 28 (Vienna: F. Tempsky, 1894): "noluit eam contristare, quam credebat posse sine suo solacio contabescere, si ab eius alienaretur animo, et omnino illa interire discordia."

this impression and attributes to Adam the same kind of self-consuming pride that had led Lucifer to be so emptily full of himself. The prideful Adam is not invested in the life of his fallen partner; he is simply taking his opportunity to take his leave of God. In this more settled reading of Augustine's, the woman's sin is a species of absent-mindedness, a lapse of judgment, and the man's sin is his defiant choice of flesh over spirit. His sin, though subsequent in time, is in fact the basis of hers.

When we try to literalize Augustine's reading, we run immediately into the problem of motive. Adam has no motive to want to break from God, for God is the source and supplier of anything he could possibly want, the woman included. If Adam is not choosing her out of ignorance—and Augustine rules out this possibility—he is certainly not choosing her for her independent worth. She has none, just as he has none. A motiveless choice is not much of a choice, and it hardly becomes more of one for being called an act of pride *(superbia)*. But apart from having to make good on a literal reading, we are allowed to notice that a movement of spirit toward flesh is originally not a choice at all, but a birth, an incarnation. None of us chooses to be born. At most, we have some choice in the birthing of someone else. A figurative reading of Genesis would frame this question about an original birth: Why think of it as a choice?

I tempted to say, based on what I have learned from Augustine's confessional psychology, that this is what God would like to know. Why are human beings so intent on undoing an incarnation? On returning flesh to will? When Augustine claims as his own life only the life that he has willed—and then out of false piety calls this life sinful—his God turns his invention into a question. What is this life of yours like? If Augustine has a good answer to this question, it is only because he really cannot, any more than anyone else can, turn flesh into will and undo a birth. All human attempts to do so have been preempted. The only will that finally counts in the matter of sin has already chosen knowledge of the flesh. If there is some original sin still to be reckoned with, it is in the human disposition to find in this choice a cause for ingratitude.

5 Thomas Aquinas on Weakness of the Will

DENIS J. M. BRADLEY

1. The Historical Background

St. Paul, speaking in the first person, characterizes his own feelings of moral weakness with unsurpassed poignancy: "For I do this, not what I will but what I hate" (Rom 7:15).[1] Commenting on St. Paul's remark, St. Thomas Aquinas observes, speaking as usual impersonally, that it is evident that men are morally weak: "The weakness of a human being is manifest from this fact that he does what he understands ought not to be done."[2] The experience of moral weakness, though, is universal, and Aquinas knew that it was long attested before St. Paul. In the fifth century B.C., it was already a common opinion, as Socrates reports disapprovingly, that "most people are unwilling to do what is best, even though they know what it is and are able to do it" (*Protagoras* 352d).[3] The last claim, if he had read it, would have riled St. Paul. In his polemic about the salvific inefficacy and exigent Christological subsumption of the Mosaic law, St. Paul effectively repudiates any view of morality and human freedom, whether religious, philosophic, or popular, that ignores or minimizes humanity's bondage to sin, from which there is no self release.[4] "Free will," in Augustine's interpretation of Pauline theology, is the problem, not the solution: "To will the good lies at hand to

1. Translation of the Latin Vulgate, which Aquinas used in his commentary: Rom 7:15: "[quod enim operor non intellego] non enim quod volo hoc ago sed quod odi illud facio." Cf. Joseph F. Fitzmyer, *Romans: A New Translation with Introduction and Commentary,* The Anchor Bible 33 (New York: Doubleday, 1993), 474, referring to the Greek text of the same verse: "The vb. *thelein,* as in classical Greek, expresses not a deliberate decision of free will *(boulesthai),* but a velleity, an inclination of the natural affective instinct."

2. *Super Epistolam ad Romanos* 7.3 n. 563, ed. Raffaele Cai, 2 vols. (Turin: Marietti, 1953), 1: 102a.

3. *Protagoras,* trans. Stanley Lombardo and Karen Bell, in Plato, *Complete Works,* ed. John Cooper and D. S. Hutchinson (Indianapolis and Cambridge: Hackett, 1997), 782.

4. Cf. Gal 2:21: "I do not nullify the grace of God; for if justification were through the law, then Christ died to no purpose."

me, but not to carry it out" (Rom 7:18).[5] Aquinas notes that the internally divided ego can be interpreted in two ways: Paul could be speaking "in the persona of a man existing in sin" or "in his [Paul's] own person, that is, of a man constituted under grace." Augustine changed his mind in favor of the latter interpretation, which Aquinas also regards as the better one.[6] For Aquinas, on either interpretation, the ego in question is the reason or intellect of the man speaking.[7] Men do what their reason tells them they ought not to do. The Pauline description, Aquinas recognizes, certainly fits the man who sins mortally through incontinence and that man could be a sinful Christian.[8] But whether Aquinas thought that a man "under grace," say St. Paul himself, can be incontinent is a question that can be deferred to the end of this paper.

St. Paul's affirmation of the will, however paradoxical his attendant view of its strictures, assumes the ancient Hebrew conviction that human agents have the freedom to obey or not even a divinely revealed and sanctioned moral law: the Mosaic Law enjoins obedience and punishes disobedience because the Chosen People can, but do not, in fact, always obey it. The presupposition of freedom is no less requisite for Aristotle's eudaimonism whose principles are more humanistic than theological. Aristotle remarks that "the origin of action—its efficient not its final cause—is choice, and that of choice is desire and reasoning with a view to an end" (*EN* 6.2.1139a31–32).[9] Only within a morality that is at least naively libertarian may one inquire about acting without self-control or "incontinently." Aristotle's account of moral weakness *(akrasia)*, however, raises more questions than answers about "freedom in regard to choice as the source of moral actions."[10]

5. Augustine, commenting on Rom 7:18 (". . . velle enim adiacet mihi, perficere autem bonum non"), insists that *liberum arbitrium* remains in the will even though the will, according to Saint Paul, cannot do what is good: see Augustine, *De diversibus quaestionibus ad Simplicianum* 1.11, ed. Almut Mutzenbecher, CCSL 44 (Turnholt: Brepols, 1970), 15, ll. 189–90: "Hic verbis videtur non recte intellegentibus velut auferre liberum arbitrium."

6. *Super Epist. ad Rom.* 7.3 n. 558, ed. Cai, 1: 101. Cf. Augustine, *Liber de diversis quaestionibus LXXXIII* 66.5, ed. Almut Mutzenbecher, CCSL 44A (Turnholt: Brepols, 1975), 158, ll. 169–78; *Contra Iulianum* 2.3.5, PL 44: 675–76; *Retractationes* 2.1, ed. Almut Mutzenbecher, CCSL 57 (Turnholt: Brepols, 1984), 88, ll. 7–15; *Contra duas epistulas Pelagianorum* 1.13.27–1.14.28, ed. Carol Urba and Joseph Zycha, CSEL 60 (Vienna: F. Tempsky/ Leipzig: G. Freytag, 1913), 445–47.

7. See *Super Epist. ad Rom.* 7.3 n. 559, ed. Cai, 1: 101: "Quod ergo dicitur primo *ego autem* etc., sic intelligendum est, ut ly *ego* pro ratione hominis intelligatur, quae est principale in homine; unde videtur unusquisque homo esse sua ratio vel suus intellectus. . . ."

8. See *De veritate* 24.12 ad 1, ed. Leon. (*Sancti Thomae de Aquino Opera omnia iussu Leonis XIII P. M. edita,* cura et studio Fratrum Praedicatorum [Rome 1882ff.]), 22/3: 718a, ll. 440–53.

9. Aristotle, *The Complete Works of Aristotle: The Revised Oxford Translation,* ed. Jonathan Barnes (Princeton: Princeton University Press, 1984), 2: 1798.

10. Joseph Owens, "The Acratic's 'Ultimate Premise' in Aristotle," in *Aristoteles: Werk*

The conceptual presuppositions and elements of the theoretical question—How is it possible to act intentionally contrary to one's own moral principles about what one ought to do?—which has been raised continuously in Western thought for over two and a half millennia, are complex and remain inescapably controversial.[11] Underlying the many issues is, prima facie, an elementary analogy. Aquinas observes that weakness of the soul *(infirmitas animae)* is an analogue of weakness of the body *(infirmitas corporis):* as the body can fail to regulate its humors, so reason can fail to regulate passions.[12] But in what way can the reason of a moral agent be too weak to regulate his passions? And how can the weak moral agent lack self-control if he or she knows what is the right thing to do? The latter question, though commonsensical, Socrates judged to be mistaken: incontinent action, as common opinion understands it, is logically impossible. Knowledge, by definition, can never be so weak that it can be "dragged around" (*Protagoras* 352b) by some passion.[13] Vice arises from ignorance; an agent never knows the better and intentionally chooses the worse. Knowledge of—or, usually, right opinion about—what is good is stronger than any opposing passion, and thus by itself sufficient for acting virtuously.[14]

Aristotle reports the famous Socratic paradox (*EE* 1.5.1216b2–25; *EN* 7.2.1145b25–27) and, apparently, rejects it (1145b27–28), by appealing to both "experience" (τὰ φαινόμενα) and "prevalent opinions" (τὰ ἔνδοξα).[15] So too Aquinas: every day we experience someone sinning knowingly from weakness.[16] Still, in explaining how it is possible that men lack mastery over their passions—that is, how *akrasia* is possible—Aristotle refines but hardly abandons Socratic "intellectualism": the ignorance of the akratic agent remains central to his explanation.[17]

und Wirkung: Vol. 1. Aristoteles und seine Schule, ed. Paul Moraux (Berlin and New York: Walter de Gruyter, 1985), 376–92, at 389.

11. For a useful introduction to the historical and systematic issues, see William Charlton, *Weakness of Will* (Oxford and New York: Basil Blackwell, 1988), 1–12.

12. See *De malo* 3.9, ed. Leon. 23: 86b, ll. 147–56.

13. See *Protagoras* 358d (ed. Cooper, 787): "Now, no one goes willingly toward the bad or what he believes to be bad; neither is it in human nature, so it seems, to want to go toward what one believes to be bad instead of to the good." Cf. *Meno* 77b–78b, and *Gorgias* 467c–79d, 492c–509d. For Plato's rejection of the self-sufficiency of knowledge for virtue, and his misgivings about Socrates' denial of incontinent action, see Terence H. Irwin, *Plato's Ethics* (New York: Oxford University Press, 1995), 116–17, 236–37.

14. See *Protagoras* 352c; *Meno* 98c.

15. See *EN* 7.1.1145b3–5. On the occasional but not universal equivalence of τὰ φαινόμενα and τὰ ἔνδοξα, see René A. Gauthier and Jean Yves Jolif, *L'Éthique à Nicomaque: Introduction, traduction et commentaire,* 4 vols. (Leuven: Publications Universitaires/Paris: Béatrice-Nauwelaerts, 1970), II–2: 588, n. 1145b3. Cf. ibid., 593, n. 1145b27–28: τὰ φαινόμενα refers to "[les] données de l'expérience."

16. *De malo* 3.9, ed. Leon., 23: 86b, ll. 173–74.

17. See *EN* 7.3.1147b14–15.

In turn, Aquinas, by introducing the causality of the will, complicates and deepens but does not repudiate Aristotle's explanation of *akrasia.*

According to some contemporary scholars—notably among them Ross, Gauthier, and Jolif—some notion of the will's distinct and irreducible role is exactly what is missing and needed in Aristotle's overly rationalist account of *akrasia.*[18] However, this criticism, which perhaps too readily assimilates the Aristotelian incontinent agent *(akrates)* with the Christian and post-Christian "weak-willed" agent, has itself been judged misguided and irrelevant when used in the hermeneutics of Greek philosophical and literary texts.[19]

While details are still being added,[20] the story of the historical invention of the will *(voluntas)* as a distinct faculty, especially its Judeo-Christian religious background, is well documented.[21] The sources of Aquinas's faculty psychology are Christian as well as classical;[22] they include the Stoics

18. See W. David Ross, *Aristotle: A Complete Exposition of His Works and Thought,* 6th ed. (London and New York: Routledge, 1995), 230: "What is missing in his [Aristotle's] formal theory is the recognition that incontinence is due not to failure of knowledge, but to weakness of will"; Gauthier and Jolif, II–2, 603: "Aristote est demeuré impuissant à sortir du schéma intellectualiste de Socrate. . . . Si l'on ignore la volonté, il faut nécessairement admettre la théorie socratique de l'incontinence."

19. Bernard Williams, *Shame and Necessity* (Berkeley and Los Angeles: University of California Press, 1993), offers an extended *apologia* for the moral acuity, linguistic resources, and conceptual rectitude of the ancient Greeks, whose literary portrayal and philosophical analysis of deliberate virtuous and vicious human actions neither mentioned nor required a power of volition distinct from practical reason itself. But the ensuing recommendation seems as much a premise as a conclusion of his *apologia:* Williams urges any critical contemporary "philosophy of action"—one that dispels the "illusion that the basic powers of mind are inherently constituted in terms of an ethical order" (46)—to discard the notion, although it is still widely held in Western culture, that a morally weak or incontinent agent is indeed weak *willed.*

20. See Susanne Bobzien, "The Inadvertent Conception and Late Birth of the Free-Will Problem," *Phronesis* 43 (1998): 133–75, who argues that Alexander of Aphrodisias, in the second century A.D., offered "the first full and unambiguous statement of the freedom to do otherwise" (143) and thus introduced into ancient philosophy "a decision making faculty" (174). Cf. the witty exaggeration of Gauthier, *L'Éthique à Nicomaque,* 1: 266: ". . . il a fallu aux hommes, après Aristote, quelque onze siècles de réflexions pour inventer la 'volonté.'"

21. See N. W. Gilbert, "The Concept of Will in Early Latin Philosophy," *Journal of the History of Philosophy* 1 (1963): 17–35; Albrecht Dihle, *The Theory of Will in Classical Antiquity* (Berkeley and Los Angeles: University of California Press, 1982); Charles H. Kahn, "Discovering the Will: From Aristotle to Augustine," in *The Question of "Eclecticism": Studies in Later Greek Philosophy,* ed. John M. Dillon and A. A. Long (Berkeley, Los Angeles, and London: University of California Press, 1988), 234–59; John M. Rist, *Augustine: Ancient Thought Baptized* (Cambridge: Cambridge University Press, 1994), 187–88; Risto Saarinen, *Weakness of the Will in Medieval Thought: From Augustine to Buridan* (Leiden: E. J. Brill, 1994); Richard Sorabji, "The Concept of the Will from Plato to Maximus the Confessor," in *The Will and Human Action: From Antiquity to the Present Day,* ed. Thomas Pink and M. W. F. Stone (London and New York: Routledge, 2004), 6–28.

22. Simplifying Dihle, Kahn schematizes four historical stages marking the conceptual emergence of *voluntas:* (1) in the third century B.C., Chrysippus introduced into Stoicism

(especially Posidonius), Maximus the Confessor (seventh century A.D.), and John Damascene (eighth century A.D.). Nonetheless, the historical commonplace that links Aristotle and Augustine remains the starting point when interpreting Aquinas. Frequency of reference shows that Aquinas himself takes—however subsequently transmuted—Augustine and Aristotle as the two main sources for his own ethical-psychological doctrines.[23] Sorabji credits Augustine with bringing together a number of previously articulated themes (notably freedom and responsibility) and rational functions (such as choice and willpower), which, once coordinated, allow for a clear identification of the will as a rational appetite for the good associated with, but distinct from reason.[24] In regard to our particular topos, Aquinas's development of *incontinentia* incorporates an original, rich, and many-sided "Augustinian" emphasis on the will,[25] all the while making constant reference to Aristotle's treatment of *akrasia*.[26]

Augustine attributes to Pelagius the doctrine that the possibility of not sinning is inseparable from human nature as created by God. So created, the human will is the source of sinning or not sinning. Contra Pelagius, Augustine uses the expression *infirmitas* (meaning *infirmitas volun-*

---

the doctrine of assent (συγκατάθεσις) to impressions (φαντασία); (2) in the first century B.C., Lucretius and Cicero used the term *voluntas* in their Latin translations of Greek philosophers; (3) in the innovative Stoicism of the first and second century A.D., Seneca emphasized that moral perfection comes from an exercise of *voluntas,* and Epictetus, writing in Greek, self-constitution or moral character through προαίρεσις; (4) A.D. 354–430, Augustine.

23. For *ST (Summa theologiae)* IaIIae, the *Index Thomisticus* gives, in descending order of frequency, the following references: "Augustinus," 722 times; "Philosophus," 365 times (and "Aristoteles," 94 times); "Gregorius," 97 times; "Ambrosius," 20 times; "Isidorus," 9 times; "Tullius" (Cicero), 5 times. For *ST* IIaIIae: "Augustinus," 908 times; "Philosophus," 751 times (and "Aristoteles," 16 times); "Gregorius," 379 times; "Tullius" (Cicero), 132 times; "Ambrosius," 125 times; "Isidorus," 89 times. Note that "Gregorius" refers to either Gregory the Great or to Gregory of Nyssa; most references to Gregory of Nyssa are actually to Nemesius of Emesa.

24. See Sorabji, "Concept of Will," 18–20.

25. See Marianne Djuth, "Will," in *Augustine through the Ages: An Encyclopedia,* ed. Allan D. Fitzgerald, O.S.A. (Grand Rapids and Cambridge: William B. Eerdmans, 1999), 881–85. While sketching its "broad range of meaning in Augustine's works" (p. 883a), Djuth mentions "three significant definitions" of will: (1) will as the free movement of the soul (*De duabus animabus* 10.14); (2) will as consent (*De spiritu et littera* 34.60); and (3) will as love (*De trinitate* 9.12.18).

26. Among recent studies, see Judith Barad, "Aquinas's Assent/Consent Distinction and the Problem of Akrasia," *New Scholasticism* 62 (1988): 98–111; G. T. Colvert, "Aquinas on Raising Cain: Vice, Incontinence and Responsibility," *American Catholic Philosophical Quarterly Supplement* 71 (1997): 203–20; Jörn Müller, "Willensschwäche als Problem der Mittelalterlichen Philosophie: Überlegungen zu Thomas von Aquin," *Recherches de théologie et philosophie médiévales* 72 (2005): 1–28; Richard Reilly, "Weakness of Will: The Thomistic Advance," *Proceedings of the American Catholic Philosophical Association* 48 (1974): 198–207; Thomas D. Stegman, "Saint Thomas Aquinas and the Problem of *Akrasia,*" *Modern Schoolman* 61 (1988/89): 117–28; and Robert Pasnau, *Thomas Aquinas on Human Nature* (Cambridge: Cambridge University Press, 2002), 241–52.

tatis) frequently.[27] A computer search of the *Index Thomisticus* produces a single instance where Aquinas also uses the same expression: "Whereas sin proceeds *ex infirmitate voluntatis humanae,* grace proceeds from the immensity of the divine goodness."[28] More frequently, one finds—notably in the *Summa theologiae* and the *De malo*—the expression *infirmitas animae:*[29] "Just as in the body the stronger the movement against the order of nature, the greater the weakness, so likewise, the stronger the movement of passion against the order of reason, the greater the weakness of the soul" (*ST* IaIIae, q. 77, a. 3, ad 1). Most frequently, Aquinas uses the synonymous expression *peccatum ex infirmitate,*[30] which appears forty-eight times in thirty-eight places, citations that require further sifting to locate those instances where the meaning of the expression precisely bears on our topic, the "weakness of the will." The expression itself is problematic; in reference to a "sin done from weakness," the weakness of the will, as Aquinas views it, seems derivative. Aquinas adheres closely to the Aristotelian line. Reason is what is first "weak": "One is sinning from passion whether innate or brought on when the judgment of reason is overcome; and this, properly speaking, is to sin from weakness."[31]

This and other Thomistic texts using the expression *peccatum ex infirmitate* focus on how passion distracts, throws off, weakens, or suppresses reason, which subsequently misdirects the will to pursue an object that, in a cooler moment, can be seen to be disordered, *contra,* not *secundum rationem.* One might infer from both early and later texts that we are, first and last of all, "weak-minded."[32] However, in those later works,

27. See, e.g., *De natura et gratia* 51.59, CSEL 60, ed. Carol Urba and Joseph Zycha (Vienna: F. Tempsky/Leipzig: G. Freytag, 1913), 276: "Ubi enim est inseparabilis possibilitas, ei accidere non potest voluntatis infirmitas vel potius voluntatis adiacentia et perfectionis indigentia." For other textual references to *infirmitas,* see Ann A. Pang-White, "The Fall of Humanity: Weakness of the Will and Moral Responsibility in the Later Augustine," *Medieval Philosophy and Theology* 9 (2000): 51–67, at 58, n. 26.

28. *Super Epist. ad Rom.* 5.5 n. 431, ed. Cai, 79b: "Quia peccatum procedit ex infirmitate voluntatis humanae, gratia autem procedit ex immensitate bonitatis divinae."

29. *Infirmitas animae:* nineteen instances (in sixteen places), seven of which are relevant: *ST* IaIIae.77.3 c; ad 1; ad 2; 77.7 arg. 3; 88.1 c; IIaIIae.33.6 arg. 1; *De malo* 3.9 arg. 15.

30. See *ST* IaIIae.77.3, ad 2: "Unde cum dicitur peccatum esse ex infirmitate, magis est referendum ad infirmitatem animae. . . ."

31. "Ex passione autem sive innata sive illata peccatur, quando propter impetum passionis, rationis judicium obruitur: et hoc proprie est ex infirmitate peccare. . . ." *In Sent.* 2.43.1.1 (*Scriptum super libros Sententiarum Magistri Petri Lombardi,* ed. Pierre Mandonnet, O.P., and Marie Fabien Moos, 4 vols. [Paris: P. Lethielleux, 1929–1947]), 2: 1094.

32. See *De malo* 3.9 ad 4, ed. Leon., 23: 87b, ll. 240–46: ". . . quandoque vero ex hoc quod [rationis iudicium] impeditur in particulari propter passionem, et tunc est peccatum ex infirmitate." Cf. *ST* IaIIae.77.2. Bonnie Kent expatiates the claim that Aquinas does not rely on weakness of will to explain "why a person acts counter to her better judgment," see "Aquinas and Weakness of the Will," *Philosophy and Phenomenological Research* 75 (2007): 70–91.

Aquinas also clearly states, perhaps in reaction to the ninth of the condemned propositions in Archbishop Tempier's Condemnation of 1270, that the "proper and intrinsic cause of sin is the will to sin."[33] This does not mean, as Lottin insisted, that Aquinas altered his doctrine of will, granting in his later works a *sua sponte* freedom to the will as efficient cause of its own movements, so as to avoid the charge of intrapsychic or "intellectual determinism."[34] However, the will does play a significant role in Aquinas's interpretation of Aristotle and, a fortiori, marks his own explanation of *incontinentia* which, nonetheless, continues to draw deeply on Aristotle.[35]

2. The Practical Syllogism of the Incontinent: Aristotle and Aquinas

Best, then, we begin, with Aristotle—that is, with Aquinas's *Sententia libri Ethicorum,* which is not a full-blown commentary, but, as Torrell describes it, a summary and doctrinal exposition of the *Nicomachean Ethics.* Aquinas wrote it contemporaneously with the *Prima secundae* (1271–1272) as a personal propaedeutic for the *Secunda secundae* of the *Summa theologiae.*[36] As always, the question remains open—since its answer can be endlessly nuanced in reference to contemporary historiographical and hermeneutic criteria—how accurate and faithful is Aquinas's reading of Aristotle?[37] I shall simply note those instances where Aquinas seems to be departing from either the letter or the spirit of Aristotle's text.

33. *ST* IaIIae.73.6: ". . . propria et per se causa peccati, quae est ipsa voluntas peccandi. . . ."

34. Odon Lottin, "Libre arbitre et liberté depuis saint Anselme jusqu'à la fin du XIIIe siècle," in *Psychologie et morale aux XIIe et XIIIe siècles,* 2nd ed. (Gambloux: J. Duculot, 1957), 11–389, at 225–43, and "La preuve de la liberté humaine chez saint Thomas d'Aquin," *Recherches de Théologie Ancienne et Médiévale* 23 (1956): 323–30. That *the will is a purely passive power necessarily moved by its object* is the ninth proposition condemned by Tempier, see Heinrich Denifle and Emile Chatelain, *Chartularium Universitatis Parisiensis,* 2 vols. (Paris: Delalain, 1889–91), 1: 487. See also John F. Wippel, "The Condemnations of 1270 and 1277 at Paris," *Journal of Medieval and Renaissance Studies* 7 (1977): 169–201.

35. See *De malo* 3.9 ad 1, ed. Leon., 23: 87a, ll. 222–25: ". . . in voluntate hominis positum est quod servetur a peccato; sed in hoc infirmatur per passionem, ut perfecte non velit, ligato rationis usu. . . ."

36. See Jean-Pierre Torrell, O.P., *Saint Thomas Aquinas, Vol. 1. The Person and His Work,* trans. Robert Royal (Washington, D.C.: The Catholic University of America Press, 1996), 227–29. However, James C. Doig plausibly argues that some individual sections of the *Sententia libri Ethicorum* "are posterior to parallel articles of the *Secunda secundae,*" *Aquinas's Philosophical Commentary on the* Ethics: *A Historical Perspective* (Dordrecht, Boston, and London: Kluwer, 2001), 229.

37. For an up-to-date rehearsal of the issues, see Christopher Kaczor, "Thomas Aquinas's *Commentary on the Ethics:* Merely an Interpretation of Aristotle?" *American Catholic*

In discussing *akrasia,* Aristotle starts by stating that there are three morally bad moral states to be avoided (vice, incontinence, and brutishness, *EN* 7.1.1145b3–5); afterwards, he confirms the first of six received opinions (ἔνδοξα) about moral evil—that lack of self-control *(akrasia)* is bad and blameworthy.[38] The incontinent man or *akrates,* as characterized in the second of these opinions, is one inclined to abandon the conclusions of his own rational calculations (1145b11) about the necessary or natural bodily goods—food and sex (7.4.1147b25–28); he is so inclined because of his excessive and bad desires (7.2.1146a10) for the pleasures of taste and, more fundamentally, touch (3.10.1118a23–32). But, thirdly, although the incontinent or akratic agent knows that his incontinent actions are morally bad, he nonetheless acts contrary to his own moral principles and thus contrary to what otherwise would be his own deliberate choices (7.4.1148a10). In Aquinas's words, although the rational faculty of the *incontinens* remains operative, incontinence occurs because passion perverts the incontinent agent's appetitive faculty by throwing his desires out of proportion.[39]

Aristotle carefully distinguishes the continent (ἐγκρατής) from the temperate agent (σώφρων)—the former has and the latter does not have excessive evil desires (7.2.1146a12)—as well as the incontinent (ἀκρατής) from the intemperate agent (ἀκόλαστος). Both the intemperate and the incontinent agent pursue the same kind of pleasures; in Scholastic terminology, the matter or object of the two vices is the same.[40] But how they pursue those illegitimate pleasures significantly differs. The intemperate or profligate agent, thinking that his pursuit of pleasure is morally good, acts from a false principle but nonetheless intentionally and consistently, in making his deliberate choices (7.4.1148a17); he has an unconscious, incurable vice. The incontinent

Philosophical Quarterly 78 (2004): 353–78; and Mark D. Jordan, "Thomas as Commentator in Some Programs of Neo-Thomism: A Reply to Kaczor," *American Catholic Philosophical Quarterly* 78 (2004): 379–86.

38. Amélie Oksenberg Rorty plausibly connects 1145b3, τὰ φαινόμενα, with the (apparent?) "distinctions between varieties of wrongdoing" mentioned at 1145a16–17—vice (κακία), incontinence (ἀκρασία), and brutality/bestiality (θηριότης), see "Akrasia and Pleasure," in *Essays on Aristotle's Ethics,* ed. Amélie Oksenberg Rorty (Berkeley and Los Angeles: University of California Press, 1980), 267–84, at 269. In the Latin text used by Aquinas, a version of the revised *translatio Lincolniensis* of Robert Grosseteste, τὰ ἔνδοξα (1145b4–5) is misleadingly translated as *probabilia:* see *SLE (Sententia libri Ethicorum)* 7.1.1145b5 [n. 921], ed. Leon., 47/2: 379. The numbering in brackets is taken from the older edition of Raimondo Spiazzi, O.P. (Turin: Marietti, 1964). As Aquinas counts them, Aristotle considers six ἔνδοξα/*probabilia;* see *SLE* 7.1 [n. 1309], ed. Leon., 47/2: 382b, ll. 232. For a convenient statement of the provenance of Aquinas's Latin text of the *Nicomachean Ethics,* see René A. Gauthier, "Saint Thomas et l'Éthique à Nicomaque," appendix in ed. Leon. 48: V–XXV.

39. See *SLE* 7.1 [n. 1295], ed. Leon., 47/2: 380b, ll. 51–54.

40. See *SLE* 7.3 [n. 1336], ed. Leon., 47/2: 391a, ll. 93–97.

man, who is weak rather than vicious, acts badly but inconsistently and intermittently. After he has succumbed, and his passion has abated, the *akrates* is conscious of his moral weakness, and even curable inasmuch as he usually repents of his morally bad actions (7.8.1150b29–36).

In regard to the Socratic paradox, Aquinas unequivocally concurs with Aristotle (7.2.1145b27–28), remarking matter-of-factly that we see people, after they are moved by anger (irascibility) or the desire for pleasure (concupiscence), doing what they antecedently knew and afterwards continue to know to be morally bad.[41] Aristotle, however, sustains the basic Socratic thesis which, suitably modified, survives in his own account of incontinence *(akrasia).* Passion does not, as Socrates rightly claims, overcome universal knowledge, but it does "drag about" particular or perceptual knowledge. Thus there is, in the reasoning of the Aristotelian *akrates,* a moment of Socratic ignorance that explains why he acts immorally. On the received view of *akrasia,* Aristotle locates the akratic moment of ignorance at the point of the particular premise within the practical syllogism.[42] But Aristotle's elliptical texts reconstructing practical reasoning leave much for his readers to sort out. Every detail of the received interpretation of the akratic practical syllogism has been challenged, but that debate far exceeds the scope of this paper. In the *SLE,* Aquinas's reading of Aristotle is broadly consonant with, although not a major source for, the received view of *akrasia,* which, despite revisionist interpretations, continues to be held by numerous scholars.[43]

The primary question, which Aristotle attempts to answer in *EN* 7.2.1145b21–7.3.1147b19, is whether and in what way the akratic agent acts knowingly?[44] Put negatively, of what is the akratic agent ignorant? Aristotle's answer, or at least its lineaments, may be sketched by distinguishing (1) universal from particular judgments, and (2) habitual or potentially usable from actually exercised knowledge. In regard to the first distinction, practical reasoning employs both universal and particular premises, whether about the object or the agent. Aristotle gives as an example of practical reasoning a decision about eating dry food (7.3.1147a4–7). Validly attaining the particular conclusion, "This piece of dry food is good for me to eat," requires two syllogistic inferences. In Aristotle's first syllogism, the major is a universal premise about the ob-

41. See *SLE* 7.2 [n. 1314], ed. Leon., 47/2: 385a, ll. 60–63.

42. Cf. Gauthier and Jolif, II–2, 606: "Ainsi, le nœud de l'argument, c'est que l'incontinent ne connaît pas actuellement la mineure du syllogisme [pratique]."

43. For a short list of some of those scholars, all anglophones, see Norman O. Dahl, *Practical Reason, Aristotle, and Weakness of the Will* (Minneapolis: University of Minnesota Press, 1984), 265, n. 2.

44. See *EN* 7.3.1146b8; *SLE* 7.2 [n. 1314], ed. Leon., 47/2: 385a, ll. 57–60.

ject, that (a) "Dry food is healthy or good for all men to eat"; the minor, a particular premise about the agent, that (b) "I myself am a man," from which derives the particular conclusion about the agent, (c) "Dry food is healthy or good for me for me to eat." A second syllogism, similarly constructed, explains why the agent can eat some particular healthy dry thing, say, a piece of dry bread. In the second syllogism, the universal premise about the object is that (d) "Bread is dry food"; the particular premise about the object is that (e) "This is a piece of dry bread," which, in conjunction with the conclusion of the first syllogism, leads to the particular conclusion about the agent (f) "This piece of dry bread is healthy or good for me to eat."

In the dry food example, there is no premise in either syllogism explicitly containing a prescription, that is, "Every man *ought* to eat dry food," licensing the conclusion, "I *ought* to eat this piece of dry bread." But without assuming or supplying such a prescriptive premise, the reference to the akratic agent, who presumably should eat this piece of dry bread, is pointless: *akrasia* is the moral failing that prevents someone from doing what, in general, he knows that he ought to do. In this first argument, Aristotle is merely concerned to show something eminently in line with the Socratic thesis about the equivalency of vice and ignorance: that the *akrates* either does not know or does not actually use his knowledge of (e). But why is the *akrates* ignorant of (e) if he knows full well premises (a) and (d)?

The second argument (7.3.1147a29–b1), which is about whether one *ought* to taste something sweet, contains a syllogism with a prescription. Again, there are two syllogisms pertinent to understanding the situation of the *akrates:* the first, a "syllogism of reason"; the second, a quasi-syllogism, the so-called syllogism of desire, or what Aquinas labels the "syllogism of the intemperate man."[45] In regard to the first syllogism, the *akrates* knows and uses the morally correct universal premise of the syllogism of reason but is either habitually ignorant or is not able to use his habitual knowledge of the minor or particular premise that falls under his universal premise; therefore, he does not draw the right conclusion. Instead, the *akrates* adopts and uses a different minor premise, one motivated by passion, not reason. Thus his reasoning is to some degree conformed to a syllogism of desire that allows him to draw a different, albeit, false conclusion. The degree of conformity, though, is a matter of some controversy.

Unfortunately, Aristotle is not sufficiently clear, at least not for some contemporary scholars, about the conclusion of the practical syllogism.

45. *SLE* 7.3 [n. 1346], ed. Leon., 47/2: 392b, l. 249.

Is the conclusion the action done or a proposition that is subsequently enacted? Actions are about particulars (1147a4), and on the received view, Aristotle identifies (1147a25–31) the right conclusion with the performance of the singular action entailed by the premises of the syllogism. In the *SLE,* Aquinas repeats what he takes to be Aristotle's doctrine; he too identifies the proper conclusion of a practical syllogism with the actual performance of the singular action entailed by the premises.[46] But is this an entirely plausible interpretation of Aristotle?

Dahl argues, with great attention to textual detail, that the Aristotelian akratic agent both knows the minor premise and infers the right propositional conclusion, but then fails to enact it. It is the latter failure that distinguishes the incontinent from the continent or temperate agent. Each of the latter, if he is not somehow externally inhibited from acting, would validly reason through his respective practical syllogism. Each would infer and then, at once, enact the propositional conclusion (f) "This piece of dry bread is healthy or good for me to eat": that is, both the continent and the temperate agent would eat this piece of dry bread. Not so the akratic agent who, according to Dahl, is prevented by some passion from enacting the sound propositional conclusion that he has, in fact, validly inferred.

Dahl presents us with a case of exceptionally "open-eyed" *akrasia.* His interpretation of the practical syllogism is close to what Aquinas sometimes says when speaking in propria persona*: ST* IaIIae, q. 13, a. 1, ad 2 precisely distinguishes the propositional conclusion of a practical syllogism from the agent's ensuing volitional choice of an action.[47] But this text, among others, marks the difference between Aquinas the Aristotelian commentator and Aquinas the Christian theologian utilizing an elaborated (non-Aristotelian) schematism of volitional acts.

For the purpose of interpreting Aquinas's doctrine of *incontinentia,* nothing important hangs on resolving the contemporary issue about where to locate the conclusion of the Aristotelian practical syllogism, that is, whether *Aristotle* thinks that the conclusion is just the performed action or (as in a theoretical syllogism) a proposition that requires subsequent enactment. Certainly Aquinas acknowledges that the practical syllogism has a propositional conclusion that really differs from the en-

46. See *SLE* 7.3 [n. 1346], ed. Leon., 47/2: 239b, ll. 239–41: "Sed in speculativis anima solum dicit conclusionem, in factivis autem statim eam operatur"; [n. 1347], 393a, ll. 269–70: "Et ita sequitur conclusio operis."

47. *ST* IaIIae.13.1 ad 2: ". . . conclusio etiam syllogismi qui fit in operabilibus, ad rationem pertinet; et dicitur *sententia* vel *iudicium,* quam sequitur electio. Et ob hoc ipsa conclusio pertinere videtur ad electionem, tamquam ad consequens." Cf. *ST* IaIIae.76.1: "Conferens enim de agendis, utitur quod syllogismo, cuius conclusio est iudicium seu electio vel operatio."

suing choice.[48] In any case, on Aquinas's view of *incontinentia*, the akratic agent only knows and uses his knowledge of the universal premises (a) and (d) in the two syllogisms of the dry bread example. The *incontinens* gets derailed at the minor premise: he misperceives fact (e), "This is a piece of dry and good or healthy bread." As Aquinas comments, the akratic agent grasps the universal "in itself"—"Dry bread is good and healthy"—but not "in the singular," in regard to *this* piece of dry bread.[49] But how can the *akrates* be ignorant of, or—if he has habitual knowledge—fail to use the particular premise which correctly applies to this case here and now?

The example of akratic misperception that Aristotle himself mentions is tasting something sweet—perhaps because every man naturally has a sweet tooth[50]—which while always pleasant is, Aquinas suggests, sometimes forbidden because it is being tasted *extra horam*, outside the appropriate time for eating sweets.[51] The negative, first premise specifies what Aristotle vaguely calls the first "universal opinion" (καθόλου δόξα, 7.3.1147a25; a31) in the mind of the *akrates*. Aristotle does not specify the first universal opinion, a lacuna that modern scholars as well as Aquinas fill in. Arguably, the forbidden sweet is forbidden not because it will satiate our appetite just before dinner-time, but because it is not good or healthy, say because it has too much sugar and will cause tooth decay or aggravate one's diabetes.[52] The quality of being healthy or not ties this example of an akratic practical syllogism to the first one about dry bread. If so, we can make Aristotle's point by expatiating the first example—eating dry, healthy bread.

48. See note 47.

49. See *SLE* 7.3 [n. 1340], ed. Leon., 47/2: 391b, ll. 156–58.

50. Cf. *SLE* 7.5 [n. 1369], ed. Leon., 47/2: 399a, ll. 20–21: ". . . dulce est naturaliter delectabile omni habenti gustum."

51. See *SLE* 7.3 [n. 1347], ed. Leon., 47/2: 393a, ll. 260–69.

52. Anthony Kenny argues that the first universal premise must be concerned "with the avoidance of tastes precisely *qua* unpleasant . . . not . . . *qua* unhealthy": so he proffers "Sweet things ought not to be tasted." See his *Aristotle's Theory of the Will* (New Haven: Yale University Press, 1979), 159. But why? Granted that both the temperate and the akratic man hold to the same moral principle that excessive pleasures of touch and taste are to be eschewed as slavish and bestial (*EN* 3.10.1118a23–26). But how are we to determine which pleasures of touching/eating—apart from some appeal to what is healthy for the *human* body—hit the mean? Unless supplemented by considerable empirical data, Kenny's proposed criterion—what best conduces to contemplation of God—seems implausibly remote from making theological choices about the right dietary regimen. The criterion, moreover, is found exclusively, on Kenny's own view of the relationship between *EN* and *EE*, in *EE* 8.1 [= 7.15] 1249b17–23. So, "Taste nothing pleasant" is, as Kenny now admits, too sweeping a universal principle to attribute to the akratic agent; "Taste nothing pleasant that is unhealthy" is not. If health is either a means to or a constituent of human flourishing, the latter principle, on Aristotelian grounds, is no less a moral principle than the former. See Kenny, 158–60, esp. notes.

The akratic agent knows that dry bread is good or healthy food to eat, and ordinarily he has no difficulty in identifying the piece of dry, healthy bread lying on a plate in front of him. But it might happen that on today's table there is also an utterly irresistible (for this *akrates*) bowl of melted butter in which to soak his hitherto dry, healthy, but gustatorily unappetizing piece of bread. Saturated with butterfat, this piece of bread is neither dry nor healthy; rationally speaking, especially if one already has high blood cholesterol, it ought not to be eaten. But it is exceedingly pleasant or delicious, and it is this fact in conjunction with his desire for pleasure that overpowers the thinking of the *akrates*. Once again, the incontinent agent must be distinguished from the intemperate agent.

In Aristotle's second example of an akratic practical syllogism, the universal premise in the mind of the *intemperate* agent is "All sweet things ought to be tasted" (7.3.1147a29). This, clearly, is a prescriptive premise. Transposed to our reworked dry food example, the intemperate man holds that "All delicious things ought to be eaten" and reasons accordingly when presented with the opportunity to eat a piece of delicious (but unhealthy) butter-saturated bread: if he is not externally constrained, the intemperate agent would at once eat *this* piece of buttery bread. And so he *must* do by a necessity that is both logical and psychological (1147a26–28). Although his argument is unsound (its first premise is false), the intemperate man's inference is valid: in that sense, he is employing a syllogism of reason.[53] The akratic agent, however, makes an invalid inference: he is employing what has been labeled a "syllogism of desire" but which, in fact, is not a valid syllogism.[54]

The Aristotelian incontinent (ἀκρατής) as well as the continent (ἐγκρατής) and temperate (σώφρων) agent knows and uses the true prescriptive universal or rule that should guide each of their dietary choices: (g) "No delicious unhealthy thing ought to be eaten." And each also holds a second universal opinion: (h) "Butter-saturated bread is delicious but unhealthy." To repeat, both (g) and (h) are true universal premises that are known to be true by the *akrates*. Yet the *akrates*, when offered a piece of butter-saturated, delicious, but unhealthy bread, reasons differently and speciously: in accordance with the revisionist model of Aristotelian practical reasoning, (i) "Everything butter-saturated is de-

53. Cf. *SLE* 7.3 [n. 1346], ed. Leon., 47/2: 392b, ll. 245–51.

54. Cf. *SLE* 7.3 [nn. 1346–7], ed. Leon., 47/2: 392b–93a, ll. 239–72: the syllogism of the *incontinens* has four premises: (1) "Every sweet thing is pleasant"; (2) "This particular thing is sweet"; (3) "No sweet thing should be eaten outside the appropriate time"; (4) "This is an inappropriate time to eat a sweet thing." Concupiscence, which at bottom is the desire for pleasure irrespective of moral decency, moves the *akrates* to act on (2) by ignoring (4).

licious" (j) "This is a piece of butter-saturated delicious bread"; (k) "This piece of butter-saturated delicious bread ought to be eaten."

In Aquinas's reconstruction, however, the *incontinens* reasons, again speciously, as follows: (i) "Everything butter-saturated is delicious"; (j) "This is a piece of butter-saturated delicious bread"; (l) concluding by actually eating this piece of butter-saturated delicious bread. Thus Aquinas equates, in his commentary, the conclusion of the incontinent agent with the incontinent action itself.[55] And so, the *akrates* immediately eats, though, on either the revisionist or received (i.e., Aquinas's) model, there is no logical necessity for him to do so: neither the propositional conclusion (k) nor Aquinas's *conclusio operationis* (l) follow from premises (i) and (j). So why does the *akrates* draw and, then, enact (k)—or as in (l) just eat—the conclusion of this invalid "syllogism of desire"? At this point, Aristotle and Aquinas press into service the second distinction between habitually possessed and actually used bits of knowledge.

The akratic agent's second universal opinion (i) "Everything butter-saturated is delicious" (corresponding to Aristotle's "Everything sweet is pleasant," 1147a32), which is descriptive not prescriptive, is not itself logically contrary to the sound rule (g) "No delicious unhealthy thing ought to be eaten." Rather, it is the minor premise subsumed under "the univeral [premise] of concupiscence,"[56] (i) "Everything butter-saturated is delicious"—namely, (j) "This is a piece of delicious butter-saturated bread"—that is operative in the reasoning of the *akrates* (1147a33). Strictly speaking, though, it is desire, not reasoning, that moves the *akrates* to pick up the piece of butter-saturated bread and eat it: desire "can move each of our bodily parts" (1147a35).

Desire, of course, also shapes the beliefs of the *akrates*. The akratic agent's reasoning is thrown off both by his excessive desire for gustatory delectations and his true beliefs—the true belief that (i) "Everything butter-saturated is delicious" and (j) "This is a piece of butter-saturated delicious bread." Together they prompt the *akrates* to act *as though* he held and had adopted the intemperate agent's universal hedonistic rule "All delicious things ought to be eaten." But, in fact, the incontinent agent does not adopt the intemperate agent's prescriptive hedonistic rule as his first universal premise. Instead, the *akrates* fixes his attention on the particular premise (j) "This is a piece of delicious butter-saturated bread" that instances his background belief, (i) "Everything butter-saturated is delicious." It is the particular premise (j) that prompts him

55. As Aquinas puts it when identifying the conclusion with the action itself: "Et ita sequitur conclusio operationis," *SLE* 7.3 [n. 1347], ed. Leon., 47/2: 393a, ll. 269–70.

56. Ibid., ll. 268–69: ". . . sed assumitur sub universali concupiscentiae [omne dulce est delectabile], ut dicatur hoc esse dulce."

actually to eat, (l)—or, on the revisionist model, enact the conclusion, (k) "This piece of butter-saturated delicious bread ought to be eaten."

For Aristotle, the akratic agent's ignorance is at the perceptual level. Under the pressure of his desires, he misperceives a singular fact—not the delicious but the *unhealthy* quality of this piece of butter-saturated bread. As Aquinas puts it, the *akrates* grasps the universal in itself, in our example, (h) "Butter-saturated bread is delicious but unhealthy," but not as instanced in *this* piece of butter-saturated bread.[57] However, Aristotle, it is often noted, distinguishes the impetuous from the weak akratic agent. Simply not having the correct information about the relevant particular premise is a characterization that best fits the actions of the impetuous *akrates.*

The impetuous *akrates* does not take the time to notice, accurately and fully, what is in front of him: this *unhealthy* piece of delicious butter-saturated bread. Not adverting to, that is, ignoring that fact, he does not deliberate, in the light of his universal principle, about this particular choice. The impetuous *akrates* may be said to reason "in ignorance" if not precisely "through ignorance."[58] If the impetuous akratic agent were to reason *inculpably* "through ignorance"—that is, because he could not know, even if he were attentive, that this particular action falls under the universal prohibition—his or her action would be involuntary, and hence not morally culpable. But what can one say about acting culpably "in ignorance" *(ignorans)?* The relevant question turns on how responsible is the impetuous *akrates* for not taking the time to notice what is in front of him—this is a piece of butter-saturated, delicious, but unhealthy bread—which is exactly the perception of the fact that could allow him to formulate the correct minor premise in what would then be a syllogism of reason. When making his choice, the impetuous *akrates* is not simultaneously aware of any conflict between reason and his desires.

Yet the situation in regard to the weak *akrates,* as critics of the received view have pointed out, is more complicated. It seems likely, in the case of the weak *akrates,* that the agent has but cannot actually use (1147a8) the information habitually known and also grasped as instanced in the particular premise "This is a piece of butter-saturated, delicious, but unhealthy bread." Revisionist interpreters note that, in a few texts in the *Nicomachean Ethics,* Aristotle's weak *akrates* apparently considers his choices while aware of the real and simultaneous conflict of his own motives, rational and appetitive. For example, *EN* 7.8.1151a1–3 apparently takes for granted direct conflicts between reason and passion.

57. See *SLE* 7.3 [n. 1340], ed. Leon., 47/2: 391b, ll. 153–58.

58. See *EN* 3.1.1110b25. In *ST* IaIIae.76.1, the distinction is between sinning "propter ignorantiam" and sinning "ignorans."

The weak *akrates* deliberates but does not stick with the conclusions he has reached through deliberation (7.7.1150b19–22). If the deliberating and succumbing occur at the same time, the weak *akrates* does what he knows to be wrong while knowing and using the particular as well as the universal premise of the rational syllogism. But does Aristotle consistently allow, as he seems to do in his other ethical treatises,[59] for this kind of knowing or "open-eyed akrasia" in the *Nicomachean Ethics?* In the *SLE,* Aquinas finds no evidence that he does; in Aquinas's reading, Aristotle hews closely to the Socratic line and only allows for unknowing or "closed-eyed *akrasia.*" Aquinas claims that the *akrates* momentarily thinks, while in the throes of passion, that *this* bad act is intrinsically good; in so doing, he is ignorant of the real good.[60]

3. Passions and the Will

Aristotle supplements his logical analysis of the "syllogism of desire" with empirical data about the somatic cause of the akratic agent's ignorance.[61] Aquinas reiterates Aristotle's physiological doctrine: the passions alter the states of our bodily organs, affecting especially the flow of blood from the heart which dilates through anger-induced warmth and contracts through fear-induced cold.[62] Because the passions can generate too much heat or cold—so Aquinas explains[63]—intense anger, fear, and sexual desire can render a man temporarily mad or, if less vehement, like someone asleep or drunk, or like an actor who, while he might repeat things by rote, is incapable of thinking clearly or judging perspicaciously about what he is saying (7.3.1147a15–23). Though neither asleep nor drunk, the *akrates* is similarly "under the influence" of intense passion; his knowledge of the particular premise relevant to making a continent choice is more potential than actual; it is not being used in the way that a sane, or wide-awake, or sober man uses his knowledge.[64]

59. See *EE* 2.7.1223b8–9; 2.8.1224b20–21. Cf. *MM* 2.6.1203b5–6. For the problem of the authenticity of *Magna Moralia,* see Terence H. Irwin, "Aristotle Reads the *Protagoras,*" in this volume, p. 00, n. 1.

60. Cf. *SLE* 7.8 [n. 1430], ed. Leon., 47/2: 415a, ll. 110–16: "incontinens . . . habet falsam aestimationem de eis [sc. delectationibus] in particulari." Although something comparable can be found in *De anima* 3.10.433b8–10, Bonnie Kent wonders, correctly, whether Aquinas is reading his own doctrine of will into Aristotle: viz., that the Thomistic will can choose only what the intellect presents as an apparent good; see "Transitory Vice: Thomas Aquinas on Incontinence," *Journal of the History of Philosophy* 27 (1989): 199–223, at 206.

61. *EN* 7.3.1147a24: the investigation into the cause of incontinence is done "naturally" (φυσικῶς).

62. See *ST* IaIIae.23.2 ad 2; *De veritate* 26.3, ed. Leon., 22/3: 756a, ll. 215–20.

63. See *SLE* 7.3 [n. 1342], ed. Leon., 47/2: 392a, ll. 183–90.

64. In *De generatione animalium* 2.1.735a9–11, Aristotle mentions, in regard to increas-

Aquinas uses a metaphor: in regard to the particular premise, the habitual knowledge of the *akrates* is not active but "fettered" *(ligatus)*.[65] Even if he does say "It is not good for me to pursue this pleasure," the incontinent man feels *(sentit)* differently in his heart than what is on his lips.[66] Here, "feeling" suggests the embodied character of the passions that block the incontinent's knowledge of the particular premise. However, beginning in his earliest works, Aquinas relates the ignorance of the *incontinens* to a willful failure to repudiate the concupiscible enticement that "absorbs the judgment of reason in regard to a particular action."[67] *ST* IaIIae, q. 6, a. 7 explicitly stresses the role of the will: the *incontinens* "wills the [concupiscible] object that he previously repudiated." Even in the *SLE,* Aquinas interposes a faculty of will distinct from reason, thus adding a new volitional element to the Aristotelian explanation of incontinence.[68] The akratic agent must actively consent to concupiscence before acting from concupiscence.

> There is one cause of all the things that a man does whether good or bad: namely, the will. For however great anger or concupiscence grows, a man rushes to doing [those things] only if there first comes the consent of the rational appetite.[69]

In his mature works, Aquinas definitely transposes—although there certainly remain occasional ambiguities albeit perhaps not a clear doctrinal shift within the *Summa theologiae*[70]—the Aristotelian discussion of

---

ing degrees of actuality, the knowledge of the geometer who is asleep, awake, and at the present time doing geometry.

65. See *SLE* 7.3 [n. 1342], ed. Leon., 47/2: 392a, ll. 179–80.

66. See *SLE* 7.3 [n. 1344], ed. Leon., 47/2: 392b, ll. 214–17.

67. See *In Sent.* 2.22.2.2, ed. Mandonnet, 2: 560: "Quaedam vero ignorantia est quae quodammodo affectum peccati consequitur, ut quando ex concupiscentia peccati, quam voluntas non reprimit, absorbetur judicium rationis de particulari operabili. . . ."

68. Cf. *SLE* 5.14 [n. 1062], ed. Leon., 47/1: 315a, ll. 154–63: "[Incontinens] habet enim per se voluntatem boni, sed per concupiscentiam trahitur ad malum. Et hoc quod dictum est, probat per hoc, quod cum voluntas sit apparentis boni, nullus vult illud quod non aestimat esse bonum; incontinens autem extra passionem existens non reputat bonum illud quod facit, unde absolute non vult illud; sed tamen operatur illud quod aestimat non oportere operari, propter concupiscentiam quae est in appetitu sensitivo, voluntas autem in ratione est."

69. *SLE* 3.4 [n. 428], ed. Leon., 47/1: 130a, ll. 65–69: ". . . sit una causa omnium quae homo facit, sive sint bona sive mala, scilicet voluntas; non enim quantumcumque ira vel concupiscentia increscat, homo prorumpit ad agendum nisi adveniat consensus rationabilis appetitus."

70. *ST* IIaIIae.53.5 ad 3 states that continence and perseverance are "solely in reason," not the appetitive power, perhaps meaning by the latter will as well as sense appetite, i.e., the concupiscible power. The latter is the view favored by Torrell, *Saint Thomas Aquinas,* 1: 245–46, who follows Gauthier's lead. In IIaIIae.53.5 ad 3, the *ratio* of the continent man is said to stand firm against the pull of concupiscence. And *continentia* is declared "species constantiae ad rationem pertinentis." Nonetheless, *ratio* here could be used as a stand-in for

akrasia to the plane of will.[71] To take one example, Aristotle denies that the *akrates* "chooses" to act incontinently, since in so acting the *akrates* deviates from the end enshrined in his own (correct) moral principles. Aquinas, however, distinguishes between the incontinent man who "sins electively" *(peccare eligentem)*—that is, sins while choosing to sin—and the intemperate malicious man who sins, in a different sense, from a deliberate choice *(ex electione)*.[72] The choice *(electio)* of the incontinent agent is the proximate cause but not the first principle *(principium)* of his sin. In the incontinent man what is uppermost or primary—the *principium* of his misdeeds—are the passions, which are in the sensible appetite, and which affect the will, to use a spatial metaphor, from the outside. While being moved by his passions, the *incontinens* chooses to satisfy them, although he could have chosen not to, at least if he has not been rendered totally irrational by the vehemence of his love or hate, or anger or fear.[73] He sins from weakness because his will is not sufficiently strengthened against an impulse of the passions by the habit of continence that governs his choices.[74] In contrast, the intemperate man sins not from weakness or lack of continence but from an interior malice; his will has become corruptly habituated by repeatedly choosing evil "on principle"—that is, by making his choices conform to the evil end that he persistently intends.[75]

---

the intellectual soul, which includes will, as its second rational power: see Ia.79.1 ad 1; *SLA (Sentencia libri De anima)* 3.8 [n. 802], ed. Leon., 45/1: 240a, ll. 108–9. The numbering in brackets is from the edition of Angelo M. Pirotta, O.P. (Turin: Marietti, 1959). Accordingly, *ST* IaIIae.58.3 ad 2, after explicitly denying that continence is in the sensitive appetite, puts it in the *pars rationalis,* but the point is that continence is an imperfect moral virtue, thus a *volitional habit* governing choices. Cf. IIaIIae.155.4 ad 3, which Torrell thinks indicates a shift inasmuch as it explicitly locates continence in the will. Doig finds the "simplicity and precision" of *SLE* 7.10 [n. 1463], ed. Leon., 47/2: 421b–22a, ll. 87–97—"subjectum utriusque [continentiae et incontinentiae] sit voluntas"—evidence that it was written after IIaIIae.155.3: ". . . continentia sit, sicut in subiecto, in illa vi animae cuius actus est electio. Et haec est voluntas . . . "; see *Aquinas's Commentary,* 228. For my reservations about Doig's view that Aquinas presents in the *SLE* his own philosophical "vision of correct moral philosophy" (XVII), see my review of *Aquinas's Commentary* in *Review of Metaphysics* 57 (2003): 402–3.

71. See *De malo* 2.3 ad 5, ed. Leon., 23: 37a, ll. 133–35: "Principaliter autem est peccatum in voluntate secundum quod malae concupiscentiae consentit."

72. *ST* IaIIae.78.4 ad 3. On the "troublesome question" of how to translate *peccare eligens,* see Kent, "Transitory Vice," 207–8.

73. *ST* IaIIae.77.8 ad 3: ". . . ratio non semper in suo actu totaliter a passione impeditur: unde remanet ei liberum arbitrium. . . ." Cf. *SLA* 2.28 [n. 621], ed. Leon., 45/1: 189a, ll. 102–5: ". . . uoluntas non ex necessitate trahitur ab appetitu sensibili, set semper ei liberum manet sequi inclinationem appetitus sensibilis uel non sequi. . . ."

74. See *ST* IaIIae.78.3–4; IIaIIae.155.3.

75. See *In Sent.* 2.43.1.4, ed. Mandonnet, 2: 1105: ". . . incontinens, quia ex passione peccat, sive infirmitate, facilius curatur quam intemperatus, qui peccat ex electione sive ex industria." *ST* IaIIae.78.4 ad 3: "Ille enim qui peccat ex passione, peccat quidem eligens, non tamen ex electione: quia electio non in eo primum peccati principium, sed inducitur

ST IaIIae, q. 77, a. 2, while carefully preserving the rationalist elements in Aristotle's account of *akrasia,* refers to the akratic's ignorance in terms of its consequences for the operation of the will: "The will would never tend to evil unless there were ignorance or error in the reason." Ignorance, to repeat, hinders the *will* in making right choices.[76] The same combination of volitional and intellectual causes, albeit the latter in more muted fashion, are retained in the *Secunda secundae.* In *ST* IIaIIae, qq. 155 and 156, Aquinas does not highlight, although it remains in the background, the Aristotelian distinction between the akratic agent's correct use of the universal and misuse of the particular premise in the practical syllogism.[77] Question 155, a. 3 speaks in volitional terms about the incontinent agent *choosing* to follow his vehement evil desires although reason—at least apart from this very act of choosing—contradicts such a choice.[78] In the same article, the reply to the second objection refers to the will as the really distinct power of the intellectual soul that mediates between reason and desire. Question 155, a. 4, ad 3 refers to the quasi-virtue of continence, which inheres in the will, as the "good of reason" *(bonum rationis)* extending to the will. Nonetheless, Question 156, a. 1 reiterates the commonplace that both the continent and the incontinent man, unlike the insane man, preserve the judgment of reason that the continent man conforms to and the weak incontinent man abandons. Like a woman, the incontinent man has a soft temperament that allows him to be easily led astray by his passions (ad 1–2)! Neither firmly hold to the judgment of reason.

4. Ignorance in Choice

One might think that the weak incontinent man's abandonment of reason should indicate for Aquinas, as it does for revisionist contemporary interpreters, a patent case of intellectually open-eyed *akrasia:* on their reading, the weak *incontinens,* unlike the impetuous *incontinens,* has deliberated, and knows full well the correct particular premise governing his choice. But it does not: here and elsewhere, Aquinas retains even

ex passione ad eligendum. . . ."; *De malo* 3.12 ad 5, ed. Leon., 23: 95a: ". . . in eo qui peccat ex malitia, uoluntas mali est primum principium peccati, quia ex se ipso et per habitum proprium inclinatur in uoluntatem mali. . . ."

76. See *ST* IaIIae.77.2: "Cum enim ad recte agendum homo dirigatur duplici scientia, scilicet universali et particulari; utriusque defectus sufficit ad hoc quod impediatur rectitudo operis et voluntatis. . . ."

77. See *ST* IIaIIae.156.3 ad 1: "Nam ignorantia incontinentis attenditur quantum ad aliquod particulare eligibile, prout scilicet aestimat hoc nunc esse eligendum. . . ."

78. *ST* IIaIIae.155.3: ". . . incontinens autem eligit sequi eas [concupiscentias pravas vehementes], non obstante contradictione rationis."

as he qualifies by reference to the will that moment of ignorance which is central to his reading of the Aristotelian account of *akrasia*.[79] Certainly the actual experience and even the desire of hoped-for bodily pleasures distracts;[80] the passion of concupiscence draws the mind's attention to itself and weakens the agent's rational focus on any other object.[81] The *incontinens,* at least while passion clouds his rational judgment (*ST* IaIIae, q. 23, a. 3), ignores an aspect of the particular choice engaging him: namely, that this particular thing, because not in accordance with right reason, is *inhonestum,* and therefore ought not to be chosen here and now. The passions of the incontinent man, inasmuch as they occlude his awareness of the self-evident principles of practical reason, corrupt the measure of prudence that he might otherwise possess.[82]

79. Even the sin of a fallen angel, who has no passions to cloud or deflect his intellectual judgment, is not perfectly knowing or "open-eyed." Passion makes the incontinent man think something evil to be good—that is, evil takes on the guise of an apparent good. Angelic sin "is [more] difficult to understand," but the angel, too, has in sinning "some mode of deception in reason," although this deception does not involve confusing a *malum ex se* with an apparent good. The angel's reason "is able to be bound" *(ligari)* not by passions, but his failure to consider all the conditions concurrently relevant to the particular choice of this good. That failure allows the angel to choose what he would otherwise know to be evil; see *In Sent.* 2.5.1.1, ed. Mandonnet, 2: 144. The angelic sin thus arises not from ignorance of "something that *secundum se* is good" but "only from the absence of considering those things that ought to be considered"—namely, whether this choice is correctly ordered "to the rule of the divine will" (*ST* Ia.63.1 ad 4). Aquinas attempts to explain why the evil angels failed to consider what they ought to have considered by reference to their pride; see *ST* Ia.63.3.

80. See *ST* IaIIae.36.2 ad 3: ". . . concupiscentia est delectabilis, quandiu manet spes adipiscendi quod concupiscitur." In regard to the sensible power of concupiscence, *concupiscentia* (the desire for some absent sensible good) is a specific passion distinguished from the passion that is its cause, *amor* (the attraction to a sensible good consequent upon the apprehension that the sensible good is naturally proportioned or conformed to the sensible appetite), and the passion that is its end, *delectatio* (the delight that comes from obtaining a desired sensible good); see ibid. 31.2 ad 3. Cf. *ST* IaIIae.25.2, ad 3: ". . . delectatio causat amorem, secundum quod est prior in intentione."

81. If intense enough, pleasure induces bodily changes that, by affecting the imagination and other bodily powers, "fetter" reason which needs to work on sensible phantasms; see *ST* IaIIae.33.3. Cf. *De veritate* 26.3, ed. Leon., 22/3: 756a, ll. 196–99: ". . . unde contingit quod laeso organo virtutis imaginativae etiam intellectus operatio impeditur, propter hoc quod intellectus indiget phantasmatibus in sua operatione."

82. See *ST* IIaIIae.47.16: ". . . prudentia non directe tollitur per oblivionem, sed magis corrumpitur per passiones. . . ." The continent man, exercising *synderesis,* the quasi-innate habit of practical rationality, clearly grasps and is rationally if not always emotively inclined toward the self-evident ends of the moral virtues (*In Sent.* 3.33.2.4 ql. 4, sol., ed. Moos, 3: 1067); because his appetites are controlled but disordered, he possesses only an imperfect form of prudence (*ST* IIaIIae.47.13). Only the man who possesses temperance and the other cardinal virtues, which rectify his passions and appetites, exercises perfect prudence; he prescribes and makes the right particular choices quickly and with pleasure (IaIIae.57.4–5; 58.5; IIaIIae.32.1 ad 1). Cf. Tobias Hoffmann, "Aquinas on the Moral Progress of the Weak Willed," in *The Problem of Weakness of Will in Medieval Thought,* ed. Tobias Hoffmann, Jörn Müller, and Matthias Perkams (Leuven, Paris, and Dudley, Mass.: Peeters, 2006), 219–45, at 226–27. Although an intellectual virtue, prudence incorpo-

Aquinas's point, however, is that reason and passion in conjunction move the *will* of the incontinent man in regard to his choices. The *incontinens* has not lost his rational moral principles but he is not universally or consistently using them; he ignores their application to this particular choice because it promises to satisfy his concupiscence. However, the incontinent, as long as he is able to think rationally, is not simply propelled, like an animal, by his sensible appetite.[83] The incontinent agent voluntarily consents, although there was no necessity to do so, to the concupiscible passion.[84] Speaking precisely, though, an agent assents to judgments reached through deliberation.[85] The incontinent agent is able to resist passion if he does not assent to the judgment that here and now passion, not the moral rule, is to be followed. Assenting to that judgment, to which *here and now* there is no acceptable alternative for the akratic, is equivalent to choosing to succumb to passion.[86]

Choice, given the nature of the will as rational appetite, is never unmotivated but necessarily directed to some real or apparent good that reason has apprehended.[87] Typically, the will first consents to a range of means reached through deliberation, but choice always presupposes a judgment (perhaps one that is long-standing or habitual and thus made with little or no immediate deliberation) about what is the most preferable *(preferendum)* among the possible courses of action.[88] Of course, the stronger the desire for some sensible good, or the more deeply ingrained the habit of pursuing and succumbing to pleasure, the easier it is for the incontinent agent to "rationalize" his particular choice.[89] Vehement desire or habit makes this particular choice to satisfy concupiscence seem the best choice, all contrary rational considerations notwithstanding.

Aquinas, no less evidently in his later works, does not embrace a radi-

---

rates, it should be noted, the operation of the will: "In omnibus autem viribus et actibus animae ordinatis hoc est commune, quod virtus primi salvatur in omnibus sequentibus; et ideo in prudentia quodammodo includitur et voluntas, quae est de fine, et cognitio finis" (*De veritate* 5.1, ed. Leon., 22/1: 137a–41b).

83. See *ST* IaIIae.15.2 ad 2.

84. See *ST* IaIIae.10.3 ad 1: ". . . potest voluntas non velle concupiscere, aut concupiscentiae non consentire. Et sic non ex necessitate sequitur concupiscentiae motum."

85. See *ST* IaIIae.15.3: "Et ideo applicatio appetitivi motus ad determinationem consilii, proprie est consensus."

86. See *ST* IaIIae.15.3 ad 3: "Sed si inveniatur unum solum quod placeat, non differunt re consensus et electio, sed ratione tantum, ut consensus dicatur secundum quod placet ad agendum; electio autem, secundum quod praefertur his quae non placent."

87. See, e.g., *ST* IaIIae.8.1; 27.2.

88. See *ST* Ia.83.3.

89. See *De virtutibus in communi* 4 ad 13, ed. P. A. Odetto (*Quaestiones disputatae*, 9th ed. [Rome and Turin: Marietti, 1953]), 719a: "Perversitas vero rationis et voluntatis ut plurimum ex passionibus accidit."

cally voluntarist account of wrong-doing. By definition, choice always follows upon judgment: "For after the determination of deliberation [*consilium*], which is reason's judgment, the will chooses; and after choice [*electio*], reason commands that power which has to do what was chosen; and then, last of all, someone's will begins the use, by executing the command of reason . . ." (*ST* IaIIae, q. 17, a. 3, ad 1). In every case of incontinence, then, satisfaction of desire is judged to be, here and now, the overriding good no matter what universal moral precept is violated. That judgment, of course, fixes on an apparent good *(bonum apparens)*, whether it be to seek pleasure or to vent anger;[90] such passion-generated judgments miss the real human good, acting in accordance with right reason, the criterion that makes this particular choice *honestum*.[91]

In Aquinas's moral psychology, the sequence of the interior intellectual and volitional acts, which are the interior psychological causes that morally determine the exterior or embodied human action—to use an abbreviated list, deliberation, judgment, choice, command, use—realigns while retaining the elements of the Aristotelian explanation of *akrasia*.[92] Ignorance continues to play a central explanatory role, again in accordance with the Aristotelian distinction between acting "from ignorance" *(propter ignorantiam)* and acting "in ignorance" *(ignorans)*.[93] But that latter ignorance is now emphatically coordinated with a volitional defect captured in the Augustinian dictum, "Sin is chiefly in the will" (*ST* IIaIIae, q. 156, a. 3). The dictum provides a new fulcrum for analyzing moral goodness in general[94] and the virtue of continence in particu-

90. Justin Gosling attributes to Aquinas the view that "[a]ll pursuit of evil has to be explained in terms of apprehension of a genuine good gone wrong" (*Weakness of the Will* [London and New York: Routledge, 1990], 81). But Aquinas's point is that an apparent good is not a "genuine good" but a moral evil *simpliciter:* ". . . voluntas non tendit in ipsum [malum] sub ratione mali. Sed quia aliquod malum est apparens bonum, ideo voluntas aliquando appetit aliquod malum" (*In Sent.* 2.25.1.2, ed. Mandonnet, 2: 649).

91. See *ST* IaIIae.59.4: "Est autem rationis bonum id quod est secundum rationem moderatum seu ordinatum."

92. For a complete list of the interior intellectual and volitional interior acts, see *ST* IaIIae, qq. 8–17. Put according to the logical order of their genesis, the sequence of interior acts is: simple intellectual apprehension of an end *(apprehensio simplex);* simple willing of the apprehended end *(volitio simplex);* volitional intending of that end through some or other possible means *(intentio);* intellectual deliberation about which of the possible means are available *(consilium);* volitional consent to the available means *(consensus);* intellectual judgment about which is the best available means *(iudicium);* volitional choice of the best available means *(electio);* intellectual command *(imperium)* to carry out the chosen action; volitional use of the intellectual or bodily faculty required to carry out the chosen action *(usus);* and volitional enjoyment of the end thus attained *(fruitio)*. For further discussion, see my *Aquinas on the Twofold Human Good* (Washington, D.C.: The Catholic University of America Press, 1997), 340–47.

93. See *ST* IaIIae.76.1; 77.2; 78.1 ad 1.

94. See *De virtutibus in communi* 7, ed. Odetto, 724a: "Bonum autem sub ratione boni est obiectum solius appetitivae partis; nam bonum est quod omnia appetunt."

lar: "That a man does well actually occurs because the man has a good will" (IaIIae, q. 56, a. 3).[95] In fact, if he has a good will, a man can be totally good inasmuch as he can then will to use all of his other powers in a good way.[96]

The incontinent man, in the light of Aquinas's analysis of volition, no longer acts as he does solely because of an intellectual defect—the state of being "in ignorance" *(ignorans)* of the "particular premise." Aquinas supplements that Aristotelian tenet. That state of ignorance is itself willful; the incontinent action is done not inculpably "from ignorance" *(propter ignoratiam)* but "in ignorance" *(ignorans),* the latter being a culpable state that could and should have been avoided—a vincible ignorance, to use the medieval qualification (IaIIae, q. 74, a. 1, ad 2).[97] Here, then, is Aquinas's new emphasis in distinguishing the incontinent from the continent man: by volitionally consenting to passion, which consent *follows upon* an erroneous judgment of reason, the incontinent man makes a bad choice in regard to the singular action in which he is engaged.[98] Aquinas makes a salient comment about the demons that is applicable to humans: "rage and concupiscence signify both the deviation of the [demon's] will from right intellectual or rational judgment and the ignorance that pertains not to speculation but to choice, in reference to which every evil-doer is ignorant."[99] The *incontinens* chooses to be in a state of ignorance by freely choosing to follow rather than to resist the inordinate inclinations of his sensible appetite.

The passions make it easy to occlude the rational judgment and choice that should follow from the agent's general moral principles.[100] No doubt, Aquinas often speaks elliptically, as though the incontinent agent directly consents to the passions. But the passions cannot directly affect the will except through the mediation of an intelligible object. Unless one is prepared to set aside the whole moral psychology of the

95. ". . . et ideo quod homo actu bene agat, contingit ex hoc quod homo habet bonam voluntatem" (*ST* IaIIae.56.3).

96. See *De virtutibus in communi* 7 ad 2, ed. Odetto, 725a.

97. See *ST* IaIIae.77.7 ad 2: "Sed passio causat ignorantiam iuris in particulari, dum impedit applicationem communis scientiae ad particularem actum. Quam quidem passionem ratio repellere potest. . . ."

98. See *De veritate* 24.12, ed. Leon., 22/3: 716a, ll. 295–6: ". . . peccatum in ipsa voluntate perficitur ante operis executionem per solum consensum"; *ST* Ia.83.3: ". . . iudicium est quasi conclusio et determinatio consilii. Determinatur autem consilium, primo quidem per sententiam rationis, et secundo per acceptationem appetitus."

99. ". . . furor et concupiscentia important obliquitatem voluntatis a recto judicio intellectus vel rationis; et ignorantiam non speculationis, sed electionis, secundum quam omnis malus est ignorans" (*In Sent.* 2.7.2.1 sol., ed. Mandonnet, 2: 187).

100. See *De malo* 3.9 ad 3, ed. Leon., 23: 87a, ll. 230–34: ". . . voluntas movetur secundum exigentiam boni apprehensi; sed quod hoc particulare appetibile apprehendatur ut bonum secundum rationis iudicium, impeditur interdum per passionem. . . ."

Prima pars, one cannot embrace the view that freedom is found in some rationally unmotivated spontaneity of the will. If it is to remain a voluntary human act, every choice, including the choice to succumb to passion, has a rational motivation;[101] the incontinent agent, unlike the temporarily or permanently insane man who is unable to exercise free judgment *(liberum arbitrium),* is not just swept off his feet.[102] Of course, the rational motivation of an incontinent choice is, spurious. The *incontinens* succumbs inasmuch as he assents to a false practical judgment prescribing that here and now it is good to follow the lead of his disordered passions.[103]

5. Contingent Choice: Intellect and Will

The incontinent agent is always moved, "in the order of formal causality or specification," by what his intellect proposes as at least an apparent good.[104] Aquinas, however, carefully notes (*ST* IaIIae, q. 9, a. 1, ad 1) that the intellect does not always move the will *ex necessitate.* From the standpoint of its formal object, truth, the intellect is necessarily moved only by a first principle, a proposition that is "always and necessarily true" (q. 10, a. 2, ad 2), or a conclusion that can be demonstrated to follow necessarily from a first principle. In regard to a contingent object, a proposition that cannot be deductively inferred from first principles, and therefore can be true or false, the intellect is moved contingently.[105] The formal object of the will, the "good in general" *(bonum commune),* can only be completely instantiated in a perfect good, the possession of which is happiness. Happiness and its constituent goods, those things that we desire by nature, are necessary objects of the will; they are not subject to free choice. But any good that is imperfect can be judged, from one angle or another, to be somehow defective; so judged, the imperfect intelligible good does not necessitate the will. Depending on how the imperfect good is viewed, we can choose or reject it.[106]

Although in Aquinas's later discussions of free choice the will has a

101. See *ST* IaIIae.77.3 ad 3: ". . . in potestate quidem voluntatis est assentire vel non assentire his in quae passio inclinat. . . ."

102. See *ST* IaIIae.77.8 ad 3: ". . . ratio non semper in suo actu totaliter a passione impeditur: unde remanet ei liberum arbitrium. . . ."

103. See *ST* Ia.82.4 ad 3: "Omnem enim voluntatis motum necesse est quod praecedat apprehensio . . ."; IaIIae.10.3: ". . . inquantum scilicet homo aliqualiter dispositus per passionem, iudicat aliquid esse conveniens et bonum quod extra passionem existens non iudicaret."

104. See, e.g., *ST* IaIIae.9.6 ad 3: ". . . homo per rationem determinat se ad volendum hoc vel illud, quod est vere bonum vel apparens bonum."

105. See *ST* Ia.82.2.

106. See *De veritate* 23.4; *ST* Ia.60.2; *De malo* 3.3; *De malo* 6.

more prominent role, this principle continues to be valid: "The whole root of freedom is grounded in reason."[107] However, the enduring centrality of this latter doctrine, in the wake of Lottin's insistent challenge, remains contested.[108] Still, there is no textual indication that Aquinas, when discussing *peccatum ex infirmitate,* changed his mind about the will's subordination to the intellect.[109] *De malo,* q. 3, a. 9, ad 7 reiterates the doctrine that every act of virtue or sin results from a "quasi-syllogistic deduction," and distinguishes the syllogisms of the continent from the incontinent agent exactly as in the *Sententia Libri Ethicorum.* Even in the much discussed sixth question of *De malo,*[110] there is no absolute spontaneity or exercise of the human will, no choice made radically independent of the intellect's prior deliberations and judgment, by which the intellect formally determines the object of the will's acts: "the will moves itself [freely] by deliberation" about contingent alternatives. God, not the human will, halts the *per se impossible,* infinite regression of such paired acts.[111] Unless passion has rendered them nonvoluntary or

107. See *De veritate* 24.2, ed. Leon., 22/3: 685b, ll. 92–100: ". . . totius libertatis radix est in ratione constituta." Cf. ibid. 24.5, ed. Leon., 22/3: 693b, ll. 67–69: ". . . secundum hoc enim libero arbitrio movemur quod libero arbitrio moveri eligimus. . . ." See also *ST* IaIIae.17.1 ad 2.

108. For a recent rehearsal of the issues, cf. David M. Gallagher, "Free Choice and Free Judgment in Thomas Aquinas," *Archiv für Geschichte der Philosophie* 76 (1994): 247–77; Daniel Westberg, "Did Aquinas Change His Mind about the Will?" *The Thomist* 58 (1994): 41–60. Gallagher shares Lottin's concerns about the early Aquinas's alleged intra-psychic or "intellectual determinism" (see above, note 34); Gallagher, but not Westberg, discovers in the later texts (the *Prima secundae* and *De malo,* q. 6) that "the will comes to have control over the specification of its own act"—presumably apart from any prior, "necessitating" rational, reflexive judgment—by exercising control over "the intellect's consideration of it" (268). In support of this claim, Gallagher distinguishes an intellectual *consideratio* (the term is used in *ST* IaIIae.10.2 c) from the judgment that actually determines the choice *(iudicium electionis).* Gallagher acknowledges (269) that "consideration," in one sense, is indistinguishable from deliberation, but then advances—in terms that seem to conflate the two faculties—that "the decisive consideration of the object occurs in the choice itself" (269). Cf. *ST* IIaIIae.53.4: "Et ideo consideratio maxime pertinet ad iudicium."

109. See *ST* IaIIae.10.3: "Inquantum ergo ratio manet libera et passioni non subiecta, intantum voluntatis motus qui manet, non ex necessitate tendit ad hoc ad quod passio inclinat."

110. Torrell, *Saint Thomas Aquinas,* 1: 201–5, 336, argues that the *De malo* was published in two stages: 1270, qq. 1–15; 1272, q. 16. Question 6 was written shortly *before ST* IaIIae, qq. 9–10.

111. See *De malo* 6, ed. Leon., 23: 149a–b, ll. 361–410: ". . . manifestum est quod uoluntas mouetur a seipsa: sicut enim mouet alias potentias, ita et se ipsam mouet. . . . uoluntas se consilio moueat. . . . Set cum uoluntas non semper uoluerit consiliari, necesse est quod ab aliquo moueatur ad hoc quod uelit consiliari; et si quidem a seipsa, necesse est iterum quod motum uoluntatis precedat consilium et consilium precedat actus uoluntatis; et cum hoc in infinitum procedere non possit, necesse est ponere quod quantum ad primum motum uoluntatis moueatur uoluntas cuiuscumque non semper actu uolentis ab aliquo exteriori, cuius instinctu uoluntas uelle incipiat. . . . id quod primo mouet uoluntatem et intellectum sit aliquid supra uoluntatem et intellectum, scilicet Deus." Cf. *ST* Ia.82.4 ad 3: ". . . non

habit predetermined, choices are usually preceded by deliberation and always by judgment,[112] and this holds true reflexively when one "judges judgments" and, as it were, "draws back" from choosing by making a second-order "free judgment" *(liberum arbitrium)* not actually to choose what one first judged the best thing to do.[113] Deliberation is what allows man to be the master of his own acts including willing.[114]

A Thomist phenomenology of deliberation and choice, one that pays great attention to the self-reflection of the intellectual and volitional powers and the mutual inclusion of their acts,[115] could fill in the introspective details of Aquinas's rather bare logical outline. Anyone attempting to do so might well recall the remark of the illustrious sixteenth-century Dominican commentator Cardinal Thomas de Vio, "Cajetanus," who observed (when commenting on *ST* Ia, q. 19, a. 1) that the will is a "difficult mystery" *(arduum arcanum)*.[116]

6. Continence and Temperance

Nonetheless, Aquinas argues for and does not merely assert his "mysterious" conception of the human will.[117] In the economy of this paper, however, I shall omit the arguments and merely reiterate three of the conclusions that Aquinas reaches: that (1) the will is an appetitive power whose

---

oportet procedere in infinitum, sed statur in intellectu sicut in primo. Omnem enim voluntatis motum necesse est quod praecedat apprehensio, sed non omnem apprehensionem praecedit motus voluntatis; sed principium consiliandi et intelligendi est aliquod intellectivum principium altius intellectu nostro, quod est Deus. . . ." See also *ST* IaIIae.109.2 ad 2.

112. *ST* IaIIae.14.4 ad 2: ". . . quando iudicium vel sententia manifesta est absque inquisitione, non requiritur consilii inquisitio." Cf. *De veritate* 24.12, ed. Leon., 22/3: 716b, ll. 347–8: ". . . quia habenti habitum iam est in eius electione finis determinatus. . . ."

113. See *De veritate* 24.2, ed. Leon., 22/3: 685b, ll. 92–100: "Iudicium autem est in potestate iudicantis secundum quod potest de suo iudicio iudicare de eo enim quod est in nostra potestate, possumus iudicare. Iudicare autem de iudicio suo est solius rationis quae super actum suum reflectitur, et cognoscit habitudines rerum de quibus iudicat et per quas iudicat; unde totius libertatis radix est in ratione constituta."

114. See *ST* IaIIae.109.2 ad 2: ". . . homo est dominus suorum actuum, et volendi et non volendi, propter deliberationem rationis, quae potest flecti ad unam partem vel ad aliam."

115. See *In Sent.* 1.17.1.5 ad 3, ed. Mandonnet, 1: 406: ". . . potentiae immateriales reflectuntur super sua objecta; quia intellectus intelligit se intelligere, et similiter voluntas vult se velle et diligere"; *ST* Ia.16.4 ad 1: ". . . voluntas et intellectus mutuo se includunt, nam intellectus intelligit voluntatem, et voluntas vult intellectum intelligere"; IaIIae.17.1: ". . . actus voluntatis et rationis supra se invicem possunt ferri, prout scilicet ratio ratiocinatur de volendo, et voluntas vult ratiocinari; contingit actum voluntatis praeveniri ab actu rationis, et e converso"; *De veritate* 22.12, ed. Leon., 22/3: 642b, ll. 109–11: ". . . intellectus cum intelligit voluntatem velle, accipit in seipso rationem volendi."

116. See *ST* Ia.19.1, ed. Leon. 4, *Commentaria in Summam theologicam D. Thomae*, 232a, II.

117. For a close examination of these relatively few texts, see Lawrence Dewan, O.P., "The Real Distinction between Intellect and Will," *Angelicum* 57 (1980): 557–93.

every act is always consequent upon the intellect's act but, nonetheless, a power really distinct from intellect and from the essence of the intellectual soul that is the subject of both powers;[118] (2) the will is the agent that moves all other powers, intellect included, to act;[119] and (3) only the will, or some power moved by the will, is the subject of those virtues which, since they not only capacitate but actually enable the agent rightly to use the capacity, are unconditionally called "virtues."[120] These three conclusions are germane to interpreting everything that Aquinas says about how continence moderates the will of the concupiscent agent.[121]

Understanding the choices of both the virtuous as well as the vicious man calls for notable precision about the conceptual distinction between speculative and practical reason, and the sometimes simultaneous but always real mutual interaction and reflection *(reflexio)* of reason and will.[122] Aquinas, in keeping with the doctrine that the operation of intellect is absolutely prior to will, allows that the *continens* is first moved by reason, inasmuch as it is speculative intellect that first apprehends the basic ends of human action. But speculative reason as such is not ordered to action, and the operation of practical reason, which is ordered to action, presupposes the will.[123] To act in accordance with practical reason—that is, to make virtuous or prudent choices about means—one must not only know, but also actually desire to attain, the ends that speculative intellect has apprehended.[124] A similar analysis can be applied to prudence. Prudence is an intellectual virtue, but its principle or starting point is in the will—that is, prudential deliberation presupposes the end to which the will tends. In order for the will to remain directed toward the right ends, it must control concupiscence, the appetite for sensible pleasure *(delectatio):* one must be temperate or at least continent.[125]

Aquinas locates the virtue of temperance in the concupiscible power.[126] The *vis concupiscibilis* is the first of the two specific powers, each of

118. See *De veritate* 22.10; *ST* Ia.59.2; 80.1.

119. See *ST* Ia.82.4; IaIIae.9.1.

120. See *ST* IaIIae.56.3.

121. See *ST* IaIIae.78.1.

122. See *ST* Ia.82.4: ". . . hae potentiae suis actibus invicem se includunt: quia intellectus intelligit voluntatem velle, et voluntas vult intellectum intelligere." See also note 115.

123. See *De virtutibus in communi* 7 ad 1, ed. Odetto, 725a.

124. See *ST* IaIIae.58.5 ad 1: ". . . ratio, secundum quod est apprehensiva finis, praecedit appetitum finis; sed appetitus finis praecedit rationem ratiocinantem ad eligendum ea quae sunt ad finem, quod pertinet ad prudentiam."

125. See *ST* IaIIae.56.3; 56.4 ad 4; *De virtutibus in communi* 4 ad 10, ed. Odetto, 719a; ibid., a. 7 ad 2 (725a).

126. See *ST* Ia.59.4 ad 3: "Temperantia autem, secundum quod est virtus humana, est circa concupiscentias delectabilium sensibilium, quae pertinent ad vim concupiscibilem."

which is aimed at a different particular good,[127] of the generic appetitive power *sensualitas*. The defining object of the concupiscible power is the sensible good and bad,[128] which considered by itself *(absolute)*—as received in the primary modality in which good or bad can be sensed—is pleasure and pain.[129] When temperance is instantiated in the concupiscible appetite, that sense appetite becomes "rectified"—moderated to the point that the power habitually follows the judgment of prudential reason, and thus desires only what the latter determines to be the medium between excessive and deficient desires and fears. The continent man, however, still is under the sway of excessive desires for sensible pleasures and excessive fears of sensible pains. It follows that the subject in which the virtue of *continentia* inheres is not the concupiscible power, but the will, since the former remains disordered by its passions.[130]

As a spiritual power that does not operate through a bodily organ, the will is not the subject of any passions;[131] the latter always involve some sort of bodily changes.[132] Aquinas, however, distinguishes corporeal from psychic passions *(passiones corporales vs. animales)*.[133] The distinc-

127. See *In Sent.* 3.17.1.1 ql. 3 ad 4, ed. Moos, 3: 533: ". . . obiectum appetitus sensibilis non est bonum simpliciter, sed est bonum particulare." The second subpower or species of sense appetite is the irascible *(vis irascibilis)* whose defining object is the sensible good or bad considered under the formality *(sub ratio)* of being somehow difficult *(arduus)* either to attain or ward off: see *SLE* 2.5 [n. 293], ed. Leon., 47/1: 91a, ll. 76–77; *ST* Ia.81.2 ad 1.

128. See *ST* Ia.81.2; IaIIae.30.1 ad 3: "Appetere autem aliquid sub ratione boni delectabilis secundum sensum, quod proprie est concupiscere, pertinet ad vim concupiscibilem"; 30.2: ". . . bonum delectabile secundum sensum est communiter obiectum concupiscibilis."

129. See *ST* IaIIae.23.1: ". . . obiectum potentiae concupiscibilis est bonum vel malum sensibile simpliciter acceptum, quod est delectatio vel dolorosum."

130. See *ST* Ia.35.2. For the subject of continence, see also note 70 above. The will is the intellectual appetite not for some particular good, whether intelligible or sensible, but for the good in general *(bonum commune)*: see *ST* Ia.59.4. When applied to the will, terms used to describe the passions—love *(amor)*, concupiscence *(concupiscentia)*, abhorence *(abominatio)*, joy *(gaudium)*, sadness *(tristitita)*, and the like—should be understood to be simple affects *(simplices affectus)*, that is, simple volitional acts that arise, not from an external agent affecting the soul, but from the will itself; see *ST* Ia.59.4 ad 2; 82.5 ad 1. Cf. *In Sent.* 3.15.2.1 ql. 2 sol., ed. Moos, 3: 486: "In appetitu autem intellectivo, est adhuc plus de ratione passionis, quia voluntas movetur a re secundum quod est bona vel mala, quae sunt conditiones rei. . . ."

131. The delight or joy *(gaudium)* in the intellectual appetite that follows upon sheer intellectual apprehension of truth, whether in regard to goods or evils, has no precise passion contrary to it; sadness *(tristitia)* arises from understanding something that is not itself directly evil or harmful to the intellect understanding it but to man, and to which, therefore, the will is averse; see *ST* IaIIae.23.4; *De veritate* 26.3 ad 6.

132. See *ST* Ia.20.1 ad 1: "Sic igitur actus appetitus sensitivi, inquantum habent transmutationem corporalem annexam, passiones dicuntur: non autem actus voluntatis."

133. Aquinas also distinguishes—in regard to their causes and how they are apprehended—exterior bodily delight *(delectatio)* and pain *(dolor)* from interior psychic joy *(gaudium)* and sadness *(tristitia)*, see *ST* IaIIae.35.7. Delight *(delectatio)* and pain *(dolor)* are "*passiones*

tion between corporeal and psychic passions contributes importantly to an understanding of incontinence, which Aquinas does not regard as a case of reason being simply overwhelmed by raw bodily passions.[134] A corporeal passion is one that begins in the alteration of a bodily organ and terminates in the sensible appetitive power of the embodied soul-form. A psychic passion begins interiorly, within the soul's apprehensive and appetitive powers whose operation causes some bodily transformation. Psychic or interiorly originated passions prove to be more potent and morally significant; they are subject to the will.[135]

7. Incontinence and Original Sin

Aquinas emphasizes the psychic origin of passions more than their corporeal instantiation: using hylemorphic terminology, the *passiones corporales* of bodily organs are the matter for the formal *passiones animales* of the soul.[136] Nonetheless, the psychic passions themselves are psychosomatic: neither purely sensible nor purely intellectual in character.[137]

---

corporales" in the concupiscible power; they result from sensibly apprehending the changes occurring in the body's sense organs. Pain is a passion caused by a bodily injury—getting cut or burned—that is apprehended primarily by the sense of touch; see *De veritate* 26.3. Cf. *De veritate* 26.4 ad 4: pain *(dolor),* strictly speaking, is not a passion because it is only the apprehension of an injury solely in the body, whereas sadness *(tristitia)* is apprehended in the appetitive power. The contrary of *concupiscentia animalis* is *fuga* or *abominatio.*

134. Joy and sadness are interior "*passiones animales*"—psychic passions caused by an interior apprehension that directly affects the concupiscible power itself and through it brings about some bodily transformation. See *In Sent.* 3.15.2.3 ql. 2 sol., ed. Moos, 3: 497: ". . . ratio tristitiae incipit in apprehensione et terminatur in affectione. Unde dolor est in sensu sicut in subjecto, sed tristitia in appetitu. Ex quo patet quod tristitia est passio animalis, sed dolor est magis passio corporalis."

135. See *ST* Ia.81.3 ad 3: ". . . sensus exteriores indigent ad suos actus exterioribus sensibilibus, quibus immutentur, quorum praesentia non est in potestate rationis. Sed vires interiores, tam appetitivae quam apprehensivae, non indigent exterioribus rebus. Et ideo subduntur imperio rationis, quae potest non solum instigare vel mitigare affectus appetitivae virtutis, sed etiam formare imaginativae virtutis phantasmata."

136. See *ST* IIIa.15.3: "Passione autem animali pati dicitur anima secundum operationem quae vel est propria animae, vel est principalius animae quam corporis . . . propriissime dicuntur passiones animae affectiones appetitus sensitivi. . . ."

137. Cf. *In Sent.* 3.15.2.2 ql. 1 sol., ed. Moos, 3: 490: ". . . hic quaeritur de tristitia secundum quod est passio animalis in parte sensitiva. . . ." The objects of the concupiscible passions are the differentiated pleasures *(delectabilia)* of sex, or the table, or games (*ST* IaIIae.60.5). *Gaudium* is a species of sensible *delectatio* (*ST* IaIIae.35.2), but it is an interior passion which arises in the concupiscible power from satisfying a rationally apprehended psychic desire *(desiderium)* or what Aquinas labels *'concupiscentia animalis,'* see *ST* IaIIae.31.3 ad 2. The latter, which is to be distinguished from the body's natural concupiscence for what sustains it, namely, food and sex, is also called *'concupiscentia spiritualis'* (*ST* IaIIae.77.5); not tied to the sense of touch, it is a higher order desire *(desiderium)* for anything that seems delectable to the imagination, such as clothing or money. Similarly, with *tristitia:* one feels sad at hearing about the death of a loved one, but the sensation of

Each one of the concupiscible passions can be morally good or bad depending upon the object, sensible or intelligible, that gives rise to the psychosomatic perturbation.[138] Reason can deliberate about the object of a passion, whether the object draws the agent to something unreasonable or makes him flee from something reasonable. If it is discordant with reason, the object of a passion is morally bad:[139] for example, being envious (feeling sorrowful) that someone else has surpassed me by attaining a good that I desire and regard as necessary for my own excellence and honor.[140]

Both corporeal/exterior and psychic/interior passions are in the sensible appetitive power. Temperance is the virtue that rectifies in the sense power itself all the passions of the concupiscible appetite.[141] The temperate person's passions are in accordance with reason: he or she feels intellectual delight or joy *(gaudium)* only in what is truly (rationally), not just apparently (sensibly) good, and sadness *(tristitia)* only in what is truly, and not just apparently evil.[142] Continence is the volitional habit that restrains the will from going along with the psychic motions *(passiones animales)* of the concupiscible power when it would be morally bad to do so. Continence, however, is an imperfect or quasi-virtue;[143] it is a psychic (volitional) habit that does not fully moderate or rectify the concupiscible power.[144] Nonetheless, its absence is morally deleterious: lacking continence, the will of the incontinent man easily succumbs to the vehement passions that assail it.

Aquinas, however, confronts quite a different problem than Aristotle in estimating the moderating effects of the virtue of continence: Thomistic man is postlapsarian man with a corrupted human nature.[145] In the prelapsarian state—the state of "original justice"—man was born temper-

---

sadness is not caused by painful motions in the ear drum. One feels sad because one imagines or remembers the loss of a friend or family member.

138. See *De malo* 10.2 ad 2, ed. Leon., 23: 22a, ll. 191–4: ". . . quando motus tristitie ex deliberatione rationis procedit, tunc non solum est sensualitatis set etiam rationis, et ideo potest esse peccatum mortale."

139. See *ST* IaIIae.24.4 ad 2: ". . . passiones quae sunt per recessum a bono, et per accessum ad malum, sunt malae."

140. See *ST* IaIIae.24.4; IIaIIae.36.1; 158.1.

141. See *ST* IIaIIae.155.3. Temperance, which rectifies the concupiscible power, is inherent therein; see IIaIIae.155.4; 58.5 ad 2.

142. See *In Sent.* 3.26.1.4, ed. Moos, 3: 825–6; *ST* IaIIae.25.4. The four principal passions are, in the concupiscible appetite, joy and sorrow; in the irascible appetite, hope and fear; see *ST* IaIIae.31.3 ad 1; ibid., ad 2; *De veritate* 26.3 ad 9.

143. See *ST* IaIIae.58.3 ad 2.

144. See *ST* IIaIIae.143.1: "Primus quidem est motus voluntatis commotae ex impetu passionis: et hunc motum refrenat *continentia,* ex qua fit ut licet homo immoderatas concupiscentias patiatur, voluntas tamen non vincitur."

145. See *ST* IaIIae.85.3.

ate; his concupiscible appetite was perfectly subordinated to reason.[146] After the fall of Adam, original justice was lost; man's appetitive powers, both rational and sensible, were no longer harmoniously cooperating with reason but became corrupted. Sensible desire, however restrained by temperance, is subject to the *fomes* or disordered inclinations that are a residual effect of the Adamic or original sin.[147] Sensual desire is natural but, in postlapsarian man, the *fomes* now inclines concupiscence *contra naturam,* that is, to what is contrary to reason.[148] In short, we find evil easy and good difficult to do. To be sure, if we are aware of them in advance, we can restrain, by an act of will, some but not all of our disordered sensual inclinations: in Aquinas's example (*ST* IaIIae, q. 74, a. 3, ad 2), we can will to divert our thoughts from bodily pleasures to scientific theorizing, only to find ourselves thinking how our discoveries can make us rich and famous. No matter how morally alert or virtuous we are, disordered concupiscible desires are unavoidable; some of them simply arise, spontaneously and without any premeditation on our part.

Neither reason nor knowledge alone can make the children of Adam either temperate or continent.[149] In the present state of fallen nature, where concupiscence perdures, grace is required to attain the natural as well as the supernatural good. Although it is possible to acquire naturally the virtues that orient man to happiness in the earthly city, the acquired virtues by themselves do not enable us to achieve in any complete way the natural human good.[150] The acquired virtues enable us to avoid, generally but not always, moral evils.[151] Without grace, neither the

146. However, the gift of original justice, not the *virtus principiorum naturalium,* kept the sensible powers harmoniously subordinated to reason; see *De veritate* 25.7, ed. Leon., 22/3: 734b, l. 63.

147. See *ST* IIIa.27.3: ". . . fomes nihil aliud est quam inordinata concupiscentia sensualis appetitus, habitualis tamen. . . ."

148. See *ST* IIIa.15.2: "Ad rationem fomitis pertinet inclinatio sensualis appetitus in id quod est contra rationem."

149. See *ST* IIaIIae.156.3 ad 2: "ad sanationem incontinentis non sufficit sola cognitio, sed requiritur interius auxilium gratiae concupiscentiam mitigantis. . . ."

150. See *ST* IaIIae.109.2: "Sed in statu naturae corruptae etiam deficit homo ab hoc quod secundum suam naturam potest, ut non possit totum huiusmodi bonum implere per sua naturalia." Cf. *In Sent.* 2.28.1.1, ed. Mandonnet, 2: 719; *De veritate* 24.14: the distinction drawn in these texts is between doing what is naturally good, without any suggestion that anything is lacking, and what is supernaturally meritorious; the latter but not the former requires grace. *In Sent.* 2.28.1.2, ed. Mandonnet, 2: 723 allows that mortal sin may be permanently avoided without grace, an opinion that Aquinas thereafter abandoned; cf. Hoffmann, 232, n. 52. *ST* IIaIIae.23.7 refers to the exercise of the natural virtues without supernatural charity as "imperfect" since they are not ordered to man's true final end, the enjoyment of God.

151. See *De virtutibus in communi* 9 ad 5, ed. Odetto, 732a: ". . . virtus acquisita facit declinare a peccato non semper, sed ut in pluribus. . . . Non enim per eas vitatur peccatum infidelitatis, et alia peccata quae virtutibus infusis opponuntur."

reason nor the will of fallen man is rightly ordered to his final end, God. Preconceived ends and preexisting habits, our "character," make it easy to sin—to turn to and love some inordinate object as though it were the final end—especially when quick decisions are called for.[152] Once in mortal sin, the sinner becomes inured with his evil condition and sins ever more easily until such moment as divine grace and the fear of some evil prompts him to deliberate and turn himself back to God. In our present state, however, habitual grace first heals—albeit imperfectly—the mind and will but not yet the carnal or sensual appetite. With a mind and will restored by grace, post-Adamic man can avoid all mortal but not every venial sin.[153] The latter continue to arise from disordered sensuality; inordinate desires can be repelled one by one, but not all of them since we cannot constantly be on guard.

St. Paul is the case in point. Aquinas thought that St. Paul was temperate;[154] the saint, by chastising his flesh, had tamed the vehement desires that afflict the continent man but even he had not completely eliminated the disorderly movement of concupiscence in the sense appetite.[155] St. Paul, like everyone else, remained subject to the *fomes*. Aquinas propounds that it would have taken a miracle for him or any other offspring of Adam to be entirely freed of the residual effects of original sin.[156] That miracle, it seems, was reserved to the Blessed Virgin Mary.[157]

> The Blessed Virgin Mary, however, was sanctified with such a wealth of grace that thenceforth she was preserved free from all sin, and not only from mortal sin, but also from venial sin. Moreover venial sin sometimes creeps up on us unawares, owing to the fact that an inordinate motion of concupiscence or of some other passion arises prior to the advertence of the mind, yet in such a way

152. See *In Sent.* 2.28.1.2, ed. Mandonnet, 2: 722; *De veritate* 24.12, ed. Leon., 22/3: 716a, ll. 301–8; *De virtutibus in communi* 10 ad 4, ed. Odetto, 736a–b.

153. On this point, there seems to be a difference between Aquinas and contemporary exegetes on the persistently radical character of human sin; cf. Fitzmyer, *Romans*, 473: "Even the Christian, if judged by the Law, could be shown to be a sinner, someone who falls under God's wrath." For a similar view, from a Protestant exegete, see C. E. B. Cranfield, *Romans*, 2 vols. (Edinburgh: T. & T. Clark, 1975), 1: 344.

154. Norman Kretzmann argues that, as Aquinas interpreted Rom 7:15, speaking as a man "under grace," was "certainly not [making] a confession of incontinence" but merely recognizing "the inescapable moral trouble that is part of the human condition," viz., the spontaneous movement of disordered concupiscence in the sensory appetite with which even the man "under grace" must contend. See his "Warring against the Law of My Mind: Aquinas on Romans 7," in *Philosophy and the Christian Faith*, ed. Thomas V. Morris (Notre Dame: University of Notre Dame Press, 1988), 172–95, at 187.

155. See *De virtutibus cardinalibus* 1 ad 6, ed. P. A. Odetto (*Quaestiones disputatae*, 9th ed. [Rome and Turin: Marietti, 1953]), 816a.

156. See *De virtutibus in communi* 10 ad 14, ed. Odetto, 737a–b: ". . . passiones ad malum inclinantes non totaliter tolluntur neque per virtutem acquisitam neque per virtutem infusam, nisi forte miraculose. . . ."

157. See *De veritate* 25.7 ad 1, ed. Leon., 23/2: 744a, ll. 78–79.

that the first motions are called sins. Hence we conclude that the Blessed Virgin Mary never committed a venial sin, for she did not experience such inordinate motions of passion.[158]

Of course, in contemplating this miracle, Aquinas's understanding of why man has a "weak will" and how it is cured, by divine grace, entirely transcends the trajectory of Aristotle's account.

158. *Compendium theologiae* 1.224, trans. Cyril Vollert (St. Louis and London: Herder, 1952), 264; ed. Leon., 42: 175b, ll. 52–62: ". . . sed beata Virgo Maria tanta habundantia gratie sanctificata fuit, ut deinceps ab omni peccato conseruaretur immunis, non solum mortali sed etiam ueniali. Et quia ueniale peccatum interdum ex surreptione contingit, ex hoc scilicet quod aliquis inordinatus concupiscentie motus insurgit, aut alterius passionis, preueniens rationem, ratione cuius primi motus dicuntur esse peccata, consequens est, quia beata Virgo Maria numquam uenialiter peccauit, quod inordinatos passionum motus non senserit."

6 Henry of Ghent's Voluntarist Account of Weakness of Will

TOBIAS HOFFMANN

Although Henry of Ghent is generally not counted among the major figures in the history of philosophy, he deserves the attention of those interested in the problem of weakness of will since he arguably offers one of the most important contributions to this problem in the Middle Ages.[1] In his own time, Henry enjoyed a high reputation as one of the leading masters in theology. He became a regent master (i.e., ordinary professor) of theology at the University of Paris in 1275 or 1276.[2] As a secular cleric he had unlimited tenure; his tenure lasted sixteen years, which for Parisian standards of the time was very long. During this time, he disputed Quodlibetal questions up to twice a year, for a total number of fifteen times. In addition, he wrote a monumental *Summa (quaestiones ordinariae)*, which remained unfinished. Both works were highly influential, existing in numerous manuscripts and being printed several times in the sixteenth and seventeenth centuries.[3] During the years after

Research for this paper was done at the Erasmus Institute of the University of Notre Dame, thanks to a generous fellowship. I also thank John Connolly and Timothy Noone for helpful comments.

1. Henry's account of *incontinentia* has been the object of recent studies. See Theo Kobusch, "Willensschwäche und Selbstbestimmung des Willens: Zur Kritik am abendländischen Intellektualismus bei Heinrich von Gent und in der franziskanischen Philosophie," in *The Problem of Weakness of Will in Medieval Thought,* ed. Tobias Hoffmann, Jörn Müller, and Matthias Perkams (Leuven, Paris, and Dudley, Mass.: Peeters, 2006), 247–62; and Jörn Müller, "Willensschwäche im Voluntarismus? Das Beispiel Heinrichs von Gent," *Archiv für Geschichte der Philosophie* 89 (2007): 1–29.

2. For Henry's biography, see Matthias Laarmann, *Deus primum cognitum: Die Lehre von Gott als Ersterkanntem des menschlichen Intellekts bei Heinrich von Gent († 1293),* Beiträge zur Geschichte der Philosophie und Theologie des Mittelalter, Neue Folge 52 (Münster: Aschendorff, 1999), 18–32. For his works, see ibid., 33–52. According to Laarmann, Henry was regent master of theology from 1275 to 1291/92; see ibid., 25. Robert Wielockx indicates slightly different dates, i.e., 1276–1292/93; see his "Henry of Ghent," in *A Companion to Philosophy in the Middle Ages,* ed. Jorge J. E. Gracia and Timothy B. Noone (Oxford: Blackwell, 2003), 296–304, at 296.

3. A critical edition, coordinated by Raymond Macken, is currently in progress: *Henrici de Gandavo Opera Omnia,* Ancient and Medieval Philosophy, ser. 2 (Leuven: Leuven Uni-

Thomas Aquinas's death (1274), Henry was one of Thomas's main critics. He was more sophisticated than Thomas's early critics in the Franciscan order.[4] He also had more institutional influence than they. According to his own witness, Henry was one of the masters of theology consulted by the bishop of Paris, Étienne Tempier, before he issued the famous condemnations of March 1277.[5] Henry's thought, in particular his moral psychology and ethic, had a great impact on late thirteenth century and fourteenth century thinkers, most notably on John Duns Scotus.

In contemporary usage, "weakness of will" is mostly taken broadly to denote the possibility of acting against one's better judgment. In the narrow sense, it is used to translate the Aristotelian notion of *akrasia* (incontinence), that is, the failure to act according to what one judges best because of passion (*EE* 2.7.1223b7–9). Weakness of will, taken in both senses, plays a prominent role in Henry's thought. In almost every one of his discussions of ethics or action theory he mentions the will's ability to desire or choose contrary to the practical judgment. For this reason, Henry deserves the appellation "voluntarist."[6] Although his voluntarist action theory and ethics significantly depart from Aristotle, Henry claims (at least early in his career) to be a faithful interpreter of Aristotle's ac-

versity Press, 1979ff.). Citations of Henry refer to the critical edition, wherever it is available, with volume number and page number. Otherwise they refer to the Renaissance edition of Jodocus Badius (Paris, 1518; repr., Leuven: Bibliothèque S.J., 1961), with folio page number.

4. The first wave of Franciscan reactions to Aquinas's thought mainly consisted of polemical writings intended to correct the "errors" contained in the *Summa theologiae*. A succinct overview of this so-called correctorium-literature is found in François-Xavier Putallaz, *Insolente liberté*, Vestigia 15 (Paris: Cerf, 1996), 93–126. See also Alexander Brungs, "Intellekt, Wille und Willensschwäche im Korrektorienstreit: Einheit des Menschen vs. Homunculi," in *The Problem of Weakness of Will in Medieval Thought*, 263–82.

5. *Quodl.* 2.9, 6: 66–67. For the condemnations of 1277, see Roland Hissette, *Enquête sur les 219 articles condamnés à Paris le 7 mars 1277*, Philosophes médiévaux 22 (Leuven and Paris: Publications Universitaires-Vander-Oyez, 1977); and David Piché, *La condamnation parisienne de 1277*, nouvelle édition du texte latin, traduction, introduction et commentaires par David Piché avec la collaboration de Claude Lafleur (Paris: Vrin, 1999). For an English translation of the articles, see "Condemnation of 219 Propositions," trans. Ernest L. Fortin and Peter D. O'Neill, in *Medieval Political Philosophy: A Sourcebook*, ed. Ralph Lerner and Muhsin Mahdi (New York: Free Press of Glencoe, 1963), 335–54.

6. The terms "intellectualism" and "voluntarism" originated in nineteenth-century German philosophy. They are now commonly used to distinguish theories that accord the primacy to intellect or to the will, respectively. The meaning of these terms varies since there are different senses of priority in the relation between intellect and will. In this paper, I employ them specifically to denote theories that see in the intellect or in the will, respectively, the ultimate determinants of acts of free decision *(liberum arbitrium)*. For useful analyses of these notions in historical perspective, see Tilman Borsche, "Intellektualismus," in *Historisches Wörterbuch der Philosophie*, ed. Joachim Ritter et al., vol. 4 (Basel and Stuttgart: Schwabe & Co., 1976), 439–44; and Sven K. Knebel, "Voluntarismus," in *Historisches Wörterbuch der Philosophie*, vol. 11 (2001), 1143–45.

count of incontinence. As a matter of fact, Henry develops the first elaborate voluntarist explanation of the Aristotelian notion of *akrasia*.[7] Moreover, we find in Henry what is probably the most extensive examination of incontinence in any Latin medieval text, apart from commentaries on the *Nicomachean Ethics.*

In Henry's action theory, the principal condition for a morally deficient action is not ignorance (as for Socrates) and the main competitors to reason are not passion and bad dispositions (as for Aristotle). What accounts for bad action is above all the will. What originally makes a will to be bad is not defective knowledge and reasoning. Rather, the shortcoming of the will is self-caused. In Henry's eyes, to deny this would imply the denial of *liberum arbitrium* (free decision). Because the will can fail to choose according to the dictate of right reason, it must be strengthened by the moral virtues.

The aim of this paper is to describe the inner logic of Henry's voluntarism and to discuss the problems inherent to it by focusing on his discussions of weakness and strength of will. Henry's account of weakness and strength of will is presented in three steps. Section 1 outlines some basic assumptions of Henry's action theory, particularly his contention that the will's ability to choose contrary to the better judgment is key to free decision. Section 2 is concerned with the relation between ignorance, passion, and moral evil. Henry at first engages this problem by discussing incontinence, and returns to it several years later, when examining the compatibility of the anti-intellectualist pronouncements of Tempier's syllabus with the so-called *propositio magistralis,* a rather intellectualist statement that Henry subscribes to by giving it a voluntarist twist. Section 3 discusses strength of will, examining virtues of the will and moral perfection.

This paper is principally based upon Henry's *Quodlibetal questions.* It is here that most of his treatments of action theory and ethics are found. His *Summa* will likewise be taken into account, yet since it does not go beyond the treatise on God, it contains less material pertinent to this paper. The first Quodlibet is particularly important for our topic. It is here that Henry elaborates the key points of his action theory. Later Quod-

7. 'Voluntarist' medieval thinkers, i.e., those who admit that the will does not necessarily choose according to what upon deliberation reason judges to be best, have different intellectual attitudes with regard to the problem of incontinence. Apart from Henry of Ghent, William of Ockham, for example, shows great interest in the philosophical analysis of incontinence, whereas Duns Scotus does not. See Matthias Perkams, "Der schwache Wille: Ockhams Theorie der Unbestimmtheit des Willens als Auseinandersetzung mit dem Problem der Willensschwäche," in *The Problem of Weakness of Will in Medieval Thought,* 305–27; and Tobias Hoffmann, "L'*akrasia* selon Duns Scot," in *Duns Scot à Paris, 1302–2002: Actes du colloque de Paris, 2–4 septembre 2002,* ed. Olivier Boulnois et al. (Turnhout: Brepols, 2004), 487–516.

libets develop these themes further, yet without significantly departing from the early doctrine.

1. Choice against Reason

During his first Quodlibetal disputation, the following question is presented to Henry: "When the intellect proposes to the will a greater good and a lesser good, can the will choose the lesser good?" (question 16).[8] Though this question does not directly concern incontinence, it is analogous to the difficulty that Aristotle discusses in reference to *akrasia:* Can one know what is best and yet choose otherwise? Henry is not concerned with showing whether—or how—one can act against better knowledge. He argues that to deny this possibility entails the denial of free decision *(liberum arbitrium).* What causes a person to act against better knowledge is not ignorance caused by passion, but rather the choice of the will to reject the practical judgment of reason. This explanation lays the foundation for Henry's entire moral thought.

It should be noted from the outset that Henry nowhere attempts to demonstrate that free decision is a reality, except by reductio ad absurdum. Without free decision, he argues, merit, demerit, exhortation, deliberation, and a number of other things that are required for virtue would be meaningless.[9]

Freedom of the Will

Though the question of *Quodlibet* 1.16 concerns the possibility that a person chooses what he or she understands to be the lesser of two goods, for Henry there are two related questions at issue. He reformulates the question twice: (1) whether the will necessarily adheres to the judgment

8. *Quodl.* 1.15 [prologue], 5: 91: "Secunda, utrum, a ratione propositis bono et meliori, possit voluntas eligere minus bonum" ("Secunda" refers to question 16).

9. *Quodl.* 9.5, 13: 121: "Et sic periret liberum arbitrium, et per consequens omnis ratio meriti et demeriti et suasionis ac deliberationis et consiliationis et ceterorum huiusmodi, quae necessaria sunt ad virtutes." See also *Quodl.* 1.17, 5: 127: ". . . a nullo alio agente impellatur [sc. voluntas] ad virtutes et vitia. . . ." For Henry's account of free decision, see Martin W. F. Stone, "Henry of Ghent on Freedom and Human Action," in *Henry of Ghent and the Transformation of Scholastic Thought: Studies in Memory of Jos Descorte,* ed. Guy Guldentops and Carlos Steel, Ancient and Medieval Philosophy, ser. 1, vol. 31 (Leuven: Leuven University Press, 2003), 201–25. See also Jos Decorte, "Der Einfluß der Willenspsychologie des Walter von Brügge OFM auf die Willenspsychologie und Freiheitslehre des Heinrich von Gent," *Franziskanische Studien* 65 (1983): 215–40; and Raymond Macken, "Heinrich von Gent im Gespräch mit seinen Zeitgenossen über die menschliche Freiheit," *Franziskanische Studien* 59 (1977): 125–82. For further references to articles by Macken, see Stone, 202, n. 2.

of reason and (2) whether freedom is guaranteed principally by the intellect or by the will.[10] With regard to these questions, Henry mentions an intellectualist view that he will reject.[11] According to this view, the will cannot deflect from what reason judges to be preferable. There is free decision *(liberum arbitrium)* only because the judgment of reason does not predetermine a single result. Free decision, according to this view, is exclusively founded upon the freedom of reason, which consists of the fact that different possibilities may be examined during the deliberation that leads to the practical judgment. Yet once the practical judgment is attained, the will inevitably adheres to it.[12] Hence the will's freedom to choose is wholly derived from reason's freedom to judge. An example is not given here, but the following one can illustrate this explanation. Being offered the choice of a dessert, a person is free to choose fruit rather than pastry only because reason can discover what speaks in favor of one choice rather than the other. If reason leans toward one option—concretely, not merely generally—the will inevitably chooses accordingly. Henry concludes that had the defenders of this view been asked the same question he was asked, they would have said that the will must necessarily choose what reason judges the greater of two goods.[13]

Henry's own account of free decision is quite different: all reason does, in Henry's view, is to propose two options and to judge which is better, and then the will freely prefers either one. A choice is virtuous if the will freely chooses what reason judges to be preferable.[14] Someone who after deliberation concludes that here and now it is better to eat fruit is still free to choose pastry, yet such a choice would not be virtuous because it is contrary to the judgment of reason.

Henry rejects the intellectualist theory he reports, which reduces the freedom of the will to freedom of reason. His refutation is guided by the

10. *Quodl.* 1.16, 5: 96: "Si autem ponamus seorsum voluntatis appetitum et seorsum rationis iudicium, hoc magis pertinet ad quaestionem, qua quaeritur, an tunc voluntas habeat liberam electionem cum iudicio vel contra iudicium rationis, vel non sed necesse sit eam adhaerere iudicio rationis sive recto sive erroneo." *Quodl.* 1.16, 5: 98: "Circa quod adhuc tota vis quaestionis vertitur, penes quid consistit illa libertas principaliter, an penes intellectum, an penes voluntatem."

11. The anonymous target of Henry's critique has not been identified to date. The adversary's view has certain resemblances to Aquinas's account of free decision (*DV* 24.1–2; *ST* Ia.83.1), but seems more thoroughly intellectualist. See Putallaz, 188–91.

12. *Quodl.* 1.16, 5: 98–101.

13. *Quodl.* 1.16, 5: 101: "Sic dicentes dicerent quod propositis maiori bono et minori iuxta iudicium rationis, non posset voluntas praeeligere minus bonum, sed necesse haberet eligere maius bonum."

14. *Quodl.* 1.16, 5: 104: "Est igitur sciendum quod ad actum electionis concurrit, ex parte intellectus scilicet, duo eligibilia proponere, ex parte voluntatis, alterum alteri praeferre, et si virtuosa sit illa electio, illud praeferre libere quod per consilium rationis iudicatum est esse melius."

conviction that any theory that founds free decision upon the intellect and not upon the will entails intellectual determinism. In support of his refutation, he makes use of an Augustinian thought experiment. In addition, he offers a consideration that excludes in principle that intellect or reason are the cause of freedom. Henry cites *in extenso* a text from Augustine's *De civitate dei,* which he applies to the case at hand:

> Suppose that two men, of precisely similar disposition in mind and body, see the beauty of the same woman's body, and the sight stirs one of them to enjoy her unlawfully, while the other continues unmoved in his decision of chastity. What do we suppose to be the cause of an evil choice in the one and not in the other? What produced that evil will? . . . The mind? Why not the mind of both? For we assumed them to be alike in both mind and body. . . . What other reason could there be than his will, given that their dispositions were precisely the same, in body and mind?[15]

Although Augustine is not concerned here with the problem of the root of free decision in the will or in the intellect, Henry appropriates this quote in this sense. He argues:

> Hence we cannot say that in one man the judgment of reason caused the will to be bad. According to the hypothesis, both men are equally mentally disposed, and therefore, if the judgment of reason had caused the will of one man to be bad, it would have made the will of the other man bad as well. Thus we must assume that over and above the freedom in reason to judge [*libertas arbitrandi*] there is in the will a freedom to choose what is judged [*libertas eligendi arbitratum*], so that the will does not choose with any necessity even what reason judges after deliberation. . . .[16]

15. "Si enim aliqui duo aequaliter affecti animo et corpore uideant unius corporis pulchritudinem, qua uisa unus eorum ad inlicite fruendum moueatur, alter in uoluntate pudica stabilis perseueret, quid putamus esse causae, ut in illo fiat, in illo non fiat uoluntas mala? Quae illam res fecit in quo facta est? . . . An uero animus? cur non utriusque? Ambos enim et animo et corpore aequaliter affectos fuisse praediximus. . . . Vnde, nisi propria uoluntate, ubi eadem fuerat in utroque corporis et animi affectio?" (Augustine, *De civitate Dei* 12.6, CCSL 48: 361, cited by Henry in *Quodl.* 1.16, 5: 101–2). (The discrepancy between the text of Corpus Christianorum and the quotation of Augustine by Henry is insignificant.) The translation, which is slightly modified, is from St. Augustine, *The City of God against the Pagans,* trans. Philip Levine, Loeb Classical Library 414 (Cambridge, Mass.: Harvard University Press; and London: William Heinemann Ltd., 1966), 29.

16. "Non ergo possumus dicere quod illam malam voluntatem fecerit iudicium rationis in uno. Fecisset enim eam eadem ratione in altero, cum aequaliter eos animo affectos fuisse ponamus. Super libertatem ergo arbitrandi in ratione oportet ponere libertatem eligendi arbitratum in voluntate, ut voluntas nulla necessitate eligat etiam quod ratio sententiat . . ." (*Quodl.* 1.16, 5: 102). Henry's position is by no means original. Albert the Great likewise considered the *arbitrium* to be independent of the *iudicium* of reason; see *De homine* 3.1 (Utrum liberum arbitrium . . .) sol., Editio Coloniensis 27/2, forthcoming.

Henry's conclusion goes beyond what Augustine had intended. In the above quote Augustine does not separate reason and will in the way Henry does. More interesting than the exegetical value of this passage is the fact that it reveals what Henry considers most important in free decision, namely, alternative possibilities of action under the exact same bodily and mental conditions in the same external circumstances.

Freedom of the Intellect

Since free decision presupposes alternative possibilities, the free preference of one option over another cannot result from reason's judgment, in Henry's view. Freedom of the will cannot be traced to freedom of reason.[17] Why not? Why does Henry exclude the possibility that reason may have alternative judgments under the same subjective and objective conditions of a given situation? This question leads us to the heart of the matter, that is, to the principal consideration that shapes the voluntaristic outlook of Henry's action theory and ethics.

According to Henry, the causality of intellect and reason, considered apart from the will's free control of understanding and reasoning, is deterministic. Intellect and reason are determined to one activity by their object. Their act is not in their control since they cannot refuse to assent to that which is found to be true:

> If we want to speak of freedom of decision in the proper and strict sense, it is in the will alone and not at all in reason, except insofar as reason is freely moved by the will to investigate different things. Cognitive reason as such is in fact not free. For it is moved by the simple objects of cognition necessarily, and it is not in its power not to apprehend these. Nor is it in its power not to assent to the connection of the [terms in] self-evident first principles and to the [demonstrative] connection [between the principles and] the conclusions. In fact, when a conclusion presents itself to reason by way of a necessary proof, it assents of necessity; when the proof is relatively manifest, it necessarily opines accordingly. . . .[18]

17. "Falsum est ergo quod tota libertas voluntatis accipitur ex parte rationis, immo est etiam ex parte sui, ut possit in contrarium iudicio rationis" (*Quodl.* 1.16, 5: 103).

18. "Unde et si proprie et stricte velimus loqui de electionis libertate, ipsa in sola voluntate est et nullo modo in ratione, nisi quatenus libere movetur ad diversa investiganda, a voluntate. Ratio enim cognitiva inquantum huiusmodi, libera non est. Necessario enim movetur simplicibus apprehensis nec est in eius potestate ea non apprehendere, similiter nec connexioni primorum principiorum per se notorum neque connexioni conclusionum non assentire, quia si conclusio apparet ei medio necessario, assentit de necessitate, si medio apparenti, valde de necessitate assentit opinando. . . ." The text continues: ". . . si debiliter apparenti, necessario assentit dubitando, nisi sit medium probabilius in contrar-

Henry certainly does not deny that reason by itself is indeterminate with regard to apprehending different objects of thought. In which sense does he consider reason's activity to be deterministic? An example may be useful here. Our eyes are indeterminate with regard to everything that appears in the spectrum of light. Yet we cannot see things differently from the way they appear. We cannot decide to see the sky as green or a lawn as blue.[19] Likewise, in Henry's view, the assent or dissent to a proposition is not self-determined by reason.[20]

In light of the deterministic causality of intellect and reason, the alternative is this: if one stipulates that each activity of the will requires a judgment of reason and that the will's choice follows the practical judgment of necessity, one must deny that in the same circumstances a different choice could have been made, for apart from an influence of the will on reason, practical judgments would come about deterministically. Conversely, if one holds that alternative choices are possible under the same circumstances, one must admit that that which determines the choice to be this (and not that) is the will, not reason. Shortly after the passage quoted above, Henry continues:

> Consequently the will does not have at all the source of freedom from reason, but primarily from itself, and because of this, the choice is free. The moral virtues and vices are not in cognitive reason as their subject, not even as their cause and principle, but only as an occasion [for the will's act].[21]

When the will chooses one of two goods, what causes it to prefer one of them are not the characteristics of the object. Nor can one hold that the will's preference is caused by reason unless one admits that the choice is deterministic. Henry concludes that the will's preference for one of

ium, ut omnis sententia rationis de connexo necessitate syllogistica concludatur" (*Quodl.* 1.16, 5: 107–8).

19. This example is my own. Elsewhere, Henry himself uses the example of seeing to support the claim that reason by itself is not free: "Arbitrium vero pertinens ad rationem servile est et nullo modo liberum, quoniam quoad actum simplicis intelligentiae omnino est passiva et determinatur per speciem intelligibilis, ut, ipsa praesente in ipsa secundum actum, non potest per ipsam non intelligere, quemadmodum oculus, praesente visibili in luce et recta oppositione, non impedita, non potest non videre" (*Summa* 45.4, 29: 124).

20. Henry's teaching with regard to the intellect's or reason's deterministic activity is constant throughout his career; see, e.g., *Quodl.* 11.7, 459rO–P. In *Quodl.* 14.5, Henry is more nuanced than in previous texts, arguing that the intellect is free, although it is moved to its act from the outside, contrary to the will which is not determined from without. The intellect's freedom is therefore much inferior to the will's freedom; see 565rB.

21. "Nullo ergo modo voluntas principium libertatis a ratione habet sed a se ipsa primo, et sic electio libera. Virtutes et malitiae morales non tantum non sunt in ratione cognitiva ut in subiecto, sed nec ut in causa et principio, sed solum sicut in occasione" (*Quodl.* 1.16, 5: 108).

the two objects is self-caused.[22] Accordingly, the will can choose what is understood to be the lesser good.[23]

The will's capacity for self-determination does not mean that acts of the will are independent of reason. The will requires the cognition of the intellect in order to elicit its act.[24] Henry carefully avoids in fact the homunculus fallacy, that is, to conceive of the will itself as a rational agent endowed with knowledge and desire, rather than to consider it merely as the appetitive power of a rational agent. There is clear division of labor between intellect and will: the intellect knows for itself and for the will, and the will desires for itself and for the intellect.[25] Intellect and will are not two agents, but the person understands and wills by means of these two powers.[26]

The intellect is thus crucial for the will's choice, but its causality is merely accidental causality, as Henry specifies. Intellect or reason provides the occasion for the choice of the will by presenting to it an object and by offering it a judgment.[27] In his later Quodlibets (*Quodl.* 9.5 and following), Henry describes this accidental causality of the intellect as a causa sine qua non (a necessary condition) of the will's act.[28] In his view, any causality other than accidental causality would undermine free decision.

The denial of any *per se* causality of reason on the will and the em-

22. "In praeeligendo ergo inter aequalia bona alterum, vel minus bonum magis bono, vel bonum ut nunc bono simpliciter, sola voluntas sibi in hoc causa est" (*Quodl.* 1.16, 5: 112).

23. "Dicendum igitur absolute quod bono et meliori proposito potest eligere minus bonum voluntas" (*Quodl.* 1.16, 5: 113).

24. *Quodl.* 1.15, 5: 93: "Absolute igitur dicendum quod voluntatis actionem necessario praecedit cognitio intellectus, sine qua praevia nihil potest velle. . . ." See also *Quodl.* 1.17, 5: 127: "Nihil enim voluntas ipsa cognoscit"; and *Quodl.* 4.22, 139vV: ". . . voluntas ex se caeca est, nec potest circa quicquam moveri amore nisi fuerit prius cognitum."

25. *Quodl.* 14.5, 566rD: ". . . quia sicut intellectus rationaliter sive rationabiliter intelligit sibi et voluntati, sic voluntas rationabiliter vult sibi et intellectui. A ratione autem qua intellectus proprie dicitur ratio, non magis dicitur voluntas rationalis quam intellectus volitivus."

26. *Quodl.* 9.5, 13: 137–38: "Is enim cuius potentiae sunt intellectus et voluntas, intelligit ipso intellectu ut aliquo sui, et similiter vult voluntate, et ideo intelligendo per intellectum bonum, per voluntatem movet se ipsum in voluntate ad volendum illud, ita quod, si intellectus et voluntas non essent potentiae eiusdem in eadem substantia animae vel naturae in corpore fundatae, sed considerentur ut quaedam diversa, quorum unum sit per se et principale intelligens et alterum sit per se et principale volens, cum voluntatis non sit cognoscere, et non contingit velle nisi cognitum, nullo modo voluntas se ipsam moveret in actum volendi." See also *Quodl.* 11.6, 455vF–56rG, and *Quodl.* 13.11, 18: 118.

27. *Quodl.* 1.16, 5: 108 and 112.

28. *Quodl.* 9.5, 13: 123: ". . . nec operatur intellectus ad hoc quod fiat in suum actum ipsa voluntas, nisi ostendendo sive offerendo ipsum obiectum, et hoc non nisi sicut causa per accidens et sine qua non."

phasis on the will's self-determination leads Henry to posit the will as a first mover of its acts of choice.[29] He admits God's primary causality with regard to the will, yet he claims that God does not move the will to a specific act, but merely causes the existence of the will.[30] Henry's theory of the self-movement of the will leads him to make some questionable metaphysical assumptions. In particular, his account of how the will can move itself from potency to act is quite weak. He claims that the Aristotelian adage *"omne quod movetur, ab alio movetur"* applies only to material things and hence not to the will. This has earned him severe criticism, most notably from Godfrey of Fontaines.[31]

Exercise and Specification

One may agree with Henry that free decision cannot be grounded in reason alone. Yet Henry seems to err in the opposite sense by reducing the contribution of reason in free decision to accidental causality. Thus it becomes hard to say for which reason the will prefers one alternative over the other. Why not root free decision in reason and will conjointly, and integrate the activity of intellect and will in an act of free decision more fully, as, for example, Thomas Aquinas did? Aquinas distinguished between the exercise of an act (to act or not) and the determination or specification of an act (to do this or that). The exercise of an act in general, and the exercise of a cognitive act in particular, depend on the will. In this sense, the will moves the intellect. The determination or specification of an act depends on the object as presented by the intel-

29. He calls the will *primus motor, primum movens,* and *movens non motum;* see *Quodl.* 1.14, 5: 85; *Quodl.* 1.16, 5: 114; *Quodl.* 3.17, 79rI; *Quodl.* 4.22, 140vA; *Quodl.* 9.5, 13: 130–31; *Quodl.* 10.9, 14: 231; *Quodl.* 11.6, 455rX, 456rF–G; and *Quodl.* 13.11, 18: 105.

30. The clearest statement is found in *Quodl.* 12.26, 16: 155–56: ". . . immo prima motio voluntatis non est nisi volitio quam habet a se, non ab alio, neque etiam a Deo . . . aut si veritatem aliquam habet, quod scilicet prima motio voluntatis non est ab ipsa voluntate sed a Deo, hoc non est nisi quia voluntas non a se ipsa, sed a Deo habet naturalem vim qua movet. . . ." See also *Quodl.* 1.16, 5: 109: 37–40; *Quodl.* 6.10, 10: 98–99; *Quodl.* 9.5, 13: 121; and *Quodl.* 13.11, 18: 131.

31. For Henry's metaphysical explanation of the self-movement of the will, see *Quodl.* 9.5, 13: 99–139, esp. pp. 131–35; *Quodl.* 10.9, 14: 229–35; *Quodl.* 12.26, 16: 154–55; and *Quodl.* 13.11, 18: 125–33. See also Roland J. Teske, "Henry of Ghent's Rejection of the Principle: 'omne quod movetur ab alio movetur,'" in *Henry of Ghent: Proceedings of the International Colloquium on the Occasion of the 700th Anniversary of His Death (1293),* ed. Willy Vanhamel, Ancient and Medieval Philosophy, ser. 1, vol. 15 (Leuven: Leuven University Press, 1996), 279–308. For Godfrey's critique, see Putallaz, 177–208. See also John F. Wippel, "Godfrey of Fontaines and the Act-Potency Axiom," *Journal of the History of Philosophy* 11 (1973): 299–317; and Peter S. Eardley, "The Foundations of Freedom in Later Medieval Philosophy: Giles of Rome and His Contemporaries," *Journal of the History of Philosophy* 44 (2006): 353–76.

lect, and thus the intellect moves the will. When an object that is good from every point of view is presented to the will, it desires it of necessity. Such a good is happiness *(beatitudo)*. No other object necessarily entails the will's adhesion, for even when it is specified by the intellect as something good, the will can move the intellect to focus on aspects that make the object appear in a different light and hence it can withhold its own consent. Giles of Rome, who was possibly a student of Aquinas at Paris, developed a similar theory, yet he uses different terms *(determinatio* instead of *exercitium; actuatio* instead of *determinatio/specificatio)* and he emphasized more clearly than Thomas the will's spontaneity with regard to the exercise of an act.[32]

Yet, according to Henry, the fundamental difficulty in the explanation of freedom remains the same, however complexly the reciprocal influence of reason and will might be arranged. Henry explicitly rejects Aquinas's and Giles's attempts to explain free decision by means of the specification-exercise distinction. Either the activity of the will (e.g., the choice of an action, or just the will's influence on the intellect's cognition) is entirely caused by a previous act of the intellect, or not. If it is, then there is no freedom at all. If not, the will has an innate freedom. *Tertium non datur.* If the will's act is caused by the intellect, then neither exercise nor specification turn out to be free since the intellect's activity is deterministic. Henry is not opposed to distinguishing between specification and exercise, but, in his view, this distinction does not explain the origin of freedom. According to Henry, the will alone freely chooses both the determination and the exercise of the act.[33]

Even to consider the object known by reason as a partial cause of the will's act would jeopardize free decision. An object known by reason and then presented to the will is a natural cause. Natural causes, as opposed to rational or free causes, are determined to a single effect, according to the Aristotelian adage *"natura ad unum, ratio ad opposita."*[34] If a natural cause were a partial cause together with the free will, the effect of this conjoint causality would be determined by the natural agent, not by the

32. For Thomas's account of free decision, see *ST* IaIIae.9.1; 10.2; 13.6; *De malo* 6; and David M. Gallagher, "Free Choice and Free Judgment in Thomas Aquinas," *Archiv für Geschichte der Philosophie* 76 (1994): 247–77. According to Gallagher's interpretation, the will can indirectly determine the specification of an action by means of the its control of cognitive acts. Peter S. Eardley opposes this interpretation, but considers it an accurate description of the doctrine of Giles of Rome; see his "Thomas Aquinas and Giles of Rome on the Will," *Review of Metaphysics* 56 (2003): 835–62.

33. *Quodl.* 9.5, 13: 122–24; *Quodl.* 10.9, 14: 238–43; *Quodl.* 11.6, 455rV–56vL; *Quodl.* 12.26; 16: 150; *Quodl.* 13.11; 18: 91–92.

34. Aristotle, *Metaphysics* 9.2.1046b4–5. For Henry's distinction between natural causes and free agents, see, e.g., *Quodl.* 10.9, 14: 255.

free will, just as a person who is falling down a cliff may have free decision, but his fall is determined by gravity, not by choice.[35]

2. Incontinence

If it is the case that the will can choose against the judgment of reason, the question that animated Aristotle's treatment of incontinence, that is, how incontinence is possible, ceases to be problematic. Under this presupposition, the phenomenon of acting against one's better judgment is a primitive fact of the psychology of intellect and will. Yet the problem of incontinence is nevertheless of great interest to Henry. What is at issue for him is not the explanation of the possibility of incontinence, but rather to elucidate how free decision *(liberum arbitrium)* is involved in incontinent action. For this, Henry will clarify whether the sinful will by which one acts incontinently is caused by ignorance, passion, or neither one. He will also argue that incontinent action involves choice, although Aristotle denies that incontinent persons act according to their choice (i.e., they do not act in accordance with the result of their deliberation). Throughout his career, Henry holds that evil has its first origin in the will, not in deficient reason.

Error and Sin

That the will can go against the judgment of reason (*Quodl.* 1.16) proves that one can freely choose to sin. Can one also freely choose to avoid sinning? Do passions and the subsequent blurring of reason lead one to commit acts of incontinence unavoidably? Henry addresses these problems in his reply to another question proposed to him in the first Quodlibetal disputation: "Is the disorder of the will caused by an error of reason, or the reverse?" (question 17).[36] According to Henry, what is at issue here is incontinence. He specifies the meaning of the question:

> The principal difficulty of the question regards the sin of the incontinent who sins from passion. The question is this: does sensual passion first infect the will

35. *Quodl.* 13.11, 18: 111. Duns Scotus holds the opposite view: when a natural cause and a free cause act jointly, their effect is determined by the free cause; see *Lectura* 2.25, nn. 73–74, *Opera omnia* (Vatican City: Typis Vaticanis, 1950ff.), 19: 254–55. Scotus mentions the example of a free person falling down, but says that this fall may be both natural and free; see *Quodl.* 16 n. 16, *Opera Omnia* (Paris: Vivès, 1891–1895), 26: 201a–b.

36. *Quodl.* 1.15 [prologue], 5: 91: "Tertia, utrum deordinatio voluntatis causetur ab errore rationis vel e converso" ("Tertia" refers to question 17). For a close analysis of *Quodl.* 1.17 and of the related questions in *Quodl.* 10, see Müller, "Willensschwäche im Voluntarismus?"

by means of the will's consent to such passion, and does the passion by means of the will obfuscate reason so that it errs in its judgment, or conversely, does the passion obfuscate first reason to cause it to err, upon which ensues inevitably a disorder of the will that desires according to the erring judgment of reason?[37]

Ignorance regarding what one ought to do in a concrete situation *(ignorantia operandorum)* is key to medieval accounts of the origin of evil. Thirteenth-century thinkers generally agree that the will, construed as rational appetite, desires its object under the aspect of the good *(sub ratione boni)*.[38] Hence evil action presupposes ignorance: when one does evil, one pursues something bad as an apparent good.

Aquinas, for example, accordingly considers ignorance or at least a lack of consideration of the badness of an action a necessary condition for incontinence.[39] To posit a cognitive defect as a presupposition for a defective will is characteristic of any intellectualist theory of free decision. According to Henry, this is also the intrinsic logic of the intellectualist account he expounded in *Quodlibet* 1.16, according to which the will cannot will or choose against the conclusive practical judgment. Those who hold this view would have to answer the question of *Quodlibet* 1.17 as such: "every order and disorder of the will proceeds from an order or disorder of reason, so that if reason and will were both well-ordered, the will cannot become disordered, without reason first getting disordered."[40] What is at stake here, in Henry's view, is whether the will can be forced to consent to sin by a defective rational judgment or whether it consents freely.[41] His concern is understandable, because in his eyes an intellectualist explanation of choice implies a chain of events that leads a person to sin without escape. Inordinate appetite of the will follows inevitably from unawareness of what ought to be done or avoided here and now, which in turn follows inevitably upon passion.[42]

37. *Quodl.* 1.17, 5: 119: ". . . de hoc est principaliter difficultas quaestionis, scilicet de peccato incontinentis qui peccat ex passione, de quo est dubitatio, utrum passio sensualis prius inficiat voluntatem pravo consensu et mediante illa obnubilet rationem ut in iudicio suo erret, vel e converso passio illa rationem primo obnubilet ut erret, et tunc necessario cogatur sequi deordinatio voluntatis appetentis secundum iudicium rationis errantis." See also ibid., p. 138.

38. See, e.g., *Quodl.* 1.16, 5: 110; *Quodl.* 3.17, 79rH; *Quodl.* 4.22, 138vQ; and *Quodl.* 12.26, 16: 153.

39. *ST* IaIIae.77.2. See also *De malo* 3.9.

40. "Tenentes hanc opinionem dicerent quod omnis ordinatio et deordinatio voluntatis procedit ex ordinatione et deordinatione rationis, ita quod si ambo, et ratio et voluntas, essent ordinata, voluntas deordinari non posset nisi prius deordinata ratione" (*Quodl.* 1.17, 5: 124).

41. "De tali autem modo necessitandi voluntatem per plenum consensum, est quaestionis difficultas" (*Quodl.* 1.17, 5: 126).

42. This sequence of events is implied, according to Henry, in the intellectualist account he rejects; see *Quodl.* 1.17, 5: 126: "Rationis autem deordinationem dicunt in incon-

In Henry's view, by contrast, the disorder of the will is in the person's power. He has established in *Quodlibet* 1.16 that it is only by means of the will that a person has control of his or her intellect. In order to prove that involuntary ignorance cannot of necessity lead to a deficient, that is, sinful, will, in other words, that inordinate appetite is due to the person's will and not merely owing to an uncontrolled sequence of events that would force the will's consent, Henry must demonstrate that the will can in fact become deficient by itself rather than because of deficient reason.

He does not deny that the will, that is, the rational appetite, can desire or choose only that which is perceived under the aspect of the good, but in his eyes this does not mean that the will necessarily follows the practical judgment of what is best or lawful, nor does this therefore imply that a deficient will presupposes an erroneous practical judgment. The will is in fact free to adhere either to the cognition of an object's goodness prior to deliberation *(simplex apprehensio)* or to follow the practical judgment after deliberation, although, by going against the judgment of reason, the will would have to resist the pull toward what reason judges best. Someone who spontaneously prefers pastry to fruit can stick to this first inclination, even though a moment later he or she judges that fruit would be healthier and better. Preferring pastry, the person would choose the lesser good, which is nonetheless a good. In that case, the individual would have to defy the reasons that speak in favor of fruit.[43]

The will's being ordered only to that which is perceived under the aspect of the good is therefore no reason to stipulate that a deficient choice presupposes deficient knowledge. But there is a good reason for the contrary view. The decisive evidence for the possibility of sin without ignorance is the case of unprecedented sin, that is, the sin of the angels and the first human sin. According to theological doctrine, ignorance (i.e., failure to know what one should know, as opposed to nescience, lack of knowledge) and error have punitive character; hence they cannot be prior to the first sin. Lucifer and Adam were not ignorant about what they were supposed to do or avoid, nor were they subject to error, yet they sinned nevertheless.[44] Henry focuses on Adam's sin, arguing that "without prior error in reason, the first man sinned by acting directly against the determinate judgment of right reason."[45] If sinning without

tinente incipere a passione appetitus sensitivi qua obnubilatur et cadit a sua recta opinione in erroneam, quam necesse est sequi, ut dicunt, appetitum voluntatis. . . ."

43. *Quodl.* 1.17, 5: 125. See also *Quodl.* 1.16, 5: 113–14; *Quodl.* 9.5, 13: 131; and *Summa* 45.4, 29: 123.

44. *Quodl.* 1.17, 5: 116 and 128.

45. ". . . nullo errore praecedente in ratione peccavit ille primus homo, sed directe agendo contra determinatum iudicium rationis rectae" (*Quod.* 1.17, 5: 128–29).

prior misconception of the good was possible for the first man, then, Henry argues, this is all the more possible for us now. In fact, the first man was in the "state of innocence" and was thus endowed with special graces that strengthened his reason and will, but under the conditions of our present life (as marked by the consequences of original sin), our power of reason and will is weakened, so that our will follows more difficultly the judgment of reason when there are averse passions.[46] Henry accordingly concludes that, on the authority of Christian faith, one must hold that

> every disorder in reason consisting in error causally proceeds from a disorder of the will consisting in vicious affection, and not vice versa, except insofar as knowledge provides the occasion for sin, because there must be knowledge before the will can act.[47]

Henry's argument is theological, yet the problem involved in it is a philosophical puzzle as well. If the erroneous belief that leads to bad action is due to negligence of acquiring the relevant knowledge or due to the failure of adequately guiding the attention of reason, then the error is voluntary and one is not excused from sin. Yet then the cause of sinful negligence must be explained. Conversely, invincible ignorance exonerates one from sin.[48] Hence the problem of the first sin cannot be explained by voluntary ignorance.

Passion, Consent, Choice

Henry's lengthy considerations about the role of ignorance in evildoing are intended to show that the cause of moral deficiency cannot be traced to anything antecedent to the deficient will itself. The will becomes sinful by itself, without prior cognitive defects. Yet the phenomenon of incontinence shows that in reality what leads to sin is not a decision of the will out of context, but temptation by a delightful object that

46. "Quod si sic posse agere tunc fuit voluntatis humanae naturae, et nunc est, licet debilior voluntas nunc sit in nobis, ut difficilius se teneat in sententia rationis rectae, passione contrariante, quam tunc, quando nulla passio fuit in homine ante peccatum" (*Quodl.* 1.17, 5: 129).

47. "Dicendum igitur est absolute, et aliter sana fide stante dici non potest, quod omnis deordinatio per errorem in ratione causaliter procedit ex deordinatione voluntatis per pravam affectionem, et non e converso nisi occasionaliter, in quantum cognitio praevia est ad voluntatem, ut praedictum est" (*Quodl.* 1.17, 5: 129). Henry examines the first angelic and human sin again in *Quodl.* 8.10, where he mainly discusses a canonical question of Scholastic treatments of angelic sin, i.e., whether sin could have occurred in the first moment of a rational creature's existence, or only after this moment. There he mentions again that error in reason is posterior to an evil will; see 323rR.

48. *Quodl.* 1.17, 5: 117 and 139; *Quodl.* 1.18, 5: 154.

solicits passions that strongly influence one's decision making. Henry still has to show that the passions' effect on the will is not mediated by the obfuscation of reason.

Henry addresses this problem in a lengthy exposition of Aristotle's account of incontinence in Book 7 of the *Nicomachean Ethics.*[49] According to Henry, the disorder of the will in incontinent action occurs gradually. Consequent to the disorder of the will, reason is obfuscated. This process culminates in the choice of the incontinent action as a result of new practical reasoning, now based upon erroneous premises.

Lamenting that Aristotle did not clearly state whether the sense appetite *(concupiscentia sensualis)* obfuscates reason directly or rather by means of the agreement of the will,[50] Henry tries to solve this problem on his own. He describes in detail the causal sequence from temptation to the sinful action. During part of the process, the incontinent does not differ from the continent; the crucial question is what marks the precise point of departure between the two. Temptation, passion, the venial sin of taking delight in the object of temptation, and a beginning clouding of reason characterize the continent and incontinent alike. Yet the continent adheres to reason, fights against passions, and defeats the temptation.[51] The incontinent, however, falls prey to the passions:

> And thus the incontinent is desirous and takes delight, although prior to the [will's] consent, he is still struggling, having as it were in front of him right reason, to which he adheres, but in the back he has the object that the sense appetite desires and finds delightful, by which his will is dragged, until, defeated, it falls into a perfect consent to the act that it is attracted to. . . . Then the person voluntarily turns his back on reason, as it were, and his face to passion. . . . And then reason is first blinded and erroneous and ignorant, as was said before.[52]

What distinguishes the incontinent from the continent is the consent to the object of delight. Once the consent is given and reason is blinded, there is no return. Now the action follows necessarily.[53] Before the will became evil by consenting to the sin, the person judged the action to be bad and was not persuaded to do it, for example, to commit adultery. After consenting, he or she is persuaded because of erring reason, now considering adultery good. At this moment, the person sins because of

49. *Quodl.* 1.17, 5: 130–50.

50. *Quodl.* 1.17, 5: 138.

51. *Quodl.* 1.17, 5: 140–41.

52. *Quodl.* 1.17, 5: 141–42: "Et sic incontinens concupiscens et delectans solum, reluctando ante consensum, quasi ab ante habet rectam rationem cui adhaeret, quasi autem a dorso habet concupiscentiam et delectabile sensus, a quo trahitur voluntas eius quousque victa cadat in consensum perfectum actus ad quem allicitur. . . . Tunc enim voluntarie quasi dorsum vertit ad rationem et faciem ad passionem, subintrans vincula passionis et tentationis. . . . Et tunc primo excaecatur ratio et errat ignorans, ut praedictum est."

53. *Quodl.* 1.17, 5: 143.

ignorance and by choice *(eligibiliter)*.[54] Henry thus concludes that passions corrupt the judgment of reason only by way of a disordered will.[55]

The Syllabus of 1277 and the Propositio Magistralis

In March 1277, that is, shortly after Henry's first Quodlibetal disputation (but possibly before the final redaction of the first Quodlibet), Archbishop Tempier condemned 219 supposedly heterodox philosophical propositions.[56] For some theologians of the time, this implied the constraint to adopt their teaching accordingly; for others, the articles of the Syllabus were a welcome sanction of their own teaching. For the most part, Henry belonged to the second group. For example, in the condemnation of article 129 (169), he could see a confirmation of his account of incontinence: "As long as passion and particular science are in act, the will cannot act against them."[57] In other words, according to authors of the Syllabus, the will is not bound to follow the practical judgment. Yet after 1285, Henry also saw himself obliged to subscribe to a proposition that seems to state the opposite, the so-called *propositio magistralis:* "There is no evil in the will without error in reason."[58] In his *Quodlibet* 10 of Christmas 1286 or Easter 1287, Henry tries to reconcile the condemnation of art. 129 with the concession of the *propositio magistralis*.[59] This attempt appears forced, but it is not my concern here to

54. *Quodl.* 1.17, 5: 146.

55. *Quodl.* 1.17, 5: 146 and 148.

56. See note 5 above.

57. "Quod uoluntas, manente passione et scientia particulari in actu, non potest agere contra eam" (ed. Piché, 118). I follow the numbering of the articles in Heinrich Denifle and Emile Chatelain, *Chartularium Universitatis Parisiensis,* 2 vols. (Paris: Delalain, 1889–1891). In parentheses, I include the numbering of the articles by Pierre Mandonnet, *Siger de Brabant et l'averroïsme latin au XIIIme siècle.* IIme partie: textes inédits, deuxième édition revue et augmentée. Les Philosophes Belges 7 (Leuven: Institut Supérieur de Philosophie de l'Université, 1908), 175–91, at 188.

58. "Non est malitia in voluntate, nisi sit error in ratione." For a thorough discussion of the *propositio magistralis* in connection with the Syllabus of 1277, see Peter S. Eardley, "The Problem of Moral Weakness, the *propositio magistralis,* and the Condemnation of 1277," *Medieval Studies* 68 (2006): 161–203. The author of the *propositio magistralis* is Giles of Rome; see *In I Sent.,* d. 17, p. 1, princ. 1, q. 1 (Venice, 1521; repr., Frankfurt: Minerva, 1968), 89M; *In I Sent.,* d. 47, princ. 2, q. 1, ibid., 237G; *Apologia,* a. 24, ed. Robert Wielockx, Opera omnia III.1 (Florence: Leo S. Olschki, 1985), 54. See also ibid., a. 51, ed. Wielockx, 59: "Numquam est malitia in voluntate, nisi sit error vel saltem aliqua nescientia in ratione." This proposition was conceded by the Parisian masters in 1285, during Giles of Rome's rehabilitation, who had been previously condemned by Archbishop Tempier. See Edgar Hocedez, "La condamnation de Gilles de Rome," *Recherches de théologie ancienne et médiévale* 14 (1932): 34–58, at 42–43 and 47–51. See also Ludwig Hödl, "'Non est malitia in voluntate . . .'. Die magistrale Entscheidung der Pariser Theologen von 1285/1286 in der Diskussion des Johannes de Polliaco, Quodl. I, q. 10. Untersuchung und Edition," *Archives d'histoire doctrinale et littéraire du moyen âge* 66 (1999): 245–97.

59. Dating according to Laarmann, 50.

discuss his argumentation in detail.[60] The interest of Henry's considerations lies rather in the fact that they show how he further develops his view regarding the effect that deficient reason and deficient will have on each other.

Henry reconciles the denial of art. 129 with the affirmation of the *propositio magistralis* by arguing that the disorder of reason and will are contemporaneous, yet ontologically the will is evil prior to the deficiency of reason.[61] If every act of the will were caused by reason, then also every defect of the will would be caused by erroneous reason, without the will being able to avoid this.[62] He thus reaffirms his teaching of *Quodlibet* 1.17 that the disorder of reason is not prior to the disorder of the will. He refines this account, however, by specifying that obfuscated reason in turn increases the malice of the will. The harm that will and reason inflict on each other becomes over time so great that the complete blinding of reason results in perfect obstinacy of the will. This leads a person to change his or her general moral and even religious convictions: someone who first believed that theft is evil and that God exists, after sinning begins to put these beliefs into doubt and ends up thinking that theft is good and that God does not exist.[63]

In sum, the problem, as Henry perceives it, is this: if there is a faulty, that is, sinful, will, the question is whether its defect is caused by whatever else than the will itself (ignorance, error, passions, habits). If it is, then the will has no control of its moral deficiency. If it is not, then an additional question must be asked: Was the sin avoidable? If it was not, then again the will had no control of its deficiency. If it was, then the will moves itself, by its own accord, to sin.

3. Strengthening the Will

When making a decision, reason is indispensable, but the will has the last say. In Henry's view, reason is subordinate to the will and inferior to it; the will is in fact not only able to reject the judgment of reason, but it

60. Henry's efforts to reconcile these apparently contradictory statements are carefully analyzed by Stephen D. Dumont, "Time, Contradiction, and Freedom of the Will in the Late Thirteenth Century," *Documenti e studi sulla tradizione filosofica medievale* 3 (1992): 561–97, at 577–91.

61. *Quodl.* 10.10, 14: 261–71; *Quodl.* 10.9, 14: 245–48; and *Quodl.* 10.13, 14: 287–89.

62. *Quodl.* 10.9, 14: 248: "Sed ponendo causalitatem semper in ratione, omnino contrariatur articulo [sc. 129]: propterea enim damnatus est ille articulus, quia sic daretur rationi quod sic pro hora necessitaret et determinaret voluntatem ut ad errorem unius sequeretur error alterius. Per hoc enim in tali actu volendi tollitur libertas liberi arbitrii in eo, quod non potest contraire."

63. *Quodl.* 10.10, 14: 260–62. See also *Quodl.* 12.14, 16: 82.

also controls reason by moving it to its exercise.[64] Hence moral development depends crucially on the will; strength of the will is no less important than strength of reason. What is strength of will for Henry and how does the will become strong? The answer is found in Henry's account of virtues of the will and of moral perfection.

Virtues of the Will

In his fourth Quodlibetal disputation, Henry is asked whether the subject of the moral virtues is the will.[65] This was a commonly debated question in the late thirteenth century. It was understood that the alternative is this: Is the location of the moral virtues the will or the sense appetite? The answer to this question affects the understanding of the nature and function of moral virtues.[66]

As an implication of his voluntarist account of free decision, Henry insists that the virtues are in the will as their subject. Precisely because of its indeterminacy, the will needs to be perfected by virtues. In fact, every potency that is indifferent and indeterminate with regard to attaining its perfection needs the habit of virtue so that it does not fail to attain its perfection because of its indeterminacy.[67] If it were the case that the will inevitably followed the practical judgment of reason, there would not be any need for virtues in the will.[68] But the will is indifferent with regard to the practical judgment; it can choose in accord with it or against it. Hence it needs a habit so that it wills to adhere to the judgment of right reason.[69]

64. *Quodl.* 1.14, 5: 88–89: ". . . voluntas rationem movet et impellit et in opus dirigit, et omnes vires animae et membra corporis. Absolute ergo dicendum quod voluntas superior vis est in toto regno animae, et ita ipso intellecto." *Quodl.* 9.6, 13: 142: ". . . quantum est ex parte superioritatis, potius ponendum est quod voluntatis est imperare, et intellectus et omnium aliarum potentiarum oboedire atque imperium voluntatis suscipere. Voluntas enim et velle contra dictamen rationis potest, et ipsam rationem cogere ut recedat a suo iudicio. . . ."

65. *Quodl.* 4.22, 138rO: ". . . utrum morales virtutes sint in voluntate."

66. See Bonnie Kent, *Virtues of the Will: The Transformation of Ethics in the Late Thirteenth Century* (Washington, D.C.: The Catholic University of America Press, 1995), 199.

67. *Quodl.* 4.22, 138vQ: "Potentia quae de se indifferens est et indeterminata respectu finis in quo debet acquirere propriam perfectionem per suam operationem, indiget habitu virtutis ut determinetur finis a quo per indifferentiam suam et indeterminationem potest sua operatione declinare et errare a fine, et propria perfectione frustrari. . . ."

68. *Quodl.* 4.22, 140vA: ". . . in voluntate non esset ponenda virtus si determinata esset naturaliter ad sequendum iudicium rationis. . . ."

69. *Quodl.* 4.22, 139rR: "Et quia in tali deliberatione voluntas indeterminata est ad utrumlibet se habens: ita etiam quod data sententia rationis adhuc potest se tenere in sua indeterminatione: et praeferre in electione sua contrarium eius quod eligendum sententiavit ratio . . . ideo ut velit assentire completa deliberatione ei quod iudicatum est recta ratione, multum indiget habitu ipsum inclinante ut velit illud." See also ibid., 140vZ.

Henry not only argues that there must be moral habits in the will to perfect it, but also that all moral habits are located in the will, while the sense appetite merely has a share in virtue. In its essence, virtue is in that which rules, whereas it is, by means of participation, in that which is ruled.[70] For Henry, the ruler of the soul is not the intellect, but the will:

> Manifestly that which not only has reason but also is a ruler is only the will. In fact, the intellect, whether it be the practical intellect or the speculative intellect, cannot rule anything, but can only offer a judgment.[71]

Even less can the sense appetite be the principle of virtue. Whereas the will (i.e., the rational appetite) is for Henry essentially rational, the sense appetite only shares in rationality. Since it is ruled by the will, the necessity of virtues does not regard above all the sense appetite.[72] Henry concludes that the moral virtues are simply and essentially in the will, whereas they are in the sense appetite only by participation and by some imprint from the will.[73] Vice and virtue are accordingly defined with reference to the will: ". . . moral virtue is nothing but a habit that inclines the will to the love of the good simply, whereas vice is the opposite habit that inclines to the love of the apparent good."[74] Thus Henry claims not only that a will perfected by virtuous habits is a strong will, but also that the moral virtues are essentially strength of will.

Weakness and Strength of Will

Even though Henry locates the moral virtues in the will, he does not reduce virtue ethics to the generic imperative to make the effort of willing what is good. He develops an impressively detailed account of the

70. Cf. *Quodl.* 4.22, 140rV.

71. *Quodl.* 4.22, 140rX: "Sed constans est quod rationem habens quod principans est, non est nisi voluntas. Intellectus enim sive sit practicus, sive speculativus, principari non habet, sed solum iudicium dare."

72. *Quodl.* 4.22, 140vA: "Falsum est etiam dicere quod vires sensitivae concupiscibilis, et irascibilis, quia non sunt determinatae secundum iudicium rationis: et propter passiones quae in eis sunt contrariae rationi: ideo indigent habitu. Quoniam licet ex se sint indeterminatae: tamen quantum est ex natura earum, necesse est eas sequi determinationem voluntatis. Et ideo sicut in voluntate non esset ponenda virtus si determinata esset naturaliter ad sequendum iudicium rationis: similiter neque in illis viribus per determinationem quam habent a voluntate." See also ibid., 141rB.

73. *Quodl.* 4.22, 140rX: "Quia ergo voluntas . . . simpliciter tamen est rationalis per essentiam: appetitus autem sensibilis est rationalis per participationem tantum: idcirco dico quod virtus moralis simpliciter et essentialiter est in voluntate et essentia habitum eius: per participationem autem et impressionem quandam in appetitu sensibili." See also 140vA, where Henry develops this point in more detail.

74. *Quodl.* 4.22, 138vQ: ". . . virtus moralis nihil aliud sit quam habitus inclinans voluntatem ad amorem boni simpliciter. Vitium autem est habitus contrarius inclinans ad amorem boni apparentis."

acquisition of moral virtues and of the connection of virtues.[75] Moral progress by means of the increase of moral virtues leads to an ever firmer adherence to the true good. The less the will's free choices are indeterminate with regard to the good, the more the person approaches perfection.

It is with regard to such moral perfection or the lack thereof that Henry employs the metaphors of "strength" and "weakness" of the will. Contrary to our contemporary usage, Henry does not equate these terms with incontinence and continence, respectively. The will is strong, according to Henry, when it is free. True freedom lies not in the capacity to choose. Despite his insistence on the will's capacity contingently to choose to act according to or against the dictate of reason, Henry does not hold that freedom itself consists of contingent choices, let alone in choices against reason. Like his contemporaries, he distinguishes between freedom of the will *(libertas voluntatis)* and free decision *(liberum arbitrium)*.[76] Free decision signifies the capacity to choose between alternative possibilities.[77] Freedom, by contrast, does not require the ability to choose, but merely the absence of constraint.[78] The more firmly and invariably one adheres to the true good, the freer one is. Accordingly human freedom is accomplished in the beatific vision, because the will of the blessed can no longer deflect from the true good.[79] The highest degree of freedom is found in God, for whom it is absolutely impossible to turn away from the ultimate end, which is God himself.[80]

Owing to original sin, the will is weakened, and it is more difficult for it to adhere to the judgment of right reason.[81] Thus it is possible that the will be defeated by the object of sense delight, as we have seen in Henry's explanation of the sin of incontinence. Nevertheless, this defeat

75. *Quodl.* 5.16–17, 185rD–93rX; *Quodl.* 12.14, 16: 79–83. See also Jean-Michel Counet, "Henri de Gand: La prudence dans ses rapports aux vertus morales," in *Henry of Ghent and the Transformation of Scholastic Thought,* 227–40.

76. *Summa* 45.4, 29: 125; *Quodl.* 10.9, 14: 235; *Quodl.* 12.26, 16: 153; *Quodl.* 14.5, 564rY.

77. *Quodl.* 10.9, 14: 235: "Liberum arbitrium autem non est nisi ubi est contrariorum libera electio." See also *Summa* 45.3, 29: 120; 45.4, 29: 125; and *Quodl.* 14.5, 564rY.

78. *Quodl.* 10.9, 14: 235: "Libertas enim est ubicumque nulla occurrit coactio, licet non sit libera electio valens ad opposita. . . ."

79. *Quodl.* 3.17, 79rK. For the necessity to adhere to the good in the beatific vision, see also *Quodl.* 9.5, 14: 135, and *Quodl.* 10.9, 14: 236.

80. *Summa* 45.3, 29: 118: ". . . in infinitum fortior et firmior sit libertas voluntatis in Deo quam in angelis, et ideo omnino invariabilis, ut nullo modo potest inclinare in motum alium quam directum in se ipsum, ut omnium finis ultimus."

81. *Quodl.* 1.17, 5: 128: "Licet enim libertas eius per peccatum modo sit debilitata, hoc nihil facit ad variationem naturae speciei." Ibid., 129: "Quod si sic posse agere tunc fuit voluntatis humanae naturae, et nunc est, licet debilior voluntas tunc sit in nobis, ut difficilius se teneat in sententia rationis rectae, passione contrariente, quam tunc quando nulla passio fuit in homine ante peccatum."

is voluntary.[82] Throughout his discussion of incontinence, Henry insists on the fact that there is free decision *(liberum arbitrium)* in incontinent actions. The will's consent cannot be necessitated; at most, a certain delight of the will may occur by necessity—yet this delight is a weakness, not necessarily a sin.[83] As long as there is free decision, one has at least a residual strength to choose among alternative actions. Whether one is continent or incontinent depends on the will.[84]

Conclusion

Weakness of will, understood as action against one's better judgment, is a fundamental phenomenon in Henry's moral psychology and ethics. It is because of the will's innate freedom that one can act contrary to what one judges best. Henry persistently defends the will's ability to choose against the practical judgment as the sole possibility to account for free decision. His reasoning seems coherent, once one admits his premises. Indeterminist free decision is real. The root of free decision cannot be the intellect, since the intellect's activity (and hence practical reasoning) is deterministic. Henry's entire moral psychology and ethics are premised on this view. Since free decision cannot spring from practical reasoning, it must be innate to the will. If the will could not go against the practical judgment, there would be no free decision.

Yet Henry does not deny that the will's choices have a motivation. Even the dismissal of the practical judgment occurs *sub ratione boni* and is therefore not unmotivated. When refusing the practical judgment, one follows the attraction of the object as it first appeared in the *simplex apprehensio,* prior to deliberation. What Henry cannot explain, however, is why one should want to dismiss the practical judgment of what deliberation has proved to be the best choice here and now. He simply posits the possibility of the second best choice (i.e., to choose according to the simple cognition) as a brute fact.

82. *Quodl.* 1.17, 5: 142, quoted above, note 52. See also *Quodl.* 1.17, 5: 150.

83. *Quodl.* 1.17, 5: 125–26: ". . . bonum autem apprehensum sub ratione veri nullo modo potest ex ratione boni cogniti necessitare voluntatem in appetendo, appetitu, dico, deliberato qui fit per consensum, licet forte posset eum necessitare ad appetendum appetitu delectante ex apprehensione simplici praecedente iudicium et sententiam rationis. Sed iste appetitus aut non est peccatum sed infirmitas quaedam in voluntate ex primo peccato, aut si est peccatum, non contingit nisi ex aliquo peccato voluntatis praecedente. . . ."

84. This is at least implicit in Henry's account; see *Quodl.* 1.17, 5: 139: "Unde si concupiscentia solummodo animum tangendo tentet et voluntas eam statim reicit, in nullo eam inficit nec in aliquo intellectum obumbrat, sed oboediente appetitu inferiori appetitui superiori, mox tentatio cessat, sicut contingit in continente." See also ibid., 142, where Henry qualifies the incontinent person's consent as voluntary: "Tunc enim voluntarie quasi dorsum vertit ad rationem et faciem ad passionem. . . ."

The examination of incontinence, that is, weakness of will in the Aristotelian sense of action against one's better judgment because of passion, is important for establishing whether free decision is also in play when passions influence one's decision. Henry insists that passions do not first cause an erroneous judgment which then entails a sinful choice. This would in fact result in a deterministic sequence of events. In a situation of temptation, the will rather decides on its own accord whether or not to pursue evil; the clouding of reason is not a condition, but rather a consequence of the evil choice.

The origin of evil action lies not in weak reason, but in a weak will. Even when reason is strong, the will can lead one to sin. Accordingly moral progress consists crucially in corroborating the will by means of virtues of the will. Virtues thus guarantee strength of will.

7 Dante: Healing the Wounded Will

GIUSEPPE MAZZOTTA

In *De vulgari eloquentia,* which was written between 1303 and the eve of 1304, after a detailed survey of the fourteen dialects into which the Italian language is subdivided, Dante formulates a theory of poetry and of the *canzone.* He considers it to be poetry's highest form because of its harmonious order. Its ideal themes, or *magnalia,* are identified as *salus, venus,* and *virtus,* which are said to embody the three inclinations or appetites of the will—the useful, the pleasurable, and the honest—and which correspond to three subject matters: *armorum probitas* (prowess in arms), *amoris accensio* (fire of love), and *directio voluntatis* (direction of the will). Dante ends the discussion by identifying these three topics of the song as the manifestation of the tripartite structure of the soul:

> And in order to make this clear, it must be observed that, as man has been endowed with a threefold life, namely vegetative, animal, and rational, he journeys as always a threefold road, for in so far as he is vegetative, he seeks for what is useful, wherein he is like nature with plants; in so far as he is animal he seeks for that which is pleasurable, wherein he is of like nature with the brutes; in so far as he is rational he seeks for what is right, and in this he stands alone, or is a partaker of the nature of the angels. It is by these three kinds of life that we appear to carry out whatever we do. . . .
>
> Now . . . if we carefully consider the object of all those who are in search of what is useful, we shall find that it is nothing else but safety. Secondly, in respect of what is pleasurable . . . this is love. Thirdly, in respect of what is right, and here no one doubts that virtue has the first place. Wherefore these three things, namely safety, love, and virtue, appear to be those capital matters which ought to be treated of supremely, I mean the things which are most important in respect of them, as prowess in arms, the fire of love, and the direction of the will. (*De vulgari eloquentia* 2.2.6–8)[1]

1. The quotations from the *De vulgari eloquentia* are taken from Dante, *De vulgari eloquentia,* ed. and trans. Steven Botterill (Cambridge and New York: Cambridge University Press, 1996).

The theoretical connection between poetic language and the powers of the will Dante posits in the *De vulgari eloquentia* overtly claims that poetry is the language of the will. It is rooted in and gives voice to the various modes of desire. It engages the faculties of the soul and exerts its influence on them. Such an insight turns into a project for Dante's future works. Its present formulation stems from a diligent, relentless quest into the tortuous and blind labyrinths of desire he had undertaken just about a decade earlier while writing his *Vita nuova*.[2]

In the pages ahead I propose to trace some of the interactions between the two questions of poetic language and the will. In the Letter to the Romans St. Paul encapsulates in stark terms the problem of the will in a manner that Dante thoroughly endorses: ". . . to will is present with me, but how to perform that which is good I find not. For the good that I would, I do not; but the evil which I would not, that I do" (Romans 7:18–19). St. Paul is addressing the issue of man's wounded will, which is the consequence of man's fallen state and by which human beings act against their better judgment. The effects of original sin, as a matter of fact, are ignorance (which technically is the wound of the intellect) and concupiscence and weakness, which are the wounds of the will and express themselves as a radical disorder thwarting the proper direction of the soul.

Throughout the *Divine Comedy,* Dante probes several forms of the will's disorder. He dramatizes the spiritual condition of sinners who transgress the hierarchy of reason over will by yielding to the pull of pleasures or who impose their own will on others. This paper aims at analyzing these issues by focusing primarily on the *Vita nuova;* on the canto of Francesca in the moral area of incontinence (*Inferno* 5); on the canto of the philosophers who yield to the lure of the power of the will, Farinata and Cavalcanti, in the area of violence (*Inferno* 10); and on the canto of Piccarda, the figure whose will comes into conflict with her brother's and who nonetheless is saved (*Paradiso* 5). Dante's poem explores the workings of the will and what could be called the "enigma of the will." But it does more than that. The *Divine Comedy* tells the story of the journey of the soul's redemption. Thus, I will argue here that for Dante art, which he understands as a transformative process, plays a central role in this journey of redemption. Art is a virtue, and for the poet it represents the highest activity. It corrects the errors of the will by providing a truer perception of the moral order.

2. I am quoting from Dante, *Vita nuova,* trans. Mark Musa (Bloomington and London: Indiana University Press, 1973). Italian quotations are from *La vita nuova,* ed. Michele Barbi (Florence: Società Dantesca Italiana, 1907).

1. Beatrice, "Accensio Amoris," and Poetry

The *Vita nuova,* an autobiographical text made of poetry and prose commentary, tells essentially the story of a double apprenticeship, a poetic apprenticeship and a sentimental education, and how each of these two experiences changes in the light of the other. The narrative begins by relating the onset of love, or what he later will call *accensio amoris,* in the chance encounter with Beatrice. Love comes through as an involuntary, sudden experience, which happens to the young protagonist and forces him to think and seek the sense of her dazzling apparition. The involuntary event takes him into two directions. On the one hand, it forces him on a quest: he seeks to understand and interpret the signs of this love, to grasp the mystery Beatrice enfolds, and to determine whether her appearance is a fortuitous accident or is meant to reveal a providential design for his life. All the resources of his mind are mobilized by the passion. On the other hand, the movement of the passion engenders in him alterations of the mind, deliriums, and hallucinations that haunt him and that he cannot manage to control. The poetry of the *Vita nuova* arises from the double-edged, contradictory nature of his experience.

The first sonnet in the *libello* (little book), as Dante calls it at the outset, recounts a strange dream. The protagonist dreams that Love, holding the lover's heart in his hand, wakes the lady from her sleep, and she eats the burning heart. The dream horrifies the young lover and he writes a sonnet that he sends out to Love's faithful subjects to help him decipher its disturbing, secret truth. In a way, because the protagonist will sink more deeply into his dreams, one can say that, however involuntary dreams are, he wills to dream in that dreams provide him with the freedom of imagination and permit him to live in the pleasurable depths of idle fictions. In this sense, his first dream-poem amounts to the very dream of poetry by the 18-year-old poet. But the dream turns also into food for thought in a specific sense: passions or dreams, however involuntary, feed his mind and force him to think and to interpret.

Two poets attempt to draw out the hidden meaning of Dante's sonnet, Guido Cavalcanti and the physician Dante da Maiano. Their interpretive reactions complement each other. Guido interprets the sonnet as a sign that love darkens the rigor of the lover's mind and that the passion produces no genuine self-knowledge. If Dante wants to reach a truth about his life, so Guido argues, he has to take the path of philosophy and give up the nightmarish fantasies of the passion. The physician, on his part, reads the sonnet as the clinical sign of the lover's diseased mind. For him, love is a sickness in which the stability of reason has been blighted by the imbalance of humors, and he recommends cold baths as a remedy.

Cavalcanti's response marks the beginning of his friendship with Dante, who dedicates the *Vita nuova* to this first of his friends. By making Guido his privileged correspondent Dante equates philosophy with the Ciceronian virtue of friendship. What connects the two is that both stand for a voluntary exercise of thought, for a rational benevolent conversation wherein minds turn together not at the mercy of somebody else's will or passion, but by making order and reason the laws of organization of the world.

The *Vita nuova* soon recounts the inadequacy of such a claim, advanced by Guido and provisionally endorsed by Dante. Neither Guido Cavalcanti nor Dante da Maiano can sufficiently explain the mystery that Beatrice comes to represent. With their stock notions about philosophy and disease they reduce love to the abstraction of a willed, objective condition, and consequently they deprive themselves of the means of understanding it. And if one poet makes love an evil of the dimmed mind, the other casts it as a question of the physics of bodies. To the pair of philosophy and friendship (or medicine and love) Dante substitutes another pair: love and poetry. He thinks that love is better than friendship because in its violent and obscure occurrence it forces truths about oneself that rational thinking cannot engender. And because these truths are involuntary, they bear the mark of a necessity.[3]

To understand this new idea of love for Beatrice, Dante undertakes the apprenticeship of art. To this end he reviews, utilizes, and absorbs all available poetic conventions of love: classical personifications of love, the rhetoric of Provençal poetry, courtly love conventions, and the Sweet New Style of Guinizelli. In order to write about her, he envelops himself in the language of others and draws his craft from the resources available in the poetic tradition. Such an apprenticeship becomes a preamble to a further quest: he looks for a unique language, one that is his own and adequately corresponds to the unique reality of Beatrice. His search for a new style deeply alters his earlier understanding of love. Because his love appears as the pursuit of a definite figure, Beatrice, poetic language cannot just play freely in an involuntary, drifting proliferation of words. He must rethink and turn to the will, impart a direction to it, and walk away from the realm and the play-acting of empty simulacra. There is in him a volition or an intention (a key word in this text) at work. In Chapter 12, Love's warning sounds clear: "Fili mi, tempus est ut

3. I have developed some of these reflections in my "The Language of Poetry in the *Vita nuova*," *Rivista di studi italiani* 1 (1983): 3–14.

pretermictantur simulacra nostra" (My son, it is time to do away with our false ideals).[4] To say that he now wills the real is tantamount to rejecting the assumption that Beatrice is merely imaginary and to acknowledge that her reality is deeper than his initial wondrous dreams about her. Her reality, however, is put into question by her death. How real can be one who is absent?

The text gives ample evidence that this shift in problems also invests Dante's poetry. At the beginning—but because he is haunted by this passion, even later—phrases come to him as if he were an empty vessel or an inspired poet. He records them. He is seized by a "desire to write a poem"[5] and decides to gain control of his words. Such a shift occurs with the poem "Donne ch'avete intelletto d'amore" (Ladies who have intelligence of love, chap. 19), which is introduced by this reflection: "Then it happened that while walking down a pathway along which ran a very clear stream, I suddenly felt a great desire to write a poem, and I began to think how I would go about it."[6] Significantly, against the solution proposed by Cavalcanti's sundering of love and philosophy, Dante's *canzone* bears witness to his new thought: love and intellect are yoked together. As Chapter 26, which is addressed to Guido, makes clear, he himself now regains both his will and his freedom: he can choose to reject a poem, he can choose the world of prose or the appropriate language of address to Beatrice, and he can choose his audience in the conviction that in poetry the voluntary and the involuntary—the willed and the inspired—converge.

In short, his poems enact the virtue of thought, which is the theme of *directio voluntatis* as was formulated in the *De vulgari eloquentia,* where *directio* is also called *rectitudo* (in Italian he writes "drittura," which means justice). One can add that the two words, *directio* and *rectitudo,* etymologically are the same. In substantive terms, *directio* implies that the will by itself alone cannot rule itself and needs reason's governance. Yet, in the *Vita nuova,* where the will turns out to be sovereign and preferable to unwilling or dreaming, Dante stumbles on the limitations and even powerlessness of the will. It is as if the initial insight into the importance of the involuntary experiences were ratified. Beatrice dies, and his will can do nothing about it. Her death plunges him into a state of dejection and it triggers an ethical drama quite common in medieval lyrics: the betrayal of the beloved. Dante betrays Beatrice's memory by turning to another woman. He yields to the temptation of believing she is not

4. *Vita nuova* 12, trans. Musa, 17.
5. *Vita nuova* 19, trans. Musa, 32; ed. Barbi, 43: "volontade di dire."
6. Ibid.

unique and irreplaceable. But the outcome of the story is the resolution to see her again. Consistently, the *Vita nuova* ends with a project of the future: ". . . I hope to write of her that which has never been written of any other woman."[7]

The ending of the *Vita nuova* adumbrates the writing of the *Divine Comedy*. In the Dedication Letter to Cangrande della Scala (Epistle 13), which functions as a general introduction of the poem and which explains the literal and allegorical principles shaping the text, Dante places the subject matter of the *Divine Comedy* under the general rubric of ethics and assigns a central thematic place to free will:

> The subject of the whole work, then, taken literally, is the state of souls after death, understood without qualification; for the movement of the whole work turns upon this and is about this. If, on the other hand, the work is taken allegorically, the subject is man, in the exercise of his free choice, meriting or demeriting the rewards or punishment of justice. (*Epistola* 13.8)[8]

The letter does not engage, nor could it (given its mode as an introductory statement to *Paradiso*) try to establish the meaning of free will and free choice, whether the human act of choice in the will is determined by reason or whether "free will" means that freedom is the fundamental character of the will. To be sure, *liberum arbitrium,* the faculty of reason and will, is attained by the pilgrim in the Garden of Eden, and, as in the Garden, the passage from the Letter to Cangrande quoted above recognizes the act of choice as the foundation of the moral life. It also establishes justice as the divine government of man, which demands man to do good and to harm no one.

From the point of view of the overarching theme of justice that has just been announced, the Letter implies that the *Divine Comedy* focuses on the complex story of a moral and spiritual education. Accordingly, because the will is the locus of sin, Dante dramatizes in Hell the wounds of the will, the sins and the proneness to sin as well as the voluntarism, which is to be understood as the belief in the primacy of the will over knowledge in acts of choice. Voluntarism, in a variety of disguises, envelops and determines Dante's representation of most human acts. Purgatory, on the other hand, displays the pilgrim's and the penitents' moral

7. *Vita nuova* 42, trans. Musa, 86.

8. "Est ergo subiectum totius operis, litteraliter tantum accepti, status animarum post mortem simpliciter sumptus; nam de illo et circa illum totius operis versatur processus. Si vero accipiatur opus allegorice, subiectum est homo prout merendo et demerendo per arbitrii libertatem iustitie premiandi et puniendi obnoxius est" (Dante Alighieri, *Opere minori II, Epistole,* ed. Arsenio Frugoni and Giorgio Brugnoli, La letteratura italiana storia e testi 5/2 [Milan and Naples: Riccardo Ricciardi Editore, 1979], 612).

education in the moral virtues. In *Purgatorio* 16.65–84, Dante expounds the centrality of free will in man's moral life. He has Marco Lombardo reject the tenet that the "will is subject to the power of the heavenly bodies," as Proposition 154 of the 219 Propositions condemned by the Archbishop of Paris, Étienne Tempier, in 1277 has it.[9] On the basis of the fact that the creation of the soul is a free and gratuitous operation, human beings' exercise of free will comes forth as the apt response to God's playful making of the human soul. And because the work of a man is learning—as a habit as well as an action—*Paradiso* focuses on knowledge, on the difficult education of the intellect striving, from height to height, from doubt to doubt, to reach the truth and to know what God is. In the last canticle reason and will, together, become the presupposition to the final vision.

2. Embodiment and the Wounded Will

In *Inferno,* one image brings into focus the condition of the pilgrim at the beginning of his spiritual adventure: he is a *homo claudus*. He has just stepped out of the darkness of the wood. In the broad daylight he tries to climb the mountain and reach the top, or the plain of truth from where he can survey the contours of the landscape. As he goes up he hobbles, "sì che 'l piè fermo sempre era 'l più basso" (so that the firm foot was always the lower, *Inferno* 1.30).[10] The feet of this *homo claudus* are the two feet of the soul, will and intellect. His "pié fermo"—as John Freccero has shown—is the left foot, his wounded will that makes the flight of the mind he is attempting impossible.[11] At the very beginning, when the pilgrim comes to the allegorical wood or "selva" (*Inferno* 1.2), he is unaware of his problems. He is clueless about how he got where he is, but he knows he wants to get himself out of the terrifying place. When he reaches the foot of a hill, he looks up at the sunlight. It is a light that "leads men aright by every path" (1.18). Fear, a passion that belongs to

9. The propositions are available in English, "Condemnation of 219 Propositions," trans. Ernest L. Fortin and Peter D. O'Neill, in *Medieval Political Philosophy: A Sourcebook,* ed. Ralph Lerner and Muhsin Mahdi (New York: Free Press of Glencoe, 1963), 335–54. The numbering of the propositions varies. According to the list established by P. Mandonnet, the proposition at hand is 154; according to the *Chartularium Universitatis Parisiensis* edited by Heinrich Denifle and Emile Chatelan, this proposition is number 162. See Roland Hissette, *Enquête sur les 219 articles condamnés à Paris le 7 mars 1277* (Leuven: Publications Universitaires/Paris: Vander-Oyez, 1977), 8.

10. The Italian quotations from the *Divine Comedy* and their translations are taken from *The Divine Comedy,* trans. Charles S. Singleton, 3 vols. (Princeton: Princeton University Press, 1970–1976).

11. John Freccero, *Dante: The Poetics of Conversion* (Cambridge, Mass.: Harvard University Press, 1986), 29–54.

the sensitive appetite and that is central to the pilgrim's state of mind, had seized him, but now it is somewhat placated. He describes himself as a shipwreck, as if he had been caught in a storm. Now his *animo* (1.25, a word that has a philosophical ring and designates the intellective powers of the mind) is in flight.

The opening scene of *Inferno* is replete with specialized Neoplatonic language. Already in the fifteenth century a Neoplatonic commentator of the *Divine Comedy,* such as Cristoforo Landino, had glossed Dante's *selva* as the translation of the Greek *hyle.* He explained it as the designation of the world of recalcitrant materiality enveloping the mind and which the mind has to flee in order to return to its original home. The pilgrim's looking up to the sun suggests the reenactment of the philosophical enlightenment, what later emerges as the flight of the mind.

If the *Divine Comedy* recounted a merely intellectual journey by the disembodied mind, the poem could convincingly end here. But the pilgrim's journey is not over. Actually, it has not even started. What is over, what ends in failure, is the myth of the philosophical, intellectual flight. The power of the mind is thwarted by the raw reality of the body:

> "E come quei che con lena affannata,
> uscito fuor del pelago a la riva,
> si volge a l'acqua perigliosa e guata,
>
> così l'animo mio, ch'ancor fuggiva,
> si volse a retro a rimirar lo passo
> che non lasciò mai persona viva.
>
> Poi ch'èi posato un poco il corpo lasso,
> ripresi via per la piaggia diserta,
> sì che 'l piè fermo sempre era 'l più basso.
>
> Ed ecco, quasi al cominciar de l'erta,
> una lonza leggiera e presta molto,
> che di pel macolato era coverta;
>
> e non mi si partia dinanzi al volto,
> anzi'mpediva tanto il mio cammino,
> ch'i' fui per ritornar più volte vòlto."
>
> (*Inferno* 1.22–36)[12]

12. "And as he who with laboring breath has escaped from the deep to the shore turns to look back on the dangerous waters, so my mind which was still fleeing turned back to gaze upon the pass that never left anyone alive. After I had rested my tired body a little, I again took up my way across the desert strand, so that the firm foot was always the lower. And behold, near the beginning of the steep, a leopard light-footed and very fleet, covered with a spotted hide! And it did not depart from before my eyes, but did so impede my way that more than once I turned round to go back."

In an essay of some years ago, Charles Singleton, reflecting on Dante's deployment of poetic and theological allegory, drew attention to the contrast in these lines between "mind" and "body" in order to argue that Dante's journey "exceeds metaphor" and is irreducible to the conventions of poetic allegory.[13] Singleton's insight led John Freccero to highlight the conceptual significance of this metaphoric transition. He argued that the failure of Dante's initial attempt to ascend the hill, indeed the failure of all journeys of the mind, resides in the laggard body to which the mind is wedded.[14] What the body means is history, the irreducible individuality of the pilgrim, the root of the passions, and the will, which, taken together, are more important than the generalized abstract promises made by philosophy. In short, the pilgrim begins his spiritual experience with the knowledge of his real destination, but this knowledge will not save him. It will not save him because, though he possesses knowledge, it does not mean that he possesses virtue. As he acknowledges the primacy of the intellect over the will, Dante must come to terms with the fears that paralyze his mind, with the beasts that threaten to rip him apart and which are to be understood as the animal forces or bodily appetites of the rational, irascible, and concupiscent appetites. He must heal the wounds of the will, which result from man's fall and which hold him back from his ends.

Consistently, Dante first confronts the wounded will within his own self. The will appears self-contradictory and divided against itself. In *Inferno* 2, he confesses to Virgil his doubts and fears: Why must he undertake this journey and who allows it? He describes himself as one who ". . . disvuol ciò che volle / e per novi pensier cangia proposta, / sì che dal cominciar tutto si tolle . . ." (2.37–39).[15]

The self-reflexiveness of these lines aims at showing the consequences of placing oneself in the prison of the will. The problem with the will consists in the fact that it cannot regulate itself. Further and paradoxically, the faculty of will and self-making shackles him. One cannot escape from it nor can one go beyond or as far as one would like. However, the pilgrim does not remain on the ground of pure will: Virgil rescues him and frees him from his fears.

13. Charles S. Singleton, *Dante's Studies I: Commedia, Elements of Structure* (Cambridge, Mass.: Harvard University Press, 1954), 11–12.

14. Freccero, 6.

15. ". . . unwills what he has willed and with new thoughts changes his resolve, so that he quite gives up the thing he had begun. . . ."

3. Francesca's Passion and the Illusion of a Pure Will

Canto 5 of *Inferno* dramatizes the dangers and complexities of the belief in the sovereignty of the will. This is the canto where lust is punished and the sinners, who have inverted the order of reason over the will (". . . i peccator carnali, / che la ragion sommettono al talento," *Inferno* 5.38–39) go endlessly round in circles, returning to the starting point. They never rest, and thus they enact their existence as pure desire (5.82), or, to put it in Augustinian language, they dramatize the restlessness of the heart forever out of place. Among the sinners from the classical and medieval world, there are queens, such as Dido, Cleopatra, and Semiramis, as well as heroes, such as Paris, Tristan, and Achilles. Dante singles out two contemporary souls, Paolo and Francesca.

He calls them: "Quali colombe dal disio chiamate / con l'ali alzate e ferme al dolce nido / vegnon per l'aere, dal voler portate; / cotali uscir de la schiera ov'è Dido, / a noi venendo . . ." (5.82–86).[16] The image of the dove, the bird that in classical lore is said to be sacred to Venus, to describe the two human beings, discloses the essence of desire as common to both animal and human behavior. In the natural world of Paolo and Francesca, the Platonic "wings of desire" are to be understood as the natural appetite, as a tendency to move toward a place where the need is satisfied. By contrast, *voler* indicates a rational, deliberate desire that characterizes a choice.

As she summarizes her love experience to the pilgrim, Francesca gives us evidence of her choice. Her speech centers on love:

> "Amor, ch'al cor gentil ratto s'apprende,
> prese costui de la bella persona
> che mi fu tolta; e 'l modo ancor m'offende.
>
> Amor, ch'a nullo amato amar perdona,
> mi prese del costui piacer sì forte,
> che, come vedi, ancor non m'abbandona.
>
> Amor condusse noi ad una morte.
> Caina attende chi a vita ci spense."
> (*Inferno* 5.100–107)[17]

16. "As doves called by desire, with wings raised and steady, come through the air, borne by their will to their sweet nest, so did these issue from the troop where Dido is, coming to us. . . ."

17. "Love, which is quickly kindled in a gentle heart, seized this one for the fair form that was taken from me—and the way of it afflicts me still. Love, which absolves no loved one from loving, seized me so strongly with delight in him, that, as you see, it does not leave me even now. Love brought us to one death. Caina awaits him who quenched our life."

Through the three tercets, as Natalino Sapegno has pointed out, the grammatical subject is a personified love: She, who dwells among queens and acknowledges God as *re* (king) (5.91), casts herself as a subject or victim enthralled to the overpowering god of love. Further, as Renato Poggioli has shown, Francesca's speech revolves around the question of desire mediated by literature.[18] She discovers, for instance, that she fell in love while reading the medieval romance of Lancelot and Guinevere. Finally, her references to love turn out to be quotations of love formulas available in texts ranging from Andreas Capellanus' *De Arte Honeste Amandi* to Guido Guinizelli's "Al cor gentil repaira" (In the gentle heart [Love] takes shelter), and to Dante's own *Vita nuova* ("Amore e el cor gentile sono una cosa," Love and the gentle heart are one thing). While these literary formulas thematically flatter the sense of the spontaneity of Francesca's passion, they show that she is possessed by literature and that her mind mirrors the love-sky of Lancelot and Guinevere that she is reading. When the romance they read tells of the kiss between the fictional lovers, the two readers read no further.

Paradoxically, when Francesca thinks she is spontaneous and free she is in bondage to fiction. When she thinks she is enthralled to love she hides her moral choice. By the paradox Dante goes to the roots of the passion and uncovers the self-delusion in her exercise of pure will. Francesca, who lives under the sovereignty of the will, reduces her real life into an imaginary life. She yields to a world of phantoms, to the magic enchantment of reading whereby she wills herself and her lover as, respectively, Guinevere and Lancelot, and in the process she derealizes her existence. She plunges into a fantasy world where she can play forever at being a queen and can live forever in a utopian condition of permanent desire.

Although her voluntarism comes through as an esthetic posture and manifests her narcissism (in that her self-absorption expects no practical results and ends in death), Francesca's frame of reference evokes the ethics of courtly love. From her exchange with Dante, we infer that she approves of and wants his approval for her choice of an ethics of gentle hearts, heroic passions, and instant pleasures. Yet the point is not simply that she substitutes one ethic for another. One may suspect that she actually attempts to do away with all ethics. She destroys within herself the bonds of time, family, and reality so that her kingdom of sheer fantasy may come into existence. She wills a glamorous esthetic life, and appropriately she ends up living eternally as a literary figure.

18. Natalino Sapegno, ed., *La Divina Commedia: Inferno,* 2nd ed. (Florence: La Nuova Italia, 1968), 61; Renato Poggioli, "Tragedy or Romance? A Reading of the Paolo and Francesca Episode in Dante's *Inferno,*" *PMLA* 77 (1957): 313–58.

4. Piccarda and the Inviolable Will

Francesca's blind surrender to her passion, her incapacity to control her will (the phenomenon of her will to will), finds its illumination and corrective counterpart in the symmetrically corresponding cantos of *Paradiso*. In the Heaven of the Moon (*Paradiso* 5) Dante encounters Piccarda, a nun, who is forced to break her vow by the political machinations of her brother, Corso Donati, and to marry. But her will was not broken by her brother's frenzy and sacrilege.

Beatrice justifies Piccarda's place in the lowest order of beatitude by claiming the autonomy of her will. No outside power can encroach upon or destroy its operation or essential freedom. Following Aristotle's *Nicomachean Ethics* 3.1 and St. Thomas Aquinas (*ST* Ia.19.6; IaIIae.77.7), who touches several times on two sorts of will, Beatrice distinguishes between the absolute and the conditional will of souls, between constrained activity and involuntary action. Her argument rests on the motive that Piccarda's absolute will remained faithful to her life in the convent, even if her conditional will yielded to coercion. She surrendered to contingent and provisional circumstances without consenting to them.

In *Paradiso* 5, Beatrice shows how Piccarda's vow made her escape all constraints and act as a free agent. What is a vow? "The word 'vow' [*votum*] derives," says St. Thomas, "from the word for will [*voluntas*]. . . . Therefore a vow consists only in an act of will" (*ST* IIaIIae.88.1–2). The etymology sustains the logical unfolding of the canto. In Beatrice's exposition, God bestows the greatest gift to human beings, and the gift is "de la volontà la libertade" (*Paradiso* 5.22), the faculty of will and judgment, which is the stamp of rationality angels and men alike share. Within the framework of God's liberality, the vow signals the restitution of the gift, which comes through as the sacrifice of the free will.

From this standpoint, Piccarda's moral drama (yielding to her brother's coercion and willpower) is secondary to the initial choice she made. In point of fact, she affirms the value and supremacy of transcendence over the order of contingency. The move shows Dante's chief purpose: he sets up moral problems so that he can point out how they can be overcome by removing self-possession and freeing oneself from the chains of estheticism. Francesca, to give consistency to the acts of her will, sacrifices the world and chooses to escape into the realm of fantasy. Piccarda divests herself of her free will and, when she is forced back into the realities of the world by somebody else's will, she can only pursue the good.

5. Cavalcanti: Political Dimensions of the Separation of Love and Intellect

The esthetic and ethical voluntarism I have been describing is not just a subjective issue, nor does it concern only Francesca, Piccarda, or Dante. In fact, a political voluntarism edges Francesca's experience, surrounded, as she is, by queens, legislators, and founders of cities. Dante tests the relation between politics and the will extensively and, poignantly in *Inferno* 10, where the sinners, on the face of it, equate questions of the immortality of the soul with the course of human history. They dissolve eternity into time and show themselves as finite, time-bound beings. That they "live" entirely within the horizon of history is made plain by the fact that sinners here inquire, with a transparent symmetrical precision, about ancestors and about the fate of their own children. I would like to turn to this canto to probe the vagaries of intellect and will.

On the face of it, the will has little to do with these sinners' fate. The pilgrim has just entered the city of Dis, where heresy—a word that comes from the Greek αἵρεσις (choice)—is punished. Here are the philosophers, among whom there is Epicurus and the Emperor Frederick II, and they are punished for not believing in the immortality of the soul. Their choice of unbelief is rooted in an intellectual judgment. Given the intellectual nature of their choice, W. H. Reade wondered whether heresy should be considered a sin at all, since, as is known, a sin must involve the will.[19] At any rate, *Inferno* 10 gets started by the traditional juxtaposition of Athens and Jerusalem, the city of philosophy and the city of revelation, which is evoked by the reference to the valley of Jehoshaphat (10.11), where the resurrection of the souls will take place at the end of time.

Once inside the walls of the infernal city, Dante meets two Florentines, Farinata and Cavalcanti, and through them he confronts Florence's persistent civil war between Guelphs and Ghibellines as well as his own past in his city. Farinata appears erect from the waist up in a tomb. His punishment fits the crime. He does not believe in the immortality of the soul. Thus, quite fittingly, he lives an eternal death. Yet he acts contemptuously toward the dead and, for that matter, toward the living, as if he actually did stand above all. He is the one to inquire about Dante's ancestors, whom he acknowledges as enemies he had twice defeated. Dante is equal to the challenge: with equal pride he responds that, though driven twice out of the city, twice they returned (*Inferno* 10.49–51).

19. W. H. V. Reade, *The Moral System of Dante's Inferno* (Oxford: Clarendon Press, 1909), 367–81.

The political squabble engaging the Guelph Dante and the Ghibelline Farinata is interrupted by Cavalcante Cavalcanti, Guido's father, who inquires about the fate of his son:

> . . . "Se per questo cieco
> carcere vai per altezza d'ingegno,
> mio figlio ov' è? e perché non è ei teco?"
>
> E io a lui: "Da me stesso non vegno:
> colui ch'attende là per qui mi mena,
> forse cui Guido vostro ebbe a disdegno."
>
> Le sue parole e 'l modo della pena
> m'avean di costui già letto il nome;
> però fu la risposta così piena.
>
> Di sùbito drizzato gridò: "Come
> dicesti: 'Egli ebbe'? non viv' elli ancora?
> non fiere li occhi suoi il dolce lume?"
>
> Quando s'accorse d'alcuna dimora
> ch'io facëa dinanzi alla risposta,
> supin ricadde e più non parve fora.
>
> Ma quell'altro magnanimo, a cui posta
> restato m'era, non mutò aspetto,
> né mosse collo, né piegò sua costa;
>
> e sé continüando al primo detto,
> "S'elli han quell'arte," disse, "male appresa. . . ."
> (*Inferno* 10.58–78)[20]

Salvation, for the old man, who clearly has his own philosophical pretensions, is completely accessible to and compatible with human intelligence. The phrase, "height of success"—an allusion to Guido's intellectual excellence—harkens back to Farinata's magnanimity (the etymology of the word is bound to sound ironic in this place where the soul is defeated), and it shows Cavalcanti's mistaken belief that Dante's journey is a philosophical or intellectual journey. By the phrase Dante

20. "'If you go through this blind prison by reason of your high genius, where is my son, and why is he not with you?' And I to him: 'I come not of myself. He who waits yonder, whom perhaps your Guido had in disdain, is leading me through here.' Already his words and the manner of his punishment had read his name to me, hence was my answer so full. Suddenly straightened up, he cried, 'How? Did you say "he had"? Does he not still live? Does the sweet light not strike his eyes?' And when he perceived that I made some delay in answering, he fell supine again and showed himself no more. But that other, that great soul at whose instance I had stopped, changed not his aspect, nor moved his neck, nor bent his side. 'And if,' he said, continuing his first discourse, 'they have ill learned that art. . . .'"

also stages his friend Guido's spiritual death as well as the reasons for it. As has been acknowledged, the speech features echoes of the rhyme scheme of Guido's love poem "Donna me prega" (A woman begs me).[21]

The poem was conceived as the answer to the queries by a fictional woman about the nature, place, and effects of love. Guido casts love as an experience that descends from the darkness of Mars, the sphere of the irascible, and dwells ". . . in quella parte dove sta memoria" (in that part where memory is), in the sensitive faculty of the soul. Practically following Isidore of Seville's etymology, "a Marte mors nuncupatur" (*Etymologies* 8.9.51), Cavalcanti describes love as a war, the activity of Mars that ends in death: "di sua potenza segue spesso morte" (death often follows its power).[22] In *Inferno* 10, where the primary thematic focus of the narrative is the civil war, this theory of love as a destructive passion underlies the reality of the civil war, just as the civil war crystallizes the essence of this love.

In "Donna me prega" love is an unrelenting passion that robs the self of any rationality and never becomes itself a rational activity. In the *Vita nuova,* as I argued earlier, Dante falls briefly into the enchanted poetic-philosophical circle of Guido Cavalcanti. In *Inferno* 10, however, Dante understands that bodies without soul are nothing, or they are like the corpse of the dead woman, Beatrice's friend, whose funeral he attends. And although Guido had advised a life of rational pursuits and had dismissed love's dark passion, Dante now intuits that Guido's theory of love is the real, though unacknowledged, source of Farinata's politics (and vice versa). His idea of *eros,* much like the other's view of politics, leads to a division within the soul as well as to the tyranny of partisan politics.

6. Political Epicureanism: Subjective Wills and Fractured Society

More precisely, Dante's exchange with Farinata and Cavalcanti highlights his notion of political Epicureanism and exposes the weakness and incoherence of that intellectual system. The commonplaces of the medieval mythography of Epicurus are available through a series of texts well known to Dante. Isidore of Seville defines Epicurus as the "philosopher who loved vanity not wisdom" (*Etymologies* 8.6.15), one who denies the

21. See Giuseppe Mazzotta, *Dante's Vision and the Circle of Knowledge* (Princeton: Princeton University Press, 1993), 107–9, for further bibliography. See also the recent essay by Maria Luisa Ardizzone, *Guido Cavalcanti: The Other Middle Ages* (Toronto: University of Toronto Press, 2002).

22. Guido Cavalcanti, *The Complete Poems,* trans. Marc A. Cirigliano (New York: Italica Press, 1992), 62.

world's government by Providence, and who believes in the corporeal nature of bodies. John of Salisbury in his *Metalogicon* attributes to Epicurus both the belief in the world's origin from atoms and the disbelief in God as the author of the world.[23] A fuller treatment of Epicurean politics, ethics, psychology, and physics is found in Cicero's *De finibus* (1.13–26). In *De finibus,* Cicero levels three major objections to Epicurus's natural philosophy, ethics, and politics. He admits that Epicurus's doctrines resemble Democritus's (1.18). At the heart of their theories stands their physics (1.17). They believe, he says, "in certain things" which they term atoms existing from all eternity. Though indivisible they are composed of parts. The motion of these atoms is such that they collide and cohere together.

This atomic theory underlies the Epicurean materialist theory of the mortality of the soul. Torquatus, Cicero's character in *De finibus,* objects to Epicurus on the grounds that he places the criteria of reality in sensation. Further, Cicero discounts the Epicurean theory of "ethical hedonism," the belief that feelings of pleasure and pain lie at the root of every act of choice. If pleasure is the end of life, then politics, which is the arena of dangerous competition, is an impossible activity. A contradiction thwarts the relation between this philosophy and the life of the city: Epicurus retreats into himself and to his garden in the company of his friends. He escapes history in the sense that he shows no interest in public life and chooses intellectual contemplation over action. Nor is there room in such a context for justice as either a transcendent norm or as a political virtue. Finally, Cicero reflects on the apparent contradiction between the Epicurean theory of pleasure and the ideal of friendship, which the Epicureans hold in high esteem, but which seems to be dismantled by their pleasure-centered ethos. The philosophers, who have retreated from the world, witness the breakdown of the city.

These contradictions, transposed to the domain of politics, color Canto 10 of the *Inferno.* It is Dante's irony, thus, to mix together Epicurus, the philosopher who retreats into the absolute, eternal order of the mind, with Farinata and Cavalcante, who dwell in the domain of historical contingency and mortality. All of them live "apart" from others (whether out of philosophical conviction or political sense of belonging to a special class) and not as parts of a unified whole. But there are other sources of contradictions. Farinata recognizes Dante from the Tuscan cadence of his language: "'O Tosco che per la città del foco / . . . di quella nobil patrïa natio, / a la qual forse fui troppo molesto'" (*Inferno*

23. John of Salisbury, *Metalogicon* 2.2, ed. J. B. Hall and K. S. B. Keats-Rohan, CCCM 98 (Turnhout: Brepols, 1991), 58.

10.22–27).[24] There is a subtle distinction at work between "città" and "patria." "Città" designates a city, whereas "patria" means fatherland or country. In a canto such as this, where fathers worry about sons, and ancestors cast a long shadow on their descendants, the term refers to one's place of origin or the particular place of one's family. "Patria," in this sense, antedates "città," which, ever since Aristotle's *Politics,* aims at the highest and comprehensive good. Ironically, this "città" is infernal.

The irony reaches even further. Both Farinata and Dante live in a world of unrelated "parts" or atomized, fragmented entities that caricature Epicurean doctrine. Dante's ancestors, Farinata says, were adverse to his party ("a mia parte," line 47). "Parte" (line 49) designates also the quarters where the factions were scattered. By the end of the canto, the old Cavalcanti, who inquires about the present but knows the past and the future, divides time into unknowable parts. In effect, and the irony is devastating for these political philosophers, his partial knowledge is no knowledge at all: the incomplete knowledge of time in its present form forfeits the possibility both of a comprehensive whole and of the completion of history. More to the point, the word "parte" figures in the opening lines of both Cavalcanti's "Donna me prega" and the *Vita nuova:* "In quella parte dove sta memoria" (In that part where memory is found) is deliberately echoed by Dante's opening words: "In quella parte del libro de la mia memoria. . . ."[25]

The two poets, who once were friends, deeply differ on how parts are related to wholes and on how bodies are related to souls. The importance of this issue for Dante emerges from *Monarchia* (1.6), where he muses on the logical connection between partial order and total order. Within that political frame of references, the part is related to the whole as to its end. The tenet echoes the argument on the relation between parts and whole developed both in Aristotle's *Physics* and in Aquinas's commentary on it. In the political Epicureanism Farinata crystallizes, the "whole" has crumbled into broken parts, and neither Farinata nor Cavalcanti sees the way of fitting the pieces into a unified totality.

A sharp image of the city emerges from these "uncivil" conversations: it is enveloped in anarchy and chaos. The canto is marked by quarrels, misunderstandings about what exactly phrases mean, interruptions, and confusions of the public with the private. Farinata, for instance, looks at life and death from the point of view of the good of the city, but he lets his partisan concerns obscure his sense of the city. Cavalcanti, on the

24. "O Tuscan, who go alive through the city of fire . . . a native of that noble fatherland to which I perhaps did too much harm."

25. *La vita nuova* 1, ed. Barbi, p. 3; cf. Musa, p. 3.

other hand, thinks only of his son's fate. And the indifference of Farinata to Cavalcanti's grief captures the reality of the city under the sway of discord, with each element believing in the compelling superior nature of its own concerns. The mixture of political relations and personal attachments belies the Epicurean principle of self-sufficiency. What these characters convey is their desire to impose their subjective wills on the chaos of the city.

Above all, the scene makes visible the workings of the will behind the claims of an apparently pure rationality. Heresy is not merely an intellectual choice. For all his magnanimity and for all the appearance that he, like a soulless being, neither moves nor is moved by the grief of others, Farinata is ruled by passions and by the will to crush his enemies. Between him and Dante there is a struggle for recognition, the desire for mastery over the submissive enemy, which makes Farinata's magnanimity edge toward pride, and disguises the hidden will to affirm his own values. By the same token, the old Cavalcanti yields to pathos over the feared premature death of his son. Finally, the tragic view of politics in the canto as a conflict without solution shows to Dante himself the ambiguities of the political project delineated in his *Monarchia.* On the one hand, *Monarchia* seeks to reconstitute political society in the light of rational philosophy, a philosophy that has mistakenly struck some as Averroistic. On the other hand, Dante takes the history of Rome—which St. Augustine views as a history of the will to power, or *libido dominandi*—as the paradigm of political excellence. In the wake of St. Augustine he sees the empire as both rooted in human sinfulness and also as a remedy to sin.

7. Art versus Usury

Francesca is the esthete who wills to transform the world into an act of the imagination and a projection of her daydreams. Farinata and Cavalcanti are the philosophers who stand for the will to power and conceal from themselves the workings of the will only to discover that reason alone dooms them to live in isolation, for reason cannot be construed as a bridge between self and others. Dante returns to the disguises and crises of the will in *Inferno* 11, where he explicitly contrasts the system of Epicurean ethics and politics by giving an exposition of the character of human life in terms of Aristotle's *Nicomachean Ethics* and *Physics,* and Aquinas's commentary on them.

The moral framework of *Inferno,* with its tripartite structure (the sins of incontinence, bestiality, and fraud) is patterned, so we are told, on the blueprint of the *Nicomachean Ethics* (*Inferno* 11.80, cf. *EN* 7.1). In listing the order of sins Virgil makes no mention of some moral violations, such as heresy (the area which the pilgrim has just crossed) and usury. Dante asks Virgil to explain the sin of usury (*Inferno* 11.95) and he complies by sketching the outline of an esthetic theory in which usury, because it is an unreal, illusory production, comes forth as a caricature of art, as a cult of shams that mocks the productive work of nature:

> "Filosofia," mi disse "a chi la 'ntende,
> nota non pur in una sola parte,
> come natura lo suo corse prende
>
> dal divino 'ntelletto e da sua arte;
> e se tu ben la tua Fisica note,
> tu troverai, non dopo molte carte,
>
> che l'arte vostra quella, quanto pote,
> segue, come 'l maestro fa 'l discente;
> sì che vostr' arte a Dio quasi è nepote.
>
> Da queste due, se tu ti rechi a mente
> lo Genesì dal principio, convene
> prender sua vita e avanzar la gente;
>
> e perché l'usuriere altra via tene
> per sé natura e per la sua seguace
> dispregia, poi ch'in altro pon la spene."
> (*Inferno* 11.97–111)[26]

Usury, the brunt of the passage, figures an unreal production, a mockery of *poiesis,* and in this sense it is juxtaposed to art as work. Aristotle's *Physics,* which debates the relationship between parts and whole (4.3–6; 7.1) and whether or not the soul moves the body, argues for a view of parts that correlate with each other. Dante's view of art as a virtue of making, of its filial relationship to the productive order of Nature, and of its discipline and educational role derives from the *Physics,* but it finds its adequate gloss in the theoretical framework of Aquinas's Proemium to his *Commentary on the Politics:*

> As the Philosopher teaches in Book 2 of the *Physics,* art imitates nature. . . . Now the principle of these things that come about through art is the human intellect, and the human intellect derives according to a certain resemblance from the

26. "'Philosophy, for one who understands it,' he said to me, 'points out, not in one place alone, how Nature takes her course from the divine intellect and from its art; and if you note well your Physics, you will find, after not many pages, that your art, as far as it can, follows her as the pupil does his master; so that your art is as it were grandchild of God. By these two, if you remember Genesis at the beginning, it behooves man to gain his bread to prosper. But because the usurer takes another way, he contemns Nature in herself and in her follower, for he puts his hope elsewhere.'"

divine intellect, which is the principle of natural things. Hence the operations of art must imitate the operations of nature. . . . For if an instructor of some art were to produce a work of art, the disciple who receives his art from him would have to observe that work so that he himself might act in like manner.[27]

The astonishing parallels between the two passages force us to say that for Dante, just as for Aquinas, art is not a form of theoretical knowledge. It fulfills the real ends of the natural world, is akin to prudence, and it belongs to the practical intellect. For Dante art counters and circumscribes the speculative subjectivity of heresy. More overtly than St. Thomas, for whom art plays a ministerial function, Dante views art as the activity bringing us back to the ground of nature, to the consideration of principles, beginning and foundation. A metaphysical, and not just a political, project underlies this paradigm of art. The conflation of Aristotle's *Physics* and Genesis evokes both Nature's beginnings and the primal condition of man's fall, where work is both a punishment and a remedy. Art is work, whereby human beings find their bearings in the world, shape Nature to their purpose, and begin anew in their effort to change the wilderness into Paradise.

This view of art's pedagogical role retrospectively discloses the flaws in the moral vision of both the "esthetic" voluntarists and the Epicurean political philosophy. Both practices, ironically without any self-consciousness, are rooted in the will. Like latter-day idealists and materialists, proponents of both strains of thought want to make the world what they say it is: a projection of their will to nothing or a projection of their megalomania. Farinata, for instance, pursues "ben far"—so the text says (*Inferno* 6.81)—an ambiguous phrase that could be translated as "doing good" or "doing well," and the ambiguity remains in whichever translation one chooses. Because the esthetes and the Epicureans have no aim beyond themselves, they end up in an essentially solitary understanding of the pleasures of art and the nature of political life. From Dante's standpoint, who never distinguishes between politics and ethics, these sciences envision no possibility of relation and coherence.

The Empire is born in sin and is a remedy to sin. Virgil's teaching about art as the corrective of the sins of incontinence (lust) and of the excesses of the speculative intellect (the heretics) and as the foundation of the moral life turns into a thread running throughout *Purgatorio* and stitching it together. No doubt, the meaning Dante attaches to art as work (in contrast to the symbolic excrescence derived from usury)

27. St. Thomas Aquinas, *Sententia libri Politicorum,* Leonine Edition vol. 48, p. A69, ll. 1–15. The translation, by Ernest C. Fortin and Peter O'Neill, is available in *Medieval Political Philosophy: A Sourcebook,* ed. Ralph Lerner and Muhsin Mahdi (New York: Free Press of Glencoe, 1963), 298.

owes much to both the *Aeneid*'s insight into work as creative desire and Genesis's theology of work. In *Purgatorio,* however, Dante addresses several aspects of the theme of the artwork.

The clearest mark of art as a basic healing virtue is evident from the double power Dante assigns to it and probes in *Purgatorio.* The moral education of the pilgrim as well as the penitent—as the encounter with Casella, the presentation of the proud sinners, the dream of the Siren, and Statius's rejection of avarice and prodigality show—puts into action the role of art. Second, as both the *Vita nuova* and the series of cantos at the heart of the poem—*Purgatorio* 16, 17, and 18—stress, art has the power to stir the phantasms of the imagination, the faculty that shapes all acts of love and knowledge.[28]

Conclusion: Healing the Wounded Will

The poetry of the *Divine Comedy* itself narrates how one takes care of one's soul and it traces the pilgrim's journey to the beatific vision after the wounds of his will have been healed (*Purgatorio* 27.140). By the end of the poem in *Paradiso* 33, the problem is not one of determining whether the will is higher than the intellect or the intellect is nobler than the will. There is no question that the intellect for Dante as for St. Thomas is a higher power than the will. Yet the two faculties necessarily move together. Furthermore, no such separation of faculties is imaginable in the divine life Dante seeks to fathom. As he approaches the beatific vision, the pilgrim does not plunge into a state whereby he loses his own self. Rather, he reaffirms his separate, ecstatic self. The mode of cognition of God at the end of the poem, however, confirms the terms of his quest: the intellectively apprehended good moves the will, and his will and desire are revolved by divine Love. While the vision's memory fades, the mind is overpowered, the logic of the geometer is futile (Dante uses geometry as the paradigm of rational knowledge), and the affections edge beyond the ordinary bounds of knowledge. It is through "disio e 'l velle" (*Paradiso* 33.143)—the intersection of desire and love, which is the will's natural end—that the pilgrim joins in God's embrace.

28. I have devoted chapter 6 of *Dante's Vision and the Circle of Knowledge* to these questions and therefore I will refrain from repeating the argument here.

8 Montaigne's Marvelous Weakness

ANN HARTLE

The first thing that Montaigne says about himself in the *Essays* is: "I am marvelously weak." How can his weakness be "marvelous"? I will attempt to show that, although Montaigne continues to use the language of the traditional, classical-medieval moral categories, he is actually introducing a new moral possibility and a new standard of human perfection. This new possibility is grounded in a rejection of Aristotelian metaphysics and results in a reordering of the traditional virtues and vices. At the same time, it is a response to Machiavelli's claim that Christianity has made the world weak. I will conclude with reflections on the essay as the new mode of philosophy that brings Montaigne's new moral possibility to light.

1. Montaigne's Weakness

Montaigne begins "Of Cruelty" with the opinion that "virtue is something other and more noble than the inclinations toward goodness that are born in us" (VS 422; F 306).[1] Virtue is more noble because it involves struggle and the difficulty of mastering the passions and appetites. Struggle and mastery seem to be essential to virtue. But as the essay moves along, that initial opinion must be modified, for Montaigne suddenly thinks of Socrates and of Cato. He cannot imagine any difficulty or constraint in their practice of virtue. The souls of these two men and their imitators have achieved "so perfect a habituation to virtue that it has passed into their nature." The vicious passions that most men experience cannot even enter these men because the strength of their souls

1. References to the French text of the *Essais* are to the edition by Pierre Villey and V.-L. Saulnier, 2nd ed., 3 vols., Quadrige 94–96 (Paris: Presses Universitaires de France, 1992). The English translation is that of Donald Frame, *The Complete Essays of Montaigne* (Stanford, Calif.: Stanford University Press, 1943). The citation (VS 422; F 306), for example, refers to p. 422 of the Villey-Saulnier edition and to p. 306 of the Frame translation. In some instances, I have emended Frame's translation.

stifles them as soon as they begin to stir (VS 425–26; F 310). Now there emerges a three-place hierarchy to supersede the initial two-place hierarchy of virtue and goodness. The highest place belongs to perfect virtue, the condition in which the individual has so "formed" himself to virtue that the very seeds of the vices are rooted out. The second place belongs to the imperfect virtue that experiences the beginnings of vicious inclinations but overcomes them by force. The third place belongs to those who simply happened to be born with an affable nature and an inborn distaste for vice (VS 426; F 310). This third condition is goodness or innocence, not virtue.

Montaigne locates himself at the lowest place in the hierarchy: he is very far from that first and most perfect degree of excellence where virtue becomes a habit, and he has not even given much evidence of the second degree of virtue. If he had been born with a more unruly disposition, it would have gone pitifully with him, for he has not experienced much firmness in his soul to withstand passions. "I do not know how to foster quarrels and conflict within me" (VS 427; F 311). Comparing himself to Socrates and to Stilpo (both of whom are said to have corrected their natural inclinations to vice through discipline and study), Montaigne says that he, on the contrary, has whatever good is in him simply by the chance of his birth. His virtue, or rather his innocence, he says, is "accidental and fortuitous" (VS 427; F 311).

By locating himself in the third and lowest place in the hierarchy, Montaigne locates himself in the place that should be weakness of will. According to the Aristotelian hierarchy, the order is divine virtue, perfect habitual virtue, moral strength, moral weakness, vice, and brutishness.[2] Montaigne preserves the categories of virtue and moral strength but then seems to substitute goodness or innocence for moral weakness. Or perhaps it would be better to say that he places goodness or innocence alongside weakness of will, for the condition of goodness or innocence is, he says, "so close to imperfection and weakness that [he does] not very well know how to separate their confines and distinguish them. The very names of goodness and innocence are for this reason to some extent terms of contempt" (VS 426; F 310).

At the same time, Montaigne's weakness looks very much like what Aristotle calls "natural virtue." In Book 6 of the *Nicomachean Ethics* Aristotle writes: "It seems that the various kinds of character inhere in all

2. Ullrich Langer, *Vertu du discours, discours de la vertu: Littérature et philosophie morale au XVIe siècle en France* (Geneva: Librairie Droz, 1999), 18–22. Langer provides conclusive evidence regarding the importance of Aristotle in discussions of moral philosophy in Montaigne's intellectual milieu.

of us, somehow or other, by nature. We tend to be just, capable of self-control, and to show all our other character traits from the time of our birth. Yet we still seek something more, the good in a fuller sense, and the possession of these traits in another way" (6.13.1144b4–8). Natural virtue is completed and perfected through intelligence. "At that point, the natural characteristic will become that virtue in the full sense which it previously resembled" (1144b13–14).[3]

Montaigne, however, does not or cannot imitate the loftiness of heroic virtue and he does not strive for the perfection of virtue that would require the rule of reason. There seems to be no distance between what he is and what he should be.[4] Throughout the essays, he presents his own weak way of coming to terms with the accidents of life and with the occasions that force us to confront evil. In "Of Husbanding Your Will" he explains that his way involves avoiding such occasions whenever possible. Some wise men who are sure of their strength have taken another way, and have not feared to test their powers of endurance in wrestling with misfortunes. But, Montaigne says: "Let us not tackle these examples; we would not come up to them. . . . For our common souls there is too much effort and harshness in that. . . . We little men must flee the storm from farther away; we must try to avoid feeling it, not try to endure it" (VS 1015; F 777). Later in the same essay, he writes: "Passions are as easy for me to avoid as they are hard for me to moderate. . . . He who cannot attain that noble impassibility of the Stoics, let him take refuge in the bosom of this plebeian stupidity of mine. What those men did by virtue, I train myself to do by disposition" (VS 1019–20; F 780).[5] Montaigne appeals to the Holy Spirit to justify his weak way. The Holy Spirit says: "Lead us not into temptation." Montaigne explains that "we do not pray that our reason may not be combated and overcome by concupiscence, but that it may not even be tested by it, that we may not be brought into a state where we even have to suffer the approaches, solici-

3. Aristotle, *Nicomachean Ethics,* trans. Martin Ostwald (Upper Saddle River, N.J.: Prentice Hall, 1999). It would make sense to say that what Montaigne means by weakness is just Aristotle's notion of natural virtue. However, since Montaigne's weakness or goodness leads to a reordering of the virtues and vices, it might be concluded that he is thinking in terms of a different meaning of "nature."

4. Hugo Friedrich, *Montaigne,* trans. Dawn Eng (Berkeley and Los Angeles: University of California Press, 1991), 227. Montaigne does not believe in the perfectibility of the human essence.

5. The idea of training his disposition looks very much like striving for the rule of reason over the natural inclinations. Yet Montaigne is making precisely that distinction between virtue and the training of the disposition. I suggest that the training of his disposition is accomplished, at least in part, by the practice of the essay itself: the essay effects a transformation that is, strictly speaking, nonrational.

tations, and temptations of sin; and we supplicate our Lord to keep our conscience tranquil, fully and perfectly delivered from dealing with evil" (VS 1016; F 777). When Montaigne introduces the distinction between virtue and the inclinations to goodness at the beginning of "Of Cruelty," he says that virtue is "more active" than goodness. His aversion to evil is expressed as a horror of vice. Thus, his avoidance of evil is very different from the active pursuit of virtue as an end.

In contrast to the strength of perfect virtue, Montaigne presents himself as weak and imperfect. How is this weakness to be distinguished from weakness of will? The reason why Montaigne's weakness is so difficult to distinguish from weakness of will is that weakness looks like cowardice. He chooses to run away from evil rather than confront it and master it. In "Of Cruelty" he refers to his hatred of the vice of cruelty as "extreme softness." The presumption seems to be that a man who is so horrified by cruelty, even to animals, must be timid, fearful, and perhaps even delicately sensual. When it is a question of the inclinations, without the direction of reason, that combination of natural inclinations looks plausible, especially in light of Aquinas's discussion of the question whether virtue is in us by nature. Following Aristotle's view that the virtues are in us by nature inasmuch as we are adapted to them, but not in their perfection, Aquinas distinguishes between "two ways in which something is said to be natural to a man; one is according to his specific nature, the other according to his individual nature." Each thing derives its species from its form and its individuation from its matter. Man's form is his rational soul and his matter is his body. Therefore, whatever belongs to him in respect of his rational soul is natural to him in respect of his specific nature; while whatever belongs to him in respect of the particular temperament of his body is natural to him in respect of his individual nature. The naturally known principles of knowledge and action are instilled in man's reason, and a natural appetite for good is instilled in his will. These principles, Aquinas says, are "the nurseries of the intellectual and moral virtues" and belong to man's specific nature. But with respect to his individual nature, each man is disposed well or ill to certain virtues according to his bodily disposition.[6]

So an individual may have a natural inclination to one or another virtue but not to all the virtues because a natural disposition that inclines to one virtue also inclines to the contrary of another virtue. For example, a man who is naturally inclined to courage will also be naturally inclined to cruelty. Since men are intended to achieve the complete good of virtue, they possess inclinations to all the virtues through reason, not

6. Thomas Aquinas, *Summa theologiae* IaIIae.63.1.

through their natural, bodily inclinations. Reason contains the seeds of all the virtues.[7]

Looked at from this perspective, Montaigne's goodness seems to be just an impossible combination of natural inclinations. He is "marvelously weak" but he is not at all cowardly because his goodness includes a certain kind of courage: he is without fear and he is not in any way servile.[8] This comes through especially in his description of the openness, frankness, liberty, and license that he exhibits in his role as negotiator between princes.[9] It takes courage to tell the prince frankly what one thinks of his actions and his character.[10] Montaigne's goodness is "so close" not only to weakness and imperfection, but also to perfect virtue: it resembles perfect virtue because there is no struggle. The same characteristic that makes it look weak also makes it resemble the extreme strength of virtue.

The Aristotelian hierarchy depends upon the direction of one's action to the end. In his *Ethics Commentary*, Aquinas distinguishes between vice in the complete sense and incontinence (which he calls vice in the incomplete sense). Vice in the complete sense means that "the reason and the appetitive faculty aim at evil." Vice in the incomplete sense means that "the appetitive faculty, but not the reason, tends to evil, which occurs in incontinence."[11] For Aristotle, the principle of action is the end on account of which we act. Aquinas explains that the incontinent person "does preserve the highest principle, which is the correct evaluation of the end."[12] Montaigne holds most vices in horror, not on account of reason, but on account of an instinct and impression that he brought away from the nursery. Indeed, his reasonings would easily give him license for actions that his natural inclinations make him hate, for his reason is more depraved than his lusts, and his habitual ways of acting are better ordered than his opinions (VS 428; F 312).[13]

7. Thomas Aquinas, *De virtutibus in communi* 8 ad 10, ed. P. A. Odetto (Rome and Turin: Marietti, 1953), 728b.

8. David Quint, *The Quality of Mercy: Ethical and Political Themes in the Essais* (Princeton: Princeton University Press, 1998), 31–32 and 122–23. Montaigne combines clemency and constancy, submission and bravery in his character. Quint also claims that Montaigne links himself with the weakness of the common people (p. 9).

9. On the quality of openness in Montaigne, see Judith N. Shklar, *Ordinary Vices* (Cambridge, Mass.: Belknap Press of Harvard University Press, 1984), 166.

10. See especially Book 3, Essay 1, "Of the Useful and the Honorable."

11. Thomas Aquinas, *Sententia libri Ethicorum* 7.4 [n. 1359], Editio Leonina 47/2: 396b, ll. 84–86. English translation: *Commentary on Aristotle's Nicomachean Ethics*, trans. C. I. Litzinger, O.P. (Notre Dame, Ind.: Dumb Ox Books, 1993), 427. Thus the vice of intemperance is worse than incontinence.

12. *Sententia libri Ethicorum* 7.8 [n. 1433], ed. Leon., 47/2: 415b, ll. 158–59; trans. Litzinger, 447.

13. Jerome B. Schneewind, *The Invention of Autonomy* (Cambridge: Cambridge University Press, 1998), 47. Montaigne's first impressions remained authoritative for him.

Consistency, which is "the end and perfection" of virtue (VS 332; F 240), would seem to be possible only through the rule and direction of reason: all of one's actions must be directed by reason to a single end. Only about a dozen men among the ancients have ever achieved this perfection: once again, Cato is his primary example. Most men "will nothing freely, nothing absolutely, nothing constantly" (VS 333; F 240). Therefore they are moved about by the winds of circumstance and by their own constantly changing dispositions. Montaigne insists on his changeability. He himself has not achieved the consistency of virtue, and that consistency would seem to be impossible for him because, on account of his inability to struggle within himself, he is not ruled by reason, but just follows his inclinations. However, a new notion of consistency emerges in the *Essays.* In the first essay of Book 3, he refers to the constant and inflexible movement of his soul which cannot be captured in the rules of any school. This constancy is his liberty and license and he refers to it as "the way of truth" that is "one and simple" (VS 795; F 603).

Montaigne begins "Of Repentance" with the claim that he is "very ill-formed" and that he would make himself very different from what he is if he had to fashion himself over again (VS 804; F 610), suggesting that he is dissatisfied with the way he has lived his life and with what he has become. But he ends that essay with the opposite view: "If I had to live over again, I would live as I have lived" (VS 816; F 620). Now he is judging himself by a different standard: "[His] conscience is content with itself—not as the conscience of an angel or a horse, but as the conscience of a man" (VS 806; F 612).

Thus a new notion of perfection also emerges in the *Essays:* "It is an absolute perfection and God-like to know how to enjoy our own being rightly" (VS 1115; F 857). This notion of absolute perfection arises against the background of his discussion of the proper relation between soul and body and his criticisms of those philosophers who despise the body and want to escape from it in order to contemplate the eternal and unchanging. "They want to get out of themselves and escape from the man. That is madness: instead of changing into angels, they change into beasts; instead of raising themselves, they lower themselves" (VS 1115; F 856).[14] Those Christian ascetics who are elevated to a constant meditation of divine things are moved by a vehement hope for "the eternal nourishment, the final and last end of Christian desires, the only constant and incorruptible pleasure" (VS 1114; F 856). Nevertheless, he

14. See also "Of Repentance," where he writes: "I have made no effort to attach, monstrously, the tail of a philosopher to the head and body of a dissipated man" (VS 816; F 619–20).

says, "these are things that I have always seen to be of singular accord: supercelestial opinions and subterranean conduct [*mœurs*]" (VS 1115; F 856).

Montaigne uses the language of weakness and imperfection, but he is displaying a moral possibility, the possibility of consistent goodness, that cannot be captured in the traditional moral categories.

2. Metaphysical Foundations

Montaigne is addressing the Aristotelian notion of moral perfection and therefore also its metaphysical basis. Perfection is fulfillment or the actualization of a potentiality. The end or final cause of a being is just the realization of the form, the complete realization of what the thing ought to be. There is one and only one form of each species or kind, and thus one perfection. In the case of the human species, perfection must involve reason because reason is what is highest in man and what distinguishes man from the other animals.

For Aristotle and Aquinas, the form of man is the rational soul. Reason is universal and the same in all men. Whereas, for Aquinas, reason contains universal principles that are the seeds of the virtues, for Montaigne, reason destroys any universal, natural principles. "It is credible that there are natural laws, as may be seen in other creatures; but in us they are lost; that fine human reason butts in everywhere, domineering and commanding, muddling and confusing the face of things in accordance with its vanity and inconsistency" (VS 581; F 438). Reason is "that appearance of discourse that each man forges in himself." Reason gives us a hundred contradictory opinions about one and the same subject. Therefore it is "an instrument of lead and wax, stretchable, pliable, and adaptable to all biases and all measures" (VS 565; F425).

Montaigne agrees with the Aristotelian-Thomistic view that reason is necessary for the practice of virtue and the attainment of perfect virtue. When he introduces Socrates and Cato as the exemplars of perfect virtue, he says explicitly that they have imitators who have achieved the same goal through the long practice of the precepts of philosophy (VS 425; F 310). Montaigne's goodness, on the other hand, is not achieved through reason or the precepts of philosophy. He is thus led to ask: "Could it be true that to be wholly good we must be so by some hidden, natural, and universal property, without law, without reason, without example?" (VS 428; F 312) Goodness cannot be imitated. There are no rules to be followed and no way to copy examples of goodness. Unlike virtue, goodness does not depend upon the rule of reason in the soul.

Montaigne's distinction between goodness and virtue entails his opposition to Aristotle on the issue of form, especially the relation between soul and body. For Aristotle, the soul is the form of the body, the efficient cause of the body's movement, and the final cause of the body, that is, the body is the instrument of the soul and exists for the sake of the activities of the soul.[15] Montaigne presents two criticisms of Aristotle's account of the soul. First, Aristotle claims that there are three principles of natural things: matter, form, and privation.[16] Montaigne ridicules the idea that privation can be a cause: "What could be more inane than to make emptiness the cause of the production of things? Privation is a negative; by what notion can he have made it the cause and origin of the things that are?" (VS 540; F 403). Montaigne's defects and deformities would seem to be privations, and he never makes any effort to overcome them. Second, Aristotle says that what naturally moves the body is "entelechy" (or actuality). Montaigne calls this a "frigid invention" that simply refers to the effect of the soul on the body but not to the essence, origin, or nature of the soul (VS 543; F 406). The context of these criticisms is Montaigne's discussion of our knowledge of natural things in the "Apology for Sebond." He concludes that "no man has ever known" how a spiritual impression can affect a solid object or "the nature of the relation and connection between these [two] wonderful springs of action" (VS 539; F 402).

Montaigne calls into question the idea that the body is ruled by the soul and is the instrument of the soul. There is no natural mastery in their relation, and that would explain why there is no struggle in him. Weakness of will is a category that makes sense only in a world in which there is hierarchy and a rightful mastery of the lower by the higher. The absence of natural mastery extends beyond the relationships among the parts of the human soul. At the end of "Of Cruelty," for example, he rejects the idea of our kingship over the animals (VS 435; F 318). This rejection of natural mastery is directly contrary, not only to Aristotle's account of human nature, but also to his justification of rule in the *Politics*.

Montaigne's references to form, scattered throughout the essays, reveal a shift in the meaning of form in two (related) ways. First, he emphasizes the imperfection of his form. In "To the Reader" he says that he wants to be seen in his simple, natural, and ordinary form, "without striving." Therefore, his defects will be an important part of his portrait (VS 3; F 2). "Of Repentance" begins: "Others form man; I tell of him, and portray a particular one, very ill-formed" (VS 804; F 610). And in "Of Cripples" he writes: "the more I am familiar with myself and know

15. *De anima* 2.4.415a22–b27.
16. See especially *Physics* 1.7.190b17–191a22.

myself, the more my *deformity* astonishes me, and the less I understand myself" (VS 1029; F 787). Second, he particularizes form especially in the idea of the master form *(forme maistresse)* which emerges in "Of Repentance." Each man, if he listens to himself, discovers in himself "a form all his own." Here he is discussing the difficulty or even the impossibility of changing one's natural inclinations through teaching. Thus true reformation is extremely difficult because the master form struggles against any education that opposes it (VS 811; F 615).

Montaigne often refers to the diversity and variety of forms, especially in reference to men and to human action. He knows no better school to "form" one's life than to have before one incessantly the diversity of many other lives, opinions, and customs, and "the perpetual variety of forms of our nature" (VS 973–74; F 744). He often discusses the common vice of judging all men by what we ourselves are, for each man thinks that the master form of nature is in him so that he makes himself the touchstone of all other forms (VS 725; F 548). The beginning of his essay on Cato the Younger is especially pertinent:

> I do not share that common error of judging another by myself. I easily believe that another man may have qualities different from mine. Because I feel myself tied down to one form, I do not oblige everybody to espouse it, as all others do. I believe in and conceive a thousand contrary ways of life; and in contrast with the common run of men, I more easily admit difference than resemblance between us. I am as ready as you please to acquit another man from sharing my conditions and principles. I consider him simply in himself, without relation to others; I mold him to his own model. . . . I have a singular desire that we should each be judged in ourselves apart, and that I may not be measured in conformity with the common examples.

At this point he introduces his weakness and thus identifies his own form with his weakness. Whereas most men praise nothing except what they think they can imitate, Montaigne says that his weakness in no way alters his high regard for the strength and vigor of those who deserve it and the inimitable loftiness of certain heroic souls (VS 229; F 169). His weakness is his form and his weakness is his deformity. His form is deformed.

The way Montaigne changes the meaning of *form* calls into question the relationship between the individual and the species and introduces a new notion of particularity. According to Aquinas's interpretation of Aristotle, each thing derives its species from its form and its individuation from matter. For Montaigne, particularity cannot be grounded simply in the body. He particularizes form itself, thereby suggesting that particularity involves the union of soul and body. Whereas, for Aristotle, the particular is not the object of knowledge because only the universal can be known, for Montaigne, his *Essays* are a philosophical attempt to reveal the intelligibility of a particular.

The philosophers achieve the perfection of virtue through deliberate imitation of the perfect form of the species, the rational soul. But Montaigne is an *accidental* philosopher. He just finds, to his surprise, that his ways of being happen to conform to many philosophical examples and discourses (VS 546; F 409). Deliberate imitation means striving for the perfection of the same form. Accidental similarity means that the form is not the same.

Montaigne's particularity is expressed in terms of the fact that he does not imitate anyone. The essays are a new form and he is a new figure. But his particularity is not "subjectivity," for his "essential form," he says, is proper to communication and to self-revelation *(production)* (VS 823; F 625). This is precisely where the will comes in. In "Of Friendship" he says that "our free will has no production which is more properly its own than that of affection and friendship" (VS 185; F 137). The will, then, is not discussed in terms of mastery of the passions but in terms of self-communication. And his self-communication is the revelation of his weakness. Thus, in one of his many allusions to his weakness and his weak way, Montaigne writes: "If my heart is not great enough, it is compensatingly open, and it orders me boldly to publish its weakness" (VS 917; F 700). The *Essays* do not conceal his imperfections any more than does his portrait which displays, not a perfect face, but his own face (VS 148; F 108). Defending himself against the charge that it is unreasonable that a man as weak as he is should make himself known so publicly, he says that in order to achieve his end and perfect his work he must only be faithful to what he is (VS 805; F 611). And explaining why he wrote the *Essays* at home among men whose Latin extended no further than their Pater Noster, he writes: "I would have done it better elsewhere, but the work would have been less mine; and its principal end and perfection is to be exactly mine" (VS 875; F 667).

Montaigne's affirmation of particularity can be seen most clearly in his rejection of philosophy's claims to offer an account of the way to the human good that can be followed by all men. "All the glory that I aspire to in my life is to have lived it tranquilly—tranquilly not according to Metrodorus or Arcesilaus or Aristippus, but according to me. Since philosophy has not been able to find a way to tranquility that is good in common, let everyone seek it in his particularity" (VS 622; F 471).

In the last book of the *Confessions,* Augustine comments on the creation of man and woman in the image and likeness of God. Genesis says that on the fifth day "God said, 'Let the earth bring forth living creatures, according to their kind: cattle, reptiles, and wild animals, all according to their kind.' So it was; God made wild animals, cattle, and all reptiles, each according to its kind." Augustine is struck by the fact that, when God creates man, he does not refer to the species. Addressing the divine author of Genesis, he says:

> You did not add *according to your kind,* as though we should imitate another who has gone the same road before us or live by the authority of some better man. For you did not say "Let man be made according to his kind," but: *Let us make man to our image and likeness,* that we may prove what is your will. . . . For when in newness of mind he sees and understands your truth, man does not need any other man to teach him to imitate his kind: but with You to teach him he sees for himself *what is your will, what is good and acceptable and perfect.* (*Confessions,* 13.22)

I suggest that Montaigne's category of particularity is not the forerunner of modern subjectivity but is a philosophical working out of the notion of particularity grounded in the individual's relation to God.

Although he rejects the Aristotelian notion of form, Montaigne does continue to speak in terms of final cause or end and, as we have seen, he does assert a notion of human perfection: to enjoy our own being rightly. His criticism of those devout souls who are elevated to a constant meditation of divine things might suggest that he is indeed entirely at home in this world (as Nietzsche says of him) and that there is only this world. But he does not deny that "the eternal nourishment" for which these devout souls hope is indeed "the final and last end of Christian desires." Montaigne is both attached to and detached from this world. In "Of Vanity" he shows his impatience with those who preach to us that we should despise the things of this world (VS 988; F 756) and he denies that he has contempt for the transitory things of this life (VS 953; F 728). Yet, describing his attitude toward death, he writes: "Never did a man prepare to leave the world more utterly and completely, nor detach himself from it more universally, than I propose to do" (VS 88–89; F 61). "Our end [he says] is in the other world" (VS 1068; F 817). Montaigne's notion of human perfection is a possibility that is grounded in faith in the goodness of creation and in the belief that our end is in the other world. His way of living this life is an acceptance of both, so that he values the things of this world for what they are but does not see them as ultimate.

3. Moral and Political Implications

Montaigne's moral innovations and his skeptical politics are in accord with these metaphysical claims. In "Of Drunkenness" Montaigne says that "even our teachers often rank sins badly" (VS 340; F 244–45).

His reordering of the virtues and vices is especially clear in the place that he assigns to cruelty as "the extreme of all vices" (VS 429; F 313) and to truth as the "first and fundamental part of virtue" (VS 647; F 491).[17] Both Aristotle and Aquinas regard cruelty as a vice and truth as a virtue, but neither places them at the extreme limits of virtue and vice.[18]

Montaigne's ranking of cruelty as the extreme of all vice follows from his denial of natural mastery and from his view of the relationship between soul and body. The condition of cruelty is the situation in which one human being is entirely at the mercy and at the disposal of another. Montaigne presents this as the extreme limit of evil. If cruelty is the extreme of all vices, then what is its opposite? Cruelty is the opposite of goodness, which is why he presents his hatred of cruelty as the outcome of his goodness. In his essay "Of Cruelty," he says that cruelty, especially in the form of torture, leads to despair. This shows us something of the kind of relationship that exists between the soul and the body. On account of the extreme and inescapable pain inflicted on the body, the individual loses all hope in the presence and the goodness of God. We Christians, he says, ought to be especially concerned to send souls away in a good state (VS 431; F 314). Thus, the place accorded to cruelty in his ranking of the vices points to the theological virtue of hope. His reordering of the traditional virtues and vices is based on the introduction of the new standard in terms of which they are measured: the virtues of faith, hope, and charity.

Montaigne approves of his father's decision to have him held over the baptismal font by the poorest people of the village (VS 1100; F 844). That might possibly account, he says, for his extreme compassion and thus for his hatred of cruelty, and for his marvelous weakness in the direction of mercy and gentleness. Whereas Cato was "a model chosen by

17. Montaigne makes a distinction between vices that involve the body and those that are "all in the soul." He starts out in "Of Drunkenness" with the utmost contempt for that vice because it is "gross and brutish" and "all bodily and earthy" (VS 340; F 245). Drunkenness overturns the understanding, stuns the body, and causes a man to lose control of himself. But by the end of the essay he takes a somewhat different attitude: drunkenness is "a weak and stupid vice, but less malicious and harmful than the others" (VS 342; F 247). In "Of the Punishment of Cowardice" he makes a similar distinction between those faults that are due to our natural weakness and those that are due to malice (VS 70; F 48). The appetites that are engendered by love "affect both the body and the soul" (VS 728; F 550) and, although most men judge that these appetites are the most violent, Montaigne holds that "the commingling of the body brings them some abatement and weakening" because these desires can be satisfied. Weakness, in this case, is a good thing. "The passions that are all in the soul, such as ambition and avarice," on the other hand, "give the reason much more to do, for it can find no help for them except in its own resources; nor are these appetites capable of satiety, but rather they grow sharper and are increased by enjoyment" (VS 729; F 551).

18. Aquinas, for example, treats cruelty under the virtue of temperance and truth under the virtue of justice; see *Summa theologiae* IIaIIae.159 and IIaIIae.109.

nature to show how far *human* virtue and constancy could go" (VS 231; F 171), Montaigne's weakness is the transformation of the traditional moral life of the virtues through the theological virtues. That is why his weakness is marvelous.

Montaigne's reordering of the virtues and vices is also his response to Machiavelli. Machiavelli distinguishes between goodness and virtue: the prince must be virtuous, but he must also "learn to be able not to be good."[19] The separation of virtue from goodness is seen most clearly in his justification of cruelty, deception, and betrayal. Montaigne ranks cruelty as the extreme of all vice and he refers to lying as "an accursed vice." In particular, he abhors what he calls "the new virtue" of dissimulation. "As for this new virtue of hypocrisy and dissimulation, which is so highly honored at present, I mortally hate it; and of all vices, I know none that testifies to so much cowardice and baseness of heart. It is a craven and servile idea to disguise ourselves and hide under a mask, and not to dare to show ourselves as we are" (VS 647; F 491).

Machiavelli's new modes and orders are necessary because, he says, Christianity has made the world weak by placing the highest good in humility, abjectness, and contempt of human things. "This mode of life thus seems to have rendered the world weak and given it in prey to criminal men, who can manage it securely, seeing that the collectivity of men, so as to go to paradise, think more of enduring their beatings than of avenging them."[20] Christianity has made the world weak because goodness is weak. That is why the prince must "learn to be able not to be good." The justification of cruelty, lying, and betrayal points to the fact that, for Machiavelli, politics is ultimate and highest. No other claims can override the claims of the political.

Montaigne is "marvelously weak in the direction of mercy and gentleness" but he also hates the cowardice of hypocrisy and dissimulation. That is, his impossible character is his answer to Machiavelli's criticism of Christianity and, at the same time, his break with the Aristotelian-Thomistic hierarchy. For the distinction between goodness and weakness is precisely that goodness is strong. The new possibility that Montaigne displays is a kind of integrity. There are things he will not do: he will not lie or deceive or betray, even for the prince who has the power of life and death over him. In her "Note" to the second edition of *Wise Blood,* Flannery O'Connor raises this very possibility of integrity when she asks: "Does one's integrity ever lie in what he is not able to do?"[21] Montaigne's goodness, innocence, and integrity show that, for him, the

19. *The Prince* 15.
20. *Discourses on Titus Livy* 2.2.
21. Flannery O'Connor, *Wise Blood* (New York: Farrar, Straus and Giroux, 1949), 5.

political realm is not ultimate. There are claims of humanity that transcend the political and that point to a standard that is higher than politics.

Montaigne's rejection of natural mastery means that there is no justification in nature for the rule of one man over another. This makes the political enterprise an inherently dangerous enterprise for a man of conscience. Montaigne's father had been mayor of Bordeaux and his son was later elected to two terms as mayor himself. His father had ruined his health and his tranquility on account of his involvement in the political turmoil of those days. That was the kind of man he was: his attitude came from a "great goodness of nature." There was never a more "charitable" soul, for he had been told that it was necessary to forget oneself for one's neighbor (VS 1006; F 769). His father interpreted the commandment to love his neighbor as a call to public life. But Montaigne does not agree. Rather, he avoids public occupations as much as possible because they present temptations to the vice of ambition (VS 795; F 603). There is little or no place for innocence in politics. Commenting on his integrity in his negotiations between princes, Montaigne says:

> This whole procedure of mine is just a bit dissonant from our forms. It would not be fit to produce great results or to endure. Innocence itself could neither negotiate among us without dissimulation nor bargain without lying. And so public occupations are by no means my quarry; what my profession requires, I perform in the most private manner I can. (VS 795; F 603)

This deflation of the claims of public service is expressed from the very beginning of the *Essays* in "To the Reader," where he sets out the purpose of his work: he has set himself only a domestic and private end, with no thought of either public service or his own glory (VS 3; F 2). And in "Of Repentance" he says that it does not matter that his life is humble and inglorious for "you can tie up all moral philosophy with a common and private life just as well as with a life of richer stuff" (VS 805; F 611). The political realm is no longer seen as the space for the appearance of the human good or the common way to the possession of the good.

Montaigne does, however, hold that there is a social bond: "We are men, and hold together only by our word" (VS 36; F 23). Lying is an ugly and accursed vice because "mutual understanding is brought about solely by way of words." Therefore, "he who breaks his word betrays human society. It is the only instrument by means of which our wills and thoughts communicate, it is the interpreter of our souls. If it fails us, we have no more hold on each other, no more knowledge of each other. If it deceives us, it breaks up all our relations and dissolves all the bonds of our society" (VS 666; F 505). Montaigne's self-disclosure is not in the arena of politics but in the bold publication of his weakness, the self-communication that is the essential act of his will.

Montaigne's lack of striving for perfection, his apparent disinterest in moral progress, and his indifference to his inability to rule his inclinations through his reason constitute a break with the classical-medieval tradition of moral philosophy. I would suggest, however, that the new moral and political possibilities intimated in this break reveal his intention to bring to perfection the Christian transformation of classical virtue through the theological virtues of faith, hope, and charity. He is, then, both a modern man and a Christian.[22]

4. The Essay as a New Mode of Philosophy

By locating goodness at the place in the Aristotelian hierarchy that belongs to moral weakness and by denying universality to "form," Montaigne makes clear that he is moving away from the Aristotelian standard of perfection and from the Aristotelian metaphysics that grounds it. Why, then, does he continue to use the language of weakness and imperfection? Goodness and innocence are "so close" to weakness and imperfection that it is difficult to delimit and distinguish them. The terms "goodness" and "innocence" are even, to some extent, terms of contempt. Montaigne continues to use the language of weakness because his philosophical practice is to use the common language. For Montaigne, meaning is not established by definition, and distinctions are not made by decree because that does not really capture anything true. Distinctions must be worked out in the common language. The essay displays distinctions, especially those that are concealed in common language.

Montaigne describes this practice as getting beyond the appearance of the first sense, or in Frame's translation, getting beyond "the first plausible meaning" (VS 312; F 227). Those who stop at the first plausible meaning are in error. They make the fundamental mistake of identifying the probable with the possible, thus limiting the possible to the probable. They are closed to the infinite variety of forms, and therefore they presume that what is ordinary and familiar to them is the essence and the limit of the possible. Montaigne's theoretical task is to go beyond the limit of the probable to the possible.

22. In *Michel de Montaigne: Accidental Philosopher* (Cambridge: Cambridge University Press, 2003), I argue that Montaigne's character is that of the great-souled man without pride, that is, an apparently impossible combination of classical, Aristotelian magnanimity and Christian humility. See especially chap. 8.

Montaigne says that his "end" is to tell what *can* happen, not what *has* happened (VS 105–6; F 75). He is interested in the manifestation of possibility, which is truth. In this respect his end is similar to that of the theologians. As Aquinas says, theology does not attempt to prove the articles of faith but to establish that "what is proposed to our faith is not impossible."[23] Montaigne's thought, however, is philosophical rather than theological. That is, he does not take the articles of faith as his first principles. He begins from experience.[24]

The possibility that emerges out of the discussion of virtue and goodness in "Of Cruelty" is left in the form of a question just because it is a possibility: "*Could it be true* that to be wholly good we must be so by some hidden, natural, and universal property, without law, without reason, without example?" (VS 428; F 312). The truth of the essay is a possibility. The essay form allows for the manifestation of possibility by getting beyond the appearance of the first sense. The first sense is that goodness and innocence are the same as weakness and imperfection. Now this possibility of complete goodness can be thought because it has been brought to light through the distinction from weakness. The *Essays* are a philosophical display of the astonishing Christian reversal: the weak things of this world confound the strong.[25]

23. St. Thomas Aquinas, *Summa theologiae* IIaIIae.1.5.

24. In "Some Aspects of the Grotesque in Southern Fiction," Flannery O'Connor says of the writer who believes that human life is mysterious that "the meaning of a story does not begin except at a depth where the adequate motivation and the adequate psychology and the various determinations have been exhausted. Such a writer will be interested in what we don't understand rather than in what we do. He will be interested in possibility rather than probability. He will be interested in characters who are forced out to meet evil and grace and who act on a trust beyond themselves . . ." (*Collected Works,* ed. Sally Fitzgerald (New York: Library of America, 1988), 813–21, at 816). In his comparison of history and poetry in the *Poetics,* Aristotle says that "the poet's function is to describe, not the thing that has happened, but a kind of thing that might happen, that is what is possible as being probable or necessary. The distinction between the historian and the poet is not in the one writing prose and the other verse; . . . it consists really in this, that the one describes the thing that has been, and the other a kind of thing that might be. Hence poetry is something more philosophic and of graver import than history, since its statements are of the nature rather of universals, whereas those of history are singulars. By a universal statement I mean one as to what such or such a kind of man will probably or necessarily say or do—which is the aim of poetry" (9.1451a37–b9, trans. I. Bywater). Aristotle identifies the possible with the probable or the necessary, whereas Montaigne does not.

25. Corinthians 1:27.

9 Descartes's Feeble Spirits

JOHN C. MCCARTHY

Few philosophers of his stature have written so sparingly about ethics and politics as Descartes. Although his correspondence inevitably touches upon such matters, there is no thematic treatment of the political in any of the four books he published, and only once in print does he enter expressly into a discussion of ethics, in the relatively brief prologue to his first book, the *Discourse on the Method for Rightly Conducting One's Reason and Seeking the Truth in the Sciences.* Since the *Discourse* proves to be the only programmatic statement of his philosophy that he saw to print, it is fitting that it should include what he calls a "morale par provision," a morality for the time being, consisting of three—or is it four?—"maxims" spelled out in as many paragraphs.[1] As he subsequently conceded, however, it was largely as a sop to certain sorts of readers that he ever troubled to broach the issue.[2] Consistent with that frank avowal is his failure to elaborate upon the *Discourse*'s sketchy moral teaching in subsequent writings.[3]

One would not expect such a thinker to have shown much interest

I am indebted to Richard F. Hassing and Tobias Hoffmann for their comments on an earlier draft of this chapter.

1. Unless otherwise indicated, references will be to the page and volume number of the *Œuvres de Descartes,* ed. Charles Adam and Paul Tannery, rev. ed., 12 vols. (Paris: Vrin, 1966–1976) [henceforth AT]; whenever possible, I shall also refer to Descartes's enumeration of the parts of the work with which I am concerned—thus, in the present instance, *Discourse* 3, AT 6: 22–28. All translations are mine.

2. See *Conversations with Burman,* AT 5: 178; also Letter to Chanut, 20 November 1647, AT 5: 86–87.

3. In a letter addressed to the Abbé Picot that was to serve as a preface to Picot's 1647 translation of the *Principles of Philosophy,* Descartes seems to have something like a definitive moral teaching in mind when he describes "the highest and most perfect morality" as the last of the three main branches of the tree of philosophy, together with medicine and mechanics (Preface, AT 9b: 14). But since the achievement of this "final degree of wisdom" presupposes "a complete knowledge of the other sciences," which on his reckoning lies many centuries off, it must be said that for all practical (or moral) purposes, the provisional morality *is* his final morality (2–3 and 20).

in the ordinary facts of everyday moral life, facts that had so often occupied his most thoughtful predecessors. Consider, for example, the common human tendency to act in ways that one knows to be contrary to one's own good. According to Aristotle, the reality of such behavior—he calls it *akratic*—is at once obvious and puzzling,[4] which is precisely why he discusses it at some length in his most extended work of moral philosophy. Christian moral theologians, who by Descartes's time had long since come to agree on Aristotle's standing as "the Philosopher," also took great interest in the theme, not only on account of the authority that the *Nicomachean Ethics* enjoyed with them, but especially because the same phenomenon seemed to concern St. Paul, who famously confessed in his Letter to the Romans that a "war" raged in his members between "the law of God" and "the law of sin." Or if the battle that the apostle's "flesh" waged against his "mind" is not perfectly of a piece with the internal division that the akratic soul experiences within himself, the theologians nevertheless were right, surely, to suppose a real affinity between the two.[5]

Aristotle's authority counted for little with Descartes, as everyone knows.[6] But insofar as Christian theology shared with Aristotelian philosophy an interest in what one might call the problem of moral weakness, he had a second reason for steering clear of that problem in addition to his diffidence regarding ethical and political disputation: although the author of the *Discourse* readily, if also anonymously, professed his commitment "constantly" to retain "the religion in which by God's grace I had been instructed since my childhood,"[7] he also let it be known with as much candor as his circumstances permitted that he judged properly theological perplexities or controversies to be useless.[8] And with one significant exception, he drew the most obvious implication from that judgment in every work he published.[9]

A closer look at the provisional morality suggests, however, that Descartes did have something to say about incontinence after all. In a state-

4. *Nicomachean Ethics* 7.2.1145b21–33.

5. Romans 7:15–25; also Galatians 5:16–25.

6. Descartes did his part to ensure that this would be one of the more open secrets of his philosophy. See the Letter to Mersenne of 28 January 1641, AT 3: 297–98.

7. *Discourse* 3, 23; but cf. *Meditations on First Philosophy*, "Seventh Replies," AT 7: 526.

8. See *Discourse* 1, 8 and *Conversations with Burman*, 176. Also see Letter to Mersenne, 18 December 1629, AT 1: 85–86, and 31 March 1641, AT 3: 349–50; Letter to Picot, 1 April 1644, AT 4: 103–4; Letter to Mesland, 2 May 1644, AT 4: 117; and Letter to Regius, July 1645, AT 4: 428–50.

9. The infamous exception is his brief foray into the theology of the Eucharist, for which see *Meditations*, "Fourth Replies," 249–56 (together with "Fourth Objections," 217, and "Letter to Dinet," 581); but also see "Sixth Replies," 428–29.

ment that serves as something of a capstone to the moral teaching of the *Discourse,* he observes that "our will does not proceed either to pursue or to flee a single thing unless our understanding represents it as good or bad," from which he infers that "it suffices to judge well to do well, and to judge one's best also to do one's best, which is to say, to acquire all the virtues, and together with them all the other goods that one can." Descartes assures us that anyone who would observe this precept, which distinctly recalls the Socratic hypothesis that virtue is knowledge, "could not fail to be contented."[10] But if judging well really is tantamount to doing well, then he must also agree with Socrates that it is impossible, strictly speaking, for an agent knowingly and willingly to act at odds with his good. Indeed, to the extent that Cartesian philosophy makes mathematical certainty the hallmark of sound judgment about any matter whatsoever, incontinence would seem to have met in the father of modern philosophy an even more tenacious opponent than it had in the Athenian philosopher of old. One might be tempted to leave matters at that were it not for the obvious difficulty of squaring Descartes's summary moral precept with orthodox Christian doctrine, to which the French thinker undoubtedly deferred, regarding sin and its irremediable consequences for our ability to know, desire, and acquire virtue or any other goods of this life in the absence of divine grace: were we to take the conclusion of the *Discourse*'s provisional morality at face value, the only "sin" would be ignorance, and the road to redemption would be study of Cartesian philosophy.

As it happens, some months before the *Discourse* appeared in print Descartes received a letter from the Reverend Father Marin Mersenne. Descartes had sent Mersenne the manuscript for comment, and his most stalwart correspondent, provoked by the passage just cited, objects to it for the reason indicated. In reply, Descartes insists that "I cannot be accused of the error of the Pelagians" because "the doing well of which I speak cannot be understood in terms of Theology, where grace is spoken of, but only of moral and natural Philosophy, where grace is not considered." Besides, he writes, he is merely following what he takes to be "the ordinary teaching of the School," according to which

> *voluntas non fertur in malum, nisi quatenus ei sub aliqua ratione boni repraesentatur ab intellectu.* Whence the saying, *omnis peccans est ignorans,* such that if the understanding never represents anything as good to the will when it is not so, the will could not fail in its choice. But the understanding often represents to it differ-

10. *Discourse* 3, 28, with *Protagoras* 352a–c, and *EN* 7.2.1145b22–28. The precept finds analogous expression in later writings, for which see, inter alia, *Meditations* 4, 58 and 59–60; and *Principles,* Preface, 3–4.

ent things at the same time; whence the saying *video meliora proboque,* which only concerns weak or feeble spirits [*les esprits faibles*], of whom I spoke on page 26.[11]

Inasmuch as it appeals to an ambiguous apprehension of the good as the source of any voluntary defection from it, Descartes's explanation, compressed though it is, would seem fundamentally in accord with the tradition. His ready adoption of a Scholastic dictum might also seem to vindicate those who think his reputation as an enemy of all Schoolmen is undeserved or at least grossly overstated. Yet one looks in vain in the letter for even a glimmer of interest in, or even awareness of, the subtle but serious disagreements to which the common doctrine gave rise. Nor is his facile separation of "nature" from "grace" terribly reassuring. What is especially curious, however, is his insistence that the tag from Ovid's *Metamorphoses*—"I see and approve the better"—pertains solely to "weak spirits," whoever they might be: Medea's lament had by this time come to be standard shorthand for akratic and sinful action alike, which is to say, the action, potentially, of virtually any human being whatsoever.[12] For reasons such as these, Gilson concluded in *La liberté chez Descartes et la théologie* that as regards the Cartesian understanding of intellect, will, and their mutual relation, "the Scholastic and theological apparatus" adopted by Descartes is "an accidental and external veneer that in no way prejudices the profound sense" of his philosophy.[13] Be that as it may, Descartes's own chosen terms, the terms of his published writings, undoubtedly provide the most direct route to his deepest intentions.[14] And as his letter to Mersenne suggests, we would best begin with his account of "les esprits faibles" if we would gain access to his most considered response to Aristotle and St. Paul regarding the nature of moral weakness. It is this that I shall attempt, in a preliminary fashion, in what follows.

11. Letter to Mersenne, April or May 1637, AT 1: 366. Descartes's ready endorsement of a Scholastic dictum is anything but representative of his usual stance toward the Schoolmen and their doctrines. A few years later, for example, he confessed to Mersenne that "nothing . . . seems to me so little likely as the philosophy of the School" (December 1640, AT 3: 256). Many other letters to him could be cited to the same effect. Or as he was reported to have said in his *Conversations with Burman,* 176, "before all else Scholastic theology should be exterminated."

12. See Risto Saarinen, "Weakness of Will in the Renaissance and the Reformation," in *The Problem of Weakness of Will in Medieval Thought,* ed. Tobias Hoffmann, Jörn Müller, and Matthias Perkams (Leuven, Paris, and Dudley, Mass.: Peeters, 2006), 329–51.

13. *La liberté chez Descartes et la théologie* (Paris: Librairie Félix Alcan, 1913), 436. As Gilson also observes, "if the mission that he believed had been entrusted to him had been the defense of religion, it would be quite extraordinary to find no trace of it in his works or correspondence. . . ." See also 440–42.

14. In his letter of 25 November 1630 (AT 1: 178), Descartes warns Mersenne not to invest his correspondence with too much importance. A letter to Morin dated 13 July 1638 (AT 1: 201–2) amply justifies the warning.

We shall first consider the place of feeble spirits in the *Discourse on the Method,* published in 1637. Although they make only three brief appearances in that writing, taken together the three contain *in nuce* almost everything Descartes has to say about them. Moreover, in comparison to the next two works he saw into print, his first publication proves to be almost expansive on the subject of feeble spirits: the *Meditations on First Philosophy,* which first appeared in 1641, refers unambiguously to the type only once, and that only in passing, and in the *Principles of Philosophy,* published three years later, they never appear at all.[15] It is only with the publication of *The Passions of the Soul,* in 1649, that he returns to the theme, and there at last he treats them in a fully thematic way.[16] It is therefore with this work that we must principally be concerned. After offering some introductory remarks about Descartes's final and nowadays unduly neglected writing, I shall examine the account it provides of the struggle between reason or will and the passions, a struggle in which the weakness of the weak is first made manifest. This is followed by a consideration of what Descartes purports to be the "moral" basis of that struggle. In the concluding section of this paper, we shall examine his treatment of weak-spiritedness as a "vice" in light of the philosopher's understanding of human "virtue."[17]

15. A straightforward comparison between the three publications is clearly not possible, given Descartes's decision to publish the latter two works in Latin. The Latin translation of the *Discourse,* approved by Descartes (see AT 6: 539), does not translate *"esprits faibles"* in a consistent way: the phrase is first rendered periphrastically (553), then as *"infirmiores animae"* (554), and finally as *"debiles animas"* (573). For most other uses of *esprit* in the *Discourse,* the Latin version favors *"ingenium."* In the *Meditations,* the only unambiguous echo of *esprits faibles* occurs at the end of the first paragraph of the "Preface," where *"debiliora ingenia"* are said not to be a suitable audience for the book (7). In the 1647 French version of the *Meditations,* which Descartes endorsed, the "Preface" was dropped in favor of a notice from "The Publisher to the Reader"; but when Clerselier, one of the cotranslators for the French edition, republished it in 1661, he added a translation of the missing section; and where the original has *debiliora ingenia,* he provides *"les esprits faibles."* See *Méditations métaphysiques* in *Œuvres philosophiques,* vol. 2, ed. Ferdinand Alquié (Paris: Éditions Garnier Frères, 1967), 390.

16. See Richard Kennington, "Descartes *Olympica,*" in *On Modern Origins: Essays in Early Modern Philosophy,* ed. Pamela Kraus and Frank Hunt (Lanham, Md.: Lexington Books, 2004), 79–104, at 100.

17. There have been several recent attempts to discover in Descartes's writings a reflection on the nature of what might loosely be called "akratic action": Byron Williston, "*Akrasia* and the Passions in Descartes," *British Journal for the History of Philosophy* 7 (1999): 33–55; Lilli Alanen, "Descartes on the Will and the Power to Do Otherwise," in *Emotions and Choice from Boethius to Descartes,* ed. Henryk Lagerlund and Mikko Yrjönsuuri (Dordrecht and Boston: Kluwer Academic Publishers, 2002), 279–98; Fabienne Pironet and Christine Tappolet, "Faiblesse de la raison ou faiblesse de volonté: peut-on choisir?" *Dialogue: Canadian Philosophical Review* 42 (2003): 627–44; and Kim Sang Ong-Van-Cung, "Indifférence et irrationalité chez Descartes," *Dialogue: Canadian Philosophical Review* 42 (2003): 725–48. However, none of these seriously attempts to unearth just what Descartes means, in his own

1. The Feeble in Spirit in the *Discourse on the Method*

Whether Mersenne was satisfied by the reply he received from Descartes it is impossible to say, for there exists no further correspondence between the two on that subject. Had he taken the trouble to reread the passage from the *Discourse* to which Descartes's letter had directed him, however, he could not have found it terribly reassuring.

The passage in question marks the second appearance of weak spirits in the work. The type is first mentioned at the beginning of Part 3. Their function in that context is to contribute to the elucidation of the first maxim of the provisional morality, according to which Descartes will govern himself, or rather his public actions, "following the most moderate opinions, and those furthest from excess that are commonly received in practice by the most sensible of those among whom I would have to live." Among such excesses he notes especially "all the promises by which one curtails something of one's freedom," a precision to which he immediately appends a disclaimer:

> Not that I disapproved of laws that, in order to remedy the inconstancy of feeble spirits, permit one, when he has some good design or plan [*dessein*] (or even, for the security of commerce, a design that is merely indifferent), to make vows or contracts that oblige him to persevere in them.[18]

The qualification pays little more than conventional respect to practices that come close to defining human convention as such.[19] Just how unconventional are Descartes's intentions in the first maxim begins to become clear from the reasons he provides for making himself an ex-

---

terms, by the "weakness of spirit" that is the locus of their studies. With the exception of Williston, moreover, they are all far too quick, in my judgment, to assimilate weak-spiritedness to *akrasia* or moral weakness or even sinfulness; and even Williston fails to appreciate just how great are the discontinuities between Descartes and his philosophical and theological precursors in this regard.

18. *Discourse* 3, 23–24.

19. In his "Commentaire historique" to his edition of the *Discours de la méthode,* 2nd ed. (Paris: Vrin, 1926), 240–41, Gilson characterizes as "highly imprudent" Descartes's pairing of vows and promises, since among Catholics, religious vows were thought to be a counsel of perfection, and not merely a remedy for human weakness. Criticism of the Catholic practice by Calvin and other reformers would, Gilson notes, have rendered Catholic ears "very sensitive" on this point. In proof, he calls attention to two letters in which Descartes attempts to respond to Mersenne on this very point (30 August 1640, AT 3: 166–67, and 18 November 1640, AT 6: 244–45). Given that Descartes could easily have corrected this alleged indiscretion in the 1644 Latin translation of the *Discourse,* his failure to do so (see 553) is all the more curious in Gilson's eyes. Descartes seems to have thought, however, that his present circumstances required or entitled him to take "prudent" exception to prudence's normal rule, for which see *Discourse* 2, 12–16.

ception to the weak-spirited rule: "I have seen nothing in the world that remains in the same state." In response to the world's unceasing flux, the Cartesian philosopher will steer what is in effect a middle course between the defective inconstancy to which the weak are prone and the excessive constancy exacted of them through the legal remediation to which they have obliged themselves. He does, however, make one promise of his own, albeit a promise only to himself, namely, "evermore to perfect my judgments and not to render them worse."[20]

As for the weakness of the weak, it surely does not here conform to the classical pattern to which Descartes had alluded in his letter; their failure in this their first appearance is not a failure to act in accordance with the good as they know it. For he admits that their promises may serve not only what is but what may well continue indefinitely to be a "good plan"; thus, if they keep their word, or rather are held to it, they will be acting deliberately, according to plan; and not despite but precisely because they are likely to do so half-heartedly, they bear a much closer resemblance to those whom Aristotle calls the enkratic, those "in control" of their inclinations, than to the incontinent, to say nothing for the time being of their kinship with, or divergence from, Christian "sinners."[21]

That weakness of spirit appears to straddle Aristotle's distinction between continence and incontinence points to more global differences between Descartes and his predecessor. The *akratic,* we may recall, are but one of six basic character types enumerated in the seventh book of the *Ethics,* all of whom would have been readily identifiable by its intended audience. Aristotle's contribution, accordingly, is not so much to invent a typology of moral character as it is to bring out essential features of recognizably distinct patterns of human agency by comparing and contrasting each of the types with all the others. He thereby seeks to prove all of the received opinions regarding the relation between knowing the good and doing it—or if not all, then most, and especially the most authoritative of such opinions.[22] Feeble spirits follow a very different trajectory. Their emergence in Descartes's text does not result from a survey of what is commonly supposed about states of character to be pursued and avoided; the type is introduced in function of Descartes's desire "once and for all to clear away [*oster*]" opinions he had previously

20. *Discourse* 3, 24. When, three pages later, he sums up the maxims of his provisional code, he underlines that they were all founded on the "plan" *(dessein)* he had "to continue to instruct himself."

21. See *EN* 7.9.1151b5–13; 7.10.1152a25.

22. *EN* 7.1.1145b2–7.

accepted, in order to correct or replace them by methodologically certified judgments.[23] As is implied, moreover, by the adjective that defines them, the weak comprise one of only two moral kinds, their counterpart being the "strong." In short, feeble spirits constitute a hitherto unrecognized human type, a Cartesian innovation. And although the *Discourse* does not explicitly reject the traditional moral typology, Descartes's failure ever to affirm or even mention it is surely a sign that he means quietly to replace it.

The kinship between weak spirits and the incontinent proves to be every bit as faint the second time they appear, in the very next paragraph of Part 3, wherein Descartes sets out the second maxim of the provisional morality, which would have him be as "firm" and "resolute" as possible, even to the point of "follow[ing] with no less constancy the most doubtful opinions," once he has committed himself to them, "than if they had been very assured." His justification for adopting such a course is sensible enough so far as it goes, namely, that "life's actions often brook no delay." Still, it is far from clear how any situation could ever be so pressing as to require that opinions in themselves indifferent or even quite dubious be treated "as very true and very certain" merely because one had, for whatever reason, once "determined" oneself "upon them."[24] Whatever else "true" and "certain" might signify in this context, it is evidently at some remove from the mathematical clarity and distinctness for which the *Discourse* is legendary. To begin to make sense of what would seem to be a thoroughly un-Cartesian standard of conduct we must consider it in light of what Descartes takes to be its utility. It is at this juncture that weak spirits again enter the scene.

The merit of his second maxim, Descartes explains, is that it will enable him henceforth to "deliver" himself "from all the repentance and remorse that customarily agitate the consciences of those weak and wavering spirits who allow themselves to go with inconstancy about, to practice as good things they judge afterward to be bad."[25] Once again, the weakness of the weak need not involve them in wrongful actions: it is perfectly compatible with the plain sense of this statement that they be guilty merely of scruples, or erroneous second guessing. But even or rather especially if the afterthoughts of a weak spirit attest to his recognition of a culpable error on his part, Descartes's censure is more than

23. *Discourse* 2, 13–14.

24. *Discourse* 3, 24–25. The Latin is even more forceful than the French: "quam maxime constans & tenax propositi semper essem, *nec minus indubitanter atque incunctanter in iis peragendis perseverarem,* quae ob rationes valde dubias *vel forte nulla* susceperam, quam in iis de quibus plane eram certus" (553, emphasis added).

25. *Discourse* 3, 24–25.

a little surprising. The notion of a troubled "conscience" is, of course, foreign to Aristotle; even so, the incontinent as he describes them do regret their misdeeds; and although regret is a sign of base character in the *Ethics*, he does not regard it as intrinsically blameworthy; to the contrary, because it arises from the incontinent agent's residual awareness of, and thus also attachment to, the good from which his deeds decline, the philosopher regards it as evidence of the possibility that the incontinent agent is curable, unlike the vicious or self-indulgent soul, whose lack of remorse suggests that he is beyond hope of reform.[26] That the *Discourse* has nothing positive to say about rueful second thoughts itself constitutes a notable departure from the Aristotelian tradition. As for the maxim's tacit dispensation from St. Paul's universal call to repentance, it is enough to recall Richard Kennington's lapidary comment: "[T]his view has no precedent in the Christian tradition."[27]

This brings us to yet another point of discontinuity between Descartes and his predecessors. The author of the *Ethics* stands silently apart from the akratic, as he does from every other form of character that he describes; the Apostle to the Gentiles, on the other hand, goes so far as to present himself as a paradigmatic example of the human self-diremption he depicts in Romans. Both authors agree, however, that the incapacity to conform one's actions to what one knows to be one's good is a real human possibility, a possibility that indicates something at once perplexing and important about human life generally. Weak spirits, in contrast, hold little or no intrinsic interest for the author of the *Discourse*. They enter the argument not so that we might ponder with Descartes what they disclose about human nature, but rather as a foil for Descartes's type, the type of the Cartesian philosopher. Yet this is not to say that they are merely bit players in his drama. Precisely because their weakness serves contrastively to display what he takes to be his "strength," they concern the heart of his moral philosophy as a whole, which turns on the distinction between the philosopher and the nonphilosopher.

To this last point someone might object that Descartes is guilty of gross inconsistency. Having claimed in the first maxim, on the basis of a tacit appeal to his strength, what amounts to an inalienable right to change his mind, does he not, in the second maxim, construe the exercise of that same right by others as proof of their weakness? Note, however, that what he rejects in the "wavering" of the weak is not their willingness to revise their judgments from time to time, which clearly is not a disposition any philosopher could fault. His concern, rather, is with

26. *EN* 7.7.1150a21–22; 7.8.1150b30–1151a28.
27. "Descartes *Olympica*," 100.

the agitation that marks their reconsiderations, as though they lacked all confidence in their judgments. It seems, then, that what unites the first two maxims is what we might call a "spirit of self-reliance" as the defining feature of Cartesian strength. For in both passages he resolves never to favor any appearance of the good—present, future, or past—over his rational capacity to discern the good for himself at any given time, and so also to call what had once seemed to him good again into question.

The final appearance of weak spirits occurs at the end of the schematic summary provided, in Part 5, of the "treatise" on physics Descartes had planned to publish before learning of the condemnation of Galileo. The thoroughly mechanistic science of nature that he goes on to describe would somehow have culminated in an account of the rational soul, about which he would have "expatiated a little," owing to the importance of the subject. It is important, he tells us, because,

> after the error of those who deny God, . . . there is nothing that puts feeble spirits more at distance from the straight path [*chemin*] of virtue than to imagine that the soul of animals is of the same nature as ours, and that consequently we have nothing to fear or to hope for after this life, anymore than do flies or ants.[28]

Given the crudely pragmatic terms in which he justifies the inquiry into rational soul, it is difficult to avoid the conclusion that the subject is otherwise unimportant for him, that the question of the soul's continuance or destruction after death is of no consequence for strong spirits. Here one might profitably recall that Descartes's confidence in his provisional morality, the observance of which would assure him "all the virtues and . . . all the other goods," had no visible connection to any hope or fear regarding his prospects after death. It is also telling that in both the paragraph before he makes that claim, and in the paragraph that follows it, he describes his life as "sweet" and "innocent."[29]

In sum, the performance of the weak-spirited in the *Discourse* never once rises to the level of incontinence. It thus does nothing to temper Descartes's implicit endorsement of the Socratic identification of knowledge and virtue. On the basis of the second maxim, moreover, we must abandon the hypothesis that he qualifies Socrates' thesis to read "clear and distinct knowledge is virtue": as regards the provisional morality at least, the measure of Descartes's certainty is not mathematics but his own resolve. Indeed, the first and final appearances of feeble spirits in the work suggest that it is they, not Descartes, who succumb to the "Cartesian" error of demanding more certainty from a subject than the nature of that subject allows. On both occasions, their pursuit of the good

28. *Discourse* 5, 59. Cf. Aristotle, *De anima* 1.2.402a1–12.
29. Cf. *Discourse* 3, 28 with 27 and 30.

is said to presume or require worldly or extraworldly assurances that he regards as unnecessary to his "doing well." Is weak-spiritedness a consequence of ignorance arising from the limits of humanly attainable certainty? Given the extreme concision he exercises in his inaugural publication one can do no more than hazard a guess.

2. The Problem of "Spirits" and "Souls" in *The Passions of the Soul*

If the problem of moral weakness has to do with how it is possible to know the good and yet fail to do and pursue it, there is no evidence from his published writings that Descartes ever took that problem very seriously. It is, however, undoubtedly an image of what was for him a genuine difficulty, namely, what it would mean to judge and to do well when perfectly clear and distinct knowledge is unavailable. That is, of course, the normal human situation, as Descartes was perfectly aware. For him as for us the normal situation is that of a being that is at once ensouled and embodied; and for such a being, what we might call the problem of knowledge concerns above all the possibility of self-knowledge, knowledge of one's nature and of the good of one's nature: knowledge of everything else is an issue for the human composite in the measure that it is related to its nature and its good. Even small gains in self-knowledge are or should be of interest to us, and often of urgent interest, even if they fall short of the clarity and distinctness promised by the study of the *res extensa* and the *res cogitans* independently of each other.

What we commonly call the passions pose a particular challenge in this regard, for as Descartes observes in his final work, whenever we experience them firsthand and for what they are, they make what is in effect a claim to a truth that is as unreliable as it is undeniable. Fear, for example, is "so close and so internal to our soul" that it is impossible to "feel" it without it being "truly such as we feel" it—which is to say, without our being truly afraid. *Ego metuo,* so to say, *ego in metu sum.* Yet "the tight alliance that exists between the soul and the body" that makes the passions so compelling also renders their real significance "confused and obscure" precisely at the moment of their greatest "truth." As a result, those who are naturally most inclined to take their passions seriously, namely, those "most agitated" by them, are also those who know them least.[30] Since, however, it belongs to "the whole nature of man" to

30. *Passions* 1.26, AT 11: 348. Descartes had already touched upon the obscure certainty of passionate experience in both the *Meditations* (see Meditation 6, 74–77; 81; and 84–85) and the *Principles* (see 1.66, 32 and 4.190, 317).

be subject to the passions, body and soul, as we shall see, not even one well versed in the rigors of Cartesian method can hope on that account to gain adequate rational access to them. *The Passions of the Soul* thus essays, in the first instance, a coherent account of the incoherences to which the passionate human whole is vulnerable. On that basis the work goes on to propose not another "method," but a series of "remedies" for this problematical state of affairs. It is in this context that Descartes sets out his most extensive account of "weak spirits."

To begin, a few general remarks about *The Passions* are in order. In addition to a "Preface," it consists of 212 articles, none more than a page or two in length and most a good bit shorter, distributed over three books. As is apparent already from its title, and as I have just anticipated, it offers what is undoubtedly Descartes's most extended reflection on the human experience of human things. Consequently, its point of departure is the passions as they are ordinarily experienced; its terms are, at least in comparison to his other works, normally drawn from common discourse; and its focus never strays far from the human composite.[31]

Yet one should not make too much of the author's common touch. In view of what he asserts to be the manifest failure of "the ancients" to teach anything "credible" about the passions, he concludes the opening article of his valedictory work by asserting that he was "obliged" to proceed as though no one before him had ever touched the subject. A still clearer sign that *The Passions* does not attempt an ascent from what is first for us to what is or purports to be first in itself occurs a page before, at the end of the Preface, wherein he announces that his "plan [*dessein*] was not to explain the passions as [*en*] orator, nor even as moral philosopher, but only as physicist [or physician: *physicien*]."[32] What he means by this is not easy to fathom. While much of the first book is given over to an outline of a highly conjectural psychophysiology, this is clearly in function of elucidating the passions as they are experienced by us. Throughout the second book, hypotheses about the bodily mechanisms at work in the passions remain prominent, yet Book 2 begins by conceding that the various "objects" of the particular passions are their "ordinary and principal causes," and it culminates in a reflection on "providence" and

31. In the Preface, 326, he prophesies that its title would win his last publication more readers than its predecessors ever enjoyed. In the event, it ran, by number of editions published, a close second to the *Principles of Philosophy* for the first five decades of its existence.

32. Preface, 326; cf. *De anima* 1.1.403a29–b16; and see Edmond Huguet, *Dictionnaire de la langue française du seizième siècle* (Paris: Didier, 1925–1973), 5: 766a, s.v. Physicien: "Celui qui étudie les choses de la nature," but also "Médecin, homme expert en médecine." Huguet adds, however, that "Plusieurs textes montrent qu'à la fin du XVIe siècle et au commencement du XVIIe ce sens [i.e., the second] avait vieilli."

"virtue." In the third book, which takes as its point of departure the role of "opinion" in constituting particular passions, the psychophysiological concerns of the first two books figure scarcely at all. Not that the argument moves progressively in the direction of a reconciliation with pre-Cartesian experience of the passions. To the contrary, the perspective of the last book proves in the decisive respect to be at greatest remove from common experience.

Curiously enough, the problem as to how the various parts of *The Passions* relate as a whole is mirrored in the course run by the word *esprits* in the work. In Book 1, subtitled "Of the passions in general, and incidentally, of the whole nature of man," the term surfaces in a brief résumé of what is "commonly known" about "the machine of the body" by those not "blinded" by "the authority of the ancients." At the end of that résumé, Descartes invokes a notion that had been in circulation since Galen or before, according to which the muscles and the senses are governed by the motions of what are "called [*qu'on nomme*] animal spirits."[33] Yet he does not merely adapt the old idea to his novel purposes. On what proves to be the first of several occasions on which he will stipulate how a term is to be understood,[34] he explains that "what I here call spirits" are "the liveliest," which is to say the "most agitated" and "most subtle" parts of the blood. And by way of purging the received theory of any lingering association with vitalism, he stresses that these parts are "nothing but bodies."[35] These spiritual corpuscles quickly assume the lion's share of the explanatory work in Cartesian physiology. Not far into Book 2, however, he abruptly and without comment presses the same word into what is for us more familiar service, and for the remainder of the work he moves with seeming insouciance from the one sense to the other.[36]

33. *Passions* 1.7, 332; and see 1.8, 333. The word *esprits* is used some dozen times in the Preface, but never does it bear the physiological meaning of Book 1.

34. *Passions* 1.10, 35. Descartes also expressly names his terms at 1.17, 342; 1.48, 367; 2.148, 442; 3.161, 453; 3.163, 455; and 3.210, 485. In addition, he "makes use" of a word *(je me sers)* in a distinctive sense at 3.182, 466 and 3.192, 473.

35. At *Passions* 1.47, 365, he repeats the point that "spirits" are purely material in nature. For the history of the term *esprits,* see Geneviève Rodis-Lewis's "Introduction" to her edition of *The Passions* (Paris: Vrin, 1957), 25–26; see also Étienne Gilson, *Index Scolastico-Cartésien* (Paris: Librairie Félix Alcan, 1913), s.v. "Esprits animaux," 99–103, for its usage in the *Commentarii Collegii Conimbricensis;* and Annie Bitbol-Hespériès, *Le principe de vie chez Descartes* (Paris: Vrin, 1990), 31–52, which underlines the novelty of Descartes's treatment of "spirits"—a point Descartes himself stresses, for which see 1.1, 327–28; 1.5–1.6, 330–31. For the sense, clearly quite unwholesome, that the distinction between "esprits forts" and "faibles" had already aquired in Descartes's time, on the other hand, see Henri Busson, *La pensée religieuse française de Charron à Pascal* (Paris: Vrin, 1933), 6–9, which directs us, inter alia, to Pascal's *Pensées* 225 (Brunschvicg ed.)/156 (Lafuma ed.).

36. The shift to the use of "esprit" in something other than a purely physiomechanical sense first occurs, in the body of the work, at 2.77, 386–87. Throughout Book 3 both

What, if anything, we are to make of such equivocation is hard to say. Although the French *esprit* has always tolerated this dual signification, as does the Latin *spiritus*,[37] Descartes's usage is puzzling all the same, especially when one considers the care he exercised in preparing *The Passions* for publication—to which he calls attention in the Preface—as also his apparent endorsement, in the body of the work, of the customary linguistic practice of designating equivocal realities by their higher or "more noble" signification, and not the reverse.[38] If, on the other hand, he trades deliberately on an ambiguity, he leaves his readers with no indication as to how he would have them solve the conundrum of putting these markedly divergent senses together in thought as one.[39]

Be that as it may, when, at the end of Book 1, Descartes insists that it is through "the outcome" *(succes)* of the "battles" *(combats)* that take place in a man between his will and his passions that he can "know the strength [*force*] or the weakness of his soul,"[40] there can be no doubt that he there has in mind the same distinction governing Book 3 in its entirety, namely, that between "strong and generous spirits" and those "low and weak." In *The Passions of the Soul,* to be weak in spirit in the end is to be a weak soul.

3. Weakness of Soul and the Soul's Proper Weapons

The battle between the will and the passions envisaged by Descartes comes as close to a recognition of the traditional problem of moral weakness as one will find anywhere in his writings. In order rightly to grasp the sort of conflict he has in mind, however, we must first say a word about the meaning of "soul" in this context, which has nothing to do with the two-substance doctrine for which Cartesianism is notorious.[41] In *The Passions* soul is, so to say, a sheerly ascriptive principle, and it is that only by default, in conformity with a "rule" *(regle)* laid down at the outset of the writing: whatever "function" that "we *experience* in us and that we *see* can also be in entirely inanimate bodies should be *attributed only* to our body," whereas anything "that is in us and that we *cannot conceive in*

"l'esprit fort/faible" and "l'âme forte/faible" are used, and at 3.164, 455, Descartes moves seamlessly from "esprit" to "âme." Also notable in this regard is his use throughout the work of the adjectives "fort" and "faible" for both animal spirits and the human spirit.

37. See Edmond Huguet, *Dictionnaire de la langue française du seizième siècle,* 3: 686a–87a. For the high Scholastic sense of *spiritus* see, e.g., Thomas Aquinas, *Summa contra gentiles* 4.23.

38. See Preface, 326, and 1.19, 343.

39. See Aristotle, *De anima* 1.2.403b30–404a17; 404b27–405a13; 1.3.406b6–26; and1.4.408a30–1.5.409b18.

40. *Passions* 1.48, 366–67.

41. The term substance is used three times in *The Passions* (1.10, 335; 1.12, 337; and 1.31, 352), always in reference to some material component of the human organism.

any way can belong to a body should be attributed to our soul."[42] Hence it is only *after* we have reviewed the body's principal mechanisms that we are invited to entertain an "easy" conclusion. "[T]here remains nothing in us that we must attribute to our soul if not our thoughts, of which there are principally two kinds [*genres*]," namely, the soul's actions and its passions, a distinction he immediately goes on to elaborate.

> Those that I call its [i.e., the soul's] actions are all our volitions [*volontez*], because we experience that they come directly from our soul, and seem to depend only on it. Whereas, contrarily, one can generally call its passions every sort of perception or knowledge that can be found in us, because often it is not our soul that makes them such as they are, and because it always receives them from the things that are represented by them.[43]

This marks the second occasion that he calls attention to his use of a term, as well he might, for it amounts to a radical transvaluation of scholastic teaching. What distinguishes one thought from another no longer turns upon differences between the various objects of our thought, or, if you will, upon the extent to which our thoughts do or do not conform to the being of that which they are given to think. The great divide between our thoughts is between those that are active, because we will them, and the passive remainder, which we merely register.

Despite or rather because of his apparent exaltation of human willing, Descartes nowhere bothers to specify what he takes to be the proper object of the will—say, the good as apprehended by the intellect, to recall the classical formulation of St. Thomas Aquinas.[44] A moment's reflection on the aforementioned ascriptive rule explains why. We plainly cannot conceive of our willing something or other as a mindlessly mechanical operation of our body. Because it is at our initiative, or rather *is* our initiative in a way, we cannot but suppose it to have issued from soul. It follows that willing is fully visible for what it is in experience, in our willing or wanting this, that, or any other thing. For that reason, however, no particular act of volition or of the will—to give a name now to the very possibility of such activity—can properly be said to be more in accord with the nature of the will than any other. Stated Scholastically, Cartesian will is fully actual at every moment of its existence. In

42. *Passions* 1.3, 329, emphasis added, with 1.2, 328. Similarly, in the next article Descartes writes "because we do not conceive that the body thinks in any way, we have reason to *believe* that every sort of thought that is in us belongs to the soul" (1.4, 329, emphasis added).

43. Ibid., 1.17, 342. The verb *vouloir* means both "to will" and "to want." Similarly, the singular substantive *volonté* does double duty for both the "will" and a particular (act of) "volition."

44. See, e.g., *Summa theologiae* Ia.19.1 and *Summa contra gentiles* 1.72.

that case, though, there neither is nor can be any measure of this will independent of any particular instance of willing. To put it bluntly, will as Descartes intends the term has no proper object.[45]

That our volitions derive so manifestly from soul also entails, paradoxically, that virtually no direct knowledge of the origins of any particular act of will is available. While they all "*seem* to depend only" on the soul from which they issue, might they also depend on the body regardless of how things seem? There is nothing in the preceding analysis to rule that out. Further on in Book 1, it is true, Descartes assures us that "the will is so free by nature that it can never be constrained," which one may be tempted to construe as an assertion of will's absolute independence from body. Yet he makes that claim immediately after having announced that the "the principal effect" of the passions is to "incite and dispose [men's souls] to will" certain things.[46] "Freedom" would then signify no more than the empty tautology that the cause of will enables it to will willingly what it wills—although from what we have seen, it could also mean that as self-conscious striving lacking any intrinsic or natural end or completion or perfection, the will resists any final determination. Either way, the "freedom" of Cartesian will is perfectly consistent with the possibility that volition somehow derives from the body. Hence the philosopher can claim, near the end of Book 1, that all the soul's "appetites," hunger and thirst included, are "volitions."[47]

The second phase of the Descartes's lexicographical revolution concerns soul as passive, which now plainly takes in what had heretofore been counted as psychic activity at its peak, namely, intellection, and above all the intellect's apprehension of that which is in itself most intelligible. The work's classification of the soul's passive thoughts appears

45. Although volition in *The Passions* is attended by none of the theological fanfare that marks the doctrine of the will in Meditation 4 (see esp. 56–62), and to a lesser extent also the *Principles* (see 1.35–42, 18–21), clear evidence of continuity between Descartes's earlier publications and his final one is not lacking. In the *Principles* volition is among the "most simple" notions given in experience as *"per se nota,"* which means that any attempt to explain it would only make it more obscure (1.39, 19–20, and 1.41, 20, with 1.6, 6; 1.10, 8; and 1.32, 17). For the *Meditations,* see esp. "Third Replies," to Hobbes (191) and "Fifth Replies," to Gassendi (377). See also *Conversations with Burman,* 159.

46. *Passions* 1.40–41, 359–60. See also, inter alia, 2.79, 387, and 2.137–38, 430–31. In 1.12, 337, the animal spirits are said to cause the nerve filaments to be "entirely free" to carry impulses from bodily appendages to the brain.

47. *Passions* 1.47, 364. Aquinas, in arguing that the will cannot be compelled, takes care also to distinguish volition, or "rational appetite," from "natural" or "sensual" appetition; see, e.g., *Summa theologiae* IaIIae.1.5, IaIIae.6 prol., and 6.4. *The Passions,* contrarily, reserves the word *appetites* exclusively for what the tradition would have known as "sensual appetites": see 1.13, 338; 1.24, 346; 1.50, 370; 2.68, 379; 2.99–100, 403; 2.105, 406; 2.107, 408; and 3.208, 484.

to be as complex as its account of the soul's activity is straightforward.[48] For present purposes it suffices to note the author's concession that "the most proper and particular sense" of the word *passions*[49] is just what that term commonly intends, though he also observes that such thoughts are best named "emotions of the soul" because no other thoughts "agitate and unsettle [*esbranlent*]" the soul so forcefully, and adds for good measure that they are "caused, maintained, and fortified by some motion of the spirits."[50] Although Cartesian soul undergoes a great deal, it is with these that *The Passions of the Soul* is chiefly concerned.

Yet if will is not naturally ordered to the good as apprehended by the intellect, on what basis can it claim just title to rule the passions? And if the passions, correlatively, merely name certain tumultuous effects the spirits have on the soul, what reason is there to think passion susceptible, at least in principle, to the will's command, to say nothing of the possibility that it gradually be formed, through habituation, to the rational heights of a virtuous agent? In fact, neither supposition is warranted in Descartes's judgment. The battles that his philosophical and theological predecessors had alleged between the higher and lower parts of the soul are imaginary, he writes in Article 47, "because there is in us only a single soul, and this soul has within itself no diversity of parts whatsoever." The same soul that is "sensitive" is "rational," and, as we have anticipated, "all its appetites are volitions."[51] In sum, there is virtually no resemblance between the battles discussed at the end of Book 1 and any of the traditional tests of the soul's strength.

Descartes does not deny that we sometimes feel at odds with ourselves. He simply rejects the standard interpretation of that feeling, which is not only erroneous, he thinks, but also conceals yet another error: what we take to be one class of experiences is actually two. By way of explaining this point, he has us imagine, in the first instance, the animal spirits "pushing" upon the infamous pineal gland, thereby causing some desire "in" the soul; we are also to picture the soul "pushing back" against the same gland, owing to the volition it happens to possess to flee the thing desired; the net result of these two distinct events, we

48. He catalogues the various kinds in *Passions* 1.19–26, 343–49.

49. *Passions* 1.21, 345; and see 1.25, 347–48.

50. Ibid., 1.27–29, 350–51. For Aquinas, passions cannot, strictly speaking, be attributed to soul except per accidens: *Summa theologiae,* IaIIae.22.1c. Cf. also IaIIae.22.2 s.c. and c., and esp. IaIIae.24.2.c., where he rejects what he takes to be Cicero's view that the passions are *pertubationes animae:* only when they "lack the moderation of reason," he argues, are they suitably so described.

51. *Passions* 1.47, 364. At 2.68, 379, he rejects the distinction between irascible and concupiscible passions. And see 1.30, 351.

are to see, is that the soul "feels itself pushed almost at the same time to desire and not desire one and the same thing." Otherwise stated, what is often taken as evidence of opposing powers within one's breast is really nothing but high-frequency waffling, divergent inclinations whose alternating influences are so nearly coincident in time that one is unaware of the difference between them. Something closer to a genuine rift within soul takes place when a thing "that excites some passion in the soul also excites certain motions in the body to which the soul does not contribute, and which it arrests or tries to arrest as soon as it perceives them." Consider, for example, a man who wills to stand fast in the face of some danger but must contend with the trembling in his legs, which are eager to move. In this as in the first case, what Descartes concedes is a quarrel of a sort between will and passion could with greater accuracy be characterized as a conflict between body and soul. For it is exclusively to the body's "functions" that we should "attribute everything that can be noticed in us that revolts against [*repugne à*] our reason."[52] In this one respect, perhaps, Cartesian moral psychology draws closer to St. Paul than to Aristotle.[53] One could not describe as authentically Pauline Descartes's appraisal, in the final three articles of Book 1, of the meaning of "body's" opposition to "soul."

The *Discourse* left us with the impression that Cartesian souls or spirits come in only two varieties, weak and strong. *The Passions* serves to correct that impression somewhat. "Strong" and "weak" now stake out a range of human possibilities. Thus, in Article 48 "the strongest souls" are said to be "those in whom the will naturally can vanquish the passions most easily, and arrest the movements of the body that accompany them."[54] Even Descartes's highest human type is subject to internal struggle, unlike the virtuous in Aristotle. Since, however, the triumph of their will over recalcitrant passion is secured with relative ease, they do not afford much evidence for the combat that here concerns us. Nor do those at the other end of the spectrum, "the weakest of all," whose sad and slavish captivity to their every urge means that they too are relatively undivided. We must therefore look to human beings of a middling sort if we are to learn more about the nature of the soul's struggles with its body. It turns out, however, that these sorts "cannot test their strength because they never make their will do battle with its own weapons [*armes*] but only with those supplied to it by some passions to resist others." And

52. Ibid., 1.47, 365–66; see also 1.34, 354.

53. Although Aristotle certainly thinks that physiological considerations can both be a sign of incontinence, and contribute to it. See *EN* 7.3.1147a10–b8; 7.5.1148b35–1149a22; and 7.8.1150b33–1151a5.

54. *Passions* 1.48, 366–67. What "naturally" signifies in this context is hardly transparent.

then for the third and last time in Book 1 he underscores a term of his art: "That which I call its own weapons are firm and determined judgments touching the knowledge of good and evil, following which it has resolved to conduct the actions of its life."[55]

Despite the echo of the second maxim of the provisional morality, the statement is surprising in several respects, beginning with its oddly periphrastic character. Why not identify the weapon in question simply as the "knowledge of good and evil"? Or if the accent is indeed to be placed not on knowledge, but on judging with firmness and determination, the instrumentalization of judgment by the will is stranger still. Would not the truth be the first casualty in such a conflict? On the other hand, if it is in their bodily operation that the passions oppose the soul, how can any judgment, true or false, hope to prevail over them?

As if to confirm our fears, in Article 49 Descartes openly allows that since false judgments are able to "rule [*reglent*]" at least some human actions, their effective use constitutes a genuine measure of the soul's "strength." Even more remarkably, he grants that judgments "founded on passions through which the will has previously let itself be vanquished or seduced" are to be counted as legitimate items in the soul's armory. To be sure, the article is entitled "that strength of soul does not suffice without knowledge of the truth," and goes on to caution that howsoever successful a false judgment may be in the short term, over the long haul only "resolutions" that are "supported by [*appuïées sur*] the knowledge of the truth" can assure that one will never have cause to regret or repent.[56] The article offers no indication, however, as to how the requisite knowledge will deliver that saving assurance. Nor does it offer any object lessons in Descartes's novel martial art. Happily, the reader does not have long to wait for such a lesson. The very next article begins, "And here it is useful to know. . . ."[57]

Exactly how the final article of Book 1 serves to develop the theme is not immediately clear. Spinoza, hardly a neophyte in the study of Cartesian philosophy, wryly mocks its argument as "more occult than any occult quality."[58] Be that as it may, Descartes first makes a series of observations: (1) that the linkage between a particular bodily motion and a particular thought—or as we might say, between a given stimulus and a given response—is not entirely fixed "according to nature's insti-

55. Ibid., 1.48, 367. This is the only use of *armes* or its cognates in the *Passions*.

56. Ibid., 1.49, 368.

57. Ibid., 1.50, 368. This is the first appearance of *utile* or its cognates in the body of the work. The word appears twice more in the present article, and with considerable frequency thereafter. In the Preface, 326, Descartes represents as all of a piece his desire to instruct himself and his desire to "put something useful down in writing" for others.

58. *Ethics*, Part 5, Preface.

tution," but can be modified through a process of "habituation" (*habitude*);[59] (2) that bodily mechanisms exist that provide for the formation of these habitual connections with little conscious involvement on our part; (3) that quite notable reconfigurations of an established pattern of stimulus and response can be established, and established quite quickly; and finally (4) that we can knowingly take control of these processes for our own purposes, even without adequate knowledge of the underlying mechanisms. As evidence for the first two claims, he points to our acquisition of a language, whereby we gradually come to recognize certain sounds as meaningful and then cease to hear them as sounds merely. As evidence for the third, he points to a human being or an animal becoming violently ill after unwittingly ingesting a favorite dish gone rancid and developing at once an aversion to that item. As evidence for the final claim, he points to a dog handler's capacity to train a setter to stop at the sight of a partridge, and then, when a gun is discharged, to run not from the report but toward the bird. "[T]hese things are useful to know," he concludes,

> for giving each the courage to learn to rule [*d'éstudier à regler*] his passions. For since one can with a little diligence [*industrie*] change the brain's motions in animals bereft of reason, it is evident that one can do still better in men; and that even those who have the most feeble souls could acquire a very absolute dominion [*empire*] over all their passions, if one employed sufficient diligence to train them and guide them.[60]

And with this he brings Book 1 of *The Passsions* to a close.

How, though, does all this serve to clarify the distinction between "the soul's own weapons" and "those supplied to it by some passions to resist others"? Once one sees that dog handling is meant to be a paradigm, the answer is clear. For of course the trainer makes use of one passion—the creature's eagerness for some "reward"—to overrule both its fear of loud noises and its appetite for quail, two other passions that left to themselves would normally oppose each other until one of them ultimately prevailed. Since it is possible to excite particular passions in

59. *Passions,* 1.50, 368. The phrase "institution of nature" first surfaces at 1.36, 357 (see also 2.90, 395; 2.94, 399; and 2.137, 430), and recalls the Scholastic *institutio naturae.* See, e.g., Thomas Aquinas, *Summa theologiae* Ia.67.4 ad 2 and Ia.92.1 ad 1. If I am not mistaken, the latter phrase functions in Aquinas as an objective genitive exclusively—presumably because he regards the causal power of nature as "instituted" by God but not itself "instituting." The "institution" Descartes has in mind serves grammatically as a subjective genitive, although it is possible he would refuse the distinction, for which see 3.198, 477; also Meditation 6, 87 with 80. For more on the institution of nature, see Robert Rethy's valuable study, "The Teaching of Nature and the Nature of Man in Descartes' *Passions de l'âme,*" *Review of Metaphysics* 53 (2000): 657–83.

60. *Passions* 1.50, 369–70.

oneself by applying oneself to a consideration of "reasons, objects, or examples" with which those passions are commonly associated,[61] the soul's own weapons would be "judgments" about the use of passion against passion, in order to marshal all the passions to its own designs. Cartesian soul, one might say, is too rational to rule the passions despotically, and they are too unreasoning to be ruled royally or politically. The philosopher therefore advises us to rule our passions indirectly, in a manner akin to the artful despotism of the Machiavellian prince.[62]

Descartes states his mind with admirable precision when he calls the soul's arms "firm and determined judgments touching the knowledge of good and evil." He also takes care to conform the act of advising his readers to the terms of the advice he offers them. What he writes in Article 50 is useful to know, he had said, because it will give us courage to study how to exercise military rule over the passions. He does not say, for it goes without saying, that he thinks that the first and best thing we can do in that regard is to continue reading *The Passions of the Soul.* He also does not say that without some encouragement we will not be likely to do what he believes to be in our own best interest. But although that, too, is clearly implied by what he writes, his reasons for thinking it are not quite so apparent. Not far into Book 2, however, we learn that by "courage" he does not mean a cardinal virtue, but one of forty particular species of passion identified in the work, that it opposes difficulties in executing some "event" *(evenement)* depending on oneself, and that its "contrary" is the passion of "cowardice" *(la lascheté).* Those who continue reading into Book 3 also learn that cowardice is "very harmful" because it "diverts the will from useful actions" and can even deprive a man of the "rights" that fall to him by virtue of his capacity freely to determine himself.[63] Putting these things together, we see that Article 50 expresses, *in actu exercito,* the very thing it explains, *in actu signato.*

And how would it arouse courage in us? Paradoxically, its thoroughly amoral content offers the key. By displaying the "mechanism" of our passions as indistinguishable, in its essentials, from that which governs canine behavior, it teaches us to look down upon them, to think less of them; and in thinking less *of* them, we will be emboldened to think more *about* them, and so learn how better to ride herd over them. The

61. See ibid., 1.45, 362–63, and 1.41, 359–60.

62. Cf. Aristotle, *Politics* 1.5.1254b2–14, and Thomas Aquinas, *Summa theologiae* Ia.81.3 with Machiavelli, *The Prince* 18. On "indirect rule" of the passions, see especially *Passions* 1.45, 362–63, "what is the power of the soul with regard to the passions"; Descartes's answer is that it is "not enough to have the will" to resist a given passion; one must "apply oneself to consider the reasons, objects, or examples" whereby one might "excite" the passion best suited to counter it.

63. *Passions* 2.59, 375–76, and 3.171–72, 460–1; 3.174–76, 462–63, and 3.152, 445.

utility of Descartes's final gesture in Book 1 proves in this way to be a fitting response to what is, for the very greatest human beings, the principal object of their compassion: the weakness they behold in those pitiable souls who, in their torpor, do nothing but complain about their "infirmity."[64] And this leads us to one final consideration about the conclusion of Book 1. Even though it holds out the possibility that even the weakest may achieve an "absolute dominion over all their passions," it does not call seriously into question the distinction between weak and strong souls. If anything, it recasts that distinction in still more drastic terms: the actions of the most feeble are to the judicious instructions of the diligent what the behavior of a dog is to the sovereign expertise of its handler. Yet even to put the matter that way is to be unduly sanguine about the prospects of the weak. Whatever hope they may have in theory of attaining to a certain self-mastery, absolute dominion over their passions is altogether unlikely in practice: there is nothing in *The Passions* to indicate that other, stronger souls would or should have any reason or inclination to assume what would doubtless be the mind-numbingly onerous task of putting the weak through their paces.[65] It is safe to conclude that Article 50 is addressed, not to the weakest of the weak, but to those middling souls who have yet to put their psychic resources properly to the test.

4. The Moral Rule of Natural Passion

As Book 1 would have it, the passions are not so much to be educated as dominated or domesticated. The first book tells us next to nothing, however, about what Descartes conceives to be the proper end of the soul's self-mastery. Only toward the end of the second book, subtitled "Of the number and order of the passions, and the explication of the six primitives," does he begin to broach that theme.

The subtitle of Book 2 is a sign that howsoever "absolute" one's dominion over the passions may become, he does not suppose them to be utterly subjugable by will, for otherwise there would be no basis for

64. See ibid., 3.187, 469–70.

65. In his translation, Stephen Voss notes rather tentatively that despite the ambiguity of the "them" with which Article 50 concludes, the pronoun "probably refers to the people, not the passions": *The Passions of the Soul* (Indianapolis and Cambridge: Hackett, 1989), 49, n. 54. To this Williston, "*Akrasia* and the Passions in Descartes," 53, objects without argument that "Voss is guilty of some exaggeration." Williston appears to have forgotten Descartes's claim, in Article 49, that the very weakest human beings "want nothing other than what their passions dictate to them," which is to say that they utterly lack the diligence that is the indispensable prerequisite for the task of self-reform. Hence the grammatical subject of the concluding sentence of article 50 is *"on"* not *"ils."*

distinguishing and ranking them. At first, it appears as though general differences between their worldly objects will provide that basis. It quickly becomes clear, however, that the object-directedness of the passions does not fully determine how they are to be differentiated and ordered. Thus, before identifying and explicating even a single one, he asserts that they all have the same natural end, or rather, natural "use" *(usage)*, namely, to "dispose the soul to will the things that nature dictates to us [*nous dicte*] to be useful, and to persist in that volition."[66] And having said that much, he hesitates for some time to say more. When he finally ventures, some eighty-five articles further on, to state the meaning of utility "according to nature's institution," the reason for his reticence is revealed: the passions are naturally ordained "to incite the soul to consent and to contribute to actions that can serve to preserve the body, or to render it in some way more perfect."[67] To put it bluntly, *The Passions* maintains that the soul is by nature for the sake of the body. At no point in Book 1 did Descartes depart so dramatically from the antecedent philosophical and theological tradition as he does here.[68] But leaving aside for the moment what it might mean for the soul to "consent" to such humble service, in what way is it to "contribute" to the preservation or perfection of the body?

Although every passion is "good according to its nature,"[69] Descartes identifies two ways in which they are often unreliable pointers to bodily well-being. In the first place, he observes, there are many things harmful to body that they do not immediately register as such, or worse still, that they initially "represent" as pleasant; correlatively, much that is genuinely useful to the body they misconstrue as "inconvenient" *(incommodes)*. Yet even when the passions target their proper objects, and do so expeditiously, they are "almost always" overemphatic: by representing things useful and harmful as "much greater and more important than they are, they incite us to seek" those things "with more ardor and care than is appropriate [*convenable*]." By way of summing up their natural "defects" *(defauts)*, he proposes an analogy the force of which markedly qualifies Book 1's encouraging paradigm of canine domesticity: "as we also see that beasts are often deceived by bait, and in order to avoid small evils, rush headlong into greater ones." The lesson we are invited to draw is simple: "[W]e should make use of experience and reason to distinguish the good from the bad, and to know their just value, in order not to

66. *Passions* 2.52, 372.

67. Ibid., 2.137, 430. Descartes begins preparing the claim as early as 1.40, 359. Just how gradual is his approach is evidenced by the similarly partial statement at 2.74, 383.

68. Cf. Thomas Aquinas, *Summa theologiae* IaIIae.46.5.

69. *Passions* 3.211, 486; but cf. 3.175–76, 462–63; 3.182, 466; 3.188, 470.

take one for the other, and not to betake ourselves to anything with excess."[70]

Were the work to end on this crudely utilitarian note, one would have to conclude that the chief difference between weak souls and strong is the difference between those who submit unthinkingly to the letter of passion's law and those whose coolly calculative subservience is to their spirit. The soul's dominion over the passions would be "absolute" only in the sense that reason, having corrected for their defects, would cease to have further grounds for opposing their lead. But can a thinker whose "method promises everything that can be hoped for from the human spirit touching the search for truth in the sciences"[71] really be committed to the belief that reason is and ought to be exclusively at bodily nature's beck and call? In the final ten articles of Book 2, Descartes draws back from the fatal precipice of reductionism—though his reasons for doing so scarcely represent a vindication of traditional views.

The natural use of the passions concerns them "inasmuch as they are related to [*se rapportent au*] the body." Recall, however, that in the measure that their functions are corporeal, they operate beneath or beyond our awareness. If we are conscious of them at all, it is only by virtue of soul. Yet although we are first aware of them, and of the body they mean to serve, as *ours,* soul also affords us the possibility of a certain distance from our passions, such that we can think critically about their urgings. In this way, we may better serve both nature's intentions for our body, so to say, and our own. On the other hand, this same self-distancing enables us to appreciate the passions aesthetically, so to speak. Abstracting from their natural use, we can come to regard them in something akin to the way a spectator views a piece of theater, and enjoy them, or at least experience them, in their own right.[72] In Article 139, accordingly, Descartes launches an examination of the passions "inasmuch as they belong to [*appartienent à*] the soul." In effect, it is precisely in entertaining the possibility that what he there describes as our "better part" be made to serve "the least" of what we are that he would have us see why the soul cannot wholly and consistently be so reduced.[73] As he goes on to show, moreover, what makes the passions humanly so problematic is not principally that their natural defects require rational emendation. The deepest problem, rather, is that the two standpoints from which

70. *Passions* 2.138, 431. On the faults or limitations of the passions, see also 2.74, 383; 2.89–90, 394–96.

71. Preface, 13.

72. The analogy is Descartes's: see *Passions* 2.147, 441, together with 2.94, 399 and 3.187, 470.

73. *Passions* 2.139, 432 with 2.137, 429.

they can, nay, must be evaluated, corporeal and psychic, do not naturally concur.

It is not to our purpose to enter into the details of Descartes's discussion of the tension between the passions as "related" to body and as "belonging" to soul.[74] To simplify matters considerably, let us compare the relative status of joy ("an agreeable emotion of the soul, in which consists the enjoyment it has of the good that the impressions of the brain represent to it as its own") and sadness ("a disagreeable languor, in which consists the discomfort [*incommodité*] that the soul receives from the evil, or defect, that the impressions of the brain represent to it as belonging to it") with regard to each of our two principal "parts."[75] Had we no bodies, *The Passions* makes bold to say, we could rightly "abandon ourselves" utterly to joy and "avoid" all sadness without fear of excess, even to the point of favoring "a false joy" over "a sadness the cause of which is true." From the body's perspective, contrarily, sadness is "primary to and more necessary than" joy, its continuance, and thus the avoidance of bodily harm, being the indispensable prerequisite to its improvement.[76] Descartes points to the possibility of a partial reconciliation of the soul's and the body's divergent interests in the passions, so to say, on the basis of the soul's inclination to join itself to, or "love," every "true good," especially when that love concerns ourselves, when it rightly "makes no distinction" between us and the goods to which it would join us.[77] For of course one's body is, after all, a part of the whole that includes "soul,"

74. The use of love, hatred, desire, joy, and sadness "insofar as they are related to the body" is set out in *Passions* 2.137, 429–30. The "use of the same passions inasmuch as they belong to soul" is treated in 2.139–42. Joy and sadness as belonging to soul are discussed in 2.141–42, 434–35.

75. "Joy" and "sadness" were introduced at *Passions* 2.61, 376, and defined at 2.91, 396–97, and 2.92, 397, respectively.

76. Because Descartes speaks here in general terms, and without reference to any particular cases of joy and sorrow, as also because he has entertained the theoretical but for the time being counterfactual possibility of experiencing joy and sorrow entirely apart from body, one may fail to realize that he here ascribes divergent significance for soul and body of passions that are at once corporeal and psychic. The point becomes somewhat clearer when he observes that while soul, left to itself, would always favor unlimited joy and love to the slightest experience of sadness and hatred, the "corporeal motions that accompany" all four passions "can be harmful to [bodily] health when they are very violent," but can also be quite "useful" to the body when they are "moderate," for which see *Passions* 2.141, 434–35. *The Passions* neither assumes nor explores the possibility of separate soul, although it does invite speculation on the theme, for which see, inter alia, 1.18, 342–43; 3.173, 461–62; and 3.212, 488.

77. *Passions* 2.139, 432. See also 2.143, 436: "About the same passions, inasmuch as they are related to desire." From this standpoint in between body and soul, as it were, false joy is more harmful than false sadness, because "the latter, by bestowing restraint and fear, disposes one in some fashion to prudence, whereas the former renders those who abandon themselves to it inconsiderate and rash."

however much lesser a part it may be. Even so, the soul's interest in the continuance of the human composite hardly suffices to resolve the tension between psychic and corporeal "uses" of the passions. It is at this juncture that the problem of morality as *The Passions of the Soul* understands it comes at last into view.

"The principal utility of morality [*la morale*]," he asserts in Article 144, consists of "the rule of desire."[78] To say nothing for the moment about the oddity of talk about morality's utility, why is desire suddenly accorded such prominence? In the preceding article he had distinguished between love, hatred, joy, and sorrow "considered precisely in themselves," where they have no effect on our actions, and inasmuch as these same passions "rule" our actions, and indeed even our "mores" *(mœurs)*, through the mediation of the desires they excite in us.[79] Our desires would especially benefit from guidance, then, because in provoking us to take action they in particular have consequences beyond the feelings that they, like every other passion, immediately stir up in us. Thus if we are ever to act in a moral way, we shall have to exercise indirect rule over our desires, governing them, as we have seen from Book 1, through the deft use of apposite "reasons, objects or examples" in order deliberately to incite whatever love, hatred, joy, or sorrow is necessary to steer those desires in the right direction.

By what compass, though, should soul or will chart a course for our desires? The question does not seem to have been an especially pressing one for Descartes. "[T]he error most ordinarily committed" with regard to our desires is not, as Aristotle and the Scholastics had supposed, to have mistaken a lesser good for a greater, or a merely apparent good for the genuine article. Mistakes of that sort are typical of the passions as naturally instituted, as we have seen. The crucial error committed with regard to desires is, rather, "that one does not sufficiently distinguish the things that depend entirely on us from those that do not so depend." Descartes concedes that one should know the object of one's desire to be good before one acts on that desire. Yet he treats what had been for the tradition the gravamen of the matter almost as an afterthought, and at no subsequent point does he discuss it in a thematic way.[80] Provided

78. Ibid., 2.144, 436.

79. Ibid., 2.143, 435–36. Earlier in Book 2, desire is distinguished from the other primitive passions by virtue of its futural orientation: 2.57, 374–75; 2.80, 387; 2.86–87, 392–93. At 2.141, 436, Descartes had asserted, in reassuringly traditional terms, that when desire "proceeds from a true knowledge, it cannot be bad, provided that it is not excessive, and that this knowledge rules it"; as we discovered in Book 1, however, the founder of modern philosophy is remarkably broad-minded about what he is prepared to count as knowledge.

80. As Rethy notes, "The Teaching of Nature and the Nature of Man," 672, n. 70.

that the things in one's power are good, then, "one cannot desire them too ardently," because doing good that depends on oneself is nothing other than to follow virtue; besides, success, and therewith also satisfaction, is virtually guaranteed when the realization of one's desire is contingent on nothing or no one else. Having specified the ordinary moral error, he then identifies a "fault" *(faute)* customarily entailed by that error: distracted by desires for what is not within our power, we desire too little what is.[81]

There are, he continues, two "remedies" against "vain desires."[82] The first, the virtue that he calls "generosity," proves to be the dominant concern of Book 3. The second, to which he dedicates Articles 145 and 146, would have us "reflect frequently" on what he calls "divine providence," though he does not call attention to his calling it so. His explanation of the second remedy constitutes what is undoubtedly one of the most obscure interludes in the entire work, the subtleties of which lie beyond our present scope. It is enough for now to note that Descartes's Providence is "like a fate or an immutable necessity."[83] Fortunately, one is tempted to say, we are spared the debilitating consequences of universal fatalism owing to the exception its "eternal decree" has made, quite unaccountably, with respect to those things that it wanted, for whatever reason, "to depend on our free decision." Everything else we are to regard as "necessary and as though fated," even if what befalls us is "evil," and even if other human beings are complicit in that evil. Since there is nothing quite so effective in quenching a desire as the conviction of its utter pointlessness, and since it is pointless to desire that what happens by necessity should happen otherwise, reflection on Providence will "easily accustom us" to limit our desires to that which Providence, in its fatal dispensation, has left to us to accomplish for ourselves.[84]

This remedy comes, it must be said, rather unexpectedly, for at no point in *The Passions* does Descartes marshal evidence for God's existence; much less does he attempt to demonstrate, from the evident goodness and order of the visible world, that He is its eternal, supreme-

81. *Passions* 2.144, 436–37.

82. Ibid., 2.145, 437, with 2.144, 137. The first of several "remedies" tendered by *The Passions* appears at 2.76, 384. See also 2.148, 442; 3.156, 447; 3.161, 454; 3.170, 460; 3.191, 473; 3.203, 481; and 3.212, 485–87.

83. Ibid., 2.145, 437. From the perspective of biblical piety, the language is singularly inept. Cf. Thomas Aquinas, *Summa contra gentiles* 3.93, on the impropriety of the use of the word *fate* by Christians; also *Summa theologiae* Ia.22.4.c., where he expressly rejects the view that God providentially causes all things to be necessarily. In *Meditations* 1, 21–2, Descartes himself distinguishes "God" from "fate."

84. *Passions* 2.145–46, 437–40. For some help in interpreting the section, see Gerhard Krüger, *Die Herkunft des philosophischen Selbstbewußtseins* (Darmstadt: Wissenschaftliche Buchgesellschaft, 1962), 33–55.

ly good, omniscient, and omnipotent creator—or, in a word, that He is providential. Stranger still, in the only other place where the word *Providence* shows up in the work, he characterizes as "impertinent and absurd" the conclusions some have drawn from the "works of God or nature" about "the conduct of the world and the secrets of Providence," and even casts quiet doubt on the appropriateness of applying the word *good* as "we deem" it to the way "all things are done."[85] Certainly there is no indication whatsoever that he would have us turn to God in prayer for guidance and assistance in knowing and carrying out His will for us.[86] In sum, Descartes's "divine providence" helps those, and apparently only those, who help themselves—if, that is, one can rightly regard as "help" the assurance born from frequent reflection on the providential conduct of the world that we would best trust exclusively to our own devices.

Having adopted this remedy, one would still be left to determine which of one's desires one can satisfy entirely by himself. Descartes cannot, on pain of contradicting himself, propose an answer to that question, even if it were within his own power to find the answer for us. Nevertheless, in the final two articles of Book 2, he does outline a general description of the scope of human power, which also serves, incidentally, to indicate what the "moral" rule of passions other than desire would look like.

From the fact that the soul can take what I have called an aesthetic distance from its passions, it is able to derive a certain pleasure, which he terms "intellectual joy." More precisely, it is enough for soul to feel the passions excited in itself in order to excite this "internal emotion" for itself.[87] Moreover, as long as a man's "conscience" cannot "reproach him with ever having failed to do everything that he judged to be best," which is what Descartes here calls "following virtue," no passion, no matter how "violent," can "disturb the tranquility of his soul." Indeed, such

85. See *Passions* 3.197–98, 476–77, and 3.201, 479, with 2.76, 385; also 3.182–83, 466–68, with 3.161, 453, and 3.195, 475; and consider "Preface," First Letter, 310 with 319. To my knowledge, Descartes uses the word *Providence* exclusively in the only writing in which he does not propose any argument for God's existence. In earlier publications, such arguments are paired with an explicit rejection of any attempt to conceive of divine causality in terms of final causes or the good. See *Discourse* 5, 42–45 with 54; *Meditations* 4, 55, and "Fifth Replies," 375; *Principles* 1.28, 15–16, and 3.2, 80–81; also *Conversations with Burman,* 158.

86. For the meaning or possibility of "prayer" in *The Passions,* cf. 2.83, 390, with 3.162, 454–55; 3.164–65, 455–56; also 3.159, 450, with 3.155, 447.

87. *Passions* 2.147, 440–41. See also 2.93, 398, where "intellectual joy" is said to derive from the "opinion" that one possesses some good; also 2.91–92, 397. On the notion of things "interior" to soul, see 1.13, 338; 1.26, 348; 2.63, 377; 2.85, 391–92; 3.187, 470; 3.204, 486. The pleasure to be had from feeling the passions operating within oneself surely anticipates Rousseau's *sentiment de l'existence.*

is his capacity to find his contentment within himself that "disturbances that come [to him] from elsewhere" even "augment his joy." For in seeing that even the most disagreeable passions "have no power to harm him," he understands that they afford him the occasion "to know his perfection," by which our author seems here to mean our psychic resilience or strength.[88] In the final expression of Cartesian philosophy, moral rule of the passions is "Stoic" only in the measure that it is also "Epicurean."

5. Virtue or Strength, Weakness or Vice

Neither strong spirits or souls nor weak are mentioned by name in Book 2 of *The Passions of the Soul.*[89] Both types are ubiquitous in the third book, which bears the subtitle "Of the particular passions." Yet the account of strength and weakness in Book 3 is prepared for by the preceding book's teaching concerning the moral or properly human "use" of the passions, a teaching that culminates, as we have seen, in a doctrine of radical self-reliance. According to Descartes's final word on the subject, a soul proves to be strong or weak to the extent that it can or cannot find satisfaction in itself alone by itself alone.

The third book is the richest of the three by far in its attention to the human details of passionate experience, and an adequate examination of the nature of weak-spiritedness as it emerges there would thus require that we give far more attention to its final sixty-four articles than is possible here. A still greater challenge is that Descartes's feeble spirits continue to function principally as pointers to their opposites; and whatever may be the case regarding other aspects of his thought, in this one case at least he maintains the classical hermeneutical principle that the lower can be accurately interpreted only in the light cast by the higher. We must begin, then, by considering if only briefly the nature of strong spirits in Book 3.

In fact, the defining feature of the type is now not so much their strength as their "generosity," a virtue the originality of which Descartes is careful to note: "I have called this virtue generosity, following the usage of our language, rather than magnanimity, following the usage of the School, where it is not well known." It is also original in a second, deeper sense inasmuch as it is "the key as it were to all the other vir-

88. Ibid., 2.148, 442, with 2.91, 397; 2.94, 399; and 2.95, 400. The perfection of soul also comes up at 3.154, 446–47, and 3.191, 473. Perfection of body is mentioned at 2.137, 430, and perfection of body or soul at 2.139, 432.

89. There is an allusion to the former type at *Passions* 2.77, 385–86, and to the latter at 2.83, 390, and 2.133, 426. See also 2.94, 399–400.

tues and a general remedy against all the disorders of the passions."[90] As we have seen, generosity was introduced as the first of two remedies for vain desires. That Descartes should discuss his first remedy in the second place, and with no retrospective glance at the alternative, is a sign of how exceptionally independent are spirits endowed with this virtue. In order to limit their desires to what they themselves can accomplish, they have no need to reflect frequently upon Providence. Indeed, they need not look outside themselves at all in order to enjoy what is, in effect, a much more direct access to the divine. For in the use they make of their free decision, and in the dominion they have over their volitions, they attain to a mastery over themselves that "renders them in a way similar to God."[91]

"Directly opposed" to the generous are, of course, those weak in spirit or soul, who are also described in a new way, namely, as "base." "Baseness," or "vicious humility," is the antipode to generosity. This novel Cartesian vice consists of two principal traits. In the first place, "one feels oneself weak or with scant resolve, and . . . cannot prevent oneself from doing things that one knows one will repent afterwards, as if one did not have full use of his free decision." We are reminded here of the second moral maxim, although the emphasis is now on the failure of the weak to affirm their capacity freely to determine themselves. The second predominant trait is that "one believes he cannot subsist by himself, nor do without many things the acquisition of which depends on others."[92] This recalls the first maxim, only now their lack of self-reliance is traced to a mistaken belief the weak have about themselves. More generally, by casting strength and weakness of spirit in terms of virtue and vice, and therewith also the praiseworthy and the blameworthy, Book 3 represents a development of sorts of earlier treatments of the distinction.

Initially, baseness looks to be but one form of human failure among the many documented in Book 3. Its catalogue of reprehensible figures includes, in addition to "the weak and the abject," "the most ignorant and the most stupid," "brutal and foolishly arrogant men," and the "bigoted and superstitious."[93] The third book also identifies a number of other vices besides "vicious humility": "fear [*peur*] or terror [*espouvante*]"; "envy," though only sometimes; "ingratitude"; and "impudence or effrontery."[94] Of these, "pride" is by far the most consequential. It also appears

90. Ibid., 3.161, 453–54. It was first mentioned in 2.54, 373–74.

91. Ibid., 3.152, 445.

92. Ibid., 3.159, 450.

93. Ibid., 3.157, 449; 3.194, 474; 3.190, 472.

94. Ibid., 3.176, 463; 3.182, 466–77, and 3.184, 468–69; 3.194, 474; and 3.207, 483–84. One could not call this list of vices traditional. Vices are mentioned in a general way at several times in Book 3.

on its face to be the excess of that of which "humility" is the defect, in conformity with the pattern of the Aristotelian mean. When examined more closely, however, there emerges a different picture of this pair.

What makes a proud man "blameworthy" is, for Descartes as for everyone else, that he erects a tower of self-esteem on unjust or unreasonable grounds, which is to say, on grounds that are either intrinsically unworthy or on grounds wholly extrinsic to oneself. But Descartes also holds, in proto-Kantian fashion, that the only legitimate basis for a person's esteeming himself is (1) "that he knows that nothing else truly belongs to him apart from his free disposition of his volitions, nor why he should be praised and blamed, if not that he uses it well or badly," and (2) "that he feels within himself a firm and constant resolution to use it well, that is, never to fail willingly [*de volonté*] to undertake and to execute everything that he judges to be best."[95] The proud, contrarily, derive their self-esteem either from praise they have been accorded by others or from having successfully competed with others for what cannot be shared with them; either way, they are dependent on others for the satisfaction of their desires, which is perhaps why Descartes also describes them as "slaves" to those same desires; and on both counts they prove to be indistinguishable from those who are "weak and base."[96]

Further evidence that pride and humility are vicious extremes that meet is that "it often happens that those who have the basest spirit are the most arrogant and haughty." This is owing to the fact that they allow themselves to be "guided [*conduits*] only by fortune," such that "prosperity" is just as likely to "puff them up" as "adversity" is to "render them humble." Consequently, they will as readily "vaunt themselves insolently" over those from whom they suppose they have nothing to fear or hope as they will "abase themselves shamelessly" before those to whom they look, in hope or in fear, for some advantage or disadvantage. In his summary comparison of these two vices with the virtue of generosity Descartes concludes, accordingly, that those most subject to excessive pride are also those most inclined to humbling themselves unduly. Pride and humility do not reside at opposing ends of a moral spectrum, they are not fixed positions, because "the movement of their passion is variable."[97]

A résumé of the other prominent features of weak spirits expressly noted in Book 3 must here suffice. They are of course prone to "irresolution," which, as *The Passions* now explains in a most un-Aristotelian

95. Ibid., 3.153, 446.

96. Ibid., 3.157–58, 448–49.

97. Ibid., 3.159–60, 450–53; for the convergence of pride and baseness see also 3.164, 455–56; 3.188, 470–71, and 3.202, 480–81.

way, "comes from too great a desire to do well," as also from "a weakness of the understanding, which, having no clear and distinct notions, has only many confused ones."[98] They are again said to be quick to "repent," but as Descartes now admits quite openly, they do so without knowing that they have done anything wrong,[99] which suggests that they are, as we would say, burdened by "guilt feelings." Because they feel themselves acutely subject to the adversities of fortune, self-love of a sort will inspire them to "represent to themselves" the evil that befalls others as likely to happen to them, with the result that they are prone to what Descartes calls "pity."[100] A still less benign expression of their nature is the cold and brooding sort of anger to which they are given, which derives, we are told, from a distorted sense of their own importance and their base dependence on things and persons; should they suffer a chance loss, they are quick to construe the harm they feel as an injury; and feeling victimized, as we would put it, they angrily seek out someone to blame.[101] Even uglier is their ingratitude toward, or rather their hatred of, those from whom, in their infirmity and neediness, they had sought and received some assistance. The explanation for this particular expression of their weakness is worth quoting in full:

> [L]acking the will to respond in kind, or despairing of being able to, and imagining that everyone is mercenary like them, and that no one does any good without the hope of being recompensed, they think they have [managed] to deceive them [i.e., their benefactors].[102]

Finally, they are apt "to sin by excess" either by "revering and dreading things that deserve only scorn" or by "insolently disdaining those that deserve most to be revered." As a result, they veer abruptly from superstition to impiety to further superstition. And on that basis, Descartes solemnly concludes that "there is no vice nor disorder [*dereglement*] of spirit of which they are not capable."[103]

Notwithstanding the many failings of the weak, and despite talk of their vices, and even their sins, the generous soul will generally regard the actions of base spirits benignly. He scorns vice, indeed he hates it, but he does not on that account allow himself to scorn or hate the vicious. Although one cannot quite say that he loves the sinner despite his sins, he certainly pities the weak because of their weakness, and is "more

98. Ibid., 3.170, 460.

99. Ibid., 3.191, 472–73. See also 3.177, 464.

100. Ibid., 3.186, 469.

101. Ibid., 3.202, 480–81.

102. Ibid., 3.194, 474.

103. Ibid., 3.164, 456. This is the only appearance of the verb "to sin" or its cognates in the work. Note that for Thomas Aquinas, *Summa theologiae* IIaIIae.92.1.c., the sin of superstition is not opposed to but simply a form of the sin of impiety.

inclined to excuse them than to blame them" for their culpable failings.[104] To be sure, his pity does not signify that he is genuinely troubled by the sufferings that the weak undergo in their weakness, or rather by the weakness they betray in their inability to bear their sufferings with "steadfastness" *(constance).* No, the spectacle affects him as though he were watching a drama on the stage, the enjoyment of which is always amplified, not diminished, by the tears it induces.[105] That he is also disposed to regard the vices of the weak as so "unreasonable" at times as to be "absurd" is, therefore, not at all inconsistent with his tender feelings for them.[106] To the contrary, it often prompts him to "gentle mockery" *(raillerie modeste)* of weak-spirited vices, which he "reproves" *(reprend)* by "making them appear ridiculous." This expression of his goodwill demonstrates how ready he is to be "useful" to others. It also shows "the cheerfulness of his temper and the tranquility of his soul," as well as the "adroitness [*adresse*] of his spirit" in being able to cloak with an agreeable appearance the unsightliness of the human failings he mocks—although as funny as he can be, it would spoil the joke were he himself to laugh out loud at that which he finds so laughable.[107] By and large, then, Cartesian virtue tends in its sublime self-reliance to regard the vices to which human weakness is prone as of too little consequence to be taken terribly seriously.[108] Not that the philosopher cynically disregards ordinary opinion regarding the praiseworthy and the blameworthy. About such matters, it is true, "the people judge very badly." Still, he will often follow their opinions rather than his own "touching the externals" of his actions, both because he "cannot live" without the people and because "it matters" to him to be esteemed by them.[109]

The view taken by the generous of human weakness goes some way toward explaining the meaning of Descartes's cryptic description, at the outset of *The Passions of the Soul,* of his intention as author. The author's

104. See *Passions* 3.154, 446; 3.156, 447–48; 3.164, 456; 3.183, 467–68; and 3.187, 470.

105. Ibid., 3.187, 470, together with 2.94, 399; 2.147, 441; and 3.212, 488.

106. Ibid., 3.157, 449; 3.198, 477.

107. Ibid., 3.180–81, 465–66, and 3.190, 471–72, together with 3.169, 458–59 and Preface, 306.

108. See 3.182, 466–67.

109. Ibid., 3.206, 483. One reason their esteem matters to the generous is indicated in 3.190, 472, wherein Descartes identifies "betraying cities, killing princes, and exterminating entire peoples, merely because they do not follow their own opinions" as among "the very greatest crimes that can be committed by men." The perpetrators of such abominations are the "bigoted and superstitious" who, "under the pretext of [*sous l'ombre*] going frequently to church, reciting many prayers," and so forth, "think themselves completely perfect and imagine themselves such great friends of God, that they can do nothing that would displease him and that everything their passion dictates to them is commendable zeal." See also 3.164, 456, and 3.207, 483–84.

plan was, as we recall, to treat the passions "neither as orator nor even as moral philosopher, but only as physicist or physician." Taken together with the unabashed instrumentalization of human pyschophysiology proposed at the end Book 1, and the reduction of "morality" to its "use" at the end of Book 2, the third book's account of weak spirits indicates just how far beneath or beyond any traditional conception of good and evil Descartes's philosophy really is. His untraditional use of traditional moral vocabulary does not disprove, it rather confirms, his willingness to abandon strictly moral descriptions of human affairs, yet it is not the self-forgetfulness of the natural philosopher that motivates his rejection of the morality of ordinary language.[110] His purpose is, rather, to maximize precisely the moral, which is to say the humanly most agreeable possibilities inherent in what he deems, at bottom, to be a thoroughly amoral universe.

However that may be, just as a generous soul is "more inclined" to excuse than to blame the weak for their shortcomings, so he is also more inclined "to believe" them due to a lack of knowledge than to a lack of goodwill. We seem, therefore, to have come full circle: from his first publication to his last, Descartes maintains that "vice ordinarily comes from ignorance," which is to say that Cartesian philosophy allows no room, at bottom, for either *akrasia* or the war between "the law of sin" and "the law of (believing) mind."[111] Yet this is not to deny that what we have called the problem of moral weakness remains a problem for Descartes. For if virtue really is knowledge, on his reckoning, and vice ignorance, on what basis does he so consistently resort to the adjectives "strong" and "weak"?

Given the psychophysiological mechanisms that Descartes supposes to be operative in every passion of the soul, he least of all is in position to rule out the possibility that at least some of what passes for "vice" is impervious to knowing remediation—because, say, it results from what will subsequently be called "mental illness." Indeed, he openly admits that both "vice" and "virtue" are passions, such that the visible differences between them can ultimately be traced to different "motions" of "the spirits," some of which "strengthen thoughts" having an "evil foundation," and others thoughts whose foundation is "just." This means, however, that it becomes awfully difficult to distinguish, on any principled basis, between bodily impulses, on the one hand, and knowledge, ignorance, and "moral" weakness or strength, on the other.[112] The philosopher did well, it would seem, to trace his reticence to cast blame back to "belief."

110. Cf. Plato, *Theaetetus* 172c–76a.

111. *Passions* 3.154, 446, and 3.160, 452.

112. Ibid., 3.160, 451–53.

What, though, of the "knowledge" and "feeling" of his own goodwill, which both enables him to "esteem himself," and ultimately "prevents him from scorning others"?[113] Esteem, he explains at the beginning of Book 3, is a passion "caused by a particular motion of the spirits" that inclines the soul "to represent to itself the value [*valeur*] of the thing esteemed." More precisely, it is a "species" of the passion of "wonder" *(admiration)*; and the value of its object is the "magnitude" *(grandeur)* of the thing esteemed, as opposed to the "pettiness" *(petitesse)* of that which is the object of scorn.[114] As we learned in Book 2, however, the passion of wonder results from encountering something "that surprises us and that we judge to be new, or very different from what we formerly knew, or from what we supposed it ought to be."[115] Thus its proper object is wholly relative to us; it is whatever happens to strike us unexpectedly; in that sense, and only in that sense, the object of wonder is admirable, and worthy of our interest. We may infer that the generous soul esteems himself because he never ceases to be surprised, in the sense of being favorably impressed, by his capacity and his inclination to act freely. It follows that in this most decisive respect he is, and will forever remain, an unknown quantity to himself.[116] That he should readily attribute his exceptional virtue to the happenstance of a "good birth" is not, therefore, a sign of false modesty on his part.[117] It simply reflects his awareness that it is not, at bottom, by his own merits that he is what he is; surpassing virtue is his thanks to who knows what. Whatever he may think about the weakness he beholds in others, it is only the faint echo of an unsuperable "belief" he has not only in but especially about himself.

113. Ibid., 3.154, 446–47.
114. Ibid., 3.149–51, 443–45, with 2.54, 373–74.
115. Ibid., 2.54, 373–74; and see 2.70, 380–81.
116. See ibid., 3.160, 453.
117. Ibid., 3.161, 453, with 3.182, 467, and 3.198, 477.

10 Kant on Weakness of Will

THOMAS E. HILL JR.

The topic of Kant and weakness of will is a large and complex one, made more difficult by the fact that Kant never gave us an explicit and thorough discussion of weakness of will. Thus we must try to reconstruct his position from his many writings on ethics, taking into account that his views, or ways of expressing them, evolved to some extent over time even in his critical period. It may also be helpful to see his view in contrast with those of certain prominent predecessors against whom he reacted. In any case the plan for my discussion is this: (1) First, without regard to Kant, I review a common conception of weakness of will and some of the philosophical puzzles that it raises. (2) Next, I sketch briefly some views about weakness of will that Kant rejected, notably the views of Hobbes and Hume. (3) Then I discuss Kant's conception of the will in general, calling attention to distinctions that are important for understanding his view. This requires considering the relations between inclinations, reason, and will and how these three are supposed to work in paradigm cases of morally good acts, morally indifferent acts, and immoral acts. (4) I turn to Kant's conception of virtue as a good will combined with developed strength of will to do what is right. (5) I take up the difficult issue of how to interpret strength and weakness of will. Kant held that our acts are not the causal product of natural forces but are based on freely chosen maxims; this view rules out familiar images of strength and weakness of will modeled on physical strength and weakness. So an alternative interpretation is needed. (6) Next I comment briefly on a puzzle raised by many commentators over the years: If the moral law is the fundamental principle of a will with negative freedom (i.e., absence of causal determination) and autonomy, how can anyone freely choose to gratify natural desires in an immoral way? Given the ap-

Earlier versions of this essay were presented at the Catholic University of America, the University of California at Riverside, and UCLA, and I am grateful to the participants at those sessions for their helpful questions and comments. I also thank Tobias Hoffmann for valuable suggestions and historical references.

parent identity between a free will and a moral will in the *Groundwork*, it may seem mysterious how anyone could *freely* will to do wrong through weakness, malice, or any other motive. So how can we be to blame when natural desires and impulses move us? (7) Finally, given Kant's assumption that we always have the capacity to do our moral duty despite our strongest inclinations, how can there be degrees of culpability and mitigation of responsibility for crimes of passion? For example, why are we less culpable, other things being equal, for weakly yielding to jealous rage than for carrying out a cold-blooded plan for revenge?

This is a large agenda, and I realize that I cannot do justice to all of the questions that I raise; but at least, I trust, we will have something to discuss.

1. A Commonsense View and Some Problems

Weakness of will is a very familiar phenomenon and yet also very puzzling. All too often we seem to know what we ought to do, care about doing what we ought, and yet do not do it. When criticized, we deny that we acted maliciously, and yet we cannot pretend that we acted in ignorance. We knew what was right and we wanted to do it, we say, but we were weak. We might mention the pressures we were under, the strong feelings prompting us, and our understandable interest in acting as we did. But we realize that these are only a partial excuse because we still could have done the right thing if we had cared enough and tried our best. Recognizing that we have a long record of acting in this and similar ways, we will admit, if we are honest, that we are weak-willed persons. We may admit this without showing any shame just to demonstrate our modesty and to provide ourselves with a generic excuse for future failures, but in our hearts we realize that our weakness of will is both a moral defect and generally a detriment to our own interests. This at least seems a quite common and intuitively sound view.

Nevertheless, the view is puzzling in several respects. For example, often when people fail to do something they can and should do, especially when this is a pattern, we begin to doubt their sincerity when they say, "I *know* and *fully understand* that I should have done it." We may wonder: If they had *really* known and fully understood that they ought to, wouldn't they have done it? Further, considering the analogy with physical strength, we may ask, "Why are they to blame at all if the failure was due to their lack of strength?" As with physical weakness, we may sometimes blame someone for not previously developing the strength his or her responsibilities demand, but that seems a separate issue. If they lacked the strength to do what they ought at a given time, then it seems they should not be blamed for failing to do it then but at most for past neglect of proper self-development. Again, from a different perspective, we might wonder whether pleading weakness of will should excuse or mitigate guilt at all. To do wrong because one's *will* is weak seems very different from doing it because of a physical disability. It is our own fault, it seems, if in the face of temptations we only will weakly to do what is right. We should will firmly, strongly, with all our might to overcome our impulses to do what we know is wrong. One might even think that to fail to do so is to be guilty twice: guilty of an immoral act and guilty for willing so weakly to avoid it. In addition, we may wonder about the relation between weak-willed acts and a weak-willed character. Is a weak-willed act the primary notion and a weak-willed character just a disposition to do weak-willed acts? Or is it perhaps the other way around, that is, that weak-willed acts are simply those characteristic of the primary notion of weakness of will as a character trait? Also, is weakness of will a general phenomenon or is it always a matter of acting contrary to one's *moral* beliefs? Don't we sometimes do what is merely imprudent or detrimental to our personal projects through weakness of will? Finally, what is a "will" anyway? We commonly explain actions in terms of desires and reasons for acting. Do we need the idea of a will in addition?

2. Some Historical Views That Kant Found Unsatisfactory

Although Kant's idea of strength and weakness of will is quite distinctive, he did not develop it in ignorance of historical precedents. Some of these are especially worth noting. First, although he does not discuss them directly, Kant apparently knew and rejected several ancient views. For example, the Socratic position was that no one could know the good and not do it.[1] Thus vice is due to ignorance, not a bad or a weak will. Plato gave us vivid metaphors for *appetites* and *passions* obeying or rebelling against *reason*,[2] but not of a *will* distinct from both that can choose between them. Aristotle tried to explain some of the phenomena that we attribute to weakness of will, but the explanations seem to turn more on distraction, short-sightedness, and lapses of focus than on willful refusal to act on the best reasons.[3] The Stoics emphasized the will and they inspired Kant in many ways, but, unlike Kant, they seemed to think that the way to virtue was to dispel or transform our troublesome desires and impulses, not to overcome them. Epictetus, for example, argues that we

1. Plato, *Protagoras* 352b–58c.
2. Cf., e.g., Plato, *Republic* 4.435b–41c.
3. Aristotle, *Nicomachean Ethics* 7.3.

should will not to desire things beyond our control,[4] not that we should walk a straight path in spite of those desires.

An idea of the will closer to Kant's developed in Christian thought that no doubt influenced him, but it was sharply challenged by Thomas Hobbes. A traditional view was that as human beings we have *reason* to discern basic moral truths, *appetites and passions* that can lead us astray, and a *free will* that is responsible for our choice when appetites and passions conflict with reason. The will becomes especially important for those who, unlike Plato and Aristotle, affirmed that every adult person has the basic capacity and responsibility to discern and do what is right and to be (fully) virtuous.[5] Given that all responsible moral agents have reason, appetites, and passions, the difference between the virtuous and the vicious could not be attributed (entirely) to the presence or absence of these factors. Besides, apart from desires that follow upon our judgments, desires and passions also came to be understood as things given to us by nature or passively "happening" to us and in us. With this understanding of desires and the assumption that everyone has the basic rational capacity to *discern* the right, many thought that the shared responsibility to *do* what is right must lie in neither desires nor reason per se but in our free capacity to choose what to do when desire and reason conflict.[6] Famously, however, Hobbes rejected this view and thereby set

4. Cf., e.g., *Arrians's Discourses of Epictetus* 1.12 and 1.15, The Loeb Classical Library 131 (Cambridge, Mass.: Harvard University Press/London: William Heinemann, 1925).

5. Medieval authors developed this point in the context of their teaching on conscience and on natural law. For basic accounts of these problems, see Timothy C. Potts, "Conscience," in *The Cambridge History of Later Medieval Philosophy,* ed. Norman Kretzmann et al. (Cambridge and New York: Cambridge University Press, 1982), 687–704; and D. E. Luscombe, "Natural Morality and Natural Law," in *The Cambridge History of Later Medieval Philosophy,* 705–19.

Many Christians, of course, added that this "basic capacity" needed to be supplemented by divine grace and the help of the Church, but this is quite different from Aristotle's denial that women, barbarians, and even Greeks without luck and good mentors could be virtuous. In *The Republic* Plato implies that the lower classes need to be told what is right by their betters; cf. 4.433c–d, 434a–b.

6. Free decision in cases of conflict between desire and reason was explained by some in terms of the will's capacity to restrain the impact of passions on reason; see, for example, Thomas Aquinas, *Summa theologiae* IaIIae.10.3. Acting against one's better judgment presupposes for Aquinas, as for Aristotle, that the judgment of what is best to do is not applied to the particular case at hand (*Summa theologiae* IaIIae.77.2 [cf. *EN* 7.3]). By contrast, the view that the will can choose to follow the sense desires even against a particular practical judgment of reason was prominent among voluntarist authors such as Henry of Ghent, *Quodlibet* 1.16, ed. Raymond Macken, Opera omnia 5 (Leuven: University Press/Leiden: E. J. Brill, 1979), 103–4; Duns Scotus, *Opus Oxoniense* 3.36.1, ed. Allan B. Wolter, *Duns Scotus on the Will and Morality* (Washington, D.C.: The Catholic University of America Press, 1986), 400; and William of Ockham, *Quodlibet* 1.16, ed. J. C. Wey, Opera Theologica 9 (St. Bonaventure, N.Y.: St. Bonaventure University, 1980), 87.

the agenda for much of the philosophical discussion of responsibility that followed. I want to sketch briefly Hobbes's view, and a variation by Hume, because they contrast sharply with Kant's view and posed a challenge that Kant needed to address.

According to Hobbes, all human behavior is causally determined in a mechanistic way by appetites, which are actually aspects of our bodies in motion.[7] These desires and aversions are often in conflict, and they can never be shaped by reason into an integrated coherent set. We are always moved by our strongest desires and aversions, and *the will* is nothing but the desire or aversion that finally causes us to act.[8] It follows that every act is a result of the agent's will: no act is involuntary, strictly speaking. It also follows that there is neither *free will* nor *weakness of will,* in the strict sense, for all of our acts are caused by our will, which is itself caused by prior motions, and we can never fail to act when we will to do so (though we may fail to achieve our objective). Acts, but not the will, can be free but only in a sense.[9] For example, we freely leave the room, as opposed to being dragged forcibly out, in that we behaved as we willed and willed what we most desired. Reason can estimate consequences of our various acts and thus influence conduct indirectly, but it has no power directly to oppose, suppress, or overcome desires and aversions. What is ordinarily called "weakness of will," then, is really just a matter of being short-sighted or impulsive, that is, being moved by appetites and aversions (including one's "will") that were not influenced by due consideration of long-term consequences. The principles (or "natural laws") of right reason are really just precepts of prudence about how to preserve oneself and further one's interests.[10] In civil society one is responsible for not acting justly, but this is just a matter of public accountability and contractually based legal liability to punishment.[11] Injustice is never a matter of freely willing, when one could do otherwise, to act to satisfy one's desires *instead of* the moral demands of reason.

David Hume, whom Kant regarded as his immediate challenger, accepted many of Hobbes's basic ideas but made them gentler and subtler. He regarded human sentiments as more varied, more other-regarding, and more socially malleable than Hobbes did. But he still conceived of reason as a fact-finder and calculator rather than as a source of moral and rational imperatives.[12] In his view desires and passions are still passive "impressions" that we feel and dispositions that we infer from pat-

7. Thomas Hobbes, *Leviathan,* 1.6, ed. Edwin Curley (Indianapolis: Hackett, 1994).

8. Ibid., 1.6.

9. Ibid., 2.21.

10. Ibid., 1.14.

11. Ibid., 1.15 and 2.27.

12. David Hume, *A Treatise of Human Nature,* 3.1.1, ed. L. A. Selby-Bigge, 2nd ed. by P. H. Nidditch (Oxford: Clarendon Press, 1978).

terns of feeling and behavior.[13] They, and only they "move us" to act. Beliefs about matters of fact, which are discovered by reason and observation, only provide the context in which sentiments move us. Strictly speaking, there are no matters of fact or imperatives of reason about what we ought to do. The will is no longer an appetite or an aversion, as it was for Hobbes, but it still is just an event in a chain of causes.[14] I act freely, in a sense, when my behavior is caused by an occurrence of a will-event in me and this was caused by my desires. As we might say, "I *did* it *freely* because I had a *will* to do it and this was because I *wanted* to do it." Again, on Hume's view a free will would be an uncaused event, and this is contrary to nature and no help to morality anyway.[15] We are responsible for acts not because a random, uncaused natural event occurred but because the acts are caused by a will that is caused by our character. Given Hume's regularity theory of causation, a will to do something does not *necessarily* result in action.[16] For example, a person who has just lost a limb may for a time try or "will" to move the limb but without success. When a limb is detached, occurrences of a will-event have no immediate causal efficacy with respect to it. The will's power, we might say, is limited in scope this way, but the failure has nothing to do with weakness of will. What we call "weak-willed acts," instead, must be simply imprudent or foolish acts: that is, objectionable acts caused by ignorance, miscalculation, or strong short-term desires contrary to our own acknowledged best interests or acts caused by immediate impulses without thought of consequences. Choosing or willing is not, strictly speaking, an *activity* that we could do weakly or resolutely, and the will is not a weak or strong *power* that could choose between desire and reason. Hume admittedly offers a more subtle account of moral virtue and responsibility than Hobbes does, but from Kant's perspective it is hampered from the outset by an untenable action theory.

Kant's theory, as we shall see, contrasts sharply with those of Hobbes and Hume. For example, according to Kant, the will is an active power of the mind, not something we passively experience. It is not a desire, strong or weak. Nor is it an inner event or "impression" that we come to recognize by introspection. We cannot understand the will as something in a series of natural causes, and so free or voluntary action cannot be reduced to behavior caused by will-events that are caused by our desires. And weak-willed acts cannot be reduced to behavior, against long-term or moral interests, caused by ignorance, miscalculation, or overpowering immediate impulses. But to see Kant's positive view, we need to review some basic elements of his action theory.

13. Ibid., 1.1.1.

14. Ibid., 2.3.1.

15. Ibid., 2.3.2.

16. Ibid., 1.3.14.

3. The Will in General, Negative Freedom, and Autonomy

A difficult but central aspect of Kant's moral theory is his idea of what human agents must be like in order to be capable of understanding and acting for moral reasons. Here the briefest summary will have to suffice. Moral agents have natural inclinations, reason, and the power to choose which to follow when inclination and reason conflict. Inclinations are natural dispositions to act, in themselves morally neutral but often temptations to act contrary to reason.[17] Reason regarding practical matters *enables us to discern* (within limits) what is prudent and what is moral. Its judgments about what we must do in a particular case depend on both rational principles and empirical facts.[18] Practical reason is also a *disposition to act* in accord with the judgments of reason.[19] The dispositions stemming from our inclinations and reason often conflict, but not always. We also have the power (or free will) to choose whether to follow inclination or reason when these conflict. At least this is what we must presuppose from the practical standpoint of an agent deliberating about what to do.[20] Granted, empirical science must think of human behavior as causally determined; but this is not inconsistent with

17. Regarding this and subsequent points in this section, see Immanuel Kant, *Groundwork for the Metaphysics of Morals,* ed. Thomas E. Hill Jr. and Arnulf Zweig (Oxford: Oxford University Press, 2002). Numbers in parentheses refer to the volume and page in the standard Prussian Academy edition, *Kant's gesammelte Schriften,* herausgegeben von der Königlich Preußischen Akademie der Wissenschaften (Berlin, 1902ff.). See especially *Groundwork,* 198–201 (4: 397–99), 215n (4: 414n). Useful commentaries include H. J. Paton, *The Categorical Imperative* (London: Hutchison, 1958), especially chaps. 8–9, 20–21, pp. 78–102, 207–22; and Henry J. Allison, *Kant's Theory of Freedom* (Cambridge: Cambridge University Press, 1990), chaps. 1–7, pp. 11–145.

18. The rational principles that lie behind moral judgments, Kant held, are expressed (in imperative form) in his various formulations of the Categorical Imperative (see *Groundwork,* 222–35 [4: 420–34]), and summarized at *Groundwork* 236–37 (4: 436–37). The rational principle behind hypothetical imperatives, Kant implies, is roughly, "One ought to take the necessary means within one's power to the ends that one wills (or abandon the ends)"; see *Groundwork,* 215–20 (4: 413–19). Partly because he thought that previous philosophers often neglected the rational principles, Kant emphasized these rather than relevant empirical facts, encouraging some critics to suppose that he thought empirical facts have no place in ethics. Particular moral judgments, however, are applications of rational principles to the agent's circumstances and so require empirical understanding. Also Kant's own arguments, especially in his later ethical writings, often presuppose at least general empirical facts about the human condition.

19. This is a theme throughout Kant's mature ethical writings. See, for example, *Groundwork,* 247–48 (4: 447–48), and Immanuel Kant, *Religion within the Boundaries of Mere Reason,* ed. Allen Wood and George di Giovanni (Cambridge: Cambridge University Press, 1998), 50–52 (6: 26–28). See also Immanuel Kant, *The Metaphysics of Morals,* translated and edited by Mary Gregor (Cambridge: Cambridge University Press, 1996), 13–14 (6: 213–14). Again, bracketed numbers refer to volume and page of the standard Academy edition.

20. *Groundwork,* 247–48 (4: 446–47).

conceiving of ourselves for moral purposes as having negative freedom and autonomy.[21] Negatively free agents can act independently of their inclinations.[22] We must presuppose that such agents also have autonomy of the will, which is a capacity and disposition to guide themselves by rational principles that are not mere hypothetical imperatives prescribing the means to their desire-based ends.[23] The fundamental moral principle expressed in the Categorical Imperative, in its various forms, expresses the standards to which any rational will with autonomy is necessarily committed.[24] Unfortunately, not every moral agent with the capacity to live by the standard actually does so. But to violate it inevitably results in an inner conflict of will, reflected in the painful self-judgments of conscience and lowered self-esteem.[25] This is because in immoral action we use our free power of choice (our *Willkür* or "will" in one sense) in a way contrary to what is required by our practical legislating reason (our *Wille* or "will" in another sense).[26] By contrast, a person who willingly follows moral principles, even when contrary to natural inclinations, has a kind of integrity and self-respect that others lack. Immoral and morally weak persons do not in the same way express their nature as rational human beings with autonomy.

4. Virtue as a Good Will with the Developed Strength of Will to Do Right Despite Obstacles

Kant's *Groundwork* was meant to be preliminary to his more comprehensive work, *The Metaphysics of Morals,* published more than ten years later. The latter is divided into the *Doctrine of Right* (concerned with law and justice) and the *Doctrine of Virtue* (concerned with personal morality).[27] Duties of virtue, he tells us, are concerned with our maxims, motives, and ends. They result from the "inner legislation" of our own reason, not from governmental legislation. We cannot be coerced to follow them, but should do so out of respect for their moral grounds—for example, the dignity of humanity in each person. Unlike juridical duties, most duties of virtue are imperfect duties: they do not prescribe specific actions but rather tell us to make it our maxim to promote certain

21. *Groundwork,* 247–57 (4: 447–58). 22. *Groundwork,* 246 (4: 446).

23. *Groundwork,* 240–47 (4: 440–47). 24. *Groundwork,* 236–41 (4: 436–41).

25. *Metaphysics of Morals,* 160–61 (6: 400–401) and 188–91 (6: 437–40); *Religion,* 27 (6: 267–68) and 178–80 (6: 184–87).

26. *Metaphysics of Morals,* 13 (6: 212) and 18 (6: 226). Gregor translates *Willkür* as *choice* and *Wille* as *will;* see Allison, 129–36.

27. For Kant's explanation of this division and the corresponding different types of duty, see *Metaphysics of Morals,* 20–22 (6: 218–21), 23–34 (6: 229–42), and 145–54 (6: 379–91).

moral ends, especially our own perfection and the happiness of others. The widest duties, such as beneficence, leave a wide "playroom" for free choice as to when, how, and to what extent to promote the end.[28] Fulfilling these duties of virtue is meritorious but omitting them is not in itself demeritorious (or culpable).[29] Neglect of duties of virtue becomes culpable when it is due to a principled refusal to accept them or a failure to apply them in a particular emergency situation in which the usually "imperfect" duty has become mandatory.[30] In these cases, predictably, our consciences will accuse us and cause us to suffer, but, generally speaking, it is not the business of others to judge and condemn us in this area.[31]

But what is it to be a virtuous person? First and foremost it requires having a *good will*—a sincere commitment and effort to do what is right.[32] This is the essential feature of a morally good person. Many other things are useful and valuable to those who have them but they are neither necessary nor sufficient for basic moral goodness. This is true, for example, of diligence, courage, intelligence, wealth, happiness, and useful accomplishments. A person with a good will is fundamentally good even if she is by nature scatter-brained, timid, stupid, unnoticed, miserable, and devoid of social achievements. A good will manifests itself when we act from duty, but we can *have* a good will even when acting at the moment from other innocent or good motives. The moral goodness of a *person* is not a function of number or kind of ("morally worthy") *acts* that the person does from duty. A commitment to morality can motivate us to do the right thing when we are tempted not to, but it can also serve as a *back-up motive* when we are doing things for other reasons. For ex-

28. *Metaphysics of Morals*, 26 (6: 233), 153–54 (6: 390–91), 168 (6: 410–11), 195 (6: 445), 202–3 (6: 453–54). Interpretations differ about the extent and kind of latitude allowed by Kant's duty of beneficence. See Mary J. Gregor, *Laws of Freedom* (Oxford: Blackwell, 1963), 95–112; Marcia Baron, *Kantian Ethics (Almost) without Apology* (Ithaca: Cornell University Press, 1995), 88–107; David Cummiskey, *Kantian Consequentialism* (New York: Oxford University Press, 1996), 105–23; and Thomas E. Hill Jr., *Human Welfare and Moral Worth* (Oxford: Oxford University Press, 2002), 201–43.

29. *Metaphysics of Morals*, 153 (6: 390).

30. For the first point, see *Metaphysics of Morals*, 153 (6: 390). The second presumably follows from applications of the Categorical Imperative directly to emergency cases of dire distress, in which aid would not be automatically made mandatory by the wide imperfect duty of beneficence, when interpreted nonrigoristically.

31. *Metaphysics of Morals*, 150–52 (6: 385–87). Their general ethical duty, like ours, is to promote the happiness of others, not their virtue, and so apart from matters concerning the law, the moral education of children, and scandalous conduct, others should be focused more on our happiness (consistent with justice) rather than our moral virtue. This perhaps surprising theme is developed in my "Kant's Anti-Moralistic Strain," in *Dignity and Practical Reason in Kant's Moral Theory* (Ithaca: Cornell University Press, 1992), 176–95.

32. *Groundwork*, 195–203 (4: 393–402). See Allen W. Wood, *Kant's Ethical Thought* (Cambridge: Cambridge University Press, 1999), chap. 1, pp. 17–49.

ample, we usually read novels for enjoyment but a person of good will is ready to stop reading if a friend suddenly needs help. Similarly, usually we take care of our children from love, not duty, but a parent with a good will is moved to continue even when stress overwhelms affection. A good will can also serve as *a filter* that rejects in advance certain immoral acts as not even options to consider. Unlike our desires, our feelings, and the *effects* of our actions, whether or not we have a good will, the commitment to act rightly is entirely up to us. At least, Kant argued, this is what we *must presuppose* as moral agents. But, as we shall see, being *virtuous* is more than having a good will. Virtue and some other features of an ideally good person cannot be acquired at will.[33]

Virtue includes a good will, but virtue as a character trait is also a *developed strength of will* to do what is right.[34] Effort, practice, and time are needed to turn a basically good will into a strong and effective will that chooses the right thing even in the presence of contrary inclinations so intense that they might sway a weaker person.[35] With practice, a person of developed virtue would overcome such obstacles with regularity and relative ease. Those who have a good will have a general policy and aim that points them in the right direction, as it were, because the principle of any good will is "to do what is right." These general good intentions, however, may sometimes fail to result in right action because of the agent's weakness of will. In this case the will generally aims at the right, so to speak, but it is weak. In a person of developed virtue, the will is both strong and aimed at the right.

5. How Are Strength and Weakness of Will to Be Understood?

Kant's conception of strength and weakness is not easy to fathom, but a few points seem clear enough. For one thing, despite the metaphors, Kant did not think of a will as an empirical force that could do battle with felt impulses and inclinations.[36] So a strong will is not (as it was for Hobbes) a desire that, in a stream of conflicting desires, hap-

33. *Metaphysics of Morals,* 158–59 (6: 397). Kant implies that being a person with cultivated "compassionate natural (aesthetic) feelings" is a goal that we have an (indirect) duty to pursue, but it is a trait that we cannot acquire at will but requires effort over time (e.g., by not avoiding sickrooms, debtor's prisons, and contact with the poor); see *Metaphysics of Morals,* 205 (6: 457).

34. *Metaphysics of Morals,* 146 (6: 380), 164–65 (6: 405–7), 166 (6: 408), 221 (6: 477). See also Allison, chap. 9, pp. 162–79; Paul Guyer, *Kant on Freedom, Law, and Happiness* (Cambridge: Cambridge University Press, 2000), 303–23; and Wood, 329–33.

35. *Metaphysics of Morals,* 158–59 (6: 397), 221 (6: 477).

36. *Groundwork,* 250–57 (4: 450–58).

pens to overpower the others and cause the resulting behavior. Willing, in Kant's view, is something we *do*, not something we *experience passively*. Second, we will to act on *maxims*, which are personal policies or general intentions referring to a kind of act, its purpose, and sometimes its underlying reason.[37] From a practical perspective, we think of ourselves as acting on a rationale that could in principle be articulated and is not reducible to a description of the empirical causes of our behavior. All acts for which we are morally responsible are supposed to be based on a maxim, whether we act dutifully or immorally, with a strong will or a weak will. Some maxims are quite specific, describing the actual intentions and aims with which we act on particular occasions. Other maxims, however, are very general, life-governing policies that guide, more or less effectively, our choice of more specific maxims. We adopt our maxims as human beings subject to the influence of both our sensuous inclinations and our morally legislative practical reason *(Wille)*. All of our maxims, however, are presumed to result from the exercise of our power of free choice *(Willkür)*.

Accordingly, weak-willed acts contrary to duty are not to be understood as the result of an agent's willing to act on a particular good maxim but lacking the power to do so.[38] Similarly, virtue or strength of a moral will is not just a matter of being committed to act on a good maxim and *being able* to do so despite obstacles. All moral agents are presumed to have *that* capacity insofar as they have freedom of will.[39] We often lack the power to ensure that our acts have the *effects* we intend, but it is presumed to be entirely up to us whether or not to choose to act

37. *Groundwork*, 202n (4: 402n), 222n (4: 421n); *Metaphysics of Morals*, 17–18 (6: 225–26), *Religion*, 48–49 (23–24).

38. Kant says that failures to fulfill an imperfect duty, provided they are not based on a principle not to comply, display "weakness," or want of virtue ("strength of resolution"). Though they are not in themselves "culpable" (as are intentional wrongdoings), nevertheless they reveal a "deficiency in moral worth," not merely an excusable disability; see *Metaphysics of Morals*, 153 (6: 390). Again, Kant says that "moral weakness" is "negative lack of virtue" where virtue is treated as "strength of soul," which is "strength of resolution in a human being endowed with freedom"; see *Metaphysics of Morals*, 148 (6: 384). Kant classifies "general weakness of the human heart" (or "frailty") with "impurity" and "depravity" as "three sources of moral evil," and in Kant's view lacking the ability to do what is right could not be a source of moral evil; see *Religion*, 53–55 (6: 29–32).

39. At least one passage might suggest that human freedom is merely a capacity *to acquire the ability to overcome opposing impulses*, but this would allow that, before we could successfully acquire the ability, our opposing impulses could completely excuse our wrongdoing, contrary to what Kant repeatedly implies. What must be acquired, I take it, is not the *basic ability* to do one's duty in the face of temptation but, as he says, *virtue*, a *strength of resolution* that we develop by "contemplating the dignity of the pure rational law and by *practicing* virtue"; see *Metaphysics of Morals*, 158–59 (6: 397).

on a maxim to try to achieve the end. *Depraved* persons act on bad maxims and without any general commitment to acting rightly.[40] Those who act rightly from *virtue* act on morally good maxims in line with their general commitment to do what is right. Those who do wrong from *moral weakness* act at the moment on an immoral maxim but contrary to their practical reason *(Wille)* and their general commitment (of *Willkür*) to act rightly. They give in to inclinations contrary to duty, but this is not a matter of a stronger *force* (their inclinations) literally *overpowering* weaker ones (their rational predisposition to morality and their general intention to be guided by it). The comparison with physical strength and weakness is misleading here. What is needed, instead, is an interpretation of strength and weakness appropriate to Kant's action theory—with its complex conception of "will" and its understanding of acts as based on freely chosen maxims.[41]

The metaphor of strength of a will to be moral might be unpacked in at least two ways.[42] First, consider the content of our commitment to morality. Like laws of the state, resolutions and principles can be clear and definite or vague and somewhat inexplicit regarding specific implications. Some even have explicit "loopholes" permitting escape from their primary provisions. Many of us do wrong because our commitment to morality is vague or even qualified. For example, we have only a rather

40. For the contrast between depravity, weakness, and impurity, see *Religion*, 52–55 (6: 29–32). Here Kant explicitly discusses *propensities* to evil, but presumably the depraved and weak persons are those who choose to fulfill rather than to overcome the corresponding propensities.

41. The best account of these matters, in my view, is Robert Johnson's "Weakness Incorporated," *History of Philosophy Quarterly* 15 (1998): 349–67. My reflections agree with his excellent discussion on most important matters, though I do not rely in the same way on a distinction between "motivation"and "values." Also at times Johnson seems to treat weakness of will as a kind of inability. For example, "The weak person we are interested in here is not simply a person who *drops* and *adopts* principles too easily, but is rather one who *cannot* live up to those she adopts and does not drop" (p. 360, my italics in the second clause).

42. Here I offer an interpretation not explicitly mandated by Kant's remarks about strength and weakness of will but guided by a concern to reconstruct, compatibly with the texts, an account of weakness of will that fits the basic requirements of his moral theory: for example, the will is not a desire or inner force that we can introspect, weakness of will is not an incapacity that excuses wrongdoing, strength of moral will is developed virtue in a person with a basically good will, morally responsible acts (good or bad) are to be understood as acts on a maxim, and we have both specific maxims (as in the *Groundwork* examples) and more generic, life-defining maxims (such as "self-love" and "duty" in the second *Critique*). The interpretation is no doubt partly influenced by my earlier attempts to make sense of weakness of will in everyday life, as manifested by several patterns in the character of weak-willed persons over time. This is reprinted as "Weakness of Will and Character" in my *Autonomy and Self-Respect* (Cambridge: Cambridge University Press, 1991), 118–37.

vague and indefinite resolve "to do good" or, anticipating potential sacrifices, we might adopt as an explicit policy the rule that "I will always to do right even against inclinations, unless the cost is really, really high." These imperfect commitments might account for a person's acting rightly in most circumstances, but occasionally failing when temptations are extraordinarily strong.

However, a qualification is needed here. Kant distinguishes *weakness*, *impurity*, and *depravity* as different grades of the natural propensity to evil.[43] The *weakness* or frailty, Kant describes as follows:

> First, the frailty [*fragilitas*] of human nature is expressed even in the complaint of the Apostle: "What I would, that I do not" i.e. I incorporate the good (the law) into the maxim of my power of choice; but this good, which is an irresistible incentive objectively or ideally [*in thesi*], is subjectively [*in hypothesi*] the weaker (in comparison with inclination) whenever the maxim is to be followed.[44]

By contrast, *impurity* is the disposition to qualify our commitment to follow the moral law, saying, for example, "I will do what is right if it also serves my interests" or "I will do my duty if the cost is not too high." Even in their basic life-defining maxims, those who yield to this disposition are not committed to treating duty as a sufficient reason for them to act. Their general policy with regard to morality is, in effect, full of loopholes. Finally, Kant says, *depravity* is "the propensity of the power of choice to maxims that subordinate the incentives of the moral law to others (not moral ones)."[45] The paradigm of a depraved person is one who systematically chooses, on principle, to act from self-interest instead of duty, when these are in conflict.

Moral regret when one does wrong is a sign of a moral weakness insofar as the regret reflects a conflict between the weak agent's immediate choice of an immoral maxim and his or her general commitment to be moral. Regret for being morally weak does not indicate that, although the particular maxim on which the agent elected to act at the time was good, regrettably the agent was unable to act on it. Rather, the regret shows that, despite maintaining a long-standing commitment or "will" to be moral, on this occasion the agent chose to indulge other, competing concerns. This reveals an irrational "conflict of will," not an inability to do what is right. Those whose basic commitments are mixed or depraved do not necessarily have this sort of conflict of will with regard to morality. They may *wish* that they could satisfy both morality and self-love, because in Kant's view they are predisposed to both. But, strictly speaking, their particular immoral choices are not in conflict with their basic, life-

43. *Religion*, 52–55 (6: 29–32).

44. *Religion*, 53 (6: 329).

45. *Religion*, 54 (6: 30).

governing maxims. In fact those maxims express their general intention (or "will") to favor inclination over duty in various circumstances.

My first suggestion is that weak-willed persons, by contrast, are committed unconditionally to doing right despite inclination, but they are typically not very clear, definite, and explicit about what specifically this implies for various particular choices. This vagueness, we might say, is a kind of "weakness" in their resolution to be moral, a weakness in the content of what they will analogous to the weakness of a vague law adopted by legislators who lack a clear understanding of its implications. A weak moral resolution of this sort enables us, especially when weak in other respects, to affirm a general, unqualified commitment to morality even though we sometimes act contrary to what that commitment, properly understood, requires. Vagueness opens a door for self-deception, inattention, and special pleading that enable us to live with a genuine conflict of will, of which we are aware enough to be responsible but not enough to prompt us to change.

A second way of thinking of moral strength requires us to distinguish *what we will* from *how seriously and resolutely we will* it.[46] Suppose two people have a *general intention* always to do what is right and the capacity to act accordingly if (as we say) they try hard enough. One person is whole-heartedly committed, treating the commitment as the highest priority, and is determined to be attentive, well focused, and clear-headed when inclinations conflict with moral responsibilities. The other person is sincere but habitually lets himself be easily distracted and indulges a tendency to make self-serving excuses. Both will to do what is right as their *life-governing policy* and have an adequate *capacity* to implement the policy in every case, but the second *wills it more weakly*.

Kant admitted that we cannot explain this commonsense idea empirically, as we might explain a person's failure to lift a certain weight as a matter of exerting too weakly a muscular capacity that one has. Nevertheless, Kant implies that a moral perspective needs a concept of this sort. Using the concept, he can suppose that both the virtuous and the morally weak person had the capacity to overcome inclinations contrary to what is right, but the virtuous, or morally strong-willed, person can do so, and typically does, more readily, easily, and confidently. Kant could even say, with Aristotle, that the virtuous person is not *tempted* to do wrong, insofar as the word *tempted* implies an initially wavering attitude characteristic of the morally weak person. This is not to say, however, that virtuous persons never experience strong inclinations contrary to

46. This second point is meant to apply even to cases in which the agents' *policy* to do what is right is clear and definite. The moral weakness here is not due to vagueness, but is to be explained in a different way.

their moral responsibilities, for extreme enduring physical pain may be required and to be inclined to stop the pain is only natural.[47]

On the interpretations suggested here, the weakness of the morally weak person is either in the content of the person's moral resolution or in how resolutely, in a sense, the person willed it. In either case, however, those who are weak-willed often make particular choices contrary to their practical reason, the "will" *(Wille)* in them that "legislates" moral standards for them irrespective of their individual choices. Thus, we could say that in the morally weak person "the will" (in this further sense) is weak in that it does not effectively govern all particular choices, as it does in the virtuous person. To say this, admittedly, is not to explain an inner mechanism at work, effective in some persons (the virtuous) but not in others (the morally weak). Rather, it is simply another way of noting that the morally weak person's particular choices, unlike the virtuous person's, do not regularly correspond with the moral commands of their practical reason. That moral weakness can be described in this way is worth noting, however, because in some passages Kant suggests that what is weak in the morally weak person is in fact the "will" in this sense *(Wille)*.[48]

6. How Can We Be to Blame When Natural Desires and Impulses Move Us?

Philosophers have often wondered how we can be responsible for our behavior if it results from natural forces, such as desires, impulses, feelings, and sentiments. The problem can take several different forms. If we regard the fundamental human desires as good, we cannot explain wrongdoing and evil simply by reference to these good desires. The main problem, then, is to say why acts motivated by some desires are praiseworthy while acts motivated by other desires are blameworthy. We would also need an account of motivation that explains why agents should be *blamed* for their objectionable behavior rather than *pitied* for the misfortune of having bad or perverse desires that overwhelm the "natural" good ones.

Kant's official position avoids these problems. Taking a broad view of "nature" as governed by causal laws, Kant rejects the idea that certain "natural" inclinations are in themselves good and others bad. He held that, although some inclinations and desires are more benign in their

47. These points about temptation and inclination in the virtuous were first suggested to me by Karen Stohr of Georgetown University.

48. *Metaphysics of Morals*, 151 (6: 387) and 164–65 (6: 405–7).

effects than others, all of them are in themselves morally neutral insofar as they belong to our sensible, empirical nature.[49] For this reason he does not rely on distinctions among such motives to explain the difference between morally culpable acts, morally indifferent acts, and acts of positive moral worth. In addition, Kant held that whether we have strong inclinations contrary to duty is often just a matter of luck (and so not our fault) and that such desires can merely *dispose,* not *compel,* us to do wrong.[50] Because we have the freedom of will to choose to satisfy desire or to follow reason, we are not to be pitied and pardoned, but held responsible, for our wrongdoing. The contrary inclinations do not literally "overpower" us but rather we choose to indulge or "give in" to them.

Nevertheless, Kant's account of desire-based wrongdoing seems to face a serious problem. At least critics have often thought so.[51] Here is the problem. In the *Groundwork* Kant argues that his supreme moral principle is the principle of a will that has the property of autonomy, which is "being a law unto itself (independently of any property of the objects of volition)."[52] Thus any rational person with autonomy wills the moral law as its principle. He also argues that autonomy is inseparable from negative freedom, which is a will's capacity to be active "independently of alien causes *determining* it."[53] This entails that anyone with a free will, in either sense, wills the supreme moral principle. Thus, it may seem, no one freely chooses to act contrary to the supreme moral principle. Those who act badly are really just caused to do so by the forces of nature, in fact by their own desires and inclinations. In other words, in "immoral" actions the will to do what is right is not just *weak,* but in fact utterly *powerless* against contrary inclinations. No one does wrong freely, and so no one is responsible for vicious and harmful behavior. This, however, is an intuitively absurd result, and it contradicts the dominant theme explicit in all of Kant's mature ethical writings. Clearly something has gone wrong.

This apparent problem rests on a serious misunderstanding. In saying that the supreme moral principle is the principle of a will that has the property of autonomy, Kant does not mean that a person who has such a will never acts immorally. To the contrary, Kant implies that autonomy

49. This is Kant's mature position (see, e.g., *Religion,* 57 [6: 35]) but it seems in tension with *Groundwork,* 229 (4: 428).

50. *Groundwork,* 199–201 (4: 397–99).

51. See, e.g., Henry Sidgwick, *Methods of Ethics,* 7th ed. (Indianapolis and Cambridge: Hackett, 1981), Appendix, pp. 511–16; and Robert Paul Wolff, *The Autonomy of Reason* (New York: Harper & Row, 1973), 122–23, 210–11.

52. *Groundwork,* 240 (4: 440) and 246 (4: 446–47).

53. *Groundwork,* 246 (4: 446).

and negative freedom are characteristics of all moral agents, good and bad.[54] In fact denying this point was the primary error of all previous moral theories, for in various different ways they assumed that heteronomy, not autonomy, was the basic feature of human wills. In Kant's view all moral agents have negative freedom, that is, the *capacity* to choose, rightly or wrongly, without being causally determined by their inclinations *(negative freedom)*. This capacity is possible only because they also have *autonomy,* which is a rational *disposition* to govern oneself by rational principles not based on contingent inclinations. This moral disposition, however, does not guarantee morally correct choice on particular occasions. The key to the puzzle lies in a distinction between two aspects of the will that Kant distinguishes explicitly only in his later writings. As noted above, in Kant's view, we have a rational legislative will *(Wille)* and a free power of choice *(Willkür)*.[55] To say we have a legislative will *(Wille)* is a metaphorical way of saying that, as moral agents, we inevitably recognize the moral law as imposing overriding rational demands on us. To say we have a free power of choice *(Willkür)* is just to say that whether or not we fulfill these demands is not causally determined but is a choice for which we are responsible. In more everyday terms, we all implicitly understand moral requirements as a *standard* that we should respect even when we violate it. Vicious people systematically refuse to let the standard constrain them. Morally weak people let themselves lapse from their general policy of doing right. For both, Kant thought, a troubled conscience is inevitable because they realize that they willfully disregard a standard that they cannot help but recognize as inherent in their own practical reason.

7. How Can There Be Degrees of Culpability?

When Kant takes an empirical point of view, he often describes human beings as morally lax, self-deceiving, self-serving, hypocritical, and weak.[56] Usually, it seems, they do wrong while professing even to them-

54. At least this is what we must presuppose from a practical standpoint. "Autonomy" here refers to a "property of the will" that is a capacity and disposition to use and follow the moral law as a rational standard that the agent with autonomy necessarily recognizes as not externally imposed. When contemporary writers write as if some people (the morally good) are "autonomous" and some (the morally bad) are "heteronomous," this would be less misleadingly expressed, if the point is Kantian, by saying that some (the good) express their rational autonomy in their choices, while others (the bad) do not, acting instead as if they were beings subject only to the laws governing beings with heteronomy of the will; see Allison, 85–99, and my *Dignity and Practical Reason in Kant's Moral Theory,* 76–122.

55. See, e.g., *Metaphysics of Morals,* 13 (6: 213–14) and 18 (6: 226–27).

56. E.g., *Religion,* 60–61 (6: 38–39).

selves that they aim to do right.[57] Principled wrongdoing and fiendish malice are rare, if not impossible, for human beings. Conscience can be dulled but not silenced. And yet Kant insists that, from a moral/practical point of view, we cannot excuse our misconduct by saying that we generally aim and want to do right and failed because of natural and universal temptations. We must take ourselves to be capable of doing our duty despite our strongest contrary inclinations. "I *really* wanted to do something else!" hardly excuses a serious neglect of responsibility. So, from a moral practical point of view, we are very often culpable regardless of our generally positive orientation toward morality.

Nevertheless, we ordinarily think that we are *less* to blame, other things equal, for the wrongs we do in moments of extreme passion or when acting rightly would require great sacrifice of our personal interests. These factors *mitigate* our culpability, we think, even though they do not completely excuse our behavior. Even Kant seems to accept this idea when, in *The Metaphysics of Morals,* he says:

> *Subjectively,* the degree to *which an action can be imputed* [*inputabilitas*] has to be assessed by the magnitude of the obstacles that had to be overcome. . . . The lesser the natural obstacles ["of sensibility"] and the greater the obstacle from the grounds of duty, so much the more is a transgression to be imputed (as culpable).—Hence the state of mind of the subject, whether he committed the deed in a state of agitation or with cool deliberation, makes a difference in imputation, which has results.[58]

The point here is that, other things equal, when our moral offense is objectively worse, then we are more culpable; and if we could have avoided the offense without much sacrifice or struggle against our passions, then again we are more culpable. In effect, strong temptations to some extent mitigate our culpability for wrongdoing.

But now the question arises: If we are fully capable of doing what is right, why should we be any less to blame because we had strong temptations to do wrong? The temptations, in Kant's view, are not marks of diminished capacity. They do not literally overpower us. We freely choose whether to yield them or not. We do not yield because the forces of reason were defeated in battle by the forces of inclination. We chose to act on the maxim to satisfy inclination when we could have done otherwise. We did wrong through weakness of will in Kant's special sense, but why is that any mitigation of our culpability?

Recall that weakness of will, as interpreted here, has at least two di-

57. See, e.g., *Groundwork,* 225 (4: 424).
58. *Metaphysics of Morals,* 19 (6: 228).

mensions: *First,* our will to do right is somewhat vague and relatively inexplicit regarding its implications. *Second,* we will it weakly: that is, we resolve half-heartedly, waveringly, off and on, without willing specifically, in anticipation, the necessary and available means. Note that although these descriptions raise questions of their own, they are not ascriptions of powerlessness, diminished capacity, or lack of adequate troops for war against inclinations. Kant uses metaphors that can easily suggest these interpretations of weakness, but he cannot intend them literally when taking the practical/moral perspective. Arguably, such metaphors are unnecessary because the two dimensions of weakness of will just mentioned are sufficient to explain why strong passions and temptations tend to mitigate culpability to some degree.

Contrast two people who tell a lie when they should not.[59] For example, they flatly deny having made a serious culpable mistake of which they are aware, and they deny it in a context where others clearly have a right to hear the truth. The first person regularly tells such lies whenever they serve his advantage, however slight. Although he sometimes feels pangs of conscience, he has decided that these are worth the rewards of getting what he wants. He is amiable and well liked and does not do anything overtly monstrous, although he would if certain opportunities arose because his commitment to self-advancement would demand it. He has relatively little to lose by telling the truth on this occasion, and yet he tells the lie readily without any strong passion driving him to do so. The second person generally aims, wants, and does do what is right, but on this occasion his moral reputation, which he has worked hard to earn, is on the line. He feels deeply ashamed and guilty about his past mistake and the harm it caused but when asked point-blank about it, he suddenly feels a huge resistance to confessing it publicly. Besides, his career is at stake, and he wants *very, very much* not to lose his distinguished and important position. He inwardly wavers, feels torn, and tries to make excuses to himself, saying, "I just *cannot* let them know I did *that!*," but he dimly realizes that he could if he tried. He tells the lie, not merely because of the psychological obstacles he faced, but because his commitment (or will) to act rightly was always somewhat vague and he willed it weakly, that is, somewhat waveringly, off and on, without an explicit commitment to take the means necessary to sustain a moral will in the face of obstacles.

Neither person, of course, is a paragon of virtue. Both are culpable

59. Any similarity to former political leaders may not be purely coincidental, even if exaggerated.

for telling the lie. But isn't the second person, for all his faults, less to blame than the first? The second fails because his will to do right was weak; the first fails because he did not actively will to do right at all. Neither was literally overpowered by temptations, but the second person's immediate passion and the threat to his personal interests help to explain his lapse despite his general commitment to morality. It is this commitment, his basic good will, that mitigates his culpability (as compared to the relatively shameless liar).

Conclusion

To summarize, my aim here has been to explore the place of moral weakness in Kant's moral theory. I first surveyed some questions raised by various popular ideas of weakness of will in general, and then briefly sketched the salient views of some of Kant's influential predecessors, especially Thomas Hobbes and David Hume. Then I reviewed the necessary background to Kant's alternative position, his special ideas of the will, negative freedom, and autonomy. These were crucial because Kant conceives of moral weakness by contrast to moral virtue, which he understands as strength of will to fulfill one's duty despite temptations. Kant, however, cannot consistently treat strength and weakness of will simply as a mental analogue of physical strength and weakness. This is because he takes all morally significant acts to be based on freely adopted maxims. These express the agents' rationale in acting—their policies, aims, and intentions—rather than causal forces that determine behavior.

The puzzle, then, was to explain, despite Kant's relatively sparse explicit discussion of moral weakness, how weakness of moral will can be interpreted consistently with the action theory implicit in his special ideas of reason, inclination, and will. One way to view moral weakness, I suggested, might be to see it as a kind of weakness (due to vagueness) in the *content* of one's resolution (or "will") to be moral. The problem here could also be expressed as a relative weakness in the agent's *rational legislative will* (or morally practical reason, *Wille*). Another possibility, I suggested, was to locate the moral weakness in *how* (weakly) one wills even clear and definite moral resolutions. These suggestions invite many further questions, but they are attempts to cash out the metaphors of strength and weakness of will consistently with Kant's ideas that we are responsible for our moral weakness and that significant moral acts are based on freely chosen maxims. The suggestions, even if further developed, would not "explain" how strong and weak wills work, but this fits with Kant's view that "the will" is ultimately beyond explanation, at least explanation of the kinds natural science or critical philosophy can reasonably hope for.

Next, I sketched a response to an old worry that Kant's texts at times imply that no one wills freely to do wrong and so no one is ever responsible for wrongdoing. Then, finally, I tried to illustrate how the conception of moral weakness suggested here might square with Kant's idea that culpability for doing wrong is mitigated, but not fully excused, by the fact that it was done under the influence of strong passions.

11 Nietzsche, the Will to Power, and the Weak Will

TRACY B. STRONG

If there is a thinker in whom the various parts of the expression "weakness of will" seem to resonate, it might be thought to be Nietzsche. "Weak" and "strong" recur constantly; the "will" seems to be one of his touchstones. If, famously, all "life is will to power" then surely power is strength of will and weakness of will is lack of a powerful will. While the word *akrasia* appears but once[1] in all of Nietzsche's writings, there is, as we shall see, discussion of wills that are in themselves weak.

Nietzsche differs from most contemporary discussion of the will in three ways. First, he rejects the notion of *the* will and speaks rather of different wills, including wills that are weak. Second, he holds that "weak" wills always in fact win out in any contest with "strong" wills. Last, he holds rationality to be the faculty that makes possible weak wills rather than that which can prevent it. I establish these claims through an analysis of key passages in the *Genealogy of Morals* and *Zarathustra* (sections 1 and 2). A question thus necessarily arises as to what would make for a will that does not have the possibility of being weak, that is in itself strong? I consider this through an analysis of Nietzsche's discussion of the "right to make promises" (section 3).

1. Constituent Elements of Talk on Weakness of Will

We do however ordinarily—at least in analytic philosophy—speak of "weakness of (the) will." What is involved in such talk? The following

Many thanks to Tobias Hoffmann for his patience and intelligence in editing this paper. I am grateful to David Allison and Babette Babich for careful readings of early drafts.

1. *Nachgelassene Fragmente*, VII–1, 578: "Viel Altruismus habe ich nöthig, um meines ego willen und seine Lust zu haben. akrasia!!" (I need a great deal of altruism for the sake of my ego and to have its joys . . . akrasia!!). Citations from Nietzsche are from the *Kritische Gesamtausgabe Werke* (Berlin: Walter de Gruyter, 1966ff.) as follows: Work, internal division in the text, KGW section and volume number (here VII–1), and page number (here 578).

three considerations shed some light on the constitutive elements of such discussion, each of which will be addressed with regard to Nietzsche's position (Section 2).

The first is loosely consequent to an understanding of human beings that is (sometimes tacitly) Christian. "We leave undone those things which we ought to have done and we do those things which we ought not to have done and there is no health in us." So much from the Book of Common Prayer, though similar statements are to be found in all branches of orthodox Christianity. Here we have a relatively straightforward statement of what becomes Davidson's discussion in his initial essay: The agent (as Davidson calls our sinner) knows what it would be better to do all things considered (including here the fate of his or her immortal soul) and yet does something else.[2] The Book of Common Prayer is in fact a bit more complex than Davidson because Anglican weakness includes *not* doing something as opposed to simply *doing something other* than that which one should have done. I note here that the Greek word that renders what Davidson gives as "continent" (ἐγκρατής) has the meaning of being "in possession of power" and in a political context (e.g., *Politics* 3.13.1284a40) is used to mean "to take a strong hold of."

The Christian analysis show us that we can only be considered incontinent *when in fact we know* that we have done something other than we should have done or that was "better" for us. If in the presence of a bottle of Maker's Mark bourbon I happily pour myself glass after glass until I fall down in a stupor to wake up the next morning with a smile on my aching head and look forward to doing it again, I am not incontinent nor is my will weak—I may indeed have, as Aristotle notes, a vice, but I am *not* weak of will.[3] My point is that weakness of will requires knowing that we should have done something other than we did and that *that* requires memory, that is, the ability to make the past present to ourselves. Thus a *temporal* consciousness is prerequisite for the possibility of weakness of will. For me to be incontinent, my past must be present to me *and* have a claim to authority.[4]

A second issue in the consideration of weakness of will can be thought to have its origins in Plato and classical Greek thought more generally. Indeed, much of the contemporary literature on the topic begins with

2. Donald Davidson, "How Is Weakness of the Will Possible," in *Essays on Actions and Events* (Oxford: Clarendon Press, 1980), 21–42.

3. *Nicomachean Ethics* 7.1.1145b1.

4. Aristotle says that one is incontinent when one has strong desires and regrets: one does what one ought not do, knows that one ought not do it both before and during, and feels bad about it afterward.

an obligatory nod to Socrates, usually the one of the *Protagoras*.[5] Importantly, however, Plato is not working, as later writers most often are, from an opposition between reason and lack of reason.[6] For Plato the self was multiple, composed of three parts that could and should be harmonized, the overall character of which was determined by the dominant part: were one to act thumotically there was precisely not weakness of will but a spirited action. When Lady Macbeth urges her husband to "screw [his] courage to the sticking-place," she is not calling for him to act rationally but rather for him to act *thumotically*.[7]

This understanding, however, also gives us something important. Incontinence cannot properly characterize a self that is multiple in the Platonic sense. Incontinence rather requires that a person act against his or her own (single) will. For there to be incontinence, a person must act without good reason against that which he or she knows to be in his or her best interest. This implies that for there to be incontinence, there must be a certain understanding of what a person is: someone capable of formulating his or her best interests. Aristotle, who wants to defend the notion of *akrasia*, argues in the *Nicomachean Ethics* that *akrasia* requires the ability to form a universal judgment (hence animals cannot be incontinent) *and* that the ability to do this requires a certain kind of character, which, if one does not have it, makes one inaccessible to the claims of reason and hence incapable of weakness of will.[8] A consideration of weakness of will thus requires turning our attention to questions of character and thus of the motility of identity.

Third, let us think of occasions in which no question of weakness of will can be relevant. These occur, among other places, in games. If the batter hits a medium-speed grounder to the second baseman while there is a man on first and only one out, it does not make sense for the second baseman to hold the ball in hand and do nothing with it, nor even to throw it directly to first base. If later he says, "I knew the right play was to second base but I just could not bring myself to do it," this does not count as weakness of will.[9] Rather it is a sign that the man *was*

5. E.g., Alfred Mele, *Irrationality: An Essay on Akrasia, Self-Deception, and Self-Control* (New York and Oxford: Oxford University Press, 1987), starts with this.

6. As George Ainslie asserts in an otherwise interesting book, *Breakdown of Will* (Cambridge and New York: Cambridge University Press, 2001), 4–5.

7. It is for this reason that some authors have questioned whether or not what Plato and even Aristotle understand by *akrasia* is in fact at all what is meant in contemporary discussions of weakness of will.

8. *Nicomachean Ethics* 7.3.1147a24–b5 (esp. b3–5) and 10.9.1179b4–31.

9. I steal the example from Stanley Cavell, *The Claim of Reason: Wittgenstein, Skepticism, Morality, and Tragedy* (New York: Oxford University Press, 1979), 311, where it serves a slightly different function.

not (doing what is called) *playing the infield in baseball.*[10] Knowledge here *is* virtue—*knowing how* to play the game means (entails, requires) throwing to the shortstop covering second.

Games are not a simple tracing of the moral world—even if Rawls sometimes spoke as if they almost were—but the example should tell us something about what kind of thing Socrates had in mind when he said to "know the good is to do it" and found himself resistant to the idea of what we have come to call weakness of will. If knowing the good entails performing it, there can be no weakness of will, merely ignorance or insurmountable hindrance. But if Socrates may be the first word on these matters, he is not, at this point, the only one.

Continuing this thought, I note that in the discussions of weakness of will in contemporary analytic philosophy, by and large *strength* of will is generally not raised as an issue. In most discussions of the matter, the opposite of "weak" is taken to be "rational." (A difference with the Socratic "ignorance-knowledge.") The opposition implicit in many discussions of weakness of will is not the one of ordinary discourse where "weak" is opposed to "strong"—unless, of course, there is a tacit melding of "strong" into "rational." Yet rationality and knowledge are not always what is at stake. One prays not to *yield* to temptation rather than to "be rational." If the problem is Satan or original sin, rationality is not the solution. So there is a final issue raised here: the relation of rational knowledge to volition and agency.

2. The Elements of Will in Nietzsche

We need therefore to keep three issues in mind as relevant to Nietzsche's critique of the idea of *the* will. First, we need to look at the question of weakness of will in temporal terms, that is, as presupposing a certain experience of time as shaping the relation of knowledge to moral agency; second, we need to consider the importance of character in matters pertaining to the will and human agency; last, we need to understand the place of rationality in this relationship.

The Will and Temporality

In the chapter "On Redemption" in *Thus Spoke Zarathustra,* Nietzsche raises the question of the relation of temporality and the will. He is con-

10. He might have been bribed, or drugged, or had a divine revelation, or any of a hundred different possibilities. See the discussion in J. L. Austin, "Pretending," in *Philosophical Papers,* ed. J. O. Urmson and G. J. Warnock, 3rd ed. (Oxford and New York: Ox-

cerned with the way that what we have been in the past shapes what we do in the present to make a future. If the will is the human faculty to construct the future and is both structured and held prisoner by its past, then the possibility of human freedom seems greatly diminished or eradicated. Nietzsche examines a number of proposed understandings of will (he includes—without naming them—Hegel, Kant, Schopenhauer, Wagner, and, I believe, his own work in *The Birth of Tragedy*) and concludes that they are all deficient in that they either simply ignore the weight of the past or too easily assert the possibility of escaping from it.[11]

Why so? The problem, he avers, is that they have all misunderstood will: "My idea," he writes in a later note, "is that the will of earlier psychology is an unjustified generalization, that this will does not exist at all, that instead of grasping the formulation of a single given will in many forms, one has eliminated the character of the will, in that one has subtracted the content, the 'whither' [*Wohin*]."[12] Nietzsche's first point is that an understanding of the will as a single entity or faculty is mistaken.[13]

I shall come back to this passage in *Zarathustra* in more detail toward the end of this paper, but for now only note that for Nietzsche none of these previous writers provide access to a realm that would escape or transfigure a human past. I argued above that for weakness of will to be possible, one must have a sense of what one should have done, that is, have a sense that another possible behavior had been possible in the past. Without a sense that one could have done something else, thus most generally a sense of time past, weakness of will is not possible. At the end of the chapter, he drops a hint that the "will that is the will to power" might possibly be able to will "backwards" and thus break the hold of time, that is, make the question of weakness of will irrelevant. How would it be possible for the will to "will backwards," that is, change the past that is the locus of the sense that one could have (in the past) done something else than what one did? What then is Nietzsche's understanding of will, which can only be correctly understood as "will to power"?

The will to power cannot be grasped as something that can be satis-

---

ford University Press, 1979), 253–71. Beyond this it is important to realize that "playing a competitive game" requires knowledge of both the constitutive and the prudential rules.

11. See the complete discussion in my *Friedrich Nietzsche and the Politics of Transfiguration*, 3rd ed. (Champaign: University of Illinois Press, 2000), chap. 8.

12. *Nachgelassene Fragmente*, VIII-3, 92.

13. This is not yet what Nietzsche means when he says there is "no will," on which see below. See also Chapter 8 in my *Friedrich Nietzsche and the Politics of Transfiguration* and Wolfgang Müller-Lauter, *Nietzsche: His Philosophy of Contradictions and the Contradictions of His Philosophy* (Urbana and Chicago: University of Illinois Press, 1999).

fied: it requires a *"Wohin"* and whatever we call will is to be understood in terms of its *Wohin* (whither). Will is thus a *bringing about* rather than something that is bought about. The will, he says, "wants to go forward and always again become master of that which stands in its way." The will to power is constant motion and finds expression as the overcoming of borders and obstacles. It does not in itself seek a *particular* state of affairs—in the English version of Freud's terminology it has "motility of cathexis"[14]—just that there *be* a state of affairs. Importantly it does not seek pleasure, nor seek to avoid pain: it is simply the "attempt to overcome, to bring to oneself, to incorporate."[15] In fact, from the standpoint of the will to power "there are no things at all, but only dynamic quanta. . . ." Nietzsche continues, "[T]he will to power, not being, not becoming, but a *pathos* is the most elementary fact from which a becoming, a working first arises."[16]

An important clue is offered by this designation of the will to power as a *pathos.* In the *Gay Science,* Nietzsche had made a distinction between *pathos* and *ethos* and suggested that as long as humans continue to think of a particular form of life they tend to think of it as an *ethos,* that is as "the only possible and reasonable thing." A true understanding, however, is that life is "pathos," as it is "not one's lot to have certain particular sensations for years. . . ."[17] *Pathos* means "that which happens to a person or a thing," "what one has experienced, good or bad"; it refers sometimes to the "incidents of things."[18] In no case does it imply a notion of growth or development, but only the different states a person or a thing may assume.[19] Will to power thus "cannot have become."[20] It is the

14. "Cathexis" is the scientized translation of Freud's *Besetzung,* which means occupying, taking a place, or being cast as a character.

15. *Nachgelassene Fragmente,* VIII-3, 152.

16. *Nachgelassene Fragmente,* VIII-3, 51.

17. *The Gay Science* 317, V-2, 229. The French edition, *Le gai savoir,* trans. Pierre Klossowski, Collection Folio essais 17 (Paris: Gallimard, 1990), 371–72, includes a passage not in the KGW to the effect that Nietzsche had occasionally thought his own life to be an *ethos* whereas it in fact was not.

18. E.g., *Phaedo,* 96a: "Now I will tell you my own experience in the matter, if you wish [ἐγὼ οὖν σοι δίειμι περὶ αὐτῶν, ἐὰν βούλῃ, τά γε ἐμὰ πάθη]." It also refers to emotion and, in rhetoric, to the appeal to emotion.

19. I am helped by the Greek-English lexicon of Liddell and Scott. It is thus not at all what is meant by *physis* and, while I cannot deal with the matter here, insofar as Heidegger wants to tie the idea of will to power to *physis* he seems to me to be mistaken. *Physis* has a number of meanings but it is centrally the natural constitution of a thing as the result of growth. Nietzsche tends to use it to refer to an achieved culture. See, e.g., *Nachgelassene Fragmente,* III-4, 347; *On the Use and Misuse of History for Life* 10, III-1, 320; and *Schopenhauer as Educator* 3, III-1, 346. *Physis* has, in other words, a teleological dimension that pathos does not have.

20. *Nachgelassene Fragmente,* VIII-2, 259.

movement itself and thus neither has being nor becoming. The most basic quality of all organisms is their attempt to incorporate that which they encounter into themselves, and thus define all that they meet. All the forms that any organism acquires it assumes, and taken as a whole they constitute its will to power. The various *Wohins* are the instances of the will to power of a particular organism. These *Wohins* can assume different qualities: among the categories Nietzsche identifies are optimism or pessimism, activity or passivity, of what he calls in *Zarathustra* being "over-rich" as opposed to lacking excess—much of his later years are spent sorting out these differences. It is thus quite sensible from this understanding to proclaim, as he does in one of his most famous remarks, that life is "will to power." The full remark is this:

> What are our valuations and tables of the good worth? What comes from their control? For whom? In relation to what?—Answer: for life. But what is life? Here is needed a new more definite formulation of the concept "life." My formula for that goes: *Leben* ["Life" or "to live"] is will to power. . . . What does evaluation mean? . . . Answer: moral evaluation is an exegesis, a *way of interpreting*.[21]

The will to power is a "way of interpreting." Indeed, elsewhere, Nietzsche is explicit: "The will to power interprets: it is a question of interpreting during the building of an organ; it sets limits, defines degrees, differences of power. . . . In truth, interpretation is a means to become master of something. The organic process presupposes continuing interpretation."[22] To interpret is to place oneself as the lens through which the observed is seen. The important thing, then, about the will to power is that it refers to the quality that living beings have to make or understand the world in their own image. Etymologically, *Macht* (as in *Wille zur Macht*) is archaically related to the same root from which we get our word *might*, which in turn has a meaning of the ability to make or do something.[23] The will to power is thus the quality that all life has *of giving form*, that is, of giving rise to the *pathoi* that are (a) life.—But *what* form?—The form that is given must be the form of the giver. Thus "cognition" itself is said to be will to power.[24] In the *Genealogy* the will to power is a "form giving . . . force";[25] elsewhere the will to power is held to interpret the "new in the forms of the old."[26]

21. *Nachgelassene Fragmente*, VIII-1, 159 (my italics).
22. *Nachgelassene Fragmente*, VIII-1, 137.
23. A *Macher* is a maker, an active leader, in both Middle High German and Yiddish.
24. *Nachgelassene Fragmente*, VII-3, 204.
25. *On the Genealogy of Morals* 2.18, VI-2, 341.
26. Nietzsche, *Die Unschuld des Werdens: Der Nachlaß*, Ausgewählt und geordnet von Alfred Bäumler, 2nd ed. (Stuttgart: Kröner, 1978), 2: 78 (not in the KGW).

This, however, means that the particular past of a willing agent so shapes that will that it simply repeats a particular pattern; changing that pattern will require changing the past of a will or determining a way not to be caught by that past. This is why the question of temporality is central to Nietzsche's discussion of the will.[27]

Character and Will

A point that emerges from the above consideration is that everyone, perhaps even every*thing*—all life—has or rather *is* will to power. We see immediately a problem relevant to the question of weakness of will: if whatever will one exercises is one's *own* or rather is what one means by one's self, what sense would it make to say that a will is at a particular moment weak? So a question raised by this investigation of "the" will must be: "What kind of beings are we?" And here it is noteworthy that Nietzsche associates weakness of will with our present moral world in general. Thus: "Today the tastes and virtues of the time diminish and debilitate the will. Nothing is so thoroughly timely as will-weakness [*Nichts ist so sehr zeitgemäss als Willensschwäche*]. . . ."[28] This is immediately referred to as quality of character: "Turned around: the need for belief, for some unconditional yes and no, is a need for weakness, all weakness is of the will [*alle Schwäche ist Willensschwäche*]: all weakness of will stems from the fact that no passion, no categorical imperative, commands." Nietzsche coins a term for such a condition: *Entselbstung*—"de-selfing," we might translate it.[29] The preliminary sense is that a weak will is associated with a need to be weak, that is, not wanting to be a self, thus unable to own, to be one's own self, to have a right to what is one's own. Such a weak will is not weak at a particular moment: weakness is its nature. Note here that Nietzsche invokes the lack of a "categorical imperative" as a quality of *Willensschwäche*—I shall consider his relation to Kant toward the end of this paper.

Given what I have said, there must be wills to power of different qualities of character (these are its *Wohins*), a will to power, for instance, that is masterly or nobly moral as well as another will to power that is slavely moral. At this point one might suppose that slaves are simply weak and

27. I leave unexamined here the complex relation of Nietzsche to the Kantian architectonic. On Nietzsche as a radical Kantian see, inter alia, the fruitful discussion in B. Babich, *Nietzsche's Philosophy of Science* (New York: SUNY Press, 1994), 78–134.

28. *Beyond Good and Evil* 212, VI-2, 149.

29. This sense is completely lost when Walter Kaufmann and R. J. Hollingdale translate it as "self-mortification," see Kaufmann's edition of *Genealogy of Morals* and *Ecce homo* (New York: Vintage Books, 1967), 118. *On the Genealogy of Morals,* 3.11, VI-2, 379.

the noble are strong. Nietzsche's position, however, is much more complex. Let us look at these two wills to power.[30]

Nietzsche's main exploration of different kinds of will to power is in the *Genealogy of Morals*. In a number of passages, Nietzsche delineates and distinguishes the quality of the will in nobles and in slaves. The nobles, he says, "do not know guilt, responsibility, or consideration." They are "born organizers."[31] In *Beyond Good and Evil*, he writes that "when the ruling group determines what is 'good,' the exalted proud states of the soul are experienced as conferring distinction and order of rank. . . . The noble type of man experiences itself as determining values; . . . it knows itself to be value creating."[32] The "noble type of man" experiences what he does as virtuous: thus insofar as one acts "nobly" one cannot have the sense that one's will is weak.

The noble moral type says—to paraphrase Alfonso Lingis's paraphrase of Bataille—"My God, am I good! How beautiful, strong, and powerful I am! You offer no possible contest for me and would be a waste of my time. You are no match for me and are bad." "Good" here means something like "worthy of being dealt with." Think of the exchange between Glaukos and Diomedes in Book 6 of the *Iliad* when the two warriors, having met on the field of battle must first determine whether or not the other is a worthy opponent (one is much younger), that is, "good" in noble moral terms, for without this there would be no reason to fight someone who is not as you are (i.e., is "bad"). They thus run through their respective genealogies to establish their worth to the other. (As it turns out, their grandparents were guest-friends and the bond is such that they do not fight but exchange battle gear.)[33] More contemporar-

30. The terms "master" and "slave" are often given negative resonance by those who read Nietzsche—memories of Nazi and racial contexts lead easily to the conclusion that Nietzsche is, as one always half suspected, whether or not a bad thinker, certainly a bad man. Yet the idea of master and slave has an obvious apparent ancestry in Rousseau ("He who believes himself to be the master of others is all the more a slave than they") and in Hegel *(Herrschaft* and *Knechtschaft).* At the time that Nietzsche was writing, Marx was developing an entire theory of history based on the interaction of the oppressor and the oppressed. Nietzsche had read the left-Hegelians and explicitly found resonances between his work and Bruno Bauer's; he may have read of Marx in other texts. See Thomas H. Brobjer, "Nietzsche's Knowledge of Marx and Marxism," *Nietzsche-Studien* 31 (2002): 298–313, and especially Howard Caygill, "The Return of Nietzsche and Marx," in *Habermas, Nietzsche, and Critical Theory*, ed. Babette E. Babich (New York: Humanity Books, 2004), 195–209. I leave aside here the differences and similarities between the Rousseau/Hegel/Marx dialectical view of the relation of master and slave and Nietzsche's genealogical one to look at what Nietzsche has to say about the master-slave relation.

31. *On the Genealogy of Morals*, 2.17–18, VI-2, 340–41.

32. *Beyond Good and Evil*, 260, VI-2, 218.

33. I should note that Glaukos apparently gets cheated ("Zeus had stolen [his] wits away")—Homer presents the whole scene in such a manner that one must read it as a doubly ironic commentary on the war itself.

ily, any of us who were chosen last to a team because of our lack of skill, or put out to play right field, have some idea of what it means to live in a masterly moral world (and remember the sense of self derived from the time where we were chosen first, or, better yet, got to do the choosing). Thus also does the concept, still surviving, of a "worthy opponent" remind us of master morality. I do not here wish to develop further the credibility of master morality as a moral form:[34] precisely its strangeness (and the fact that I move most easily to sports examples), is testimony to the fact that we now think of morality generally only in its "good and evil" form.

Yet what happens? Here it is important to understand that "good/evil slave morality" is quite different from "good/bad noble morality," not simply the latter stood on its head. The slave says in effect "My goodness, do I suffer! You make me suffer, you are evil and I am the opposite of you and therefore am good. Why do you make me suffer?" The definition of self of the slavely moral is thus the conclusion of a dialectical argument. Several things are worth noting: First, this situation is not all that different from what Hegel described in the *Phenomenology* where the self is attained by a progressive differentiation first from nature and then from others. Second, this form of attaining identity—this form of moral agency—*requires* oppression. That is, unless I suffer, I will have nothing to negate. Hence it is important for the continuity of my self that I maintain a source of suffering and nothing that I do should or may put an end to the possibility of suffering. Over time, Nietzsche argues, humans incorporate the source of suffering into themselves; they become their own oppressor (this is how he interprets the idea of original sin): he will trace this dynamic through various stages in the second and third books of the *Genealogy*.

Slave morality is thus *not* just the noble morality stood on its head—a reversal of the structures of domination. It is structured in a different manner and thus is a different way of being in the world. Nietzsche works this out in a parable of the eagle and the lamb.

It is in fact not surprising that the lamb dislikes the eagle. After all, for no apparent reason every so often a bird of prey swoops down and carries off one of the flock. Since it is not clear that this is in response to something one has done wrong, it is also quite possible that one day this might happen to anyone. The lamb clearly would like to put an end

34. It has been done, if not in Nietzsche's terms, by Alasdair MacIntyre in his consideration of Homer in *After Virtue,* 2nd ed. (Notre Dame: University of Notre Dame Press, 1984).

to this situation. The eagle is evil; the lamb is the opposite of the eagle, thus it must be "good."[35] But the bird keeps swooping down.

What the lamb must want is for the eagle not to behave as an eagle, to be ashamed of its desires, of itself; the lamb wants the eagle to acquire another, new, character such that it would choose not to carry off the lambs. On the face of it this is silly. As Nietzsche continues, "to demand of strength that it *not* express itself as strength, that it *not* be a will to overpower, to cast down, to become master, a thirst after enemies, oppositions and triumphs, is just as absurd as to require weakness to express itself as strength."[36] *The lamb wants, however, precisely this "absurdity," that is, weakness of will on the part of the eagle.* He wants the eagle's will to be weak, that is, he wants the eagle not to act in accord with what he, the eagle, considering all things, knows to be his nature. For Nietzsche, in other words, weakness of will is not as traditionally understood the failure to act according to reason even when the desires are adverse, but rather for Nietzsche it means that one fails to act in accord with one's own nature.

As Nietzsche's little parable starts, the eagle has no other will than the will of an eagle. So what we learn here from Nietzsche is that weakness of will requires the *acquisition* of *specific* qualities of character, ones that are not, as it were, natural to a particular being. What does the lamb require of the eagle? He requires, first, that the eagle need a *reason* for doing what it does; second, he requires that the eagle have a *choice* in doing what he does (this follows from and requires the first); this requires, next, that there be an *independent common framework* in terms of which both the eagle and the lamb can make judgments; and this requires finally that the eagle be *reflective*.[37] The lamb wants the eagle to be rational.

Rationality and Will

These considerations lead us to the third element. They correspond to the acquisition by the eagle of reflective rationality ("Why am I doing

35. Note that in the passages explicating these terms Nietzsche puts "good," "evil," and "bad" in scare quotes.

36. *On the Genealogy of Morals*, 1.13, VI-2, 292.

37. Note that we have returned to Aristotle on *akrasia*. This is the related to the interesting argument made by Richard Holton in his "Intention and Weakness of Will" (*Journal of Philosophy* 96 [1999]: 241–62), in which he concludes that weakness of will "consists in over readily revising an intention when it is in the agent's power to desist from that revision." Holton does not, however, consider in what that power might consist. Holton notes also that one could be akratic but not weak of will, in that one might have an intention to do other than what one might think best and (if one acted on it) not be weak of will (the president, enraged at the enemy, is determined to launch a missile strike); see 255–56.

this?"), that is, to the acquisition of those qualities for which Nietzsche attacked Socrates. In Nietzsche's reading, Socrates sought to get people to give reasons for their beliefs. The Greek found that *"das Unbewußte"* (not so much the "unconscious" but how one assesses the world) could not account for itself. So Socrates, in the *agora* as in the theater, Nietzsche avers, wanted reasons for why individuals or characters act or think as they do, and this made it impossible for him to accept tragedy as tragedy. "Whereas," Nietzsche writes in the *Birth,* "in all productive men the instinct is precisely the creative-affirmative power and consciousness [*Bewusstsein*] operates in a critical and dissuasive way, in Socrates the instinct becomes a critic and consciousness the creator. . . . Here the logical nature is, by a hypertrophy, developed . . . excessively."[38] As Nietzsche remarked in an early public lecture, a remark that shocked his audience: *"Wenn Tugend Wissen ist, so muß der tugendhafte Held Dialektiker sein"* (If virtue is knowledge, then the virtuous hero must be a dialectician).[39]

If we take these thoughts back to the problem of weakness of will, it appears that weakness of will is something that *one needs to learn* in order to have it. The eagle will continue to want to carry off the lamb, but having been subject to dialectical frustration, he will change his mind and not do what he desires but rather what is "good"—in the "good/evil" sense of good. Most considerations of weakness of will hold that one's will is weak when one does not do what one thinks in one's best interest, all things considered.[40] Here, however, the transformed eagle becomes weak precisely in taking account of all things. In this case, though, he has had to learn to take these things into account. The noble qua noble cannot have a weak will because for him *character is in fact destiny*—I go back to my earlier examples of situations where there is no weakness of will.

It is thus the case that the lamb requires that the eagle exhibit at

Contrariwise, argues Holton, if the president then takes his finger off the button he will be weak of will but not acting contrary to what he thinks best (weakness of will but not *akrasia*).

38. *The Birth of Tragedy,* 13, III-1, 86.

39. *Sokrates und die Tragödie,* III-2, 23.

40. One might argue that it is not a matter of best interest but rather one of what is right. Thus strength of will would have to do with the strength to do what is right. The Nazi guard claims that he was simply carrying out his duty, claiming strength of will. Hannah Arendt's rebuke, which for many readers is insufficient, consists in pointing out how little strength of any kind is involved in the ordinariness of doing what is expected of one and which everyone else does as well. Our own general rebuke of Heidegger is that he should have had the strength of will (and the moral vision that is equivalent to our own vision, so a kind of moral pretzel-scope, hindsight in advance) to have done the right thing anyway, even if, no matter if, it is *not* in his own best interest. Davidson avoids these problems by setting the question in terms of interest, not in terms of what is right. Thanks to Babette Babich for a discussion on these matters.

least what Gary Watson identifies as "a normal amount of self-control,"[41] self-control defined in terms *external* to what the eagle is as eagle. In Nietzsche's reversal, weakness of will consists in controlling oneself in terms of an external and given framework; strength of will is thus to do *what is one's own,* no matter what the expectations. Hannah Arendt's rebuke of Eichmann rested on her claim that doing what was expected of him, his duty as he best understood it, was precisely what Eichmann should not have done. Evil is banal. The good is singular.

The matter does not stop here. The weakness of will of the slave is in fact the source of its victory over the noble or the strong. For what happens is that the *Unbewußtheit* of the noble is unable to resist the dialectics of the slave: *The victor is always the weak.*[42] Nietzsche is quite clear on this: the ability to induce the knowledge that one could have done otherwise in effect is the ability to place a person under the demands of a choice not made in time past. For Nietzsche, the weak person—that is, the person who from his or her own viewpoint "could have" acted otherwise—is actually the victor because of the fact that he can blame someone else. Eventually, for Nietzsche, the genius of Christianity will be to find in oneself the source of oppression: hence the problem of maintaining the constant source of oppression necessary to slave morality is permanently and irretrievably solved in this world. The only way out will be a redemption from oneself. The point of Nietzsche's analysis here is the recognition that the victory is always to the weak—that the quality of character that allows one to be weak of will is the source of strength. And the source of the triumph of slave morality over the noble morality will always derive from the fact that the slave is *rational.* Nietzsche thus has stood the standard analysis of weakness of will on its head or back on its feet: rationality, which was to counter weakness of will, is for him the central and defining quality of those who *have* weak wills, and this, seemingly paradoxically, is the source of their domination over those whose will is strong.[43]

41. Gary Watson, "Skepticism about Weakness of Will," *Philosophical Review* 86 (1977): 316–39. The question here is as to the status of "normal."

42. Thus Marx foresaw the victory of the proletariat. Neither Nietzsche nor Marx were Social Darwinians.

43. This recasts Davidson's distinction between "conditional prima facie evaluative judgments" and "evaluative judgments sans phrase" (Davidson, 40). Davidson retains the notion of irrationality as central to weakness of will. The *akrates* acts without reason by not letting his "sans phrase" judgment prevail. He or she is "surd"—without voice or reason as to why. Note that "surd" has the same meaning as Nietzsche's "absurd." Davidson had some anxieties later about this claim of surdian irrationality or more accurately about the whole question of rationality in these matters. In a subsequent article he argues that the explanation of irrationality also requires something like Freud's conception of the mind,

The slavely moral type responds to the presence of a generalizable, hence reasoned, external or internalized threat of oppression. The slavely moral type can thus not stand for him- or herself because that self depends on a dialectical relationship to someone or something other, to a fixed and general framework. This is the reason that Nietzsche refers to this condition as one of *Entselbstung,* as if slavely persons had nothing that was theirs, as if they did not have a self of their own. Such beings do not in fact have, one might say, the right to their actions, those actions are not really their own.[44]

It is in this sense that the will of the slavely moral is powerful and triumphs over the master precisely because it is weak. By "powerful" Nietzsche means something like "having on one's terms, be those terms authentic or not." By "weak" he means here "not authentically one's own." This, however, does not get us very far. What does it mean for an act not to be authentically one's own (a central question one might put to Davidson)? Where Davidson and others see the *akrates* as acting "surd"[45]—without voice or reason—Nietzsche sees him as not having a being that is his own. Nietzsche's analysis thus calls into question the notion that rationality can provide a counter to weakness of the will—in fact, for Nietzsche, rationality makes weakness of will possible.[46]

But then how can one not yield to the seductions of a weak will? Why on Nietzsche's analysis, would one, for instance, keep a promise? It is this problem that is often at the basis of accusations that Nietzsche's thought is amoral or irrationalist.

---

viz., that the mind is multiple, that something like agency occurs in different "parts" of the mind and that what happens in one part of the mind can lead to changes in another part of the mind. (Freud remarks, for instance, that we are responsible for the content of our dreams; see his "Moral Responsibility for the Content of Dreams," in *The Standard Edition of the Complete Psychological Works of Sigmund Freud,* ed. and trans. J. Strachey [London: Hogarth, 1961], 19: 131–34.) An actor would then act against the principle that he ought to act on the principle he holds best. Thus, Davidson needs to claim, a mental act may *cause* a mental act without being a *reason* for it. See Davidson, "Paradoxes of Irrationality," in *Philosophical Essays on Freud,* ed. Richard Wollheim and James Hopkins (Cambridge: Cambridge University Press, 1982), 289–305. I was reminded of this article by Robert Dunn, *The Possibility of Weakness of Will* (Indianapolis: Hackett, 1987). Dunn's final position (that there is no logical problem about weakness of the will "because it is perfectly possible for us to be un-integrated in a certain way, namely not to have any volitions to act that correspond to our felicitous all out present tense summary evaluations about our own actions" [125]) seems a relative of Davidson's later essay. The accumulation of five predicates testifies to me the difficulty in maintaining the idea of *the* will.

44. We have an entry here into what Kant was after when he began his essay "What Is Enlightenment?" by asserting the importance of attaining one's *own way.*

45. Davidson, "How Is Weakness of the Will Possible?" 40.

46. See the emphasis on habit over rationality as a path to continence in Victor L. Worsfold, "Akrasia: Irremediable but Not Unapproachable," in *Philosophy of Education 1996,* found online at www.ed.uiuc.edu/EPS/PES-Yearbook/96_docs/worsfold.html.

3. The Right to Keep Promises and the Will

I want to turn to an analysis of Nietzsche on promising, for on the face of it according to Nietzsche there should be no reason to keep a promise. After all when one keeps a promise one allows oneself to be bound by an act in one's past—something that Nietzsche seems to seek to escape from. Nietzsche argues that one has to *become* a person who has the right to keep promises, that keeping a promise is not something that one does out of acquiescence to a universal standard (e.g., rationality). If the eagle had to change his character to acquiesce to the lambs, so also must human beings acquire a new character in order to be the kind of person who keeps promises.

We might profitably think here of the question of the weakness of will as a question of the relation of an agent to a performative. If I promise to meet you at the train station but do not appear because I have succumbed to a desire for a pastrami sandwich at the Silver Diner, I have not only broken my promise but in an important sense I have shown myself as a person in some sense incapable of actually making (what is properly called) a promise. (It does no good to say that I might "keep my promise" on some future occasion: promisers are made of sterner stuff; I am not a person who has the right to promise if I find that sometimes I can keep it and sometimes not.) The performative—that is my promise—required something of me that I did not perform, hence I was not what I am.[47] This is the basis for Nietzsche's view that not anyone can actually promise, that is, incarnate his or her own words as recurring presence, no matter what; not all can mean what they say. A person who does not hold to his promise is, in this understanding, not responsible to himself and is *"entselbstet."* Performatives thus have a particular relation to temporality in that they transfigure a quality of a past into a new present. If under certain conditions I say "I do" I am in no way any longer an unmarried person. Tellingly, when Austin discusses the "infelicities" or "unhappinesses" of performatives—when they do not work, as it were—he brings the matter down to "non-responsibilities."[48] By this he appears to mean failing to have the quality of being able actually to mean what you say, to speak in such a manner that your words are transparently your own. The question of character thus is centrally relevant.

Having this quality—being able actually to mean what one says—is the role that Nietzsche thinks is reserved for the philosopher-legislator,

47. It is always possible that I would not be what I am—that I might be pretending—to be, in Austin's example, a hyena; see Austin, "Pretending," 256. But I might also lose track, perhaps permanently, of what I am. Cf. Arendt on Eichmann, above, 242n40 and 243.

48. J. L. Austin, "Performative Utterances," in *Philosophical Papers*, 232–52, at 238–40.

that is, he or she who can authentically use the words "Thus shall it be," where "authentically" means that they become actual, and thus the individual is transformed or, as Nietzsche sometimes says, "transfigured." (Saying "Thus it shall be" is itself a performative.) This is not as esoteric as one might think. It is simply the question of refoundation, of reconstituting oneself as a person, a body, a people, perhaps even of what Stanley Cavell has called the "education of grownups"—I would argue that it is a fundamental modern political question.[49]

How might it work in Nietzsche's understanding? What is movement toward being able to bind oneself in fact to one's word(s), be spoken for by one's language (to move toward Heidegger)? For one's words to be one's own one must be able actually to mean what one says. The question of making one's words one's own is the question that Nietzsche pursues in the second essay in the *Genealogy of Morals,* most especially in the first several sections on the "right to make promises" and the "sovereign individual."

The question there is why and how an individual should ever want to acquire the "right to make promises." After all, why should one want to bind oneself to a future that one might well regret?[50] How can one? As Nietzsche poses it, the question of weakness of will can be brought back to the question of why and how it is that one should ever *be able* to so bind oneself, or to find oneself bound.

The movement of the text in the first three sections of the second essay in *On the Genealogy of Morals* is a first key.[51] In each of them, Nietzsche describes the possibility of a particular kind of being-in-the-world (the right to make promises, the sovereign individual, the acquisition of conscience) and then circles back to give an account for the genealogy of that quality. Thus the right to make promises requires first the development of calculability, regularity, and necessity.[52] The sovereign individual requires the development of a memory. This is the acquisition of a temporal dimension to the self. Each of these qualities is what Nietzsche

49. Cavell, *The Claim of Reason,* 125. See the discussion in Sandra Laugier, *Recommencer la philosophie: La philosophie américaine aujourd'hui* (Paris: Presses universitaires de France, 1999).

50. Nietzsche's questions thus transcends the standard answers that have been given to this question (sentiment, objective good, utility, contractarianism, and rational agreement).

51. It is worth noting that most readings of the second essay of the *Genealogy* pass over the first two sections and go immediately to section 3 on conscience. See, e.g., Werner Stegmaier, *Nietzsches Genealogie der Moral* (Darmstadt: Wissenschaftliche Buchgesellschaft, 1994), 131ff. He gets to the question of the sovereign individual on p. 136, without however the sense of the genealogical development that Nietzsche sees.

52. *On the Genealogy of Morals,* 2.1, VI-2, 305.

calls a "late" or "ripest" fruit, the coming into being of which, therefore, has required ripening.

Nietzsche is quite clear that the earlier developments are the *means to making possible* a "sovereign individual" (for instance). Nietzsche refers to this as a "preparatory task" and includes in it what he calls human "prehistory." What is key here is the understanding of history: the past has made possible the present, but has not necessarily monotonically determined it. The resources for a variety of different presents are all in the past, if we can deconstruct the past we have received and reassemble it.

What quality does the sovereign individual—whom I take here to be an individual who has earned the right and capacity to say what he or she is—have? Nietzsche details a number of qualities in *On the Genealogy of Morals*, 2.2, all of which sound like or are intended to sound like the *megalopsuchos* of Aristotle.[53] Yet there is a difference between Nietzsche's sovereign individual and the great soul in Aristotle, for the sovereign individual is the result of an achievement, a process by which a consciousness has become instinct.[54] What is important though for us here is the insistence that Nietzsche places on the "*right* to make promises."[55]

We are returned with that consideration to the question of performatives—of which promising is the standard example. Yet what Nietzsche has done is to make the matter much deeper. Standard accounts of weakness of will hold that a person who does not keep a promise is incontinent *(ceteris paribus)*. They assume that there is no question of one's *right* to make a promise. When Nietzsche asks as to the *right* to make a promise, it is as if the expectation is that I will not to enact my words, that is, I will act weakly, because I am not sovereign over myself.

What, then, would or could keep me from not keeping my promises (from being weak of will) if, as we have established, rationality is for Nietzsche of no actual avail? Nietzsche's point is not so much to oppose rationality as to point out that *rationality is not why we keep promises*. While

53. See *Nicomachean Ethics*, 4.3.

54. Cf. this passage from *On the Use and Misuse of History for Life*, 3, III-1, 267: "The best we can do is to confront our inherited and hereditary nature with our knowledge of it, and through a new, stern discipline combat our inborn heritage and implant in ourselves a new habit, a new instinct, a second nature, so that our first nature withers away. It is an attempt to give oneself, as it were a posteriori, a past in which one would like to originate in opposition to that in which one did originate—always a dangerous attempt because it is so hard to know the limit to denial of the past and because second natures are usually weaker than first."

55. One of the very few commentators to focus on this is Randall Havas, *Nietzsche's Genealogy: Nihilism and the Will to Knowledge* (Ithaca: Cornell University Press, 1995), 193ff., who does so with an eye to the move from "animality" to "humanity," which I think misleading. He is on sounder ground on p. 196, where he relates the idea of "right" to that of the responsibility for intelligibility.

it may be rational to keep promises, it is not in the nature of promises to be kept *because* one has a reason to do so—I do not need a reason to keep my promise. (If you ask "Why should I keep my promise?" you will find that, sooner or later, reasons come to an end. If you ask that, you do not know what a promise is.)[56] Nietzsche says that promising requires that I have "mastery over circumstances, over nature, and over all more short-willed and unreliable creatures."[57] Those who have the right to promise are like "sovereigns" because they can maintain their promise in the face of accidents, even in the "face of fate." To have the right to a promise is to have taken upon oneself, as oneself, all the circumstances present and future in which the promise may occur. It is to maintain that promise—the requirement that the present extend into the future—no matter what befalls. Thus when Kaufmann and Hollingdale translate the key passage—*"für sich als Zukunft gut sagen zu können"* as "able to stand security for his *own* future,"[58] one may pass by Nietzsche's point, which is that one should be "able to vouch for oneself *as a* future." One must earn entitlement to one's "own."

What this means is that a person who has the right to make promises does not regard his or her action as a choice between alternatives but as a manifestation of what he or she is, as something he or she *must* do, where there is no gap possible between intention and action.[59] A promise is a declaration of what I am, of that for which I hold myself responsible: as it is not a choice, there is no possibility of what gets called weakness of will. As Cavell says: "You choose your life. This is the way an action Categorically Imperative feels. And though there is not The Categorical Imperative, there are actions that are for us categorically imperative so far as we have a will."[60]

This is what it means for Nietzsche to "have" a categorical imperative, as in the passage to which I drew attention above. In this, and despite obvious echoes, Nietzsche's categorical imperative is not identical to Kant's. In the *Grundlegung zur Metaphysik der Sitten* and elsewhere Kant argues that one cannot break a promise because to do so would in effect deny the point of the entire institution of promising. Kant took this position with its very strong denial of the relevance of intention, because, as he argued, any breaking of a promise or uttering of a lie for contin-

56. See the discussion in Hanna F. Pitkin, "Obligation and Consent, II," *American Political Science Review* 30 (1966): 39–52.

57. *On the Genealogy of Morals,* 2.2, VI-2, 309.

58. In their edition (see above, note 29) of the *Genealogy,* p. 58.

59. Were there to be—say I was acting out of fear—then I would be acting fearfully and not precisely promising.

60. See the discussion in Cavell, 309.

gent reasons (say, as with Sartre, you were being asked by the Gestapo the location of the partisan they were seeking) would mean that you claimed to know precisely what the consequences of your action would be. Since such a claim was epistemologically impossible, it followed that one must be bound by the only certainty one might have, that of one's non-temporally-limited reason.[61]

Kant's reason for keeping a promise or not telling a lie was consequent to the interplay of a fixed and actually rational self and an incompletely graspable world. The difference in Nietzsche's analysis of the right to keep promises comes in his insistence that not only is the external world not knowable, but neither is the self. The self is not given for Nietzsche: it is rather the effect of actions undertaken and thus is motile. The self endures, for him, only as what it has the power to be responsible to. Hence the binding of the self to a promise can only be rightfully accomplished by a power "over oneself and over fate" and must penetrate below the level of assessment—where it remained with Kant—to become part of the assessor of him- or herself, of what Nietzsche calls *"das Unbewusste."* This means that promising must be part of what I am, for me to have the right to it. In this sense, it is part of one's present and not one's past.[62] Nietzsche's categorical imperative builds "sovereign individuals"; Kant's "autonomous individual" is a cousin but is built *in terms of* the Categorical Imperative.

Nietzsche is also clear—now contra Kant, and post-Kantians from Rawls to Habermas—that the self that is so committed is committed also to all the pain and all the reversals that will and may occur—pains that can be seen in his exploration of what he calls "mnemotechnics." In this, the sovereign individual in Nietzsche will find an instantiation in Weber's person who has the vocation for politics and who can remain true to his vocation, "in spite of all."[63] (I might note here that the insistence on the necessity of the pain and cruelty of existence was already central to the argument in the *Birth of Tragedy*.) Pain and cruelty are en-

61. Immanuel Kant, *Grundlegung zur Metaphysik der Sitten,* in *Kant's gesammelte Schriften,* herausgegeben von der Königlich Preußischen Akademie der Wissenschaften (Berlin, 1902ff.), 8: 402–3; "Über ein vermeintliches Recht aus Menschenliebe zu lügen," 8: 427.

62. See the discussion in my "Texts and Pretexts: Reflections on Perspectivism," Chapter 10 in the second and third editions of my *Friedrich Nietzsche and the Politics of Transfiguration.*

63. Cf. Max Weber, *The Protestant Ethic and the Spirit of Capitalism,* trans. Talcott Parsons (Los Angeles: Roxbury, 1998), 115: "They [i.e., good works] are the technical means, not of purchasing salvation, but of getting rid of the fear of damnation. . . . Thus the Calvinist . . . himself creates his own salvation, or, as would be more correct, the conviction of it. But this creation cannot . . . consist in a gradual accumulation of individual good works to one's credit, but rather in a systematic self-control which at every moment stands before the inexorable alternative, chosen or damned."

demic to the possibility of life—they are part of what make the sovereign individual possible.

Conclusion

In a note from 1885 Nietzsche writes: "Basic idea: new values must first be created—we must not be spared that! The philosopher must be a lawgiver to us. New types. (As earlier the highest types [e.g., Greeks] were bred: this type of 'accident' to be willed consciously.)"[64] So the question that Nietzsche raises for us in relation to weakness of the will is that of the qualities that it is necessary to have in order to have weakness of will and of the politics by which those qualities are acquired. If rationality produces or is a quality of the weakness of will it cannot be the solution. But if rationality cannot be the basis of keeping one's promise (which is what Nietzsche tells us), what can possibly be the case that ensures that someone will keep his or her promise? What does it mean to be a person with the "right to make a promise"? If rationality is not the answer to the question—hence his praise of the body against Plato—what is the quality of a person who becomes what he or she is? If the problem with weak wills is *Entselbstung*, what is the basis of *Verselbstung?*

The answer is that nothing can "ensure" that I keep my promise except that *I* must. If I look for something outside me to ensure that I keep my promises I have not right to promise. Unless I make promising mine, I cannot promise. This is *Verselbstung:* to become actually the person you have come to know you are: it is as such that the claim of time past and thus the possibility of weakness of will is abolished. From his youth on, one of Nietzsche's touchstone passages was from Pindar's Second *Pythian Ode:* "Γένοι' οἷος ἐσσὶ μαθών," rendered by Barbara Fowler as "Be what you know you are,"[65] and by Alexander Nehamas as "Having learned, become who you are."[66] As the voice of his "Gewissen," his knowing conscience, Nietzsche tells us: *"Du sollst der werden, der du bist."*[67] "You should become the one you are."[68] We learn from Nietzsche that

64. *Nachgelassene Fragmente,* VII-3, 255.

65. *Archaic Greek Poetry: An Anthology,* selected and trans. Barbara Fowler (Madison: University of Wisconsin Press, 1992), 279.

66. Alexander Nehamas, *The Art of Living: Socratic Reflections from Plato to Foucault* (Berkeley and Los Angeles: University of California Press, 1998), 128. I am indebted for this and the previous citation to Babette Babich, "Nietzsche's Imperative as a Friend's Encomium: On Becoming the One You Are, Ethics, and Blessing," *Nietzsche-Studien* 32 (2003): 29–58, at 30–31.

67. *The Gay Science,* 270, V-2, 197.

68. There is a considerable literature about what in Nietzsche's renderings happens to the μαθών. Babich's paper (note 66) deals with this very effectively. One can point out

to be weak of will is not only not to become what one is, but also not to be able ever to know what that is, for there is for no one a preexisting self that can become one's own.[69] Weakness of will, for Nietzsche, is not having a self that has become one's own. Weakness of will cannot, for Nietzsche, be prevented by rationality. If one has a question for one's will, it will be weak, the victory of the "ought" over the "must."

also that by placing the imperative as that which the conscience says, Nietzsche has incorporated it.

69. *Nachgelassene Fragmente,* VIII-3, 71.

12 A Libertarian View of Akratic Action

ALFRED R. MELE

According to a common conception, paradigmatic akratic actions are free, intentional actions that are contrary to a conscious belief that the agent has at the time, to the effect that it would be best to *A* (or best not to *A*)—best from the perspective of his own values, desires, beliefs, and the like, as opposed, for example, to a common evaluative perspective that he does not endorse. I dub such a belief a *CB;* that saves a lot of ink. My label in *Irrationality* for paradigmatic akratic action, on this conception, is *strict akratic action.*[1] Typically, the *CB* is rationally acquired.[2]

One important question about strict akratic actions is whether they are conceptually possible. Another is how particular strict akratic actions are to be explained, if actions of this kind are not only possible but actual. A common assumption in the literature on akratic action is that free actions are possible. What some skeptics about akratic action claim is that no action contrary to the agent's *CB* can be free.[3] Theorists who are confident that they understand what free action is may try to ascertain whether any intentional actions contrary to the agent's *CB* meet their standards for free action. Theorists who lack confidence on the point at issue but wish to tackle the conceptual and explanatory questions about strict akratic action would do well to seek answers that are neutral regarding what they take to be the various live options about

I am grateful to Josh Gert and an audience at the Catholic University of America for comments on a draft of this paper. This paper derives partly from Alfred Mele, *Free Will and Luck* (New York: Oxford University Press, 2006), chaps. 3 and 5.

1. Alfred Mele, *Irrationality: An Essay on Akrasia, Self-Deception, and Self-Control* (New York and Oxford: Oxford University Press, 1987), 7.

2. On exceptions, see Alfred Mele, "Motivated Irrationality," in *The Oxford Handbook of Rationality,* ed. Alfred Mele and Piers Rawling (New York: Oxford University Press, 2004), 240–56, at 246.

3. See, e.g., R. M. Hare, *Freedom and Reason* (Oxford: Clarendon Press, 1963), chap. 5; Plato, *Protagoras,* in *The Dialogues of Plato,* trans. Benjamin Jowett (Oxford: Clarendon Press, 1953); David Pugmire, "Motivated Irrationality," *Proceedings of the Aristotelian Society* 56 (1982): 179–96; and Gary Watson, "Skepticism about Weakness of Will," *Philosophical Review* 86 (1977): 316–39.

free action. For example, although any incompatibilist about determinism and free action will reject compatibilist accounts of akratic action, an incompatibilist who is undecided whether free action requires agent causation or instead only ordinary event (and state) causation should pursue the questions about akratic action in a way that leaves both options open.

In *Irrationality*, I argue that akratic action is conceptually possible and I develop a view about how token strict akratic actions are to be explained. There, I assume that compatibilism is true—that is, that determinism is compatible with free action. In this paper, for the sake of argument, I assume that compatibilism is false. Some incompatibilists contend that no one acts freely,[4] but most incompatibilists hold that at least some of us sometimes act freely. The latter philosophers—libertarians—divide into three broad kinds: there are noncausal, agent-causal, and event-causal libertarians.[5] In *Motivation and Agency*, I argue that any view of actions according to which actions may be uncaused is deeply problematic.[6] So I set noncausal views of free action aside here. Agent-causal libertarians assert that agents themselves—as opposed, for example, to agents' motivational and representational states—are causes of free actions. Contemporary agent-causal libertarians motivate their view partly by arguing that event-causal libertarianism is subject to a devastating problem about control or luck that agent causation solves.[7] Elsewhere, I argue that agent-causal libertarianism fares no better in this connection.[8] So, partly in light of independent worries about agent causation, I set agent-causal libertarianism aside here too. That leaves event-causal libertarianism. The purpose of this paper is to explore what event-causal libertarians should say about strict akratic actions. Since

4. See Richard Double, *The Non-Reality of Free Will* (New York: Oxford University Press, 1991); Derk Pereboom, *Living without Free Will* (Cambridge: Cambridge University Press, 2001); and Galen Strawson, *Freedom and Belief* (Oxford: Clarendon Press, 1986).

5. For important noncausal libertarian views, see Carl Ginet, *On Action* (Cambridge: Cambridge University Press, 1990), and Hugh McCann, *The Works of Agency* (Ithaca, N.Y.: Cornell University Press, 1998), chap. 9. Timothy O'Connor, in *Persons and Causes* (New York: Oxford University Press, 2000), and Randolph Clarke, in *Libertarian Accounts of Free Will* (Oxford: Oxford University Press, 2003), present the most fully developed agent-causal libertarian views, and Robert Kane, in *The Significance of Free Will* (New York: Oxford University Press, 1996), does the same for event-causal libertarianism.

6. Alfred Mele, *Motivation and Agency* (New York: Oxford University Press, 2003), chap. 2.

7. See Clarke and O'Connor. Whereas most agent-causal libertarians prefer their agent causation straight—see, e.g., Roderick Chisholm, "The Agent as Cause," in *Action Theory*, ed. Myles Brand and Douglas Walton (Dordrecht: Reidel, 1976), 199–211; O'Connor; and Richard Taylor, *Action and Purpose* (Englewood Cliffs: Prentice-Hall, 1966)—Clarke mixes it with event causation in a theory of the production of free actions.

8. Alfred Mele, "Libertarianism, Luck, and Control," *Pacific Philosophical Quarterly* 86 (2005): 381–407.

free decisions have a central place in this literature, I focus on strict akratic decisions.

Strict akratic action is defined, again, as free, intentional action that is contrary to the agent's *CB*. In *Motivation and Agency*, I argue that decisions to do things—practical decisions—are themselves actions: specifically, momentary mental actions of intention formation.[9] An agent who refrains from *A*-ing and freely and intentionally *B*-s even though his *CB* favors *A*-ing acts akratically. So, in normal cases, does an agent who freely *decides* to *B* rather than to *A* despite having a *CB* that favors *A*-ing. That is, the decision itself is an akratic action. That very decision, in normal cases, is contrary to the agent's *CB* in a straightforward sense. For a decision to *B* to be a strict akratic action, the agent need not consciously believe that a better option than *deciding* to *B* is open to him; the *CB* that an alternative to *B*-ing is a better course of action will do, other things being equal.[10]

1. Fluky Action and the Problem of Present Luck

Akratic action is typically contrasted with, among other things, *compelled* intentional action contrary to the agent's *CB*.[11] For example, if a certain compulsive hand-washer's washing his hands now is contrary to his *CB* but he is compelled to wash them by an irresistible desire to do so, his hand washing is not a strict akratic action because it is not a free action. Typical event-causal libertarian views open the door to the possibility that another kind of intentional action contrary to the agent's *CB* also is not strict akratic action. I call it *fluky* action. Introducing it will take some time.

According to libertarians and other incompatibilists, an agent who did not *A* at *t* was able at *t* to *A* at *t* only if in another possible world with the same laws of nature and the same past up to *t*, he *A*-s at *t*. On this view, if agents in deterministic worlds are able to do anything at all, they

9. Mele, *Motivation and Agency*, chap. 9.

10. In special cases, alternative decisions, as opposed to alternative courses of nondecisional action that the agent can decide between or among, are rendered salient for the agent. If an agent believes that a mind reader will reward him with a good book for deciding at *t* to raise only his left hand at *t* + *n* (whether or not he actually raises it) and will reward him with a good bottle of whiskey for deciding at *t* to raise only his right hand at *t* + *n*, he may reflect on which decision it would be better to make. If he consciously believes that the former decision would be a better one to make than the latter, but freely makes the latter, he decides akratically. (Presumably, the focus of the practical reflection would be whether it would be better to bring it about that he has a good book or a good bottle of whiskey.)

11. See Alfred Mele, "Akratics and Addicts," *American Philosophical Quarterly* 39 (2002): 153–67.

are able to do only what they actually do. For in any world with the same past and laws as *S*'s deterministic world, *Wd*, *S* behaves exactly as he does in *Wd*. Typical libertarians contend that freedom requires an ability to do things that one does not actually do. Libertarians have, in this connection, the option of endorsing either stronger, nonhistorical requirements on free action or weaker, historical requirements.[12] For example, they can claim that an agent freely *A*-ed at *t* only if, at *t*, he was able to do otherwise than *A* then, or they can claim instead that an agent who was not able to do otherwise at *t* than *A* then may nevertheless freely *A* at *t*, provided that he earlier performed some relevant free action or actions at a time or times at which he was able to do otherwise than perform those actions. I call any free *A*-ings that occur at times at which the past (up to those times) and the laws of nature are consistent with the agent's not *A*-ing then *basically free actions*. In principle, libertarians can hold that an agent's basically free actions that are suitably related to his subsequent *A*-ing confer freedom on his *A*-ing even though he was not able to do otherwise than *A* then. It is open to libertarians to accept or reject the thesis that the only free actions are what I am calling basically free actions. Exactly parallel options are open on moral responsibility, and to save space I simply report that the kind of free action at issue in this article (whether or not "free" is qualified by "basically") is the kind most closely associated with moral responsibility.[13]

Libertarians have options regarding which abilities they require for basically free *A*-ing. One view is that an agent performs a basically free *A*-ing at *t* only if he was able at *t* to perform an alternative *free* action then. Attention to it leads quickly to the issue of fluky action.

Consider the following case. In world *W*, Ann sincerely promises to flip, in one minute, at high noon, the coin she is holding. In so promising, she expresses an intention to flip it at noon. No unexpected substantial obstacles arise, and no excuses for not flipping the coin come to mind. Ann also has no intention not to flip the coin at noon, no intention to wait until later to flip it, no intention to hurl it into the bushes then, and so on. Moreover, Ann is convinced, rightly, not only that she has a good reason to do what she promised but also that she has no significant reason for not tossing the coin or for deciding to do anything other than toss it. The only thing that in any sense speaks in favor of her not flipping the coin is a very weak desire to discover what it would

12. Alfred Mele, *Autonomous Agents* (New York: Oxford University Press, 1995), 207–9.

13. Incidentally, it is possible to take a historical line on moral responsibility while embracing the nonhistorical requirement I mentioned on free action. See, for an instance of this, Robert Kane, "Two Kinds of Incompatibilism," *Philosophy and Phenomenological Research* 50 (1989): 219–54.

feel like to break a promise for no good reason. Ann occasionally has what she regards as silly desires and she sees this as one of them. The intention expressed in Ann's promise persists until she tosses the coin, at noon, as does her *CB* in favor of tossing it then.

Suppose that Ann's tossing the coin was a basically free action.[14] Then, according to the libertarian position on ability under consideration now, Ann was able to perform an alternative free action at noon. Perhaps in some possible world that does not diverge from *W* before noon Ann decides at noon—just as she is beginning to flip the coin—to continue holding it and does not flip it. Is there enough time for this? Yes, if Ann's beginning to toss the coin precedes the coin's leaving her hand by enough milliseconds to permit the possibility of her holding on to it. If, for example, overt actions begin in the brain just after proximal intentions are acquired, there is enough time for this.[15]

As shorthand for the expression "Ann performed a noontime coin flip," I use the expression "Ann *C*-ed." It is useful to have a label for possible worlds with the following features: they do not diverge from *W* before noon, and in them Ann does not *C* and decides on some alternative course of action at noon. I call them *N-worlds.* Pick an *N*-world *Na* in which Ann decides at noon to hold the coin for another minute and continues holding it. Her making that decision at noon rather than *C*-ing, as she does in *W*—that difference—seemingly is not explained by anything. *Na*'s divergence from *W* begins with Ann's deciding at noon to hold the coin. So there is no difference between *W* and *Na* to account for the difference at issue. If nothing accounts for the difference, the difference is just a matter of luck. Also, insofar as it is better, other things being equal, to keep one's promises than to break them, Ann can be said to have *better* luck in *W* than in *Na.* Now, if the difference is just a matter of luck, Ann arguably is not morally responsible for deciding at noon to hold on to the coin. After all, given exactly the same laws of nature and antecedent conditions, in a world in which she has better luck at noon, she instead *C*-s, as promised. Knowing this, one may be disinclined to blame Ann for breaking her promise. This disinclination is evidence of an inclination to

14. According to a restrictivist position on free action, Ann is in no position to act freely, given how little there is to be said for doing otherwise than tossing the coin at noon. See Peter van Inwagen, "When Is the Will Free?" *Philosophical Perspectives* 3 (1989), and "When the Will Is Not Free," *Philosophical Studies* 75 (1994). For an excellent critique of restrictivism, see O'Connor, 101–7.

15. See Frederick Adams and Alfred Mele, "The Intention/Volition Debate," *Canadian Journal of Philosophy* 22 (1992): 323–38, and Myles Brand, *Intending and Acting* (Cambridge, Mass.: MIT Press, 1984), 20. Proximal intentions include intentions to *A* straightaway, intentions to start *A*-ing (e.g., start running a mile) straightaway, and intentions to continue doing something that one is doing.

believe that Ann is not morally responsible for deciding to hold on to the coin. That Ann is not morally responsible for this in turn suggests that, in *Na,* she did not freely decide at noon to hold on to the coin and did not freely break her promise. The issue that I have just raised is an aspect of what I call *the problem of present luck.* I return to it in Section 2.

The inclination to let Ann off the hook for breaking her promise gains considerable support from the fact that the only thing that in any sense speaks in favor of her not tossing the coin at noon and her deciding not to toss it then is a very weak desire to discover what it would feel like to break a promise for no good reason—a desire she regards as silly. In *Na,* at noon, under the conditions identified, Ann abandons the intention expressed in her promise and decides not to toss the coin. Her decision is not only irrational, it is downright strange.

Ordinary akratic decisions are typically deemed irrational. In virtue of their clashing with the agent's rational *CB,* such decisions are subjectively irrational (to some degree, if not without qualification). There is a failure of coherence in the agent of a kind directly relevant to assessments of the agent's rationality. Now, in ordinary cases of akratic decision, the decision is motivated by substantial desires. People tend not to find it especially surprising that someone with a strong desire for a cigarette or a shot of whiskey would decide accordingly despite believing that it would be better to abstain. But they would find it very surprising that an agent who takes promise making seriously, as Ann does, decides to break a promise when the only thing that speaks in favor of breaking it and of deciding to break it is a weak desire that the agent regards as silly. Ann's decision in the present scenario is plausibly viewed as a manifestation of a breakdown of agency that goes beyond the irrationality of ordinary akratic decisions. Evidently, Ann's particular constitution as an indeterministic agent is such that she is subject to breakdowns of this kind, and she suffers such a breakdown in *Na.* If Ann is not responsible for this defect in her constitution as an agent, she seems not to be responsible for this manifestation of it. To make the case for pity stronger, it may be supposed that Ann is aware of her defect and does everything in her power to minimize the chance of its being manifested on this occasion.

In short, although Ann's decision at noon in *Na* is contrary to her *CB,* it seems too fluky to count as an akratic decision. Ann's problem seems to be, not weakness of will, but bad luck. How should an event-causal libertarian go about attempting to justify the claim that akratic decisions are distinguishable from fluky decisions contrary to the agent's *CB?* Should such a libertarian try to show that, actually, there is no cross-world luck at all at the time of action in cases of strict akratic decisions and that the difference between akratic decisions and fluky decisions contrary to the agent's *CB* lies in that fact? Is an alternative tack more promising?

2. Luck-Embracing Libertarianism and the Problem of Present Luck

I am about to invent an event-causal libertarian view that embraces cross-world luck at the time of action as essential to basically free action and attempts to stare down the problem of present luck. I call it *luck-embracing libertarianism,* or *LEL* for short. Some of its central elements are sketched in this section. In Section 3, I develop the view further in connection with fluky action.

A very brief review of a portion of the recent history of the problem of present luck will prove useful. Bruce Waller raises an interesting worry about luck in criticizing the view of free will once advocated by Robert Kane.[16] Kane summarizes Waller's objection as follows:

> "Suppose two persons had exactly the same pasts and made exactly the same efforts of will," says Waller, but one does the moral or prudential thing while the other does not. Given that their pasts were exactly the same up to the moment of choice, as indeterminism requires, wouldn't that mean that the outcome was a matter of luck? One of them got lucky and succeeded in overcoming temptation, the other failed. Would there then "be any grounds for distinguishing between [them], for saying that one deserves censure for a selfish decision and the other deserves praise for generosity? If they are really identical, and the difference in their acts results from chance, then it seems irrational to consider one more praiseworthy (or more blameworthy) than the other should be."[17]

Kane replies that efforts to resist temptation in free agents are *indeterminate,* and because that is so we cannot

> imagine the same agent in two possible worlds with exactly the same pasts making exactly the same effort and getting lucky in one world and not the other. Exact sameness or difference of possible worlds is not defined if the possible world contains indeterminate efforts or indeterminate events of any kinds.[18]

Elsewhere, I argue that this appeal to indeterminacy does not help, even if it is granted that exact sameness and difference are not defined:

16. See Bruce Waller, "Free Will Gone Out of Control," *Behaviorism* 16 (1988): 149–67, at 151; and Robert Kane, *Free Will and Values* (Albany: SUNY Press, 1985).

17. Kane, *The Significance of Free Will,* 171.

18. Ibid., 172.

Kane's appeal to the indeterminacy of an effort makes it more difficult to formulate crisply the "objection from luck" to libertarianism. But the spirit of the objection survives. If John's effort to resist temptation fails where $John_2$'s effort succeeds, and there is nothing about the agents' powers, capacities, states of mind, moral character, and the like that explains this difference in outcome, then the difference really is just a matter of luck. That their efforts are indeterminate explains why the outcomes of the efforts might not be the same, but this obviously does not explain (even nondeterministically or probabilistically) why John failed whereas $John_2$ succeeded.[19]

Kane responds by modifying his view to include the agent's making an effort to choose the tempting course of action.[20] According to his modified view, in basic instances of free decision, agents simultaneously try to make each of two competing decisions, and throughout the process it is causally open which attempt will succeed. In his view, an agent who is tempted to act contrary to his *CB* may try to decide in accordance with his *CB* while also trying to decide to take the tempting course of action. Whether he decides akratically or not is a matter of which effort succeeds. (Readers who have trouble with the idea that agents *try to decide* to *A* may suppose that the agent is trying to bring it about that he decides to *A*.)[21] Kane's earlier claim about exact sameness and difference no longer plays a role.

I illustrate this feature of Kane's position with a story. Bob lives in a town in which people bet not only on football games but also on such things as whether the opening coin toss will occur on time. After Bob agrees at 11:55 A.M. to toss a coin at noon to start a football game, Carl, a notorious gambler, offers him $50 to wait until 12:02 to toss it. Bob is tempted by the $50, but he also has moral qualms about helping Carl cheat bettors. He judges it best on the whole to do what he agreed to do, and, as Kane would have it, he tries to decide to toss the coin at noon while also trying to decide to wait until 12:02 to toss it. The latter effort is successful: at noon, Bob decides to toss the coin at 12:02 and to pretend to be searching for it in his pockets in the meantime. In a possible

19. Alfred Mele, "Ultimate Responsibility and Dumb Luck," *Social Philosophy and Policy* 16 (1999): 274–93, at 280. Also see Alfred Mele, "Kane, Luck, and the Significance of Free Will," *Philosophical Explorations* 2 (1999): 96–104; and Ishtiyaque Haji, "Indeterminism and Frankfurt-Type Examples," *Philosophical Explorations* 2 (1999): 42–58.

20. Kane, "Responsibility, Luck and Chance: Reflections on Free Will and Indeterminism," *Journal of Philosophy* 96 (1999): 217–40.

21. A smoker who thinks that he would have a reasonable chance of kicking the habit if only he were to decide to kick it may also believe that making that decision would be very difficult for him. He might consult a therapist for advice about what he might do to bring it about that he decides to kick the habit.

world that does not diverge from the actual world before noon, Bob decides at noon to toss the coin straightaway and acts accordingly.

The problem of present luck stares us in the face. The cross-world difference between Bob's deciding at noon to toss the coin in two minutes and his deciding at noon to toss it straightaway is just a matter of luck. According to the alternative event-causal libertarian view that I will develop, *LEL*, the psychology that Kane postulates is a much greater problem than present luck. Proponents of *LEL*—"*LELs*" for short—doubt that agents ever try to decide to *A* while also trying to decide to do something else instead. They want a more credible view of what happens in agents in the sphere of akratic and continent action.

A sketch of some background for a psychologically more credible view is in order now. In *Springs of Action,* I argue that a common route from the acquisition of a *CB* in favor of *A*-ing to an intention to *A* is a default route.[22] The basic idea is that "normal human agents are so constituted that, in the absence of preemption," acquiring a *CB* in favor of *A*-ing "issues directly in the acquisition of an intention to *A*."[23] In simple cases involving little or no motivational opposition, the transition from *CB* to intention is smooth and easy. In such cases, having acquired a *CB* in favor of *A*-ing, agents have no need to think further about whether to *A;* nor, given the agents' motivational condition, is there a need to exercise self-control in order to bring it about that they intend to *A*. No special intervening effort of any sort is required. The existence of a default procedure of the sort at issue in normal human agents would help to explain the smoothness and ease of the transition. Indeed, we should expect an efficient action-directed system in beings who are capable both of acquiring deliberative *CB*s and of performing akratic actions to encompass such a procedure. Special energy should be exerted in this connection only when one's *CB* encounters significant opposition. When one akratically fails to intend in accordance with one's *CB,* opposition is encountered: something blocks a default transition; something preempts the default value of the *CB.*

In *Springs of Action* I also distinguish among three kinds of case in which an agent's *CB* is opposed by competing motivation: (1) a default process unproblematically generates a continent intention even in the face of the opposition; (2) a continent intention is formed even though the default route to intention is blocked by the opposition; (3) the motivational opposition blocks the default route to intention and figures in the production of an akratic intention.[24] What I needed was a principled

22. Alfred Mele, *Springs of Action* (New York: Oxford University Press, 1992), chap. 12.
23. Ibid., 231.
24. Ibid., 233–34.

way of carving up the territory. I suggested that a continent intention is produced (in the normal way) by default, as opposed to being produced via a distinct causal route, when and only when (barring causal overdetermination, the assistance of other agents, science fiction, and the like) no intervening exercise of *self-control* contributes to the production of the intention.[25] (Sometimes opposing motivation is sufficiently weak that no attempt at self-control is called for.) If the move from *CB* to intention does not involve a special intervening effort on the agent's part, the intention's presence typically may safely be attributed to the operation of a default procedure.

Self-control also figures importantly in explaining why, when a default route from *CB* to intention *is* blocked, we sometimes do, and sometimes do not, intend on the basis of our *CB*s. Barring the operation of higher order default processes, overdetermination, interference by intention-producing demons, and so on, whether an agent intends in accordance with his *CB* in such cases depends on his own efforts at self-control. In simple cases of self-indulgence, he makes no effort at all to perform the action favored by his *CB* or to form the appropriate intention. In other cases, an agent whose *CB* favors *A*-ing might attempt in any number of ways to get himself to *A* or to get himself to intend to *A*. He might try focusing his attention on the desirable results of his *A*-ing or on the unattractive aspects of his not *A*-ing. He might generate vivid images of both or utter self-commands. If all else fails, he might seek help from a behavioral therapist. Whether his strategies work depends on the details of the case.[26]

Consider the following case.[27] Because she has had one shot of whiskey already—and very recently—at a party and needs to drive home soon, Drew believes that it is best to switch now to coffee. She believes both that she can switch from whiskey to coffee now and that she can have another whiskey instead; in Drew's opinion, it is up to her which of these she does. She knows that it is risky to drive under the influence of two shots and she believes that, in light of the risk, her reason for having a second shot—that she would enjoy it—does not justify having one. Although Drew believes that she should switch to coffee, she thinks "I've had a bit too much to drink before, and all has gone well. It really would be best to switch to coffee, but I'll indulge myself. Just one more

25. Ibid., 233.

26. Parts of this paragraph and the preceding two are borrowed from *Springs of Action*, 231–34. For a discussion of the practical potential of strategies such as these in effective self-control, and of pertinent empirical literature on the topic, see *Irrationality*, 23–24 and chaps. 4–6. For more on intentions by default, see *Springs of Action*, chap. 12.

27. From my "Akratics and Addicts," 156.

shot, then a cup of coffee, then I'll drive home." Still believing that it would be best to switch to coffee now, Drew decides to drink another shot and drinks one. She does not feel compelled to drink. She feels that she is deciding freely and that she is freely drinking the whiskey. Drew makes no attempt to exercise self-control in support of her acting as she believes best, even though she has a modest desire to make such an attempt.

If strict akratic action is possible, this would seem to be a case of it. Imagine that the story just told is instantiated in a possible world with the same natural laws as the actual world and the same past up to the moment at which Drew decides to drink another shot. In the actual world, at that very moment, Drew decides to switch to coffee (and she switches). In another possible world with the same past and laws she remains undecided about what to do a little longer. Suppose that Drew's brain works indeterministically in a way that helps to account for the possibility of these worlds. Is that consistent with Drew's having freely decided to switch to coffee and with her being morally responsible for that decision? *LELs* answer *Yes*. How well can they support that answer?

As *LELs* see it, the occurrence of basically free akratic and continent actions entails cross-world luck at the time of action and such luck does not preclude freedom or moral responsibility. In their view, various relevant probabilities are grounded primarily in various features of Drew's psychological condition at the time, *t*, at which she acquires her *CB* in favor of switching to coffee. Relevant probabilities include the probabilities that Drew will straightaway decide to drink another whiskey, straightaway decide to switch to coffee, straightaway decide to exercise self-control in support of switching to coffee, and remain undecided for a time about what to do. The features of Drew's psychology that partly ground or account for these probabilities include the strengths of various desires she has at *t*: for example, her desire to drink another whiskey, her desire to avoid increasing her chance of being in an accident as she drives home and her chance of being pulled over by the police and arrested for driving under the influence, her desire to avoid breaking the law, and her desire to exercise self-control in support of her acting as she believes she should. Other pertinent psychological features include, but are not limited to, Drew's degree of confidence at *t* that switching to coffee would be best and the strength of any generic desire she may have at *t* to do whatever she thinks is best. *LELs* point out that these features do not come out of the blue and that they are products in part of Drew's past behavior. For example, it is very plausible that the strength of Drew's desire at *t* to avoid increasing the chance of an accident is influenced by her beliefs about previous occasions on which she drove under the influence, beliefs that she would lack if she had not engaged in this risky behavior in the past.

In remarking on Drew's past behavior, *LELs* are not overlooking the point that if luck is in play in agents' present basically free actions, this also is true of their past actions of these kinds. *LELs* maintain that agents play an indeterministic role in shaping the probabilities that they will act continently and that they will act akratically insofar as they play an indeterministic role in shaping things that ground these probabilities. Many agents have a capacity for present influence on relevant future probabilities of action, and it is often true that their past behavior has influenced present probabilities of action. Regarding influence of the former kind, notice that someone who has just acquired a *CB* in favor of *A*-ing may have, in addition to a probability that he will straightaway decide to *A* or nonactionally acquire an intention to *A* and a probability that he will straightaway decide to pursue a tempting course of action instead, a high probability of remaining undecided for a while. While he is undecided, there may be a chance that he will try to bring it about that he intends to do what he believes he should. If he tries in a promising way to do this, he thereby increases the probability that he will *A*. Other things being equal, an agent who makes such an effort at self-control has a better chance of continently *A*-ing than he would have if he were to make no such effort. To be sure, if the attempt is a basically free action, then there was a chance that the agent would not make it at that time. These observations do not undermine the claim about present influence.

Past influence on present probabilities of action is considerable. For example, the strengths of Drew's desire for another whiskey and her desire not to increase the risk of an accident are likely to have been influenced by past decisions she made in similar situations, by her reflection on the consequences of those decisions, and by decisions about future behavior made partly on the basis of such reflection. Of course, if these decisions are basically free actions, there was a chance, when Drew made them, that she would not make them. But these facts do not undermine the claim that they influence the strengths of present relevant desires.

Part of what *LELs* are driving at in their claims about influence is that probabilities of actions—practical probabilities—are not, in general, imposed on the agents. Through their past behavior agents shape present practical probabilities, and in their present behavior they shape future practical probabilities. The relationship between agents and the probabilities of their actions is very different from the relationship between dice and the probabilities of outcomes of tosses. In the case of dice, of course, the probabilities of future tosses are independent of the outcomes of past tosses. However, the probabilities of agents' future actions are influenced by their present and past actions.

LELs like to emphasize the opportunity that agents have to learn from their bad luck—especially from basically free decisions contrary to their rational *CB*s. An agent who executes such a decision—say, a decision to drive under the influence—with bad consequences may learn from reflection on the consequences. (Of course, a drunk driver who kills himself in a car crash has no opportunity to learn from his mistake.) Another agent who drives under the influence against his *CB* but gets home safely and without being arrested may learn from reflection on what might have happened if he had been less fortunate. And both agents can think, effectively, about how to decrease the probability that they will drive under the influence again.[28]

LELs maintain that in the vast majority of cases of basically free actions, agents have some responsibility for the relevant probabilities. They have, for example, some responsibility for the chance that they will act akratically and for the chance that they will act continently. These chances are not dictated by external forces, and they are influenced by basically free and morally responsible actions the agents performed in the past. *LELs* take these claims to soften worries about present luck, but they realize that they have more work to do.

As I have mentioned, it is open to libertarians to hold that an agent's basically free actions that are suitably related to later actions of his that are not basically free confer freedom on those later actions. *LELs* take this position. They see an agent's being able to perform some actions whose proximal causes do not deterministically cause the actions as a necessary condition for his having a kind of initiatory power that they value. For them, the importance of this initiatory power is not limited to cases in which it is exercised; it is also important insofar as the basically free actions that depend on its exercise confer freedom on some subsequent actions. This point merits emphasis because *LELs*—who are not only theorists but also are agents—would like to make themselves such that their considered judgments about what it is best to do are consistently part of a mix that *deterministically* causes corresponding intentions that, in turn, are part of a mix that deterministically causes corresponding attempts.[29] They hold that they would make such deter-

28. Agents in deterministic worlds also can learn from events associated with their bad luck, but, of course, they cannot perform basically free actions.

29. Some *LELs* hold that it is the neural realizers of these judgments and intentions that do the causal work rather than the judgments or intentions themselves, but I ignore this complication here. Henceforth, unless I indicate otherwise, readers should understand assertions of mental causation disjunctively, as assertions that either the mental item at issue or its neural realizer does the causal work.

ministically caused attempts freely, the freedom being of the conferred variety. And they believe the same of actions that are successful attempts of this kind.

Given that *LELs* would like to make themselves into agents of the kind just described, why do they value the ability to perform basically free actions? Because they value a measure of independence from the past, a kind of independent agency that includes the power to make a special kind of explanatory contribution to some of their actions and to their world—contributions that are not themselves ultimately causally determined products of the state of the universe in the distant past. Basically free actions are not such products. Nor are the deterministically caused actions that *LELs* would like to enable themselves to perform: these actions, if suitably influenced by past basically free actions, are not ultimately causally determined products of the state of the universe in the distant past.

In short, *LELs* value the power to perform basically free actions, but they also value working to make it the case that they are not subject to luck in an important practical sphere, even though success in this effort would cut them off from *further* basically free actions in this sphere. This is not paradoxical, as is most easily seen from a common perspective on moral credit. Aristotle's virtuous agent has made himself such that akratic action is not psychologically possible for him, and this agent is regarded as deserving moral credit for his virtuous actions.[30] Some ordinary libertarians find it very intuitive that such an agent deserves moral credit for the actions that flow from his virtuous constitution only if he deserves some moral credit for that constitution and that he deserves credit in the latter connection only if some basically free actions of his played a significant role in his making himself as he is.

LELs appeal to the game blackjack as a very rough analogy of part of what they have in mind. Players compete only with the dealer, whose every move is dictated by the rules. Unlike the dealer, the players have options: for example, they can hit (request another card), stand (refuse additional cards), double their bets in certain situations, and split pairs into two hands. Blackjack involves a mixture of luck and skill. What cards one gets is a matter of luck, and skilled players have memorized and are guided by reliable tables about when they should hit, stand, and so on. Very skilled players keep track of the cards they have seen—they "count cards"—and they adjust their playing strategy accordingly.

Just as luck—though not necessarily indeterministic luck—is an es-

30. See Aristotle, *Nicomachean Ethics* 7.9.1151b34–7.10.1152a8 in light of *Nicomachean Ethics* 2.1.

sential part of (legal) blackjack, being subject to present luck, according to *LELs,* is an essential part of being an agent who is capable of performing basically free actions. But whereas luck is an ineliminable part of (legal) blackjack, *LELs* seek, as agents, to eliminate luck in an important sphere. Now, the blackjack player who wants to maximize his chances of winning (legally, of course) should learn how to minimize the potential consequences of bad luck and to maximize the potential consequences of good luck. So he should learn to count cards, and he should memorize a good set of blackjack tables and play accordingly. What should *LELs* do about luck, given their aspirations as agents? One thing they should do, apparently, is to try to become so self-controlled that there is no longer a chance that they will act akratically.

How should *LELs* respond to the claim that the influence of agents' actions on their present probabilities of action is of no use to *LELs* because an agent's being subject to cross-world luck at the time of action precludes his acting freely at that time no matter how the pertinent probabilities came to be as they are? Return to the case of Ann and the coin. Ann is rightly convinced both that she has a good reason to toss the coin at noon as she promised and that she has no significant reason not to do what she promised. The only thing that speaks in favor of deciding not to toss it then is a very weak desire to discover what it would feel like to break a promise for no good reason, and Ann regards that desire as silly. In the actual world, *W,* Ann tosses the coin at noon. In a possible world *Na* with the same past and laws as *W,* she decides at noon to hold on to the coin. In that world, as I have explained, Ann seems to suffer a breakdown of agency that is beyond the sphere of akratic action. The objection to *LEL* under consideration entails not only that Ann's decision in *Na* is unfree but also that Ann does not freely toss the coin in *W. LELs* accept the claim about *Na:* they do not see actions that are manifestations of radical breakdowns of agency as free. But they are well within their rights to ask why they should agree that Ann does not freely toss the coin in *W.*

Their opponents might claim that an agent performs a basically free action only if he could have performed an alternative basically free action at the time. However, if some Frankfurt-style cases are successful, they undermine this requirement, and the requirement is rejected on independent grounds even by some traditional libertarians.[31] An argument would certainly need to be advanced for it.

31. See Clarke, 125–26. The thesis that there are Frankfurt-style cases that undermine not only this alleged requirement but also some less demanding alleged libertarian requirements on basically free action is defended in Alfred Mele and David Robb, "Rescuing Frankfurt-Style Cases," *Philosophical Review* 107 (1998): 97–112, and "BBs, Magnets and

Some critics of *LEL* might ask how the possibility of performing an unfree action can be relevant to basically free action. I defend an answer elsewhere.[32] A short version of it is that this alternative possibility is conceptually sufficient for the falsity of determinism and therefore is sufficient for the satisfaction of one important necessary condition for the truth of libertarianism, a condition linked to a kind of initiatory power that libertarians value. Opponents who deem that answer unsatisfactory should defend their opinion about it.[33]

A critic of *LEL* might claim that even if it is possible for agents to *A* as a basically free action in cases in which the only alternative actions open to them at the time are unfree actions, it is impossible for agents to *A* as a basically free action when their alternatives to *A*-ing include a free action favored by the agent's *CB*. Such a critic might hold, for example, that all basically free actions are performed in accordance with the agent's *CB* and that akratic action is impossible because action contrary to one's *CB* necessarily is unfree. This, of course, is far from obviously true; again, an argument is needed.[34]

It may be objected that *LELs* are not entitled to make any claims about the influence of past basically free actions on present probabilities of action until they have shown that there is good reason to believe that basically free actions are possible. However, *LELs* should reply that the point they have been making in that connection is simply that we should not believe that basically free action is impossible on the grounds that agents' probabilities of action are externally imposed or that agents are related to their present probabilities of action roughly as dice are related to present probabilities about how they will land if tossed.

Can *LEL* accommodate basically free akratic actions? If indeterministically caused actions contrary to the agent's *CB* were like outcomes of tosses of dice, they might plausibly be regarded as only apparently akratic and actually unfree. If agents were to house neural randomizers with unchanging probabilities of continent and akratic action or with probabilities that change independently of what agents learn from their mistakes and successes, they would be subject to luck in a way that seems to preclude their being basically morally responsible for actions contrary to their *CB*s and to preclude their performing basically free akratic actions. But *LELs* postulate neural equipment of a kind that agents are

Seesaws: The Metaphysics of Frankfurt-Style Cases," in *Freedom, Responsibility, and Agency*, ed. Michael McKenna and David Widerker (Aldershot: Ashgate, 2003), 127–38.

32. Alfred Mele, "Soft Libertarianism and Frankfurt-Style Scenarios," *Philosophical Topics* 24 (1996): 123–41.

33. There is such a defense in John Fischer, "*The Metaphysics of Free Will:* A Reply to My Critics," *Journal of Social Philosophy* 29 (1998): 157–67.

34. For criticism of such arguments, see my "Akratics and Addicts."

capable of molding through reflection and efforts of self-control. They contend that morally responsible agency is possible and that, over time, agents can take on increased moral responsibility for their probabilities of action in the sphere in which *CB*s clash with temptation, probabilities that evolve in ways sensitive to what agents have learned and to their efforts at self-control.

How does an agent come to be morally responsible for anything? This is a question for any theorist who believes that at least some human beings are morally responsible agents. More fully, how do we get from being neonates who are not morally responsible for anything to being the free, morally responsible agents we are now, if we are indeed free and morally responsible agents? I return to this question in Section 4 and observe now that one thing that is required is an ability to adjust our behavior in light of what we learn from our past behavior. *LELs* are claiming that this ability includes an ability to mold our probabilities of akratic and continent action. (This is not to say that agents themselves typically think in terms of molding probabilities.)

3. Strict Akratic Decisions and Bizarre Breakdowns

How, according to *LELs,* do basically free akratic actions differ from actions manifesting radical breakdowns of agency, as in the world in which Ann strangely decides at noon to hold on to the coin? Two kinds of radical breakdown scenario may be distinguished: those in which the agent's focal action is contrary to his *CB,* and those in which it is not. Consider a case of the second kind. Cathy, who is in her mid-fifties, had always been a sweet, harmless person. She had never liked her loud, obnoxious neighbor, George, but she had never wanted to hurt him. Today, as Cathy is doing her normal Saturday morning gardening, it strikes her that the world would be at least a slightly better place without George and that killing him would be a good thing to do today, and she acquires a desire to kill him. As Cathy continues her pruning, digging, and watering, she spends an hour or so devising a plan for killing George. Later, she attends her customary Saturday tea and bridge session, takes her granddaughters to a movie, and goes home to finish preparing a meal for her grandkids and their parents. After saying goodnight to her visitors and watching the 10:00 P.M. news, Cathy executes her plan for George's murder. She slips her hands into some new latex gloves, breaks into George's house, sneaks into his bedroom, and stabs him through the heart with a knife she found in his kitchen. She then walks home, destroys the gloves, crawls into bed, and falls asleep.

This is all very strange, and the fact that the murder was wildly out of line with Cathy's history and character contributes to the strangeness. Why, we want to know, did Cathy do what she did? We might be given a reasons explanation of a standard kind: Cathy killed George because she wanted to make the world at least a slightly better place and believed that killing him would accomplish that. But that is not what we want to know. Evidently, Cathy was moved to kill George by, among other things, the desire and belief just mentioned. But why?

Readers may be expecting an answer featuring a fanciful kind of hypnosis, brainwashing, or psychosurgery. But, in fact, there was simply an extremely improbable indeterministically caused pair of glitches in Cathy's head that day—so improbable that this sort of thing had never happened before on Earth. Normally, when Cathy has thoughts about doing something or other that for her would be very strange—for example, speeding in her car just for the fun of it or seducing a friend's husband—she simply sets it aside as a fleeting fantasy. As a consequence of her first glitch that day, the thought of killing George was not set aside. As a consequence of the second, Cathy became so bizarrely fixated on and emotionally detached from the thought of killing George that killing him seemed to her to be an absolutely normal, unpleasant activity—rather like filling out her income tax forms. If we had to attach an everyday label to Cathy's psychological condition at the time of the killing it would be "insanity." One final detail: it was possible the whole day, even as Cathy was in the process of executing her deadly plan, that she would snap out of her bizarre psychological condition, but there was nothing she could do to snap herself out of it.

An adjustment to Cathy's scenario turns it into a case of acting contrary to one's *CB*. The only difference (aside from differences for which this one is logically sufficient in the context) is that in addition to believing that killing George would be a good thing to do today, Cathy believes that, on the whole, it would be better not to kill him today. What tips the scales in the direction of the latter belief for Cathy is the belief that killing George at the end of a long and busy day would be very tiring. (Last month, Cathy judged that it would be best not to fill out her income tax forms at the end of a long, busy day, but she did it anyway.)

What led to the stories about Cathy was the question how, according to *LELs*, basically free akratic actions differ from actions manifesting radical breakdowns of agency. One difference between actions of the former kind and Cathy's killing George, apparently, is that the former are not relatively direct products of extremely improbable but enormously powerful flukes. A related difference—the connection being the power of the fluke—is that Cathy's insanity gets her off the hook for the killing. Cathy seems not to be morally responsible for the killing and not to have performed it freely, in a sense of *freely* closely associated with moral responsibility. However, basically free actions are, by definition, free in that sense, and the agents of such actions are morally responsible for them (in all cases in which the action has moral significance).

If, holding Cathy's psychological condition and behavior fixed, they had been products of a fanciful kind of unsolicited brainwashing, hypnosis, or psychosurgery, the scenario would have featured an *extreme takeover* rather than an extreme breakdown. In one version of an extreme takeover scenario, the killing is contrary to Cathy's *CB*. Even so, the etiology of the killing precludes its being an akratic action. It also is noteworthy that extreme scenarios of the breakdown and takeover varieties do not afford agents the opportunity to learn from their experience in the way that scenarios featuring garden-variety akratic actions do (provided that the akratic actions do not result in the agent's death or incapacitation). Agents can typically learn from their akratic mistakes and make progress in dealing with similar temptations in the future. Subjects of extreme breakdowns and takeovers can hope that they are never again subjected to such forces, but they cannot learn how to deal with these forces.

Ann's strangely deciding at noon to hold on to the coin despite her promise and her assessment of her situation may seem not to be momentous enough to sustain a diagnosis of temporary insanity. However, even if that impression is correct, it may be that as far as intrinsic features alone of the pertinent glitches are concerned, Ann is the locus of glitches of the same kind as Cathy's. If the two agents' glitches are related in this way, then Ann's strange decision to hold on to the coin can be made much more momentous by adjusting the stakes while holding the intrinsic features of her glitches fixed. In an adjusted scenario, Ann would love to have a million dollars and she knows that the reward for tossing the coin at noon, as she promised to do, is a million dollars. With that much at stake and only a very weak desire—which she regards as silly—to learn what it feels like to break a promise for no good reason speaking in favor of holding on to the coin, Ann's deciding not to toss it would seem to be a product of temporary insanity. The decision is not merely irrational and not merely surprisingly irrational; it is shockingly and astoundingly irrational. Akratic decisions are much more consonant with psychological normalcy.

In *Irrationality,* I offer a compatibilist account of the possibility of strict akratic action and a compatibilist theory about how strict akratic actions are caused. The account and theory rest partly on two theses, both of which I defend there:

(1) The motivational strength of our desires is not always in line with our evaluation of the "objects" of our desires (i.e., the desired items).

(2) Typically, *CB*s are formed, in significant part, on the basis of our evaluation of the objects of our desires.

(Notice that both theses are consistent with incompatibilism.) Given (1) and (2), an agent may have a stronger desire to *A* than to *B* even though his *CB* favors *B*-ing rather than *A*-ing. If such an agent proceeds to act on the stronger desire, he acts contrary to his *CB*. If his action is intentional and free, he acts akratically. The same is true of the agent's *deciding* in accordance with the stronger desire in this case—his deciding to *A*. If he *freely* decides to *A*, his decision is an akratic action. If it is assumed that there is a tight—even if indeterministic—connection between an agent's strongest proximal motivation at a time and what he does at that time, a key to understanding how we can act akratically is understanding how preponderant motivation and better judgment can part company.[35] I will not rehearse my compatibilist view of akratic action in any detail here. The point I want to make is that *LELs* can apply a modified version of it to basically free akratic decisions. The main difference is that the actual or imagined phenomenon that *LELs* have in their sights is a *basically* free species of action and therefore depends on the falsity of determinism.

4. Little Agents

In Section 2, I asked how we get from being neonates, who do not even act intentionally, much less freely and morally responsibly, to being free, morally responsible agents. In *Autonomous Agents,* I sketch a pair of overlapping answers to this question—one for compatibilists and the other for libertarians.[36] The main question for *LEL* in this connection is whether it can accommodate the possibility of a neonate's developing into an agent capable of performing basically free actions for which he is basically morally responsible.

Normal parents eventually come to view their children as having some degree of moral responsibility for what they do. The word *degree* is important here. Normal four-year-olds are not as well equipped for impulse control as normal eight-year-olds, and they have a less developed capacity for anticipating and understanding the effects of their actions. When normal four-year-olds snatch an appealing toy from a younger sibling's hands, most people take them to be morally responsible and blameworthy for that, but not as responsible and not as blameworthy as

35. Proximal motivation includes motivation to *A* straightaway, motivation to start *A*-ing straightaway, and motivation to continue doing something that one is doing.

36. *Autonomous Agents,* 227–30.

their normal eight-year-old siblings are for doing the same thing. (This is true at least of most people with a robust memory of significant dealings with children of these ages.) A simple way to account for this difference in how people regard these children is in terms of their grip on the fact that, given the differences in the children's emotional and intellectual development, resisting an impulse to snatch a toy tends to be significantly harder for the younger children.

In some cases, four-year-olds may have an urge to snatch a toy from a younger sibling and nonactionally acquire an intention to do so. In others, they may have an urge to snatch it, think (very briefly) about whether or not to do so, and decide to take it. Consider the first time a normal child, Tony, makes a decision about whether to snatch a toy from his younger sister. He has occasionally acted on nonactionally acquired intentions to grab his sister's toys, but this time he gives the matter some thought and makes a decision. Tony knows that his father is nearby; and, on the basis of some unpleasant experiences, he associates taking the toy with his sister's screaming and his father's scolding him. He decides not to snatch it and feels a little frustrated. Imagine that Tony's father saw that he was tempted to take the toy and was inconspicuously watching his son to see what he would do. When he saw Tony move away from his sister and pick up something else to play with, he praised him for his good behavior. The father was not simply trying to reinforce the good behavior; he believed that Tony really deserved some credit for it.

Suppose now that owing to Tony's being an indeterministic decision maker and to his being tempted to take the toy, there was a significant chance at the time that he would decide to take it. In another world with the same past and laws of nature, that is what he decides to do, and he proceeds to grab the toy (with predictable results). Does that entail that Tony has no moral responsibility at all for deciding not to take the toy? Well, he is only a child; and if he can be morally responsible for anything, he can be so only in ways appropriate for young children, if moral responsibility is possible for young children. It does not seem at all outlandish to believe that Tony would deserve, from a moral point of view, some blame in the world in which he decides to snatch the toy and acts accordingly—but blame appropriate to his age and the nature of his offense, of course. If he does deserve some such blame, he has some moral responsibility for the decision. Similarly, the father's belief that Tony deserves some moral credit for his good decision is far from outlandish. If he does deserve such credit, it is of a kind appropriate to his age and the nature of his action, and he has some moral responsibility for the decision.

The difference at t (the time of Tony's decision) between the actual world and a world with the same past and laws in which Tony decides at *t* to snatch the toy is just a matter of luck. That should be taken into account when asking about Tony's moral responsibility for deciding not to take the toy. Only a relatively modest degree of moral responsibility is at issue, and the question is whether the cross-world luck—or the luck together with other facts about the case—entails that the degree is zero. I doubt that the knowledge that all actual decision-making children are indeterministic decision makers like Tony would lead us to believe that no children are morally responsible at all for any of their decisions.

Views according to which agents' past decisions can contribute to their moral responsibility for their present decisions naturally lead us to wonder about the earliest decisions for which agents are morally responsible. When we do wonder about that, we need to keep firmly in mind how young these agents may be and how trivial their good and bad deeds may be by comparison with the full range of good and bad adult deeds. Tony's making the right or the wrong decision about the toy is not that big a deal, and that is something for theorists to bear in mind when trying to come to a judgment about whether Tony is morally responsible for his decision. If, when pondering whether an indeterministic decision maker can make a first decision for which he is morally responsible, a theorist is focusing on scenarios in which adults make decisions about important moral matters, cross-world luck at the time of decision should strike the theorist as at least seriously problematic on grounds associated with worries presented earlier. But this focus is very wide off the mark.

Galen Strawson describes true or real moral responsibility as "*heaven-and-hell* responsibility," a kind of responsibility such that, if we have it, "it makes sense to propose that it could be just—without any qualification—to punish some of us with (possibly everlasting) torment in hell and reward others with (possibly everlasting) bliss in heaven."[37] Obviously, no sane person would think that little Tony deserves torment in hell—eternal or otherwise—for his bad deeds or heavenly bliss for his good ones. But Tony might occasionally deserve some unpleasant words or some pleasant praise; and, to use Strawson's expression, "it makes sense to propose" that Tony has, for some of his decisions, a degree of moral responsibility that would contribute to the justification of these mild punishments and rewards—even if those decisions are made at times at which the past and the laws leave open alternative courses of action, owing to Tony's being an indeterministic decision maker.

37. Galen Strawson, "The Bounds of Freedom," in *The Oxford Handbook of Free Will,* ed. Robert Kane (New York: Oxford University Press, 2002), 441–60, at 451.

If no one can be morally responsible for anything, then, of course, Tony is not morally responsible to any degree for deciding not to take the toy. But if people are morally responsible for some things, they have to develop from neonates into morally responsible agents; and Tony's decision not to take the toy is a reasonable candidate for an action for which this young agent is morally responsible.[38] If Tony is basically morally responsible to some degree for deciding not to take the toy, and if an agent is basically morally responsible for an action only if he does it freely, then Tony freely decides not to take the toy.

Perhaps I have not been sufficiently explicit about certain themes in my discussion of little Tony. Moral responsibility is very commonly and very plausibly regarded as a matter of degree. *If* young children and adults are morally responsible for some of what they do, it is plausible, on grounds of the sort I mentioned, that young children are not nearly as morally responsible for any of their deeds as some adults are for some of their adult deeds. When we combine our recognition of that point with the observation that the good and bad deeds of young children are relatively trivial in themselves, we should be struck by the implausibility of stringent standards for deserved moral praise and blame of young children—including standards the satisfaction of which requires the absence of present luck. And once even a very modest degree of moral responsibility is in the picture, *LELs* can begin putting their ideas about the shaping of practical probabilities to work.

What *LELs* say about agents' shaping of their practical probabilities is meant to help us understand, among other things, how we get from being little free agents like Tony to being the mature free agents we are, if, in fact, we are free agents. The free agency at issue is an incompatibilist kind. The process, if it is real, would seem to be very gradual; and I will not try to trace it. *LELs* claim that, other things being equal, as the frequency of the indeterministically caused free actions of little agents increases and as the range of kinds of situations evoking such free actions expands, the agents take on greater moral responsibility for associated practical probabilities of theirs and for their morally significant free actions. This, *LELs* say, helps to account for the fact that the moral credit and blame that little free agents deserve for their indeterministically caused free actions tends to increase over time.

38. Some readers may regard Tony as not sufficiently cognitively developed to have any degree of moral responsibility for his pertinent actual and counterfactual deeds. Some such readers may be satisfied if, for example, Tony were to believe the universal proposition that it is wrong for any child to take a toy away from another child just because he wants to play with it. I am willing to be accommodating.

5. Conclusion

LELs grant that if, in the actual world, an agent decides at *t* to *A*, whereas in another possible world with the same laws of nature and the same past, he decides at *t* not to *A*, then the cross-world difference at *t* is just a matter of luck. But they hold that the fact that the difference is just a matter of luck is compatible with its being true that the agent decided freely and morally responsibly at *t*. To be sure, other event-causal libertarians and agent causationists can make this compatibility claim too. According to *LELs*, the main problem with the most detailed event-causal libertarian view on offer, Kane's, is not that it is subject to the problem of present luck, but rather that its account of what agents do in cases of basically free action is unsatisfactory. Kane's doubled trying maneuver fails to solve the problem of present luck anyway, and there is good reason to believe that no real agent who lacks a serious brain disorder tries to decide to *A* while also trying to decide to do something else instead. (The same goes for trying to bring it about that one decides to *A* while also trying to bring it about that one decides to do something else instead.)[39] *LELs* have a similar attitude toward agent-causal libertarianism. As they see it, the only thing that this view might have seemed to have going for it is that it might secure a kind of enhanced control that solves the problem of present luck. But *LELs* are convinced that agent causationists leave the problem intact.[40] So in light of independent worries about agent causation, they set it aside.

I have sketched a libertarian view of basically free action that accommodates strict akratic decisions. A thorough assessment of the view is too large a project for a single paper, but I believe that libertarians would do well to attend not only to what happens at the time of action and to what might have happened instead at that time but also to agents' past actions and to their capacities for learning from actions and consequences associated with their bad and good agential luck. This expansive temporal perspective on agents—one that takes seriously not only the time of an agent's action but also the agent's past and future—sheds light on possibilities for a libertarian view of free agency that merits further investigation.

39. For critical discussion of Kane's new view, see Clarke, 82–92, and Mele, "Libertarianism, Luck, and Control."

40. See Mele, "Libertarianism, Luck, and Control."

13 Conflicts of Desire

ALASDAIR MACINTYRE

To be human is to suffer from unresolved, or at least from imperfectly resolved, conflicts of desire. Yet we are of course under considerable pressure to suppress the expression of such conflicts, so that we may be able to function in a socially acceptable way in a variety of contexts, making choices, pursuing projects, acting and responding to the actions of others, in coherent and what are taken to be normal ways. In order to be able to function acceptably and effectively we need almost all of the time to present ourselves to ourselves as well as to others as unified or very nearly so, and not as divided selves. So in every culture there is generated some image of what is taken to be the normal undivided self, a social artifact that enables us both to interpret others and to present ourselves to others as interpretable.

The normal self is understood as one who makes judgments and choices, pursues projects, and acts and responds to the actions of others in a principled and consistent way—except for what are taken to be very occasional lapses. There are of course individuals who fall outside the bounds of normality thus understood: the alcoholic, the psychotic, the gravely neurotic, the autistic. But, so far as individuals who suffer from none of these conditions are concerned, their lapses from normal coherent and principled functioning are treated as occasional, exceptional, out of character, in need of special explanation, rather than as what they generally in fact are: signs of deep fissures and fractures in the self.

The normal self with its occasional lapses is then a socially important fiction, one that commonly has great power over us. And it is this fiction that gives much of its interest to, even if it did not generate, the philosophical problem often characterized as that of weakness of will. To be sure, in its first and original version the problem was a theoretical response by Aristotle to Socrates' claim that no one willingly errs, that genuine knowledge of the good wholly precludes bad action. But it is not only philosophical considerations that have given continuing life to the problem, so that it has remained central to moral enquiry over an extraordinarily long period, but also a presumption prior to all theorizing that action in conformity with what are taken to be one's best founded judgments as to what one ought to do does not stand in need of explanation, but that actions at odds with those judgments stand in need of special explanation. Or, to put it another way, actions in character are taken to have an intelligibility that actions taken to be out of character lack. It is this presumption that I am going to argue against, rejecting with it the conception of character that informs it.

Social fictions are generally more powerful than philosophical arguments. So that, although most of this paper will be given up to argument, it is important also to say something about what gives this social fiction its power and why to unmask and displace it would cause psychological unease and discomfort. I shall proceed as follows. First, I will give a brief—too brief—account of the relationship of actions, reasons for action, and desires. Then I will say something about the nature of conflicts of desire and their place in our lives, as a prologue to considering and rejecting a currently influential view of what it is to be a rational agent and to order one's desires rationally, the view elaborated by rational decision theorists. I will propose a different account of practical rationality, one that is, I hope, able to accommodate the place that conflicts of desire have in our lives. And finally I will suggest why attempts to think about ourselves in the light of that account will be apt to encounter psychological resistance.

I

It is important to say how the word *desire* is going to be used in this paper. Sometimes in everyday English usage we ascribe wants or desires solely on the basis of the performance of some action. Someone does something and we ask "What did he want to do that for?" This is not how I am going to use such words as *want* or *desire.* As I will use these verbs, it is true of someone that she or he acted from some desire, only if her or his failure to achieve the object of that desire does or would result in some feeling of frustration or disappointment. Desires are individualized by their objects and the frustration or disappointment must have as its intentional object the lack or absence of whatever it was that was desired. My use of *desire* also differs from Hume's, since Hume uses *desire* to name just one of the passions, whereas, as I use it, desire is a constituent of every passion. To be angry or resentful is to respond to some frustration or disappointment in respect of desire. To be joyful or elated is to respond to the achievement of some object of desire.

Are all actions motivated by desire thus understood? There are clearly actions not so motivated, of at least three kinds. Waiting to go into a meeting, I stroll in the corridor, whistling a half-remembered tune. Is either my strolling or my whistling motivated by some identifiable desire? It would be absurd to think so. A different kind of case is that in which we are afflicted by lack of desire—there is nothing that we particularly want to do or to achieve, no object that strikes us as desirable. Listlessly we go through the motions of our everyday activities, unmotivated by any identifiable desire. Thirdly and much more commonly we all of us, in performing the routine actions of our everyday lives, getting out of bed, brushing our teeth, putting on our clothes, and so on, do these things with minimal attention and without any identifiable desire motivating us. Notice, however, that in all three types of cases, that of the idle time-passing action, that of those afflicted by lassitude, and that of routine everyday activity, we act as we do only until or unless we are motivated by some desire to do otherwise. Absence of desire is a key part of the explanation of our action in all three cases. We act as we do only because we have no desire to act otherwise. So desire is of crucial importance to our motivation even in these cases.

Some philosophers have argued in respect of all actions other than these that only desire motivates and that therefore the having of a sufficiently good reason for action cannot motivate by and of itself. Others have argued that the having of a sufficiently good reason can motivate by and of itself and that therefore it is not true that only desire motivates. I shall want to argue that, apart from the types of case that I have put on one side, only desire motivates, but that the nature of desire is such that we can become agents who, when we have a sufficiently good reason to act, are motivated by that reason.

We need first to think about how we come to distinguish between objects that we have reason to desire and objects that we do in fact desire. As children we desire many things that we are rightly told are not good for us: to eat junk food, to grab other children's toys, to watch TV. The first is damaging to our health, the second to our capacity for social relationships, the third to the development of our intellectual and aesthetic powers. If we learn what parents and other adults want us to learn, we learn not only that it is bad for us to have these things, but bad also to go on wanting them. To eat healthy food, keep one's hands off other people's possessions, and read Lewis Carroll or C. S. Lewis, while all the time wishing that one was doing otherwise, is also inimical to the development of bodily, social, intellectual, and aesthetic powers. We not only have good reason to want certain things, we also have good reason to want to want them, good reason to want to want what is for our good.

But having reason to want, even having reason to want to want, is never by itself sufficient to generate desire. What else is needed?

For this we need to develop three kinds of habit: a habit of stopping and thinking before we act on a desire, a habit of feeling as much of a sense of achievement about letting some desires go unsatisfied as satisfying others, and a habit of being able to give ourselves wholeheartedly to the achievement of desires that are for our good, just because and insofar as they are for our good. Every normal human being has by nature the potentiality for acquiring these habits and by doing so transforming and redirecting her or his desires, although for some this acquisition is difficult, while for others it is relatively easy. And some have excellent teachers and role models, while others do not. What is true of everybody, however, is that the development of the relevant habits and the transformation and redirection of our desires is not something that happens once for all. It takes place over long periods of time and during that time part of what we discover are new obstacles and distractions.

Let us catalogue some of these difficulties by reminding ourselves of four familiar contrasts. The first is between objects of desire that are achievable in the short term and objects of desire to be achieved only in some longer term. It is notoriously dangerous to satisfy one's desires for what is immediate, so that one becomes unable to achieve future goals. But it is also dangerous to sacrifice the present to the future, so that the achievement of the object of desire is always deferred. And there are no rules to guide one here in making one's choices between present and future satisfactions, but only the exercise of fallible judgment.

A second contrast is between the care of oneself and the care of others. Without a suitable regard for others one will be unable to develop the types of social relationship and the type of character that are required if one is to be able to achieve one's own good. It is notoriously dangerous to sacrifice others to the satisfaction of one's desires for oneself, but it is also dangerous to sacrifice oneself for the sake of satisfying the desires of others. Yet the dangers here are different from those that derive from the first contrast. For here the tension is between, on the one hand, thinking in terms of *either* the-pursuit-of-my-good-at-the-expense-of-others *or* the-pursuit-of-the-good-of-others-at-the-expense-of-my-good and, on the other hand, thinking in terms of the pursuit of goods that are neither mine nor theirs, but ours, both mine and theirs, the common goods of human beings. For my care for family members or friends or strangers in need is in fact integral to my care for myself as someone in relationship to those others, someone who achieves her or his own good in achieving both what is good for me and what is good for those others. But this is something that we have to learn and we are so constituted that, even when we have understood it and to some significant measure embodied it in our lives, we are still apt to lapse into either the vices of selfishness or the vices of altruism, for the desires that find expression in those vices tend to survive, even when unrecognized.

A third contrast presents different possibilities of error and frustration. Even when we have successfully identified certain objects of desire as goods, and as goods that it is appropriate for us to pursue here and now, we are apt to care for these goods either too little or too much. Both excess and defect are signs of disorder in our desires. To care for something too little is to be too easily diverted from attempting to achieve it, to be too willing to give up on it. To care for something too much is to place it too high on the rank ordering of our goods, to project onto it a desirability that it does not in reality possess, and so to delude ourselves into believing that we have better reasons for putting on one side other projects and purposes than in fact we do.

Both these failures have extreme versions: that of treating something as the ultimate object of one's heart's desire, when it lacks the characteristics that such an object would have to possess, and that of treating nothing as the ultimate object of one's heart's desire because of a belief that such an ultimate object is an impossible object. The first of these attitudes involves illusion and disappointment, the second a desperate fear of illusion together with an insistence that nothing can be finally satisfying, an insistence designed to enable one to avoid disappointment. This of course is not the only strategy for avoiding disappointment. One way to ensure that one always gets what one wants is always to want only what one gets. Diminished desires and diminished expectations that issue in this often pathetically low level of satisfaction are sometimes the result of prolonged deprivation. Ferdinand LaSalle, the nineteenth-century German social democrat, spoke of "the damned wantlessness of the poor."

This condition of wantlessness is not so much a matter of treating this or that object of desire as less desirable than it is as of a lack of any but minimal desire for any object. And so we arrive at a fourth contrast, that between having too few and too weak desires and that of having too many and too strong desires, so in the latter case being too open to movement in too many directions, to a life of zigzags rather than one of deliberate progress. Here, as in the other three cases, we need to steer a course between two bad extremes and here again individuals differ in how difficult it is for them to steer such a course, either because of their biochemistry or because of their early childhood upbringing. Yet, no matter how favorable these are and no matter how good the habits that we develop, we are all of us liable to suffer from continuing contradictory influences that are the result of imperfect resolutions of tensions between incompatible desires. Where we differ from one another is both in the extent to which we are subject to such influences and in the degree to which we are aware of them, able to confront them, and to make choices that are not distorted by them. But how are we to do this? One answer to this question we owe to the exponents of rational decision theory.

II

To be practically rational, according to rational decision theorists, is to have rank-ordered one's preferences and assigned numbers to their relative strengths, to have assigned numerical probabilities to the outcome of each alternative course of action open to one, and to choose that course of action that scores highest when one combines the relevant numbers. It would, for example, be rational to choose a course of action such that there was a very high probability of satisfying some preference that ranked high in one's ordering rather than a course of action directed toward the satisfaction of some preference that one ranked a little higher, but where the probability of a favorable outcome of any course of action designed to achieve it was near zero. By so choosing one maximizes one's expected utility. To rank-order one's preferences is a matter of answering the question for each of what costs one would be prepared to pay to secure the satisfaction of that particular preference: the higher the cost, the higher the ranking of that preference. Such ordering has to conform to three conditions. First, a certain kind of asymmetry must hold, so that if I prefer *x* to *y*, then I must not prefer *y* to *x* or be indifferent as between *x* and *y*. Second, in the set of outcomes being considered, every outcome must be connected to every other by some state of the agent's preferences, so that of any outcome compared with any other we can say which of these two the agent prefers or if the agent is indifferent between them. Third, to these asymmetry and connectivity conditions we have to add a transitivity condition. If an agent prefers *x* to *y* and *y* to *z*, then the agent must prefer *x* to *z*, and if the agent prefers *x* to *y*, but is indifferent between *y* and *z*, than the agent must prefer *x* to *z*.[1]

Given an ordering of our preferences that satisfies these conditions and an adequate method for assigning probabilities to outcomes—and there are alternative ways of doing this—we can determine which course of action will maximize the satisfaction of these preferences. A back-

1. For an excellent and full account, see Michael D. Resnik, *Choices: An Introduction to Decision Theory* (Minneapolis: University of Minnesota Press, 1987).

ground assumption is that our preferences will remain stable at least over the period during which we are engaged in trying to secure the maximum degree of satisfaction of this particular set of preferences. And it is of course the case that our estimation of probable outcomes will generally be more accurate the shorter the period between our choice and the expected outcome of our action. But these are not so much difficulties for the theory as limits on the powers of rational choice thus conceived. And there are of course many types of situation in which it is uncontroversial that to proceed as rational choice theory dictates is to proceed reasonably. But there are two large questions to be raised if that theory is taken to be as an account of rationality as such.

The first concerns its inability to find any place for a concept of rational desire, a concept of objects of desire that we have reason to desire. The exponents of rational decision theory as a theory of practical rationality treat our preferences, and with them also our desires, as given, as surd realities from which rational decision making begins. In so doing they remind us of course of Hume, although their rhetoric is very different. Where Hume announces dramatically that "[r]eason is, and ought only to be the slave of the passions, and can never pretend to any other office than to serve and obey them" (*Treatise of Human Nature,* 2.3.3), they less dramatically presuppose an account of reason in our practical lives that is wholly instrumental, enabling us to satisfy as efficiently as possible the preferences by which we happen to be motivated. What we lack on both views is any practically effective conception of our individual and common goods that would allow us to distinguish between preferences and desires that it would be good that we should satisfy and preferences and desires of which this is not true.

What is it, then, at the level of practice to have such a conception of one's goods? It is to know how to engage in two kinds of rank ordering and not just one, a rank ordering, on the one hand, of preferences and desires and, on the other, of goods. Examples of these types of rank ordering and of the conflicts that they may and often do generate are familiar to everyone who has reflected on the difference between how they would live, if they acted as their present desires and preferences bid them, and how they would live if they were directed toward the good of their own bodily health. If I consulted only my own preferences, I would omit my annual physical examination with all the tests, some of them invasive, that generally lead to no particular result. I would consume large quantities of rich food and drink. And I would take only sporadic exercise. But I know that to live like this would be to be inadequately concerned with the good of my health. That good provides me with a standard, and if I have developed the prudential habits and the desires that I need, will motivate me to act for the sake of that good.

To this the reply may be: insofar as you are motivated by your conception of your good, this is in each particular case just one more preference, to be rank-ordered together with your other preferences. This is therefore a type of case that rational decision theory can easily accommodate, although in characterizing your preference as one for your own good health, nothing more could be meant by "good" than perhaps "such as would be found desirable by many people." But this reply misses the point. For, when I say that bodily health is a good, I make an assertion about a matter of fact, something that is true or false independently of my preferences and desires. What kind of matter of fact is this?

Members of every animal species, except for the very simplest, pass through some natural line of development. And at each stage of their development they may flourish or fail to flourish. To flourish is for an animal to develop and to exercise its specific powers, so that it attains those goals that are its in virtue of its nature. And for rational animals, human beings, those powers are physical, moral, aesthetic, and rational. It is moreover the work of reason to govern, so far as it can, the exercise of our nonrational powers. And it is the work of reason to instruct us, among other things, as to what we do and do not have good reason to desire. To say that I have good reason to do whatever contributes to my flourishing is therefore to say that I have good reason to act only on good reasons, for to flourish is to act, so far as possible, only on good reasons.

Put this another way. Someone who is puzzled as to whether she or he has good reason to do what contributes to her or his flourishing has an inadequate grasp of the concept of human flourishing and such an inadequate grasp is itself a symptom of failure to flourish. It can therefore be the case that someone has good reason to desire, to choose, or to act in some particular way, without having any desire so to desire, to choose, or to act, and moreover without any awareness that this is so. But this is a possibility that those who take rational decision theory to be an account of practical rationality as such exclude from view. And, by excluding it, they exclude any possibility of a practically effective critique of desire that is not itself desire-based.

A second objection to rational decision theory as an account of practical rationality concerns the insistence by rational decision theorists on consistency as a requirement of rationality, a requirement embodied in the asymmetry, correctivity, and transitivity conditions that I noted earlier. And they are far from alone in thinking that in both theoretical and practical reasoning consistency is an obvious requirement. To this I reply that consistency must indeed be a goal of both rational enquiry and rational practice, but that there is always a danger of imposing a requirement of consistency prematurely. In theorizing we may well find ourselves with apparently good reason to affirm two or more inconsistent positions, but not yet know which to reject and which to affirm. In some contexts we find ourselves driven to the conclusion that *p*, while in other contexts we find ourselves driven to the conclusion that *q*, which we know very well entails *~p*. We never of course allow ourselves at any time and in any context to assert $p \cdot q$ without qualification. Nonetheless, an observer might seem to have reason to accuse us of inconsistency. Yet, if we were to try to rebut this accusation by a premature resolution of the issue, rejecting *p* in order to affirm *q* or vice versa, we might well find later on that we had closed some door to theoretical progress.

So it can be too an occasion with desires. Of two or more alternative and incompatible goals defining alternative and incompatible courses of action we may find ourselves in some contexts driven to the conclusion that we have sufficiently good reason to desire one and in other contexts equally driven to conclude that we have sufficiently good reason to desire the other. We never of course allow ourselves to conclude that we have sufficiently good reason to desire the conjunction of these incompatible sets of reasons. But once again an observer might seem to have reason to impute inconsistency. And once again if we were to try to rebut this accusation by abandoning one of these goals we might well find later that we had made a premature and unfortunate choice. Sometimes, then, rationality requires us to live on the edge of practical as well as of theoretical inconsistency, something of which rational decision theory seems to be able to offer no account.

Having recognized this we need to return to the question of what the relationship is between, on the one hand, having a good reason to act and, on the other, being motivated so to act, just because there is good reason to act. What we first need to understand, if we are to answer this question, is how we learn to desire what it is that we have reason to desire, a third notion that rational decision theory cannot accommodate. When we are infants our desires are for the immediate satisfaction of our own most strongly felt needs and they are clamorous. We begin, that is to say, at one extreme of each of the four contrasts that I identified earlier. Interaction with caring adults, especially and overwhelmingly our mothers, moves us away from those extremes, so that we learn to defer satisfaction, to become minimally patient, to respond to expressions of desire or need by others, and to have a wider range of types and strengths of desire. Mothers shape their children's desires, sometimes perhaps being too anxious to satisfy the child, sometimes perhaps teaching the child to be too compliant, but generally negotiating their way between these extremes and teaching the child how to negotiate her or his own way between them. So children begin to learn that they have reason to desire this and not that, to desire this strongly and that only moderately, to have neither too many nor too few desires. And learning to desire what we have reason to desire and as we have reason to desire is inseparable from learning how to rank-order goods, since to say of something that it is better than something else is to say that we have more or better reason to desire it.

Here again of course we are at odds with those whose conception of practical rationality is drawn from rational decision theory. Just because they can find no place for the concept of *having good reason to desire* and just because they understand the resolution of inconsistencies as a precondition for practical reasoning, rather than as something to be achieved by practical reasoning, so too they cannot find a place for such notions as those of learning how to desire and, in the course of that learning, learning how to resolve conflicts of desire.

This learning can be something that continues through the whole of one's life or it can be something that breaks off at some point, so that thereafter we leave our desires unexamined and our conflicts unresolved. And sometimes it may scarcely begin, so that we are liable to be passive in our responses to numerous stimuli that we encounter, victims of our own desires and of our conflicts of desire, a state that it is the intention of advertisers to induce in as many of us as possible. Advertising, like a good deal of contemporary political rhetoric, is not designed to engender calm reflection of the form "Do I really want this? And, whether I do or not, do I have good reason to want it?" yet it is only through such reflection, continued throughout our lives, that we over time through our rank ordering of desires and goods and through our resolution of conflicts acquire a more or less spelled-out conception of what a life would be that was directed toward the achievement of what is good and best for us as human beings, of *the* good and *our* good.

III

The progress toward such a conception is not, however, a straightforward one. For at different stages in our lives the issues presented by such questions as whether or not to focus on the short term at the expense of the longer term and whether or not to narrow down one's interests or to widen them may take very different forms. And having learned how to answer them more or less adequately at one stage in our lives is no guarantee that we will know how to answer them equally well at subsequent stages. Even when we have identified some misdirection of desire and know what must be done to redirect that desire, desire is not always immediately amenable to redirection even in the best of us. Occasional lapses from what we know to be best are therefore part of the normal human condition. They are not necessarily signs of a weak will, but may instead testify to the strength of some desire that we have not yet sufficiently transformed or redirected. So many of the cases that have been considered under the rubric "weakness of will" should instead have been considered under the rubric "strength of desire"—but not all. What, then, is the difference between them?

Weakness of will in someone is not so much a matter of the lapse itself, but of someone's attitude to her or his lapses. When we act other than as we know to be best, we may stop short, stand back, and express disappointment and, if appropriate, contrition, so making the lapse an occasion for resolving to do better. Or we may pass over it, excuse ourselves, and hurry on to something else. The differences between these two is a difference in direction. To will rightly is to be directed toward our good, since the will is appetite for the good. And to fail to be so directed is a failure of, a weakness in, will.

To be directed toward our good is then compatible with certain kinds of lapse, although certainly not with others. Actions that involve gratuitous violence toward others or treachery and betrayal of a friend, even when apparently out of character, are never mere lapses. They exhibit untamed and untrained desire. But we should not infer that someone who is never tempted to perform such actions or indeed any actions that violate the prohibitions of the moral law is therefore directed toward her or his good. Their condition may instead be simply one of absence of desire of any significant strength, including absence of desire for their own good, an unhappy condition that we need to distinguish from moral rectitude, even when its outward appearance is the same as that of moral rectitude.

To have a strong and sustained desire for one's good is compatible with large misconceptions of what one's good is and this in part because of the complexity of the concept of one's good. So each individual life embodies a narrative in which, if we do well, we move through a series of less than adequate understandings—sometimes gross misunderstandings—of our good and, that is to say, less than adequate understandings of what we will have to achieve if we are to perfect our lives according to the standard of specifically human flourishing. It is the mark of a desire for the good that insofar as we identify something hitherto desired as involving a misunderstanding or even a less than adequate understanding of our good, we become dissatisfied with that object of desire and our desire moves beyond it in search of another more adequate object, indeed in search of a fully adequate object. I move beyond thinking that this particular job, that particular set of material possessions, the enjoyment of this friendship or of the achievement of this child could in some way complete my life toward a thought of what I conceive of originally perhaps as something I know not what, something that would perfect and satisfy my life without qualification. To speak of this is on, for example, Lacan's view to speak of an illusion. But here I shall simply assume that Lacan is mistaken, for my immediate concern is not with what end would or would not complete the narrative of my or your life, but with the nature of our progress toward that end.

That progress will seldom, if ever, be straightforward for reasons that I have already suggested. Let me give just one example. Some of us, perhaps all of us, have within ourselves both a tendency toward risk taking and a tendency toward caution. In some the risk taking is so pronounced a trait that caution becomes something urged on the self by others and perhaps by an internalized voice, an other to whom either too little or too much heed may be paid. In others it is caution that has the upper hand, so that impulses toward risk taking are apt to be instantly suppressed. But for individuals of both types learning involves recognizing the need to strike a balance, to find a mean, and this need is something of which individuals characteristically become aware when they fall into disorder and frustration because of either too great risk taking or excessive caution. But they also learn, sometimes painfully, that one cannot hit on the mean between risk taking and caution once and for all so that thereafter one always or almost always gets it right. As one's circumstances change, as one finds oneself in new and unfamiliar contexts in which a balance has to be struck, one learns that what is now demanded of one by way of risk taking and caution may be so different from what was demanded in previous contexts that past experience hinders rather than helps. So that one also has to learn how to be neither too dismissive of nor too reliant on one's own past experience. And such complexities of learning are possible only for those whose desires have been ordered and directed in a particular way. To say what that particular way is is also to say something important about practical reasoning.

Someone who, as a rational agent, is moving toward her or his good through the conflicts engendered by her or his desire to take appropriate risks and desire to be properly cautious has to reckon with at least three motivations that may have to be integrated in choice and action. She or he may have an inclination to take the same bold and unexpected step toward her or his goal, one that, if it succeeds, will make further steps much easier, but that, if it fails—and there is a significant chance of failure—will make it necessary to begin all over again. She or he may also have an inclination to take a more arduous and much slower way of reaching her or his objective, but one that has less chance of failure. Yet in addition she or he will have a desire for her or his own good, a good the achievement of which requires that she or he becomes a particular kind of person, someone whose desires are rightly proportioned to their objects. So that a rational agent has to ask what kind of person she or he will be shown to be by her or his choice between risk taking and caution, and whether that is the kind of person that she or he needs to be, if she or he is to achieve her or his good. She or he has to ask, that is, whether in this respect she or he has reason to desire what and as she or he does desire. And this is possible only if and insofar as her or his desire for her or his good is her or his overriding motivation.

The desire for one's own good is a desire to desire only what one has good reason to desire. If we lacked any such desire, we would lack any motivation to transform and redirect our other desires, so that what we in fact desire might come to coincide with what we have good reason to desire. And it is in part because they can find no place for this desire for our own good in their account of the psychology of human agents that so-called internalists, who hold that the only practically effective reasons for action derive from within the set of our present desires (broadly construed), remain vulnerable to the criticisms of so-called externalists, who hold that we can be motivated to act in this or that particular way by having sufficiently good reasons so to act, independently of the state of our desires, and that such externalists remain similarly vulnerable to internalist criticism. The prudent reasoning and motivation of genuinely rational agents are fully intelligible only if we ascribe to such agents a desire for their own good.

What, then, is the structure of the practical reasoning of such agents? We can best answer this question by considering first an example that Aquinas employs in his discussion of incontinence, then Davidson's criticism of Aquinas's use of that example, and finally how the issue between Davidson and Aquinas should be addressed. Aquinas argues that someone under the influence of a passion may ignore the truth of the major premise of the relevant practical syllogism and supply instead an alternative major premise for a practical syllogism that will permit him to yield to the passion (*Summa theologiae* IaIIae, q. 77, a. 2). So someone envisaging a genuinely pleasing act of fornication supplies himself with a true minor premise, 'This will be pleasant,' supplies as a major premise 'Pleasure is to be pursued,' and concludes 'This act is to be pursued,' turning his mind away from other premises that he knows to be true, the minor premise, 'This is an act of fornication,' and the major premise 'No act of fornication is lawful,' judgments to which when not directed by passion he assents, and with them what follows from them, that 'This act is unlawful,' and therefore not to be performed.

Davidson has two closely related criticisms of Aquinas.[2] The first is that we need to represent the condition of the incontinent agent not just by two, but by three arguments. For if an agent were to rehearse the two rival arguments with their incompatible conclusions what he would arrive at is a blank contradiction, which cannot be a prescription for action. And of course, even if he attempts to proceed beyond the two arguments to a further third argument yielding a practical conclusion, he cannot do so via a blank contradiction. Hence we need to reword the two arguments as well as to go beyond them. And so Davidson reconstructs the two arguments, making of the principles that supply the major premises not unconditional, but merely prima facie assertions. With Davidson's reconstruction we do not need to be concerned. For Davidson's critique of Aquinas misses the point instructively. What Davidson has not recognized is the importance of time in Aquinas's representation of the arguments of the incontinent human being. And in omitting this element Davidson is following the example of almost all writers on practical reasoning.

Consider someone who, unlike the incontinent man, rehearses to himself each of the two practical arguments identified by Aquinas. He will do so successively, taking whatever time he needs, and in, as it were, different voices. He will be in dialogue with himself and at the point in time at which he has rehearsed only these two arguments his dialogue will be as yet incomplete. How then should he continue? He may of course not continue, but instead break off the dialogue, recognize that if he stops here he is faced with a blank contradiction and resolve matters by a choice, either, as passion bids, to do what is unlawful, or instead to obey reason and the natural law and put aside the bidding of pleasure. If he does the latter, it will surely be as a result of a habit, that of responding to moments of this kind by stopping and thinking, so that he is able to carry his dialogue with himself one stage further. With what thought might it continue? Perhaps with the thought of Aristotle and Aquinas that the pleasures of the good human being are not the same as those of the bad and that to find the unlawful pleasant is a sign of something in himself that still needs remedying.[3] If he does continue

2. Donald Davidson, "How Is Weakness of the Will Possible," in *Essays on Actions and Events* (Oxford: Clarendon Press, 1980), 21–42.

3. *Nicomachean Ethics* 10.5.1176a.10–24; Aquinas, *Sententia libri Ethicorum* 10.8 [nn. 2059–63], Editio Leonina, 47/2: 576a–b. English translation: *Commentary on Aristotle's*

in this way, his lapse into temptation, even if not into action, becomes an occasion not only for an immediate practical conclusion, but also for further reflection.

Practical reasoning, then, commonly takes the form of temporally extended dialogue and the history of any practical reasoner is a history of ongoing dialogues, always with her- or himself and often, if she or he is prudent, with others. The dialogues with her- or himself are expressions both of conflicting desires and of rival sets of judgments as to what she or he has reason to desire. They will be dialogues to which others are invited to contribute, if the agent follows the dictates of reason, partly because it is often from others that we are able to learn how to correct the one-sidedness and partiality of our own particular point of view and to see things as they are, rather than as our desire-driven phantasies represent them, and partly because in so many of our enterprises we need to consult with others about their and our common good.

Accounts of practical reasoning generally ignore its dialogical character, just as they ignore the dimension of time. What they do provide is a statement of the final stages of practical reasoning, those that more or less immediately precede choice and action. And this is understandable, since generally all that honest and self-aware agents themselves provide when put to the question, whether as explanation or as justification for their choices and actions, is the reasoning of this final stage. But we also need to know how this final stage was arrived at.

This is not always a matter of those states of mind and desires that were immediately prior to this final stage. What determined the final stage of my reasoning on some particular occasion may or may not have occurred immediately beforehand. It is often the case that crucial dialogues that resolved tensions between conflicting desires, in the light of judgments about what we have good reason to desire, took place at some time well in advance of those situations whose practical reasoning they determine. And it is always the case that the patterns of our practical reasoning on particular occasions are the outcome of a lifelong history of conversations with ourselves and others, devoted to resolving conflicts of desire and to arriving at judgments about what we have reason to desire.

IV

What, then, is the case that I have advanced against what I take to be conventional conceptions of weakness of will? It is twofold. First, I have

Nicomachean Ethics, trans. C. I. Litzinger, O.P. (Notre Dame, Ind.: Dumb Ox Books, 1993), 616–17.

claimed that lapses and inconsistencies are in fact characteristic of the normally virtuous individual, of the normally genuinely virtuous individual, that is. They are signs not of weakness of will, but of that imperfect ordering of our desires that continues to mark the lives of the very best of us.

Second, I have suggested that what matters is not so much the occurrence of these lapses, important though that is, but our responses to them. Insofar as we are virtuous, we will take note of them, reflect on them, and try to make sure that they do not recur. But if we either pass over them, failing to take note, or actively assent to them, then we have taken a direction that is other than that toward our good and there is something amiss with the will, a weakness, a lack of strength to persevere in directedness toward our good, something that may properly be called "weakness of will."

I said at the beginning of this paper that the conventional view of weakness of will presupposed a socially influential conception of the normal self and that the alternative account that I was going to offer is one that there would be resistance to accepting. Now that I have sketched that alternative account it is possible to ask why this is so. Apart from my reference to Davidson's criticism of Aquinas, I have put forward my alternative account in an idiom that owes as little as possible to Aquinas, even though his thesis that every wrong act "proceeds from inordinate desire" (*Summa theologiae* IaIIae.77.4) is presupposed in my argument. I have, for example, spoken of strength of desire rather than, as Aquinas does, of weakness in not resisting such desire (IaIIae.77.3). And my hope has been by so doing to present philosophical arguments and a philosophical conclusion that are and are seen to be independent of any theological assertions or presuppositions. But at this point some reference to Thomist theology cannot be avoided. Consider what Aquinas says as to whether human beings without grace can avoid sin (IaIIae.109.8).

Without grace, says Aquinas, human beings can avoid each, but not every, act of sin. Any one particular act of sin could have been avoided. The agent did not have to perform it. Nonetheless, in the life of any human being there cannot but be acts of sin, acts that violate the precepts of the natural law. The human condition without grace is such that a normal human life is one in which lapses from principles to which agents are firmly committed occur recurrently. Aquinas, that is to say, describes what I have described as the normal human condition as the condition of original sin. But this is something that moral theorists are generally unwilling to allow, something indeed that normal human beings are deeply reluctant to acknowledge. For to agree that this is so would be to acknowledge that there is a humanly unbridgeable gap between what we know that we ought to do and what we do, a gap that can disappear only through the action of grace. The conception of the normal self presupposed by conventional views of weakness of will has the effect of disguising this aspect of the human condition. It functions as a defense against a theological understanding of human nature. Small wonder then that it is seldom put in question.

Bibliography

AUTHORS BEFORE 1900

Albert the Great. *Alberti Magni Opera Omnia.* Münster: Aschendorff, 1951– (Editio Coloniensis).

Aristotle. *Aristotle's Metaphysics: A Revised Text with Introduction and Commentary.* Edited by W. David Ross. 2 vols. Oxford: Clarendon Press, 1924.

———. *The Complete Works of Aristotle: The Revised Oxford Translation.* Edited by Jonathan Barnes. Princeton: Princeton University Press, 1984.

———. *Magna Moralia.* Übersetzt und kommentiert von Franz Dirlmeyer. Werke in deutscher Übersetzung 8. Berlin: Akademie-Verlag, 1964.

———. *Opera.* Edited by the Academia Regia Borussica, Berlin, 1831–.

Augustine. *The City of God against the Pagans.* Translated by George E. McCracken et al. 7 vols. Loeb Classical Library 411–17. Cambridge, Mass.: Harvard University Press/London: William Heinemann Ltd., 1957–1972.

———. *Confessions.* Text and commentary by James J. O'Donnell. 3 vols. Oxford: Clarendon Press, 1992.

———. *Confessions.* Translated by Henry Chadwick. New York: Oxford University Press, 1991.

———. *Contra duas epistulas Pelagianorum.* Edited by Carol Urba and Joseph Zycha. Corpus Scriptorum Ecclesiasticorum Latinorum 60. Vienna: F. Tempsky/Leipzig: G. Freytag, 1913.

———. *Contra Iulianum.* Patrologina Latina 44: 641–874.

———. *De civitate Dei.* Edited by Bernard Dombart and Alphonse Kalb. 2 vols. Corpus Christianorum Series Latina 47–48. Turnholt: Brepols, 1955.

———. *De diversis quaestionibus ad Simplicianum.* Edited by Almut Mutzenbecher. Corpus Christianorum Series Latina 44. Turnholt: Brepols, 1970.

———. *De Genesi ad litteram.* Edited by Joseph Zycha. Corpus Scriptorum Ecclesiasticorum Latinorum 28. Vienna: F. Tempsky, 1894.

———. *De libero arbitrio.* Edited by W. M. Green. Corpus Christianorum Series Latina 29. Turnholt: Brepols, 1970.

———. *De natura et gratia.* Edited by Carol Urba and Joseph Zycha. Corpus Scriptorum Ecclesiasticorum Latinorum 60. Vienna: F. Tempsky/Leipzig: G. Freytag, 1913.

———. *De nuptiis et concupiscentia.* Edited by Carol Urba and Joseph Zycha. Corpus Scriptorum Ecclesiasticorum Latinorum 42. Vienna: F. Tempsky, 1902.

———. *De spiritu et littera.* Edited by Carol Urba and Joseph Zycha. Corpus Scriptorum Ecclesiasticorum Latinorum 60. Vienna: F. Tempsky/Leipzig: G. Freytag, 1913.

———. *Liber de diversis quaestionibus LXXXIII.* Edited by Almut Mutzenbecher. Corpus Christianorum Series Latina 44A. Turnholt: Brepols, 1975.

———. *Œuvres de Saint Augustin.* Bibliothèque augustinienne. Paris: Desclée de Brouwer, 1936–.

———. *Retractationum libri II.* Edited by Almut Mutzenbecher. Corpus Christianorum Series Latina 57. Turnholt: Brepols, 1984.

Chrysippus. *Chrysippi fragmenta moralia.* In *Stoicorum veterum fragmenta,* vol. 3, edited by Hans Friedrich August von Arnim. Leipzig: Teubner, 1903.

Cicero. *De finibus bonorum et malorum.* With an English translation by H. Rackham. Loeb Classical Library 40. Cambridge, Mass.: Harvard University Press, 1983.

Dante Alighieri. *De vulgari eloquentia.* Edited and translated by Steven Botterill. Cambridge and New York: Cambridge University Press, 1996.

———. *The Divine Comedy.* Translated by Charles S. Singleton. 3 vols. Princeton: Princeton University Press, 1970–76.

———. *La divina commedia.* Edited by Natalino Sapegno. 2nd ed. 3 vols. Florence: La Nuova Italia, 1968.

———. *La vita nuova.* Edited by Michele Barbi. Florence: Società Dantesca Italiana, 1907.

———. *Opere minori.* Edited by Pier Vincenzo Mengaldo et al. 2 vols. La letteratura italiana storia e testi 5. Milan and Naples: Riccardo Ricciardi Editore, 1979.

———. *Vita nuova.* Translated by Mark Musa. Bloomington and London: Indiana University Press, 1973.

Descartes, René. *Discours de la méthode.* Avec introduction et notes par Étienne Gilson. Paris: Vrin, 1926.

———. *Œuvres de Descartes.* Edited by Charles Adam and Paul Tannery. Rev. ed. 12 vols. Paris: Vrin, 1966–1976.

———. *Œuvres philosophiques.* Edited by Ferdinand Alquié. Paris: Éditions Garnier Frères, 1963–.

———. *The Passions of the Soul.* Translated by Stephen Voss. Indianapolis and Cambridge: Hackett, 1989.

Diogenes Laertius. *Vitae philosophorum.* Edited by H. S. Long. Oxford: Clarendon Press, 1964.

Epictetus. *The Discourses as Reported by Arrian.* Translated by W. A. Oldfather. 2 vols. Loeb Classical Library 131. Cambridge, Mass.: Harvard University Press/London: W. Heinemann, 1925–1928.

Galen. *De placitis Hippocrates et Platonis.* In *Posidonius,* Vol. 1: *The Fragments,* edited by Ludwig Edelstein and I. G. Kidd. Cambridge: Cambridge University Press, 1972.

Giles of Rome. *Apologia.* Edited by Robert Wielockx. *Opera omnia* III.1. Florence: Leo S. Olschki, 1985.

———. *In primum librum Sententiarum.* Venice, 1521. Reprint, Frankfurt: Minerva, 1968.

Guido Cavalcanti. *The Complete Poems.* Translated by Marc A. Cirigliano. New York: Italica Press, 1992.

Henry of Ghent. *Henrici de Gandavo Opera Omnia.* Edited by Raymond Macken et al. Ancient and Medieval Philosophy, Series 2. Leuven: Leuven University Press, 1979–.

———. *Quodlibet.* Edited by Jodocus Badius. Paris, 1518. Reprint, Leuven: Bibliothèque S.J., 1961.

Hobbes, Thomas. *Leviathan.* Edited by Edwin Curley. Indianapolis: Hackett, 1994.

Hume, David. *A Treatise of Human Nature.* Edited by L. A. Selby-Bigge. 2nd ed. with text revised and variant readings by P. H. Nidditch. Oxford: Clarendon Press, 1978.

Isidore of Seville. *Isidori Hispalensis episcopi Etymologiarum sive originum libri XX.* Edited by W. M. Lindsay. 2 vols. Oxford: Clarendon Press, 1911.

John Duns Scotus. *Duns Scotus on the Will and Morality.* Selected and translated with an introduction by Allan B. Wolter. Washington, D.C.: The Catholic University of America Press, 1986.

———. *Opera omnia.* Paris: Vivès, 1891–1895.

———. *Opera omnia.* Edited by Carolus Bali et al. Vatican City: Typis Vaticanis, 1950– (Editio Vaticana).

John of Salisbury. *Metalogicon.* Edited by J. B. Hall and K. S. B. Keats-Rohan. Corpus Christianorum Continuatio Mediaevalis 98. Turnhout: Brepols, 1991.

Kant, Immanuel. *Groundwork for the Metaphysics of Morals.* Edited by Thomas E. Hill Jr. and Arnulf Zweig. Oxford: Oxford University Press, 2002.

———. *Kant's gesammelte Schriften.* Edited by the Königlich Preußische Akademie der Wissenschaften. Berlin, 1902–.

———. *The Metaphysics of Morals.* Translated and edited by Mary Gregor. Cambridge: Cambridge University Press, 1996.

———. *Religion within the Boundaries of Mere Reason and Other Writings.* Edited by Allen Wood and George di Giovanni. Introduction by Robert Merrihew Adams. Cambridge: Cambridge University Press, 1998.

Machiavelli, Niccolò. *Discourses on Livy.* Translated with an introduction and notes by Julia Conaway Bondanella and Peter Bondanella. New York: Oxford University Press, 1997.

———. *The Prince.* Edited by Quentin Skinner and Russell Price. Cambridge and New York: Cambridge University Press, 1991.

Mill, John Stuart. *Utilitarianism.* Edited by George Sher. 2nd ed. Indianapolis: Hackett, 2002.

Montaigne, Michel de. *The Complete Essays of Montaigne.* Translated by Donald Frame. Stanford, Calif.: Stanford University Press, 1943.

———. *Les essais.* Edited by Pierre Villey and V.-L. Saulnier. 2nd ed. Quadrige 94–96. Paris: Presses universitaires de France, 1992.

Nietzsche, Friedrich. *Die Unschuld des Werdens: Der Nachlaß.* Ausgewählt und geordnet von Alfred Bäumler. 2nd ed. 2 vols. Stuttgart: Kröner, 1978.

———. *Kritische Gesamtausgabe Werke.* Berlin: Walter de Gruyter, 1966–.

———. *Le gai savoir.* Translated by Pierre Klossowski. Collection Folio essais 17. Paris: Gallimard, 1990.

———. *On the Genealogy of Morals; Ecce Homo.* Translated by Walter Kaufmann and R. J. Hollingdale. Edited, with commentary by Walter Kaufmann. New York: Vintage Books, 1967.

Ovid. *Metamorphoses.* Translated by Frank J. Miller. Revised by G. P. Goold. 2 vols. Loeb Classical Library 42–43. Cambridge, Mass.: Harvard University Press/ London: William Heinemann Ltd., 1977–84.

Photius. *Bibliotheca.* Edited by René Henry. Paris: Les belles lettres, 1991.

Plato. *Complete Works.* Edited by John Cooper and D. S. Hutchinson. Indianapolis and Cambridge: Hackett, 1997.

———. *The Dialogues of Plato.* Translated by Benjamin Jowett. Oxford: Clarendon Press, 1953.

———. *Opera.* Edited by John Burnet. Oxford: Clarendon Press, 1900–1907.

Plotinus. *Enneas.* In *Plotini opera,* edited by Paul Henry and Hans-Rudolf Schwyzer. Paris: Desclée de Brouwer/Brussels: Édition universelle, 1951–1973.

Plutarch. *De Stoicorum repugnatiis.* In *Stoicorum veterum fragmenta,* vol. 3, edited by Hans Friedrich August von Arnim. Leipzig: Teubner, 1903.

Porphyry. *De regressu animae.* In *Porphyrii philosophi fragmenta,* edited by Andrew Smith. Stuttgart: Teubner, 1993.

———. *Vita Plotini.* In *Plotini opera,* vol. 1.

Proclus. *The Platonic Theology.* Translated by Thomas Taylor. 6 vols. London: A. J. Valpy, 1816. Reprint: Kew Gardens, N.Y.: Selene Books, 1985–1986.

Sidgwick, Henry. *Methods of Ethics.* 7th ed. Indianapolis and Cambridge: Hackett, 1981.

Spinoza, Baruch. *Ethics.* Edited and translated by G. H. R. Parkinson. New York: Oxford University Press, 2000.

Stobaeus. *Eclogues.* Edited by Hans Friedrich August von Arnim. Stoicorum veterum fragmenta 3. Leipzig: Teubner, 1903.

Tempier, Étienne. *La condamnation parisienne de 1277.* Nouvelle édition du texte latin, traduction, introduction et commentaires par David Piché avec la collaboration de Claude Lafleur. Paris: Vrin, 1999.

———. "Condemnation of 219 Propositions." Translated by Ernest L. Fortin and Peter D. O'Neill. In *Medieval Political Philosophy: A Sourcebook,* edited by Ralph Lerner and Muhsin Mahdi, 335–54. New York: Free Press of Glencoe, 1963.

Thomas Aquinas. *Commentary on Aristotle's Nicomachean Ethics.* Translated by C. I. Litzinger, O.P. Notre Dame, Ind.: Dumb Ox Books, 1993.

———. *Compendium theologiae.* Translated by Cyril Vollert. St. Louis and London: Herder, 1952.

———. *De virtutibus cardinalibus.* Edited by P. A. Odetto. *Quaestiones disputatae.* 9th ed. Rome and Turin: Marietti, 1953.

———. *De virtutibus in communi.* Edited by P. A. Odetto. *Quaestiones disputatae.* 9th ed. Rome and Turin: Marietti, 1953.

———. *Sancti Thomae de Aquino Opera omnia iussu Leonis XIII P. M. edita,* cura et studio Fratrum Praedicatorum. Rome 1882– (Editio Leonina).

———. *Scriptum super libros Sententiarum Magistri Petri Lombardi.* Edited by Pierre Mandonnet, O.P., and Marie Fabien Moos. 4 vols. Paris: P. Lethielleux, 1929–1947.

———. *Super Epistulas S. Pauli Lectura.* Edited by Raffaele Cai. 2 vols. Turin: Marietti, 1953.

Thomas de Vio (Cajetan). *Commentaria in Summam theologicam D. Thomae.* Editio Leonina.

William of Ockham. *Opera philosophica et theologica.* Edited by Gideon Gál et al. 17 vols. St. Bonaventure, N.Y.: St. Bonaventure University, 1967–1988.

AUTHORS AFTER 1900

Adams, Frederick, and Alfred Mele. "The Intention/Volition Debate." *Canadian Journal of Philosophy* 22 (1992): 323–38.

Ainslie, George. *Breakdown of Will.* Cambridge and New York: Cambridge University Press, 2001.

Alanen, Lilli. "Descartes on the Will and the Power to Do Otherwise." In *Emotions and Choice from Boethius to Descartes,* edited by Henryk Lagerlund and Mikko Yrjönsuuri, 279–98. Dordrecht and Boston: Kluwer Academic Publishers, 2002.

Allison, Henry J. *Kant's Theory of Freedom.* Cambridge: Cambridge University Press, 1990.

Annas, Julia. *An Introduction to Plato's Republic.* Oxford: Clarendon Press, 1981.

———. *Platonic Ethics, Old and New.* Ithaca: Cornell University Press, 1999.

Austin, J. L. "Performative Utterances." In *Philosophical Papers,* edited by J. O. Urmson and G. J. Warnock, 3rd ed., 232–52. Oxford and New York: Oxford University Press, 1979.

———. "Pretending." In *Philosophical Papers,* edited by J. O. Urmson and G. J. Warnock, 3rd ed., 253–71. Oxford and New York: Oxford University Press, 1979.

Babcock, William. "Augustine's Interpretation of Romans (AD 394–396)." *Augustinian Studies* 10 (1979): 55–74.

———. "Augustine on Sin and Moral Agency." *Journal of Religious Ethics* 16 (1988): 28–55.

Babich, Babette E. "Nietzsche's Imperative as a Friend's Encomium: On Becoming the One You Are, Ethics, and Blessing." *Nietzsche-Studien* 32 (2003): 29–58.

———. *Nietzsche's Philosophy of Science.* New York: SUNY Press, 1994.

Barad, Judith. "Aquinas's Assent/Consent Distinction and the Problem of Akrasia." *New Scholasticism* 62 (1988): 98–111.

Baron, Marcia. *Kantian Ethics (Almost) without Apology.* Ithaca: Cornell University Press, 1995.

Billings, Grace Elvina Hadley. *The Art of Transition in Plato.* Menasha, Wis.: George Banta, 1920. Reprint, New York: Garland, 1979.

Bitbol-Hespériès, Annie. *Le principe de vie chez Descartes.* Paris: Vrin, 1990.

Bobonich, Christopher. "Akrasia and Agency in Plato's *Laws* and *Republic.*" *Archiv für Geschichte der Philosophie* 76 (1994): 3–36.

———. *Plato's Utopia Recast: His Later Ethics and Politics.* Oxford: Clarendon Press, 2002.

Bobonich, Christopher, and Pierre Destrée, eds. Akrasia *in Greek Philosophy: From Socrates to Plotinus.* Philosophia Antiqua 106. Leiden: E. J. Brill, 2007.

Bobzien, Susanne. "The Inadvertent Conception and Late Birth of the Free-Will Problem." *Phronesis* 43 (1998): 133–75.

Borsche, Tilman. "Intellektualismus." In *Historisches Wörterbuch der Philosophie,* edited by Joachim Ritter et al., 4: 439–44. Basel and Stuttgart: Schwabe & Co., 1976.

Bradley, Denis J. M. *Aquinas on the Twofold Human Good: Reason and Human Happiness in Aquinas's Moral Science.* Washington, D.C.: The Catholic University of America Press, 1997.

———. Review of *Aquinas's Philosophical Commentary on the Ethics: A Historical Perspective,* by James C. Doig. *Review of Metaphysics* 57 (2003): 402–3.

Brand, Myles. *Intending and Acting.* Cambridge, Mass.: MIT Press, 1984.

Broadie, Sarah W. *Ethics with Aristotle.* New York: Oxford University Press, 1991.

Brobjer, Thomas H. "Nietzsche's Knowledge of Marx and Marxism." *Nietzsche-Studien* 31 (2002): 298–313.

Brown, Peter. *The Body and Society: Men, Women, and Sexual Renunciation in Early Christianity.* New York: Columbia University Press, 1988.

Brungs, Alexander. "Intellekt, Wille und Willensschwäche im Korrektorienstreit: Einheit des Menschen vs. Homunculi." In *The Problem of Weakness of Will in Medieval Thought,* edited by Tobias Hoffmann, Jörn Müller, and Matthias Perkams, 263–82. Leuven, Paris, and Dudley, Mass.: Peeters, 2006.

Burns, J. Patout. *The Development of Augustine's Theory of Operative Grace.* Paris: Études augustiniennes, 1980.

Busson, Henri. *La pensée religieuse française de Charron à Pascal.* Paris: Vrin, 1933.

Carone, Gabriela Roxana. "*Akrasia* in the *Republic:* Does Plato Change His Mind?" *Oxford Studies in Ancient Philosophy* 20 (2001): 107–48.

Cavadini, John C. "Feeling Right: Augustine on the Passions and Sexual Desire." *Augustinian Studies* 36 (2005): 195–217.

Cavell, Stanley. *The Claim of Reason: Wittgenstein, Skepticism, Morality, and Tragedy.* New York: Oxford University Press, 1979.

Caygill, Howard. "The Return of Nietzsche and Marx." In *Habermas, Nietzsche, and Critical Theory,* edited by Babette E. Babich, 195–209. New York: Humanity Books, 2004.

Chappell, T. D. J. *Aristotle and Augustine on Freedom.* New York: St. Martin's Press, 1995.

Charles, David. *Aristotle's Philosophy of Action.* London: Duckworth, 1984.

Charlton, William. *Weakness of Will.* Oxford and New York: Basil Blackwell, 1988.

Chisholm, Roderick. "The Agent as Cause." In *Action Theory,* edited by Myles Brand and Douglas Walton, 199–211. Dordrecht: Reidel, 1976.

Clarke, Randolph. *Libertarian Accounts of Free Will.* Oxford: Oxford University Press, 2003.

Colvert, G. T. "Aquinas on Raising Cain: Vice, Incontinence and Responsibility." *American Catholic Philosophical Quarterly Supplement* 71 (1997): 203–20.

Cooper, John M. "The Magna Moralia and Aristotle's Moral Philosophy." *American Journal of Philology* 94 (1973): 327–49. Reprinted in *Reason and Emotion: Essays on Ancient Moral Psychology and Ethical Theory,* 195–211. Princeton: Princeton University Press, 1999.

Counet, Jean-Michel. "Henri de Gand: La prudence dans ses rapports aux vertus morales." In *Henry of Ghent: Proceedings of the International Colloquium on the Occasion of the 700th Anniversary of His Death (1293),* edited by Willy Vanhamel, Ancient and Medieval Philosophy, ser. 1, vol. 15, 227–40. Leuven: Leuven University Press, 1996.

Courcelle, Pierre. *Recherches sur les Confessions de Saint-Augustin.* Paris: E. de Boccard, 1950.

Cross, R. C., and A. D. Woozley. *Plato's* Republic: *A Philosophical Commentary.* London: Macmillan, 1964.

Cummiskey, David. *Kantian Consequentialism.* New York: Oxford University Press, 1996.

Dahl, Norman O. *Practical Reason, Aristotle, and Weakness of the Will.* Minneapolis: University of Minnesota Press, 1984.

Davidson, Donald. "How Is Weakness of the Will Possible?" In *Essays on Actions and Events,* 21–42. Oxford: Clarendon Press, 1980.

———. "Paradoxes of Irrationality." In *Philosophical Essays on Freud,* edited by Richard Wollheim and James Hopkins, 289–305. Cambridge: Cambridge University Press, 1982.

Decorte, Jos. "Der Einfluß der Willenspsychologie des Walter von Brügge OFM auf die Willenspsychologie und Freiheitslehre des Heinrich von Gent." *Franziskanische Studien* 65 (1983): 215–40.

Denifle, Heinrich, and Emile Chatelain. *Chartularium Universitatis Parisiensis.* 2 vols. Paris: Delalain, 1889–1891.

De Stryker, Emile. "The Unity of Knowledge and Love in Socrates' Conception of Virtue." *International Philosophical Quarterly* 6 (1966): 428–44.

Dewan, Lawrence. "The Real Distinction between Intellect and Will." *Angelicum* 57 (1980): 557–93.

Dihle, Albrecht. *The Theory of Will in Classical Antiquity.* Berkeley and Los Angeles: University of California Press, 1982.

Djuth, Marianne. "Will." In *Augustine through the Ages: An Encyclopedia,* edited by Allan D. Fitzgerald, O.S.A., 881–85. Grand Rapids and Cambridge: William B. Eerdmans, 1999.

Doig, James C. *Aquinas's Philosophical Commentary on the* Ethics: *A Historical Perspective.* Dordrecht, Boston, and London: Kluwer, 2001.

Dorter, Kenneth. "The Divided Line and the Structure of Plato's *Republic.*" *History of Philosophy Quarterly* 21 (2004): 1–20.

———. *The Transformation of Plato's* Republic. Lanham, Md.: Lexington Books, 2006.

Double, Richard. *The Non-Reality of Free Will.* New York: Oxford University Press, 1991.

Dumont, Stephen D. "Time, Contradiction and Freedom of the Will in the Late Thirteenth Century." *Documenti e studi sulla tradizione filosofica medievale* 3 (1992): 561–97.

Dunn, Robert. *The Possibility of Weakness of Will.* Indianapolis: Hackett, 1987.

Eardley, Peter S. "The Foundations of Freedom in Later Medieval Philosophy: Giles of Rome and His Contemporaries." *Journal of the History of Philosophy* 44 (2006): 353–76.

———. "The Problem of Moral Weakness, the *propositio magistralis,* and the Condemnation of 1277." *Mediaeval Studies* 68 (2006): 161–203.

———. "Thomas Aquinas and Giles of Rome on the Will." *Review of Metaphysics* 56 (2003): 835–62.

Fischer, John. "*The Metaphysics of Free Will:* A Reply to My Critics." *Journal of Social Philosophy* 29 (1998): 157–67.

Fitzmyer, Joseph F. *Romans: A New Translation with Introduction and Commentary.* The Anchor Bible 33. New York: Doubleday, 1993.

Fortenbaugh, William W. *Aristotle on Emotion.* London: Duckworth, 1975.

Fowler, Barbara. *Archaic Greek Poetry: An Anthology.* Selected and translated by Barbara Fowler. Madison: University of Wisconsin Press, 1992.

Frankfurt, Harry. "Freedom of the Will and the Concept of the Person." *Journal of Philosophy* 68 (1971): 5–20.

Freccero, John. "Autobiography and Narrative." In *Reconstructing Individualism:*

Autonomy, Individuality, and the Self in Western Thought, edited by Thomas Heller, Morton Sosna, and David E. Wellbery, 16–29. Stanford: Stanford University Press, 1986.

———. *Dante: The Poetics of Conversion.* Cambridge, Mass.: Harvard University Press, 1986.

Fredriksen, Paula. "Paul and Augustine: Conversion Narratives, Orthodox Traditions, and the Retrospective Self." *Journal of Theological Studies,* n.s., 37 (1986): 3–34.

Freud, Sigmund. "Moral Responsibility for the Content of Dreams." In *The Standard Edition of the Complete Psychological Works of Sigmund Freud,* edited and translated by J. Strachey, 19: 131–34. London: Hogarth, 1961.

Friedrich, Hugo. *Montaigne.* Translated by Dawn Eng. Berkeley and Los Angeles: University of California Press, 1991.

Fries, Horace. "Virtue Is Knowledge." *Philosophy of Science* 8 (1940): 89–99.

Gallagher, David M. "Free Choice and Free Judgment in Thomas Aquinas." *Archiv für Geschichte der Philosophie* 76 (1994): 247–77.

Gauthier, René A. "Saint Thomas et l'Éthique à Nicomaque." In *Sententia Libri Politicorum: Tabula Libri Ethicorum,* cura et studio Fratrum Praedicatorum. Editio Leonina 48: V–XXV. Rome: ad Sanctae Sabinae, 1971.

Gauthier, René A., and Jean Yves Jolif. *L'Éthique à Nicomaque: Introduction, traduction et commentaire.* 4 vols. Leuven: Publications Universitaires/Paris: Béatrice-Nauwelaerts, 1970.

Gerson, Lloyd P. *Knowing Persons: A Study in Plato.* Oxford: Oxford University Press, 2003.

———. "Platonic Dualism." *Monist* 69 (1986): 352–69.

Gilbert, N. W. "The Concept of Will in Early Latin Philosophy." *Journal of the History of Philosophy* 1 (1963): 17–35.

Gill, Christopher. *Personality in Greek Epic, Tragedy, and Philosophy.* Oxford: Clarendon Press, 1996.

Gilson, Étienne. *Index Scolastico-Cartésien.* Paris: Librairie Félix Alcan, 1913.

———. *La liberté chez Descartes et la théologie.* Paris: Librairie Félix Alcan, 1913.

Ginet, Carl. *On Action.* Cambridge: Cambridge University Press, 1990.

Gomperz, Theodor. *Greek Thinkers: A History of Ancient Philosophy.* 4 vols. London: John Murray, 1901–1912.

Gosling, Justin. *Weakness of the Will.* London and New York: Routledge, 1990.

Gregor, Mary J. *Laws of Freedom.* Oxford: Blackwell, 1963.

Guthrie, W. K. C. *A History of Greek Philosophy.* 6 vols. Cambridge: Cambridge University Press, 1962–81.

Guyer, Paul. *Kant on Freedom, Law, and Happiness.* Cambridge: Cambridge University Press, 2000.

Haji, Ishtiyaque. "Indeterminism and Frankfurt-Type Examples." *Philosophical Explorations* 2 (1999): 42–58.

Hare, R. M. *Freedom and Reason.* Oxford: Clarendon Press, 1963.

Hartle, Ann. *Michel de Montaigne: Accidental Philosopher.* Cambridge: Cambridge University Press, 2003.

Havas, Randall. *Nietzsche's Genealogy: Nihilism and the Will to Knowledge.* Ithaca: Cornell University Press, 1995.

Hill, Thomas E., Jr. *Human Welfare and Moral Worth: Kantian Perspectives.* Oxford: Clarendon Press, 2002.

———. "Kant's Anti-Moralistic Strain." In *Dignity and Practical Reason in Kant's Moral Theory*, 176–95. Ithaca: Cornell University Press, 1992.

———. "Weakness of Will and Character." In *Autonomy and Self-Respect*. Cambridge: Cambridge University Press, 1991.

Hissette, Roland. *Enquête sur les 219 articles condamnés à Paris le 7 mars 1277*. Philosophes médiévaux 22. Leuven and Paris: Publications Universitaires-Vander-Oyez, 1977.

Hocedez, Edgar. "La condamnation de Gilles de Rome." *Recherches de théologie ancienne et médiévale* 14 (1932): 34–58.

Hödl, Ludwig. "'Non est malitia in voluntate . . .'. Die magistrale Entscheidung der Pariser Theologen von 1285/1286 in der Diskussion des Johannes de Polliaco, Quodl. I, q. 10. Untersuchung und Edition." *Archives d'histoire doctrinale et littéraire du moyen âge* 66 (1999): 245–97.

Hoffmann, Tobias. "Aquinas on the Moral Progress of the Weak Willed." In *The Problem of Weakness of Will in Medieval Thought*, edited by Tobias Hoffmann, Jörn Müller, and Matthias Perkams, 219–45. Leuven, Paris, and Dudley, Mass.: Peeters, 2006.

———. "L'*akrasia* selon Duns Scot." In *Duns Scot à Paris, 1302–2002: Actes du colloque de Paris, 2–4 septembre 2002*, edited by Olivier Boulnois, Elisabeth Karger, Jean-Luc Solère, and Gérard Sondag, 487–516. Textes et Études du Moyen Âge 26. Turnhout: Brepols, 2004.

Hoffmann, Tobias, Jörn Müller, and Matthias Perkams, eds. *The Problem of Weakness of Will in Medieval Thought*. Recherches de Théologie et Philosophie médiévales—Bibliotheca 8. Leuven, Paris, and Dudley, Mass.: Peeters, 2006.

Holton, Richard. "Intention and Weakness of Will." *Journal of Philosophy* 96 (1999): 241–62.

Howland, Jacob. "The *Republic*'s Third Wave and the Paradox of Political Philosophy." *Review of Metaphysics* 51 (1998): 633–57.

Huguet, Edmond. *Dictionnaire de la langue française du seizième siècle*. 7 vols. Paris: Didier, 1925–1973.

Inwood, Brad. *Ethics and Human Action in Early Stoicism*. Oxford: Clarendon Press, 1985.

Irwin, Terence H. *Plato's Ethics*. New York: Oxford University Press, 1995.

———. "Some Rational Aspects of Incontinence." *Southern Journal of Philosophy* 27 suppl. (1988): 49–88.

———. "Will, Responsibility, and Ignorance: Aristotelian Accounts of Incontinence." In *The Problem of Weakness of Will in Medieval Thought*, edited by Tobias Hoffmann, Jörn Müller, and Matthias Perkams. Leuven, Paris, and Dudley, Mass.: Peeters, 2006.

Joachim, H. H., and D. A. Rees. *The Nicomachean Ethics: A Commentary*. Oxford: Clarendon Press, 1951.

Johnson, Robert. "Weakness Incorporated." *History of Philosophy Quarterly* 15 (1998): 349–67.

Jordan, Mark D. "Thomas as Commentator in Some Programs of Neo-Thomism: A Reply to Kaczor." *American Catholic Philosophical Quarterly* 78 (2004): 379–86.

Kaczor, Christopher. "Thomas Aquinas's *Commentary on the Ethics:* Merely an Interpretation of Aristotle?" *American Catholic Philosophical Quarterly* 78 (2004): 353–78.

Kahn, Charles H. "Discovering the Will: From Aristotle to Augustine." In *The Question of "Eclecticism": Studies in Later Greek Philosophy,* edited by John M. Dillon and A. A. Long, 234–59. Berkeley and Los Angeles: University of California Press, 1988.

———. *Plato and the Socratic Dialogue: The Philosophical Use of a Literary Form.* Cambridge: Cambridge University Press, 1996.

———. "Plato's Theory of Desire." *Review of Metaphysics* 41 (1987): 77–103.

Kane, Robert. *Free Will and Values.* Albany: SUNY Press, 1985.

———. "Responsibility, Luck and Chance: Reflections on Free Will and Indeterminism." *Journal of Philosophy* 96 (1999): 217–40.

———. *The Significance of Free Will.* New York: Oxford University Press, 1996.

———. "Two Kinds of Incompatibilism." *Philosophy and Phenomenological Research* 50 (1989): 219–54.

Kennington, Richard. "Descartes *Olympica.*" In *On Modern Origins: Essays in Early Modern Philosophy,* edited by Pamela Kraus and Frank Hunt, 79–104. Lanham, Md.: Lexington Books, 2004.

Kenny, Anthony J. P. *The Aristotelian Ethics.* Oxford: Clarendon, 1978.

———. *Aristotle's Theory of the Will.* New Haven: Yale University Press, 1979.

———. "The Practical Syllogism and Incontinence." *Phronesis* 11 (1966): 163–84.

Kent, Bonnie. "Aquinas and Weakness of the Will." *Philosophy and Phenomenological Research* 75 (2007): 70–91.

———. "Transitory Vice: Thomas Aquinas on Incontinence." *Journal of the History of Philosophy* 27 (1989): 199–223.

———. *Virtues of the Will: The Transformation of Ethics in the Late Thirteenth Century.* Washington, D.C.: The Catholic University of America Press, 1995.

Knebel, Sven K. "Voluntarismus." In *Historisches Wörterbuch der Philosophie,* edited by Joachim Ritter et al., 11: 1143–45. Basel and Stuttgart: Schwabe & Co., 2001.

Kobusch, Theo. "Willensschwäche und Selbstbestimmung des Willens: Zur Kritik am abendländischen Intellektualismus bei Heinrich von Gent und in der franziskanischen Philosophie." In *The Problem of Weakness of Will in Medieval Thought,* edited by Tobias Hoffmann, Jörn Müller, and Matthias Perkams, 247–62. Leuven, Paris, and Dudley, Mass.: Peeters, 2006.

Kretzmann, Norman. "Warring against the Law of My Mind: Aquinas on Romans 7." In *Philosophy and the Christian Faith,* edited by Thomas V. Morris, 172–95. Notre Dame, Ind.: University of Notre Dame Press, 1988.

Krüger, Gerhard. *Die Herkunft des philosophischen Selbstbewußtseins.* Darmstadt: Wissenschaftliche Buchgesellschaft, 1962.

Laarmann, Matthias. *Deus primum cognitum: Die Lehre von Gott als Ersterkanntem des menschlichen Intellekts bei Heinrich von Gent († 1293).* Beiträge zur Geschichte der Philosophie und Theologie des Mittelalter, Neue Folge 52. Münster: Aschendorff, 1999.

Lamberigts, Mathijs. "A Critical Evaluation of Critiques of Augustine's View of Sexuality." In *Augustine and His Critics,* edited by Robert Dodaro and George Lawless, 179–81. London: Routledge, 2000.

Langer, Ullrich. *Vertu du discours, discours de la vertu: Littérature et philosophie morale au XVIe siècle en France.* Geneva: Librairie Droz, 1999.

Laugier, Sandra. *Recommencer la philosophie: La philosophie américaine aujourd'hui.* Paris: Presses universitaires de France, 1999.

Lesses, Glenn. "Weakness, Reason, and the Divided Soul in Plato's *Republic*." *History of Philosophy Quarterly* 4 (1987): 147–61.

Long, A. A. *Stoic Studies*. Cambridge: Cambridge University Press, 1996.

Lottin, Odon. "La preuve de la liberté humaine chez saint Thomas d'Aquin." *Recherches de Théologie Ancienne et Médiévale* 23 (1956): 323–30.

———. "Libre arbitre et liberté depuis saint Anselme jusqu'à la fin du XIIIe siècle." In *Psychologie et morale aux XIIe et XIIIe siècles*, 2nd ed., 11–389. Gambloux: J. Duculot, 1957.

Luscombe, D. E. "Natural Morality and Natural Law." In *The Cambridge History of Later Medieval Philosophy: From the Rediscovery of Aristotle to the Disintegration of Scholasticism, 1100–1600*, edited by Norman Kretzmann et al., 705–19. Cambridge and New York: Cambridge University Press, 1982.

MacDonald, Scott. "Primal Sin." In *The Augustinian Tradition*, edited by Gareth B. Matthews, 110–39. Berkeley and Los Angeles: University of California Press, 1999.

MacIntyre, Alasdair. *After Virtue: A Study in Moral Theory*. 2nd ed. Notre Dame: University of Notre Dame Press, 1984.

Macken, Raymond. "Heinrich von Gent im Gespräch mit seinen Zeitgenossen über die menschliche Freiheit." *Franziskanische Studien* 59 (1977): 125–82.

Mandonnet, Pierre. *Siger de Brabant et l'averroïsme latin au XIIIme siècle*. 2 vols. Les Philosophes Belges 6–7. Leuven: Institut Supérieur de Philosophie de l'Université: 1908–1911.

Mazzotta, Giuseppe. *Dante's Vision and the Circle of Knowledge*. Princeton: Princeton University Press, 1993.

———. "The Language of Poetry in the *Vita nuova*." *Rivista di studi italiani* 1 (1983): 3–14.

McCann, Hugh. *The Works of Agency*. Ithaca: Cornell University Press, 1998.

McDowell, John H. "Incontinence and Practical Wisdom in Aristotle." In *Essays for David Wiggins: Identity, Truth and Value*, edited by Sabina Lovibond and S. G. Williams, 95–112. Oxford: Blackwell, 1996.

Mele, Alfred. "Akratics and Addicts." *American Philosophical Quarterly* 39 (2002): 153–67.

———. *Autonomous Agents*. New York: Oxford University Press, 1995.

———. *Free Will and Luck*. New York: Oxford University Press, 2006.

———. *Irrationality: An Essay on Akrasia, Self-Deception, and Self-Control*. New York and Oxford: Oxford University Press, 1987.

———. "Kane, Luck, and the Significance of Free Will." *Philosophical Explorations* 2 (1999): 96–104.

———. "Libertarianism, Luck, and Control." *Pacific Philosophical Quarterly* 86 (2005): 381–407.

———. "Motivated Irrationality." In *The Oxford Handbook of Rationality*, edited by Alfred Mele and Piers Rawling, 240–56. New York: Oxford University Press, 2004.

———. *Motivation and Agency*. New York: Oxford University Press, 2003.

———. "Soft Libertarianism and Frankfurt-Style Scenarios." *Philosophical Topics* 24 (1996): 123–41.

———. *Springs of Action*. New York: Oxford University Press, 1992.

———. "Ultimate Responsibility and Dumb Luck." *Social Philosophy and Policy* 16 (1999): 274–93.

Mele, Alfred, and David Robb. "BBs, Magnets and Seesaws: The Metaphysics of

Frankfurt-Style Cases." In *Freedom, Responsibility, and Agency*, edited by Michael McKenna and David Widerker, 127–38. Aldershot: Ashgate, 2003.

———. "Rescuing Frankfurt-Style Cases." *Philosophical Review* 107 (1998): 97–112.

Moline, Jon. *Plato's Theory of Understanding*. Madison: University of Wisconsin Press, 1981.

Müller, Jörn. "Willensschwäche als Problem der Mittelalterlichen Philosophie: Überlegungen zu Thomas von Aquin." *Recherches de théologie et philosophie médiévales* 72 (2005): 1–28.

———. "Willensschwäche im Voluntarismus? Das Beispiel Heinrichs von Gent." *Archiv für Geschichte der Philosophie* 89 (2007): 1–29.

Müller-Lauter, Wolfgang. *Nietzsche: His Philosophy of Contradictions and the Contradictions of His Philosophy*. Urbana and Chicago: University of Illinois Press, 1999.

Murphy, N. R. *The Interpretation of Plato's* Republic. Oxford: Clarendon Press, 1951.

Nehamas, Alexander. *The Art of Living: Socratic Reflections from Plato to Foucault*. Berkeley and Los Angeles: University of California Press, 1998.

Nettleship, R. L. *Lectures on the Republic of Plato*. 2nd ed. London: Macmillan, 1901.

O'Brien, Denis. "Plotinus on Matter and Evil." In *The Cambridge Companion to Plotinus*, edited by Lloyd P. Gerson, 171–95. Cambridge: Cambridge University Press, 1996.

———. *Plotinus on the Origin of Matter*. Naples: Bibliopolis, 1991.

O'Connor, Flannery. "Some Aspects of the Grotesque in Southern Fiction." In *Collected Works*, edited by Sally Fitzgerald, 813–21. New York: Library of America, 1988.

———. *Wise Blood*. New York: Farrar, Straus and Giroux, 1949.

O'Connor, Timothy. *Persons and Causes*. New York: Oxford University Press, 2000.

O'Donnell, James J. *Augustine: A New Biography*. New York: HarperCollins, 2005.

Oksenberg Rorty, Amélie. "Akrasia and Pleasure." In *Essays on Aristotle's Ethics*, edited by Amélie Oksenberg Rorty, 267–84. Berkeley and Los Angeles: University of California Press, 1980.

———. "The Limits of Socratic Intellectualism: Did Socrates Teach Arete?" In *Proceedings of the Boston Area Colloquium in Ancient Philosophy*, edited by John Cleary, 2: 317–30. Lantham, Md.: University Press of America, 1987.

Ong-Van-Cung, Kim Sang. "Indifférence et irrationalité chez Descartes." *Dialogue: Canadian Philosophical Review* 42 (2003): 725–48.

Owens, Joseph. "The Acratic's 'Ultimate Premise' in Aristotle." In *Aristoteles: Werk und Wirkung*, Vol. 1: *Aristoteles und seine Schule*, edited by Paul Moraux, 376–92. Berlin and New York: Walter de Gruyter, 1985.

Pang-White, Ann A. "The Fall of Humanity: Weakness of the Will and Moral Responsibility in the Later Augustine." *Medieval Philosophy and Theology* 9 (2000): 51–67.

Pasnau, Robert. *Thomas Aquinas on Human Nature*. Cambridge: Cambridge University Press, 2002.

Paton, H. J. *The Categorical Imperative*. London: Hutchison, 1958.

Penner, Terence. "Knowledge vs. True Belief in the Socratic Psychology of Action." *Apeiron* 29 (1996): 199–230.

———. "Plato and Davidson: Parts of the Soul and Weakness of the Will." *Canadian Journal of Philosophy*, Suppl. 16 (1990): 35–74.

———. "Socrates on the Strength of Knowledge: *Protagoras* 351B–357E." *Archiv für Geschichte der Philosophie* 79 (1997): 117–49.

Pereboom, Derk. *Living without Free Will*. Cambridge: Cambridge University Press, 2001.

Perkams, Matthias. "Der schwache Wille: Ockhams Theorie der Unbestimmtheit des Willens als Auseinandersetzung mit dem Problem der Willensschwäche." In *The Problem of Weakness of Will in Medieval Thought*, edited by Tobias Hoffmann, Jörn Müller, and Matthias Perkams, 305–27. Leuven, Paris, and Dudley, Mass.: Peeters, 2006.

Pironet, Fabienne, and Christine Tappolet. "Faiblesse de la raison ou faiblesse de volonté: Peut-on choisir?" *Dialogue: Canadian Philosophical Review* 42 (2003): 627–44.

Pitkin, Hanna F. "Obligation and Consent, II." *American Political Science Review* 30 (1966): 39–52.

Poggioli, Renato. "Tragedy or Romance? A Reading of the Paolo and Francesca Episode in Dante's *Inferno*." *PMLA* 77 (1957): 313–58.

Potts, Timothy C. "Conscience." In *The Cambridge History of Later Medieval Philosophy: From the Rediscovery of Aristotle to the Disintegration of Scholasticism, 1100–1600*, edited by Norman Kretzmann et al., 687–704. Cambridge and New York: Cambridge University Press, 1982.

Pugmire, David. "Motivated Irrationality." *Proceedings of the Aristotelian Society* 56 (1982): 179–96.

Putallaz, François-Xavier. *Insolente liberté*. Vestigia 15. Paris: Cerf, 1996.

Quint, David. *The Quality of Mercy: Ethical and Political Themes in the* Essais. Princeton: Princeton University Press, 1998.

Reade, W. H. V. *The Moral System of Dante's* Inferno. Oxford: Clarendon Press, 1909.

Reilly, Richard. "Weakness of Will: The Thomistic Advance." *Proceedings of the American Catholic Philosophical Association* 48 (1974): 198–207.

Resnik, Michael D. *Choices: An Introduction to Decision Theory*. Minneapolis: University of Minnesota Press, 1987.

Rethy, Robert. "The Teaching of Nature and the Nature of Man in Descartes' *Passions de l'âme*." *Review of Metaphysics* 53 (2000): 657–83.

Rist, John M. *Augustine: Ancient Thought Baptized*. Cambridge: Cambridge University Press, 1994.

Rosen, Stanley. "The Role of Eros in Plato's *Republic*." *Review of Metaphysics* 18 (1965): 452–75.

Ross, W. David. *Aristotle: A Complete Exposition of His Works and Thought*. 6th ed. London and New York: Routledge, 1995.

Rowe, Christopher J. "A Reply to John Cooper on the *Magna Moralia*." *American Journal of Philology* 96 (1975): 160–72.

Saarinen, Risto. *Weakness of the Will in Medieval Thought*. Leiden: E. J. Brill, 1994.

———. "Weakness of Will in the Renaissance and the Reformation." In *The Problem of Weakness of Will in Medieval Thought*, edited by Tobias Hoffmann, Jörn Müller, and Matthias Perkams, 329–51. Leuven, Paris, and Dudley, Mass.: Peeters, 2006.

Schneewind, Jerome B. *The Invention of Autonomy*. Cambridge: Cambridge University Press, 1998.

Scolnicov, Samuel. *Plato's Metaphysics of Education.* London: Routledge, 1988.

———. "Reason and Passion in the Platonic Soul." *Dionysius* 2 (1978): 35–49.

Scott, Dominic. "Plato's Critique of the Democratic Character." *Phronesis* 45 (2000): 19–37.

Shklar, Judith N. *Ordinary Vices.* Cambridge, Mass.: Belknap Press of Harvard University Press, 1984.

Singleton, Charles S. *Dante's Studies I:* Commedia, *Elements of Structure.* Cambridge, Mass.: Harvard University Press, 1954.

Sorabji, Richard. "The Concept of the Will from Plato to Maximus the Confessor." In *The Will and Human Action: From Antiquity to the Present Day,* edited by Thomas Pink and M. W. F. Stone, 6–28. London and New York: Routledge, 2004.

———. *Emotion and Peace of Mind: From Stoic Agitation to Christian Temptation.* Oxford: Oxford University Press, 2000.

Stegmaier, Werner. *Nietzsches Genealogie der Moral.* Darmstadt: Wissenschaftliche Buchgesellschaft, 1994.

Stegman, Thomas D. "Saint Thomas Aquinas and the Problem of *Akrasia.*" *Modern Schoolman* 61 (1988–1989): 117–28.

Stewart, John Alexander. *Notes on the* Nicomachean Ethics. 2 vols. Oxford: Clarendon Press, 1892.

Stone, Martin W. F. "Henry of Ghent on Freedom and Human Action." In *Henry of Ghent and the Transformation of Scholastic Thought: Studies in Memory of Jos Decorte,* edited by Guy Guldentops and Carlos Steel, Ancient and Medieval Philosophy, Series 1, Vol. 31, 201–25. Leuven: Leuven University Press, 2003.

Stowers, Stanley. *A Rereading of Romans: Justice, Jews, and Gentiles.* New Haven: Yale University Press, 1994.

Strauss, Leo. *The City and Man.* Chicago: Rand McNally, 1964.

Strawson, Galen. "The Bounds of Freedom." In *The Oxford Handbook of Free Will,* edited by Robert Kane, 441–60. New York: Oxford University Press, 2002.

———. *Freedom and Belief.* Oxford: Clarendon Press, 1986.

Strong, Tracy B. *Friedrich Nietzsche and the Politics of Transfiguration.* 3rd ed. Champaign: University of Illinois Press, 2000.

Stump, Eleonore. "Persons: Identification and Freedom." *Philosophical Topics* 24 (1996): 183–214.

Taylor, Charles. *Sources of the Self.* Cambridge, Mass.: Harvard University Press, 1989.

Taylor, Richard. *Action and Purpose.* Englewood Cliffs: Prentice-Hall, 1966.

Teske, Roland J. "Henry of Ghent's Rejection of the Principle: 'Omne quod movetur ab alio movetur.'" In *Henry of Ghent: Proceedings of the International Colloquium on the Occasion of the 700th Anniversary of His Death (1293),* edited by Willy Vanhamel, Ancient and Medieval Philosophy, ser. 1, vol. 15, 279–308. Leuven: Leuven University Press, 1996.

Torrell, Jean-Pierre. *Saint Thomas Aquinas.* Translated by Robert Royal. 2 vols. Washington, D.C.: The Catholic University of America Press, 1996–2003.

Vlastos, Gregory. *Socrates, Ironist and Moral Philosopher.* Ithaca: Cornell University Press, 1991.

Waller, Bruce. "Free Will Gone Out of Control." *Behaviorism* 16 (1988): 149–67.

Watson, Gary. "Skepticism about Weakness of Will." *Philosophical Review* 86 (1977): 316–39.

Weber, Max. *The Protestant Ethic and the Spirit of Capitalism.* Translated by Talcott Parsons. Los Angeles: Roxbury, 1998.

Westberg, Daniel. "Did Aquinas Change His Mind about the Will?" *The Thomist* 58 (1994): 41–60.

Wetzel, James. Review of *Augustine: A New Biography,* by James J. O'Donnell. *Journal of Early Christian Studies* 13 (2005): 528–30.

———. "Will and Interiority in Augustine: Travels in an Unlikely Place." *Augustinian Studies* 33 (2002): 139–60.

Wielockx, Robert. "Henry of Ghent." In *A Companion to Philosophy in the Middle Ages,* edited by Jorge J. E. Gracia and Timothy B. Noone, 296–304. Oxford: Blackwell, 2003.

Williams, Bernard. *Shame and Necessity.* Berkeley and Los Angeles: University of California Press, 1993.

Williston, Byron. "*Akrasia* and the Passions in Descartes." *British Journal for the History of Philosophy* 7 (1999): 33–55.

Wippel, John F. "The Condemnations of 1270 and 1277 at Paris." *Journal of Medieval and Renaissance Studies* 7 (1977): 169–201.

———. "Godfrey of Fontaines and the Act-Potency Axiom." *Journal of the History of Philosophy* 11 (1973): 299–317.

Wolff, Robert Paul. *The Autonomy of Reason.* New York: Harper & Row, 1973.

Wood, Allen W. *Kant's Ethical Thought.* Cambridge: Cambridge University Press, 1999.

Worsfold, Victor L. "Akrasia: Irremediable but Not Unapproachable." In *Philosophy of Education 1996.* Available online at www.ed.uiuc.edu/EPS/PES-Yearbook/96_docs/worsfold.html.

Contributors

Denis J. M. Bradley is a professor in the Department of Philosophy at Georgetown University. He has written on Aquinas's ethics, the history of the faith-reason problematic in the Middle Ages, the relationship of Aquinas's metaphysics to post-Kantian transcendental philosophy, and Thomistic understanding of philosophical pluralism.

Kenneth Dorter is a professor of philosophy at the University of Guelph. His most recent book is *The Transformation of Plato's* Republic (Lexington Books, 2006), which discusses in greater detail the themes of his paper in the present volume.

Lloyd Gerson is a professor of philosophy at the University of Toronto. He is the author or coauthor of many articles and books on ancient philosophy, particularly focusing on the works of Plato, Aristotle, and Plotinus. His most recent book is *Ancient Epistomology* (Cambridge University Press, forthcoming).

Ann Hartle teaches philosophy at Emory University. She is the author of *Michel de Montaigne: Accidental Philosopher* (Cambridge University Press, 2003) and is currently working on a study of Montaigne and the origins of modernity.

Thomas E. Hill Jr. is Kenan Professor at the University of North Carolina at Chapel Hill. He has published many articles on moral and political philosophy, with a particular emphasis on the thought of Kant. With Arnuf Zweig, he has coedited a new edition of Kant's *Groundwork for the Metaphysics of Morals* (Oxford University Press, 2002).

Tobias Hoffmann is an associate professor of philosophy at the Catholic University of America. He has published on thirteenth- and fourteenth-century authors, with a special focus on Thomas Aquinas and Duns Scotus. He recently coedited (with Jörn Müller and Matthias Perkams) *The Problem of Weakness of Will in Medieval Philosophy* (Leuven: Peeters, 2006).

Terence H. Irwin is a professor of ancient philosophy at the University of Oxford and a fellow of Keble College. He specializes in Greek philosophy and has written extensively on Plato, Aristotle, Greek ethics, moral philosophy, and Kant. He is currently working on a book about the history of ethics.

Alasdair MacIntyre is a senior research professor of philosophy at the University of Notre Dame. His most recent publication is *Selected Essays,* 2 vols. (Cambridge University Press, 2006).

John C. McCarthy is an associate professor of philosophy at the Catholic University of America. He has published on St. Augustine, Pascal, Husserl, scientific reductionism, and the scope of natural theology. He is the editor of *Modern Enlightenment and the Rule of Reason* (Washington, D.C.: The Catholic University of America Press, 1998).

Giuseppe Mazzotta is Sterling Professor of Italian at Yale University. An authority on Dante, his works include *Dante Poet of the Desert: History and Allegory in the* Divine Comedy (Princeton University Press, 1979) and *Dante's Vision and the Circle of Knowledge* (Princeton University Press, 1993). He recently provided an editorial commentary on Michael Palma's translation of the *Inferno* (New York: Norton, 2008). He also serves as president of the Dante Society of America.

Alfred R. Mele is the William H. and Lucyle T. Werkmeister Professor of Philosophy at Florida State University. He is the author of *Irrationality* (Oxford University Press, 1987), *Springs of Action* (Oxford University Press, 1992), *Autonomous Agents* (Oxford University Press, 1995), *Self-Deception Unmasked* (Princeton University Press, 2001), *Motivation and Agency* (Oxford University Press, 2003), and *Free Will and Luck* (Oxford University Press, 2006).

Tracy B. Strong is a distinguished professor of political science at the University of California, San Diego. He has published extensively on such topics as political theory, political science, aesthetics, and literature. His books include *Friedrich Nietzsche and the Politics of Transfiguration; The Idea of Political Theory: Reflections on the Self in Political Time and Space;* and *Jean-Jacques Rousseau and the Politics of the Ordinary.* He is currently working on a book about aesthetics and politics in the early twentieth century.

James Wetzel is a professor of philosophy at Villanova University, where he holds the Augustinian Endowed Chair in the Thought of Saint Augustine. He writes extensively on Augustine and late antique philosophy and is broadly interested in the love-hate relationship between theology and philosophy in the Western tradition.

Index of Names

Adams, F., 256n
Ainslie, G., 233n
Alanen, L., 179n
Albert the Great, 120n
Allison, D., 231n
Allison, H. J., 216n, 217n, 219n, 226n
Ambrose, Saint, 66n, 86n
Ammonius Saccas, 42
Andreas Capellanus, 148
Annas, J., 7n, 10n, 45n
Arendt, H., 242n, 243, 245n
Aristotle, xin, xii, xiv, xv, 2, 22–43, 45n, 46–49, 50, 52n, 54, 55n, 56n, 57, 60–61, 62n, 63, 68, 83–86, 88–97, 99–100, 111, 114, 116–18, 125n, 126, 130, 149, 154–57, 160, 161n, 162–63, 165–67, 170, 174n, 176, 178, 181, 183, 184n, 188n, 192, 195n, 200, 212–13, 223, 232–33, 241n, 247, 265, 276, 289
Augustine, xiii, xiv, 58–81, 82, 83n, 85n, 86, 87n, 120, 155, 168
Austin, J. L., 234n, 245

Babcock, W., 58n, 79n
Babich, B. E., 231n, 238n, 242n, 250n
Barad, J., 86n
Baron, M., 218n
Bauer, B,, 239n
Billings, G. E. H., 14n
Bitbol-Hespériès, A., 187n
Bobonich, Ch., xin, 3n, 45n
Bobzien, S., 85n
Borsche, T., 116n
Bradley, D. J. M., xiv, 82, 99n, 103n
Brand, M., 256n
Broadie, S. W., 23n
Brobjer, T. H., 239n
Brown, P., 75
Brungs, A., 116n
Burns, J. P., 58n
Busson, H., 187n

Carone, G. R., 3n, 17n
Cavadini, J. C., 64n
Cavell, S., 233n, 246, 248
Caygill, H., 239n
Chadwick, H., 64n
Chappell, T. D. J., 62n
Charles, D., 23n, 39n, 41n
Charlton, W., 84n
Chatelain, E., 131n
Chisholm, R., 253n
Chrysippus, 49, 50n, 51, 85n
Cicero, 86n, 153, 191n
Clarke, R., 253n, 266n, 275n
Colvert, G. T., 86n
Cooper, J. M., 22n
Counet, J.-M., 135n
Courcelle, P., 66n
Cross, R. C., 10n
Cummiskey, D., 218n

Dahl, N. O., 23n, 90n, 92
Dante Alighieri, xv, 71n, 138–58
Davidson, D., ix, 47n, 232, 242n, 243n, 244, 288, 289, 291
Decorte, J., 118n
Democritus, 153
Denifle, H., 131n
Descartes, R., xin, xvi, xvii, 175–209
De Stryker, E., 3n
Dewan, L., 107n
Dihle, A., 62n, 85n
Diogenes Laertius, 49n
Djuth, M., 86n
Doig, J. C., 88n, 99n

Dorter, K., xii, 1, 16n
Double, R., 253n
Dumont, S. D., 132n
Duns Scotus, J., 116, 117n, 126n, 213n

Eardley, P. S., 124n, 125n, 131n
Epictetus, 50n, 52n, 86n, 212
Epicurus, 8, 10, 150, 152, 153

Fitzmyer, J. F., 82n, 113n
Fortenbaugh, W. W., 45n
Fowler, B., 250
Frankfurt, H., xiii, 44, 51
Freccero, J., 71n, 144, 146
Fredriksen, P., 58n
Freud, S., 6, 13, 236, 243n, 244n
Friedrich, H., 161n
Fries, H., 3n

Galen, 49, 50n, 187
Gallagher, D. M., 106n, 125n
Gauthier, R. A., 84n, 85, 89n, 90n, 98n
Gerald Odonis, xin
Gerson, L. P., xiii, 3n, 42, 44n, 54n
Gert, J., 275n
Gilbert, N. W., 85n
Giles of Rome, 125, 131n
Gill, C., 45n
Gilson, É., 178, 180n, 187n
Ginet, C., 253n
Godfrey of Fontaines, 124
Gomperz, T., 8n
Gosling, J., 103n
Gregor, M. J., 217n, 218n
Gregory of Nyssa, 86n
Gregory the Great, 86n
Guido Cavalcanti, 152
Guido Guinizelli, 141, 148
Guthrie, W. K. C., 3n, 10n
Guyer, P., 219n

Habermas, J., 239, 249
Haji, I., 259n
Hare, R. M., ix, 252n
Harte, V., 41n
Hartle, A., xvi, 159, 173n
Havas, R., 247n
Hegel, G. W. F., 235, 239n, 240
Heidegger, M., 236n, 246
Henry of Ghent, xv, 115–37, 213n
Hierocles of Alexandria, 42
Hill, T. E., Jr., xvii, 210, 218n, 221n, 226n
Hissette, R., 116n, 144n
Hobbes, T., xvii, 210, 213–15, 219, 229
Hocedez, E., 131n
Hödl, L., 131n
Hoffmann, T., ix, xin, xv, 101n, 112n, 115, 117n
Hollingdale, R. J., 238n, 248n
Holton, R., 241n
Homer, 240n
Howland, J., 20n
Huguet, E., 186n, 188n
Hume, D., xvii, 210, 214–15, 229, 277, 282

Inwood, B., 49n, 50n
Irwin, T. H., xii, 3n, 20n, 22, 23n, 45n, 84n, 97n
Isidore of Seville, 86n, 152

Joachim, H. H., 39n
John Buridan, xin
John Damascene, 86
John of Salisbury, 153
Johnson, R., 221n
Jolif, J. Y., 84n, 85, 90n
Jordan, M. D., 89n
Julian of Eclanum, 58, 69, 79

Kahn, C. H., 3n, 25n, 33n, 45n, 85n
Kane, R., 253n, 255n, 258–60, 275
Kant, I., xi, xvii, xviii, 210–30, 235, 238, 244n, 248–49
Kaufmann, W., 238n, 248
Kennington, R., 179n, 183
Kenny, A. J. P., 22n, 23n, 26n, 48n, 55n, 93n
Kent, B., 87n, 97n, 99n, 133n
Knebel, S. K., 116n
Kobusch, Th., 115n
Kretzmann, N., 113n
Krüger, G., 201n

Laarmann, M., 115n, 131n
Lacan, J., 287
Lamberigts, M., 64n
Landino, C., 145
Langer, U., 160n
LaSalle, F., 280

Laugier, S., 246n
Lesses, G., 3n, 45n
Lingis, A., 239
Locke, J., xin
Long, A. A., 50n
Lottin, O., 88, 106
Lucretius, 86n
Luscombe, D. E., 213n

MacDonald, S., 79n
Machiavelli, N., 159, 171, 195n
MacIntyre, A., xix, 240n, 276
Macken, R., 115n, 118n
Mandonnet, P., 131n, 144n
Marx, K., 239n, 243n
Maximus the Confessor, 86
Mazzotta, G., xv, 138, 141n, 152n, 158n
McCabe, M. M., 41n
McCann, H., 253n
McCarthy, J. C., xvi, 175
McDowell, J. H., 23n
Mele, A., xviii, 233n, 252, 253n, 254n, 255n, 256n, 258, 259n, 260, 261n, 266n, 267n, 270–71, 275n
Mersenne, M., 177, 180
Mill, J. S., 8n
Moline, J., 45n
Montaigne, M. de, xvi, 159–74
Müller, J., xin, 86n, 115n, 126n
Müller-Lauter, W., 235n
Murphy, N. R., 7n

Nehamas, A., 250
Nemesius of Emesa, 86n
Nettleship, R. L., 8n
Nietzsche, F., xviii, 5, 169, 231–32, 234–51

O'Brien, D., 54n
O'Connor, F., 171, 174n
O'Connor, T., 253n, 256n
O'Donnell, J. J., 66n, 67n, 68
Oksenberg Rorty, A., 3n, 89n
Ong-Van-Cung, K. S., 179n
Ovid, 178
Owens, J., 83n

Pang-White, A. A., 87n
Pascal, B., 187n
Pasnau, R., 86n
Paton, H. J., 216n
Paul, Saint, xiii–xiv, 58–59, 62, 67, 77–78, 82–83, 113n, 139, 176, 178, 183, 192, 222
Pelagius, 86
Penner, T., 23n, 46n
Pereboom, D., 253n
Perkams, M., xin, 117n
Photius, 42n
Piché, D., 116n
Pindar, 250
Pironet, F., xin, 179n
Pitkin, H. F., 248n
Plato, xii, 1–21, 23–29, 33n, 41n, 42–46, 47, 49–50, 51n, 52n, 53–54, 55n, 56, 82n, 84n, 208n, 212, 213, 232, 233n, 250, 252n
Plotinus, xiii, 42, 51, 66n, 70
Plutarch, 51n
Poggioli, R., 148
Porphyry, 42, 66n
Posidonius, 49, 86
Potts, T. C., 213n
Proclus, 51
Pugmire, D., 252n
Putallaz, F.-X., 116n, 119n, 124n
Pythagoras, 26

Quint, D., 163n

Rawls, J., 234, 249
Reade, W. H. V., 150
Reilly, R., 86n
Resnik, M. D., 281n
Rethy, R., 194n, 200n
Rist, J. M., 63, 85n
Robb, D., 266n
Rosen, S., 20n
Ross, W. D., 24n, 25n, 85
Rousseau, J.-J., 202n, 239n
Rowe, C. J., 22n

Saarinen, R., xin, 61n, 85n, 178n
Sapegno, N., 148
Sartre, J.-P., 249
Schneewind, J. B., 163n
Schopenhauer, A., 5, 235
Scolnicov, S., 3n
Scott, D., 45n
Seneca, 86n
Shklar, J. N., 163n

Sidgwick, H., 225n
Singleton, Ch. S., 146
Socrates, xii–xiii, 1–35, 38–42, 82, 84, 90, 117, 177, 184, 233–34, 242, 276
Sorabji, R., 51n, 64n, 85n, 86
Spinoza, B., xin, 193
Stegmaier, W., 246n
Stegman, T. D., 86n
Stewart, J. A., 40n
Stobaeus, 50n
Stohr, K., 224n
Stone, M. W. F., 118n
Stowers, S., 59n
Strauss, L., 20n
Strawson, G., 253n, 273
Strong, T. B., xviii, 231, 235n, 249n
Stroud, S., ixn
Stump, E., 44n

Tappolet, C., ixn, xin, 179n
Taylor, C., 51n
Taylor, R., 253n
Tempier, É., 88, 116–17, 131, 144
Teske, R. J., 124n
Thomas Aquinas, xin, xiv–xv, 82–114, 116, 119n, 124–25, 127, 149, 154–58, 162–63, 165, 167, 170, 174, 188n, 189, 190n, 191n, 194n, 195n, 197n, 201n, 206n, 213n, 288, 289, 291
Thomas de Vio (Cajetan), 107
Torrell, J.-P., 88, 98n, 99n, 106n

Virgil, 158
Vlastos, G., 24n
Voss, S., 196n

Wagner, R., 235
Waller, B., 258
Watson, G., 243, 252n
Weber, M., 249
Westberg, D., 106n
Wetzel, J., xiii, xiv, 58, 62n, 68n
Wielockx, R., 115n
William of Ockham, 117n, 213n
Williams, B., 85n
Williston, B., 179n, 180n, 196n
Wippel, J. F., 88n, 124n
Wolff, R. P., 225n
Wood, A. W., 218n, 219n
Woozley, A. D., 10n
Worsfold, V. L., 244n

Xenophon, xin